29 **Hahn and Economic Methodology**
Edited by Thomas Boylan and Paschal F. O'Gorman

30 **Gender, Growth and Trade**
The miracle economies of the postwar years
David Kucera

31 **Normative Political Economy**
Subjective freedom, the market and the state
David Levine

32 **Economist with a Public Purpose**
Essays in honour of John Kenneth Galbraith
Edited by Michael Keaney

33 **Involuntary Unemployment**
The elusive quest for a theory
Michel De Vroey

34 **The Fundamental Institutions of Capitalism**
Ernesto Screpanti

35 **Transcending Transaction**
The search for self-generating markets
Alan Shipman

36 **Power in Business and the State**
An historical analysis of its concentration
Frank Bealey

37 **Editing Economics**
Essays in honour of Mark Perlman
Edited by Hank Lim, Ungsuh K. Park and Geoff Harcourt

38 **Money, Macroeconomics and Keynes**
Essays in honour of Victoria Chick, volume 1
Edited by Philip Arestis, Meghnad Desai and Sheila Dow

39 **Methodology, Microeconomics and Keynes**
Essays in honour of Victoria Chick, volume 2
Edited by Philip Arestis, Meghnad Desai and Sheila Dow

40 **Market Drive and Governance**
Reexamining the rules for economic and commercial contest
Ralf Boscheck

41 **The Value of Marx**
Political economy for contemporary capitalism
Alfredo Saad-Filho

42 **Issues in Positive Political Economy**
S. Mansoob Murshed

43 **The Enigma of Globalisation**
A journey to a new stage of capitalism
Robert Went

44 **The Market**
Equilibrium, stability, mythology
S.N. Afriat

45 **The Political Economy of Rule Evasion and Policy Reform**
Jim Leitzel

46 **Unpaid Work and the Economy**
Edited by Antonella Picchio

47 **Distributional Justice**
Theory and measurement
Hilde Bojer

48 **Cognitive Developments in Economics**
Edited by Salvatore Rizzello

49 **Social Foundations of Markets, Money and Credit**
Costas Lapavitsas

50 **Rethinking Capitalist Development**
Essays on the economics of Josef Steindl
Edited by Tracy Mott and Nina Shapiro

51 **An Evolutionary Approach to Social Welfare**
Christian Sartorius

52 **Kalecki's Economics Today**
Edited by Zdzislaw L. Sadowski and Adam Szeworski

53 **Fiscal Policy from Reagan to Blair**
The left veers right
Ravi K. Roy and Arthur T. Denzau

54 **The Cognitive Mechanics of Economic Development and Institutional Change**
Bertin Martens

55 **Individualism and the Social Order**
The social element in liberal thought
Charles R. McCann Jnr

56 **Affirmative Action in the United States and India**
A comparative perspective
Thomas E. Weisskopf

57 **Global Political Economy and the Wealth of Nations**
Performance, institutions, problems and policies
Edited by Phillip Anthony O'Hara

58 **Structural Economics**
Thijs ten Raa

59 **Macroeconomic Theory and Economic Policy**
Essays in honour of Jean-Paul Fitoussi
Edited by K. Vela Velupillai

60 **The Struggle Over Work**
The "end of work" and employment alternatives in post-industrial societies
Shaun Wilson

61 **The Political Economy of Global Sporting Organisations**
John Forster and Nigel Pope

62 **The Flawed Foundations of General Equilibrium Theory**
Critical essays on economic theory
Frank Ackerman and Alejandro Nadal

63 **Uncertainty in Economic Theory**
Essays in honor of David Schmeidler's 65th birthday
Edited by Itzhak Gilboa

64 **The New Institutional Economics of Corruption**
Edited by Johann Graf Lambsdorff, Markus Taube and Matthias Schramm

65 **The Price Index and its Extension**
A chapter in economic measurement
S.N. Afriat

66 **Reduction, Rationality and Game Theory in Marxian Economics**
Bruce Philp

67 **Culture and Politics in Economic Development**
Volker Bornschier

68 **Modern Applications of Austrian Thought**
Edited by Jürgen G. Backhaus

69 **Ordinary Choices**
Individuals, incommensurability, and democracy
Robert Urquhart

70 **Labour Theory of Value**
Peter C. Dooley

71 **Capitalism**
Victor D. Lippit

72 **Macroeconomic Foundations of Macroeconomics**
Alvaro Cencini

73 **Marx for the 21st Century**
Edited by Hiroshi Uchida

74 **Growth and Development in the Global Political Economy**
Social structures of accumulation and modes of regulation
Phillip Anthony O'Hara

75 **The New Economy and Macroeconomic Stability**
A neo-modern perspective drawing on the complexity approach and Keynesian economics
Teodoro Dario Togati

76 **The Future of Social Security Policy**
Women, work and a citizen's basic income
Ailsa McKay

77 **Clinton and Blair**
The political economy of the third way
Flavio Romano

78 **Marxian Reproduction Schema**
Money and aggregate demand in a capitalist economy
A.B. Trigg

79 **The Core Theory in Economics**
Problems and solutions
Lester G. Telser

80 **Economics, Ethics and the Market**
Introduction and applications
Johan J. Graafland

81 **Social Costs and Public Action in Modern Capitalism**
Essays inspired by Karl William Kapp's theory of social costs
Edited by Wolfram Elsner, Pietro Frigato and Paolo Ramazzotti

82 **Globalization and the Myths of Free Trade**
History, theory and empirical evidence
Edited by Anwar Shaikh

83 **Equilibrium in Economics**
Scope and limits
Edited by Valeria Mosini

84 **Globalization**
State of the art and perspectives
Edited by Stefan A. Schirm

85 **Neoliberalism**
National and regional experiments with global ideas
Edited by Ravi K. Roy, Arthur T. Denzau and Thomas D. Willett

86 **Post-Keynesian Macroeconomics**
Essays in honour of Ingrid Rima
Edited by Mathew Forstater, Gary Mongiovi and Steven Pressman

87 **Consumer Capitalism**
Anastasios S. Korkotsides

88 **Remapping Gender in the New Global Order**
Edited by Marjorie Griffin Cohen and Janine Brodie

89 **Hayek and Natural Law**
Eric Angner

90 **Race and Economic Opportunity in the Twenty-First Century**
Edited by Marlene Kim

91 **Renaissance in Behavioural Economics**
Harvey Leibenstein's impact on contemporary economic analysis
Edited by Roger Frantz

92 **Human Ecology Economics**
A new framework for global sustainability
Edited by Roy E. Allen

93 **Imagining Economics Otherwise**
Encounters with identity/difference
Nitasha Kaul

94 **Reigniting the Labor Movement**
Restoring means to ends in a democratic labor movement
Gerald Friedman

95 **The Spatial Model of Politics**
Norman Schofield

96 **The Economics of American Judaism**
Carmel Ullman Chiswick

97 **Critical Political Economy**
Christian Arnsperger

98 **Culture and Economic Explanation**
Economics in the US and Japan
Donald W. Katzner

99 **Feminism, Economics and Utopia**
Time travelling through paradigms
Karin Schönpflug

100 **Risk in International Finance**
Vikash Yadav

101 **Economic Policy and Performance in Industrial Democracies**
Party governments, central banks and the fiscal–monetary policy mix
Takayuki Sakamoto

102 **Advances on Income Inequality and Concentration Measures**
Edited by Gianni Betti and Achille Lemmi

103 **Economic Representations**
Academic and everyday
Edited by David F. Ruccio

104 **Mathematical Economics and the Dynamics of Capitalism**
Goodwin's legacy continued
Edited by Peter Flaschel and Michael Landesmann

105 **The Keynesian Multiplier**
Edited by Claude Gnos and Louis-Philippe Rochon

106 **Money, Enterprise and Income Distribution**
Towards a macroeconomic theory of capitalism
John Smithin

107 **Fiscal Decentralization and Local Public Finance in Japan**
Nobuki Mochida

108 **The 'Uncertain' Foundations of Post-Keynesian Economics**
Essays in exploration
Stephen P. Dunn

109 **Karl Marx's *Grundrisse***
Foundations of the critique of political economy 150 years later
Edited by Marcello Musto

110 **Economics and the Price Index**
S.N. Afriat and Carlo Milana

111 **Sublime Economy**
On the intersection of art and economics
Edited by Jack Amariglio, Joseph W. Childers and Stephen E. Cullenberg

112 **Popper, Hayek and the Open Society**
Calvin Hayes

113 **The Political Economy of Work**
David Spencer

114 **Institutional Economics**
Bernard Chavance

115 **Religion, Economics and Demography**
The effects of religion on education, work, and the family
Evelyn L. Lehrer

116 **Economics, Rational Choice and Normative Philosophy**
Edited by Thomas A. Boylan and Ruvin Gekker

117 **Economics Versus Human Rights**
Manuel Couret Branco

118 **Hayek Versus Marx and Today's Challenges**
Eric Aarons

119 **Work Time Regulation as Sustainable Full Employment Policy**
Robert LaJeunesse

120 **Equilibrium, Welfare and Uncertainty**
Mukul Majumdar

121 **Capitalism, Institutions and Economic Development**
Michael Heller

122 **Economic Pluralism**
Robert Garnett, Erik Olsen and Martha Starr

123 **Dialectics of Class Struggle in the Global Economy**
Clark Everling

124 **Political Economy and Globalization**
Richard Westra

125 **Full-Spectrum Economics**
Toward an inclusive and emancipatory social science
Christian Arnsperger

126 **Computable, Constructive and Behavioural Economic Dynamics**
Essays in honour of Kumaraswamy (Vela) Velupillai
Stefano Zambelli

127 **Monetary Macrodynamics**
Toichiro Asada, Carl Chiarella, Peter Flaschel, Reiner Franke

128 **Rationality and Explanation in Economics**
Maurice Lagueux

Rationality and Explanation in Economics

Maurice Lagueux

Routledge
Taylor & Francis Group
LONDON AND NEW YORK

First published 2010
by Routledge
2 Park Square, Milton Park, Abingdon, Oxon OX14 4RN

Simultaneously published in the USA and Canada
by Routledge
605 Third Avenue, New York, NY 10017

Routledge is an imprint of the Taylor & Francis Group, an informa business

Typeset in Times by Wearset Ltd, Boldon, Tyne and Wear

British Library Cataloguing in Publication Data
A catalogue record for this book is available from the British Library

Library of Congress Cataloging in Publication Data
Lagueux, Maurice.
Rationality and explanation in economics/Maurice Lagueux.
p. cm.
Includes bibliographical references and index.
1. Rational expectations (Economic theory) 2. Reason–Economic aspects.
3. Economics–History. I. Title.
HB3731.L34 2010
339–dc22

2009035804

ISBN 13: 978-0-415-55121-2 (hbk)
ISBN 13: 978-0-203-85647-5 (ebk)

To Gisèle, Olivier, Fabienne and Emilia

Contents

Preface and acknowledgements

A book bearing on the central concept of a discipline, which in one way or another connects with the most controversial questions raised in its methodology can hardly be the fruit of a brief period of time. Therefore, many ideas exposed in this book were progressively put together over nearly three decades, during which first versions of them were tentatively presented in conferences such as those organized by HES (History of Economic Society) and ESHET (European Society for the History of Economic Thought), and then reworked and reformulated, largely thanks to comments obtained at these occasions. Then, some of them were reshaped to be published in various journals such as the *Erasmus Journal for Philosophy and Economics* (2008), *Cahiers d'économie politique* (2005), *Journal of Economic Methodology* (2004), *Dialogue* (2001a), *Philosophiques* (1998b), *Theory and Decision* (1994), and *Methodus* (1993c) or in collective books such as *Y a-t-il des lois en économie?* (2007), *Karl Popper: A Centenary Assessment* (2006b), *Quebec Studies in the Philosophy of Science* (1995) and *Perspectives on the History of Economic Thought* (1993a). I am grateful to editors of these journals and books for publishing these papers, which allows me to benefit from still new useful comments from anonymous reviewers and readers.

However, when the time came to write a book based on these ideas, this early material was necessarily not only adapted in order to realize a fully unified book and, in certain cases, rewritten in English after having been published in French, but it was almost completely reformulated in a succession of stages. Some conclusions were slightly, and sometimes substantially, modified. Different elements of the content of some papers turned out to be more logically adapted to being rethought as elements of different chapters. Complete sections of earlier papers were suppressed; a large number of brand new developments were added in each chapter in such a way that a very significant part of the content of the book has nothing to do with any of my previous publications. In fact, it is mostly some arguments that I still find particularly appropriate and a few examples that I consider still telling enough that I have recycled in this book after a proper rewording and adaptation to the new context.

A work devoted to methodological and philosophical problems raised by a science such as economics is first addressed to philosophers interested in economics and to economists who find it worthwhile to pay attention to the principles on which the discipline that they practise is based. However, these questions might interest many others including graduate and undergraduate students; therefore I did all that I could to make it accessible to laypersons who might be interested in such topics.

It is impossible to express my gratitude to all those who, through their comments and objections offered at different stages in the long gestation period of this book, have forced me to significantly improve the formulation of the ideas that were to find their way into its content. Nonetheless, I would like first to express particular thanks to two colleagues with whom I had the chance to discuss at length many of the ideas that I tried to defend in this work. I am thinking about Robert Nadeau and the late Michel Rosier. I benefited from discussing with Robert Nadeau most of the ideas that I propose in this book. Moreover, for more than 15 years, I was involved with him in a research group of which he was the efficient animator and which provided me with the occasion both to exchange views with a large number of guests including many of those whose ideas I refer to in this book and to defend preliminary versions of my own ideas with participants whose comments were made still more appropriate due to the fact that, according to the rule of the group, participants had the opportunity to read the relevant texts in advance. As for my frequent, animated and always helpful discussions with Michel Rosier, they were tragically interrupted by his premature death, but his extremely friendly comments and objections have continued to inspire me long after this sad event.

I would also like to express quite special thanks to Daniel Hausman, Philippe Mongin and Bernard Walliser, whose advice and comments when I prepared either earlier papers or the book itself were particularly precious. Let me also mention the names of some others, either students, colleagues, commentators of conference papers or very well known economists or philosophers who, at different periods, and in different ways and contexts, were kind enough to communicate some reactions to preliminary versions of ideas that were to find their way in this book. Many of them have surely forgotten that they were brought in some way to react to my modest contributions, but the following alphabetically ordered list, which could unfortunately not include the names of many others whose comments were also helpful, is nonetheless representative of the set of other persons to whom I want to express my gratitude: Roger Backhouse, Gary Becker, Carlo Benetti, Peter Boetke, Lawrence Boland, Hubert Brochier, Luigino Bruni, Bruce Caldwell, Gilles Campagnolo, Paul Christensen, William Coleman, Jocelyne Couture, Stéphan D'Amour, John Davis, Daniel Desjardins, Tyler Desroches, Gilles Dostaler, William Dray, Paul Dumouchel, Jon Elster, Marc-André Gagnon, Yvon Gauthier, Yves Gingras, Daniel Gougeon, Dan Hammond, Shaun Hargreaves Heap, Robert Hebert, Ken Hoover, Richard Hudson, Israel Kirzner, Gérald Lafleur, Richard Langlois, Clément Lemelin, Robert Leonard, Pierre Livet, Paisley Livingston, Gary Madison, Uskali Mäki, Mathieu Marion, Catherine Martin, Sheila Mason, Alfred Mele, Philip Mirowski, Christopher Morris, Benoît Pépin, Veronica Ponce, Jean Robillard, Menno Rol,

Alex Rosenberg, Don Ross, Paul-Martel Roy, Malcolm Rutherford, Pierre Salmon, Christian Schmidt, Bertram Shefold, Lucas Sosoe, Bernt Stigum, Richard Sturn, Isabelle Thiss, François Tournier, Bas van Fraassen, Alex Viskovatoff, Jack Vromen and Amos Witzum. It goes without saying that none of them can be held responsible for the shortcomings of the book.

English not being my native language, I am also grateful to the English-speaking graduate students at Université de Montréal who have revised my texts over the last two decades: William Milnes, Erik Litwack, Andrew Connochie, Olaf DeWinter, Bruce Maxwell, Niall Mann, Bruce Toombs, Matthew Brown, William Colish and Aviva Shiller. A special thanks goes to the latter who has edited most of the final draft of the book. All of them have considerably contributed to making my English less defective. However, it was not possible to require them to modify the structure of a text whose language deficiencies remain indisputably mine.

I am also grateful to the SSHRC (Social Sciences and Humanities Research Council) (Ottawa), FQRSC (Fonds québécois de la recherche sur la société et la culture) (Quebec) and Université de Montréal for the grants that they provided me over the years, which have made the research required for the preparation of this work possible financially.

Last but not the least, I must thank my wife, Gisèle, who encouraged me to finish this book and has patiently supported the fact that I spent so much of my time in front of my computer. Many thanks also to my son, Olivier, who was very helpful when this computer started to create unexpected problems instead of remaining the wonderful instrument that is so useful in the realization of books of this kind.

Introduction

Few economists would deny that the rationality principle plays a fundamental role in economics and in all social sciences, but the nature of this principle and the way it operates in economics are far from consensual. Though this principle was more or less explicitly defined by various authors, it remains almost impossible to characterize it in a way that can be generally accepted as fully satisfactory.[1] Of course, one can say that it is the principle according to which people are rational, but rational in what sense? What kind of rationality should one have in mind when maintaining that this principle plays such a significant role? It is true that most economists would answer this question with the help of an apparently crystal clear concept, either maximization or consistency. But these notions referred to in economic models should be considered as idealizations of a certain rationality that is attributed to actual agents who make decisions and perform actions. Therefore, when they are engaged in a debate that forces them to refer to human rationality as such, economists usually realize how hard this notion is to encapsulate. To mention only one example, in his debate with Daniel Kahneman, Charles Plott observed that the concept of rationality 'lacks scientific precision and as a result is a source of needless controversy and misunderstandings' (Plott 1996b: 220). How can we characterize this rationality which presumably guides human actions? Are agents making their choices in such a way that they maximize their utility in each or most of their choices? Are they maximizing this utility according to an objective measure or simply according to what they *consider* to be useful for them? Are they simply disposed to act in ways that they judge appropriate according to the circumstances? What kind and what amount of information is required to allow agents to make such relatively appropriate choices? Are we assuming that their expectations are based on the conclusions of the most reliable economic theories? Should we postulate that they themselves are in a position to rationally impute choices to other players in economic games in order to choose accordingly? Are they managing to be consistent in all of their choices or are they rather trying to optimally adapt themselves to changing situations irrespective of their previous choices? Should we consider that agents change their minds and adapt their choices to new situations only when the prevailing situation becomes unbearable in such a way that they simply manage to remain in a satisfying situation?

What do rationality and the rationality principle mean?

Since answers to such questions vary widely among economists and philosophers, it is not surprising that the exact meaning of the concept of rationality involved in each of these questions cannot be easily defined. In fact, it is throughout the present book that a satisfactory picture of this concept will be progressively developed through discussions of some of the most significant topics in the methodology of economics. However, since a provisory notion of rationality is required to start the analysis, let us look at whether relatively uncontroversial features associated with rationality can provide such a notion, in which it seems sensible not to include too much. Let us tentatively admit that people are said to act rationally when their actions are motivated by intentions that can be construed as reasons. From a methodological point of view, what makes reasons interesting is the fact that they can normally be understood by economists, sociologists, archaeologists and other social scientists, since these researchers are presumed to be rational as well.

Of course, the notion of reason may raise suspicions because agents are frequently tempted to rationalize their actions and justify them by invoking good reasons that tend to be more honourable than their real motivations. As Marx and Engels lucidly observed, confusing 'what somebody professes to be and what he really is' (Marx and Engels 1947 [1846]: 43) was a source of fatal illusions for historians of his time and eventually for contemporary social scientists as well. However, one should not be bothered too much by this, because when they implicitly invoke the rationality principle in the development of their analyses, economists are rarely interested by what agents *say* about their actions. Rather, they assume that these actions correspond to means for satisfying what they suppose to be the agents' goals. Put otherwise, they assume that these actions are appropriate to the situation from the point of view that they suppose to be the agents' one. They never ask consumers whether they buy a given basket of goods because they prefer these goods to the money they part with to buy them; they simply suppose that they act this way for this reason. Because buying is clearly an appropriate action for one who prefers a good over the corresponding sum of money, economists estimate that they understand the rationality of actions of this type. After all, it is precisely when actions do not seem to be appropriate to the satisfaction of an assumed goal that we conclude that we do not understand their rationale. The preceding considerations, vague as they are, imply that rational actions must 'make sense' and that the reasons accounting for these actions can be considered explanatory, a fact that illustrates, while still weakly, that the rationality principle cannot be dissociated from the very idea of an explanation since it is precisely because reasons have some explanatory power that the rationality principle is so significant for economics.

Note that the reasons invoked for explaining the actions need not be very sophisticated. It might be that paying less for a given good is preferred to paying more for it, which satisfactorily explains why someone tends to choose the cheapest one between two similar goods. Many might prefer to characterize more straightforwardly the rationality principle by assuming that, at least in the realm of economic analysis, this principle claims that people normally tend to act in ways that correspond to their best interests. It might usually be true, since satisfying one's best interests constitutes a quite understandable reason, which may have motivated one to act in line with reaching this goal, but such satisfactions and interests can be associated with so many types of behaviours that it is not really possible to characterize them in a univocal way. Even though paying less provides generally more satisfaction than paying more for a given good, it is quite possible that paying *more* provides a greater satisfaction than *paying less at the extra price* of spending time and energy to find the cheaper alternative or of losing the friendship of a sympathetic shopkeeper. Thus the notion of rationality seems to be doomed to remain forever vague and difficult to define. In this context, one of the main goals of this book is to contribute to reducing this vagueness and to explain why, in this matter, it is not possible to formulate a perfectly precise definition, something that, when attempted by economists, has produced deceptive results as will be shown.

For now, let me illustrate with a very simple example in what sense the rationality principle allows us to explain social phenomena and, on the basis of this explanation, to make sometimes highly accurate predictions. If I look through my window at the passing cars on the street outside, I can predict with a remarkably high degree of accuracy that these cars will continue straight ahead and will not turn right or left before the next street corner. I can also predict that, at this transversal street, some of them will turn right but none left, this street being one-way. Admittedly, there are no mechanical laws that exclude such events from taking place. There is nothing in the design of a car that forces it to turn at a specific place and there is no reason to think that a neurological mechanism in the brains of the drivers forces them to drive in this way. In fact, were this the case, since these mechanisms would remain inaccessible to one who is looking at the street through a window, they would not help to predict the behaviour of the cars.

Nonetheless, I am confident that the drivers are not stupid enough to drive their cars into the sidewalk or to turn the wrong way down a one-way street; thus, it is the fact that I postulate that they are rational and not stupid that allows me to explain the observed regularity in the behaviour of the cars. It is true that this use of the rationality principle is not an absolutely reliable basis for predictions. Unfortunately, such predictions turn out to be wrong once in a while, because some drivers do stupid things, but most of the time they do not. In any case, in spite of its limitations, this principle was seen as reliable enough to be adopted as one of the founding principles of the social sciences. True, it is difficult to deny that such a principle sounds rather weak, but we should not be too quick to denigrate it. Meteorologists would probably appreciate having a similar principle at their disposal allowing them to predict with a fair degree of accuracy that clouds will progress along straight lines up to a definite point where some of them will turn right but not left. But clouds are not rational agents. Consequently, in the absence of such a simple predictive tool, meteorologists must look for other kinds of causal mechanisms that can improve their relatively inaccurate predictions. In contrast, economists, can at least draw on the rationality principle, and they have done so a great deal. Since the goals (or interests) of economic agents, while sometimes much more difficult to identify than the immediate interests of drivers, are on average relatively easy to characterize, economic theories have generally and fruitfully been based on this principle.

Though such a principle may appear a bit vague and almost empty, the important point, as we will see, is that it may be meaningfully and very fruitfully applied to human agents, and possibly in a somewhat less demanding version, to the most intelligent animals,[2] but not to plants, stones or clouds. Some methodologists would prefer that economists search, as meteorologists do, for deterministic and non-intentional explanations instead of relying on the imperfectly reliable rationality principle. Such explanations might be based on the neurological workings of human brains and I will have to come back to this point later in the book. However, up to now, one may say that attempts to explain *economic phenomena themselves* with the help of facts established in neurology were rarely very convincing and illuminative; therefore relatively few economists have devoted much of their time to the development of this approach, which, while highly promising from some points of view, is not very rewarding when it comes to explaining what economists usually aim to explain. This is the reason why the rationality principle is so indispensable in social sciences. It seems implausible, at least for the present time, to explain typical human behaviour by resorting to a deterministic analysis of neurophysiological processes according to which people must behave in some strictly determinate ways, though it is quite plausible to draw on the fact that people, in most usual situations, *act* in a relatively rational way and consequently in a more or less determinate way. If it is admitted that, in a given set of circumstances, a sufficiently determinate action is clearly what should normally provide a basic satisfaction of people's assumed wants, this principle can be used as a kind of surrogate for laws that have brought success to the natural sciences. Indeed, when the question is either to *explain that* one actually performed some act *A*, or to *predict whether* one would do *A* in a given set of circumstances, it is almost immaterial whether *A* was done by the force of a law according to which everyone does *A* in such circumstances, or because one who is not stupid would surely do *A* when it is clearly in one's best interest to do *A* in those circumstances.

It will be appropriate to revisit the question of laws later in this introduction, but for now, let us first try to circumscribe the notion of rationality a little more. If it is so difficult to characterize the sort of rationality that is required by the rationality principle and even to characterize with some precision the type of behaviour that should be excluded by this principle, it might be because the degree of rationality involved is astonishingly minimal. I say that this kind of rationality is minimal because it just requires that, for example, entrepreneurs not be so thoughtless as to produce more and more units when it is clear that they apparently lose a lot of money every time they produce a new unit, which is roughly similar to requiring that someone be only so mindful as to turn off the tap when the bathtub is full! One might even say that the required rationality is minimal to the point that not complying with it would be equivalent to acting out of sheer stupidity. Therefore, claiming that agents are not stupid after all, and that their actions generally make sense, may turn out to be an expressive and useful way of drawing attention to the essential requirements of this principle. Indeed, people are not usually stupid enough to perform actions that work against *what they consider* the best thing to do in typical economic situations. Of course, they frequently perform actions that are far from being the best thing to do in their situation but, since there is no question of postulating that they are omniscients, I claim that the rationality principle simply requires that they usually act rationally in function of what they *consider* to be the best thing to do. Nonetheless, they are normally sensitive enough to variations of situations to modify their course of action when they assess that the latter becomes detrimental to the attainment of their goal. Put otherwise, people are not stupid like those organisms that would always react the same way regardless of changes in the situation. More importantly, their evaluation of the situation is based on their experience, which means that, while generally being unable to immediately detect the optimal position, they do what they consider appropriate and if they are disappointed by unsatisfactory results, they normally adjust their actions as much as they can in order to improve their situation, insofar as they judge that such frequently painful adjustments are worthwhile. Human beings rarely maximize and are far from being consistent; they hesitate, make mistakes, change their mind, regret, suffer from myopia; nonetheless, they are not stupid, and they normally make decisions and perform actions that make sense given their goals. While very imperfect, this degree of rationality is sufficient for *explaining* most economic phenomena.

Is the rationality principle a predicament for economics?

Indeed, such is the rationality that can be attributed to human agents. However, most economists would probably not be very happy with this kind of analysis of the notion of rationality. Understandably enough, economists, who generally aim to promote the *scientific* character of economics, estimate that being based on a principle whose meaning remains vaguely defined in spite of many attempts to analyse its working constitutes a kind of predicament for their discipline, which they prefer not to emphasize. The problem is that if one tries to determine precisely when choices, decisions or actions can be called rational, one is almost necessarily involved in the manipulation of hardly definable concepts, which are largely inherited from a 'folk psychology', such as intentions, desires, preferences, objectives, satisfaction, utility, etc. Given this ambiguity of the concept of rationality, when economists attempt to characterize the content of the rationality principle, they are more or less forced to adopt either an openly false, a purely tautological or a desperately vague formulation. Indeed, suggesting that the principle claims that human beings always make decisions and perform actions either in a strictly consistent way or in an optimal way that maximizes their gains in utility is clearly false, since it is undeniable that actions performed by human beings very frequently turn out to be erratic and inconsistent. Economists might avoid any risk of falsity by construing the principle as the claim that any action is necessarily rational in the sense that agents choose to perform only actions that they *perceive* as being capable of procuring for them more satisfaction than not performing them, but it would be at the price of promoting a purely tautological principle. Indeed, actions would have this trait almost by definition, given that a behaviour will not count as an action at all if it was driven by something other than whatever satisfaction is consciously associated with this eventual action in the agent's perception. In order to avoid both falsity and tautology, economists might choose to describe rationality along the lines proposed above, which imply that rational actions make sense because they are usually appropriate to situations faced by agents in the sense that they are progressively and consciously adapted to changing situations through sensible responses to the experience of unsatisfactory results. But for most economists, the price for avoiding tautology and falsity in this fashion would be the adoption of an intolerably vague definition of rationality.

I will discuss this perception of vagueness later in the book, but for the time being let us follow economists who have to choose between tautology, vagueness and falsity. Over more than a century, they have hesitated between these alternatives but, by the middle of the twentieth century, most of them had decisively rejected tautology and vagueness and accepted making room for a fundamental principle that can unfortunately not be said to be true. After all, an empirical science being incompatible with a tautological basis and mathematical formalization being incompatible with vagueness, it is easily understandable that members of a community who, more or less explicitly, aim to emulate mathematical-minded physicists chose to purge the bases of their discipline from anything which can be said to be tautological or vague. In a period in which economists turn more and more of their ingenuity towards the construction of theoretical economic models – preferably based on axiomatic foundations – and expect to see their conclusions used as guides by entrepreneurs and political leaders, what is important for them is to derive precisely formulated conclusions from their models. Indeed, such conclusions can be submitted to more or less compelling empirical tests and have more of a chance of being seen as persuasive enough to influence policies. Therefore, they decisively concluded that such an objective could hardly be met with theories relying on tautological or vague principles.

For sure, falsity is also inimical to science and a principle according to which agents always make optimal decisions is clearly false if economic agents are supposed to be human beings. Nonetheless, from the point of view of the model builder, the epistemic status of the principles on which such models are based was judged more or less irrelevant by comparison with the purity, the precision and the fecundity of axioms from which the model can be derived. In this context, the continuously repeated objections denouncing the unrealistic character of a theory that attributes maximizing capacities to human beings and especially to entrepreneurs appeared rather old-fashioned to most neoclassical economists. According to the latter, such objections have been dealt with a long time ago when Fritz Machlup (1946, 1947) and a few other economists (for example, Alchian 1950: 217) more or less triumphantly underscored the pedestrian and irrelevant character of arguments based on empirical inquiries concerning entrepreneurial behaviour, which were systematically opposed to the more and more sophisticated models of neoclassical economics. Still more to the point, this kind of objection seemed to have been totally defeated when Milton Friedman (1953) brilliantly defended the thesis according to which an economics that aims to be a positive science does not have to care about the realism of assumptions insofar as it makes successful predictions. As is well known, this thesis was immensely influential among economists, despite the considerable number of objections that it has raised among methodologists of economics.

Therefore, though most economists pay lip service to the rationality principle, rare are those who find it worthwhile to devote important intellectual resources to discussing the very nature of this principle or to find out what its exact function in economic theory is. They clearly prefer to conclude that, thanks to the well defined concepts with which they are used to working, economic models can be developed without being involved in the conundrums associated with the hardly definable rationality principle. More precisely, the role traditionally attributed to the rationality principle in its original meaning has been taken over by principles that are considered to be better fitted variants of this principle. These preferred ways of encapsulating the notion of rationality through mathematical maximization or logical consistency, since they import less psychological content by avoiding ambiguous references to human behaviour, look like purely technical requirements that are judged more appropriate to the needs of modern economics. Thus, what is frequently still called 'rationality' and which works as a fundamental principle is presented in a formulation that, thanks to the notions of maximization and consistency, has been domesticated in order to satisfy the need for developing the formal models that tend to constitute the core of modern economics. It is because this formalization of the concept of rationality has clearly contributed to obliterating the latter's essential meaning and role in economic explanations that documenting and discussing the consequences of this fact will be one of the main topics of this book.

Why economic rationality is necessarily instrumental after all

In spite of their importance, the debates evoked above were far from being the only ones that had the notion of economic rationality as an object. Therefore, it is important to discuss at least another one of them in order to dissipate a possible confusion regarding the content of this hard-to-define notion. Among the views that are generally accepted by economists, the idea according to which economic rationality is purely an instrumental rationality is an undoubtedly prevalent one. However, while generally admitted as a methodological tenet, this view tends to be perceived as embarrassing or even as deceiving and unacceptable by certain economists among those who consider that economics is not concerned only with increasing material wealth. Indeed, instrumental rationality seems to be subordinated to an instrumentalization of economic life, which, since it seems to be associated with successful accumulation at any rate of material wealth, is easily charged with highly pejorative connotations. Therefore, making decisions according to instrumental rationality is easily associated with the mean behaviour of one who is only interested in maximizing utility understood in a strictly economic sense. However, the objections referred to above, regarding the relevance of reducing economic rationality to maximization, do not imply that the same suspicion must affect the idea of instrumental rationality insofar as the latter is properly characterized. In fact, the blame addressed to instrumental rationality is largely due to odd and deceitful semantic associations. What do we mean when we say that economic rationality is instrumental? Simply, that decisions are made and actions taken insofar as they are rationally judged appropriate means (or instruments) for reaching a goal. In order to clarify the implications of this way of understanding instrumental rationality, let us ask what kind of rationality *would not* be instrumental. It is surely not when one voluntarily chooses to use means that do not allow for the reaching of one's goal, because this would, rather, correspond to sheer irrationality. Obviously, we refer to a kind of rationality that is not instrumental when the question at stake is not to adapt means to goal, but to rationally determine goals themselves.

Whatever the most appropriate name for this last kind of rationality, let us call it value-rationality, following a tradition that goes back to Max Weber's thought. There is no doubt that it is rational, in some sense, to grant a particular value to what is judged good, to value life over death, happiness over misfortune, benevolence over cruelty, virtue over vice, etc. It is difficult not to declare irrational one who, on principle, claims to prefer death over life; such a person would be spontaneously considered as foul. Hitler, the overused example in such matters, is frequently, and probably very rightly, pictured in such a way, which means that, since we cannot find any superior and acceptable goal that could explain his behaviour, we cannot understand or explain how he could have developed and entertained ideas as stupid and irrational as those to which he devoted his life. Nonetheless, one may reasonably say that insofar as his (irrational and inexplicable) goal was to create a unified Aryan race, his actions can be judged as perfectly (*instrumentally*) rational, but surely not value-rational. However, it is not the role of economics, and not even the role of psychology, to determine what is value-rational: this is the role of ethics. Even though economists, especially when they devote themselves to welfare economics, are sometimes involved in ethical considerations quite legitimately and argue for values that they consider rational, they are not thereby *explaining* economic phenomena with the help of this reference to rationality. Now, if rationality and the rationality principle are so fundamental for economics, it is, as we have seen, because they play an essential role in economic explanation. Thus, while economists should not reduce rationality to instrumental rationality, the rationality that is involved in the rationality principle and that allows us to *explain* economic phenomena is instrumental rationality and not value-rationality.

Of course, an economist may find it important to explain, for example, why an altruistic person values what is good for other people so much, but if the explanation provided is really explanatory, it could hardly be based on rationality as such. Rationality may quite legitimately be invoked in this context, but it would no longer be explanatory. Let us take an example to illustrate what I mean by no longer being explanatory. I see someone driving at an excessive speed on a quiet street, risking being involved in a grave accident, and I look for an explanation for this behaviour. A rational explanation might be that the driver, who is conducting a seriously wounded child to a hospital, wants to arrive there as soon as possible. Why going to a hospital? Obviously, because the driver wants the child receive the best care and survive. If the alleged facts are exact, these answers are both perfectly correct explanations based on *instrumental* rationality: the idea is that one just took the best means according to one's beliefs in order to satisfy one's desire, namely to save a life. But if I raise the question '*why* should we desire saving a life?', the answer will probably be that life is of a superior value and that it is totally irrational to question this view. Indeed, a broader notion of rationality suggests that, especially in the case of a child, life should be indisputably preferred to death, but this 'rational' view is in no way an explanation. Indeed, the questioner asks why life is worth so much, and the answer provided is that life is better than death. Such an answer may reflect the ethical conviction of a sane and rational person, but why should we consider that it is an explanation?

Jon Elster referred to a somewhat similar distinction, when he opposed broad to thin theories of rationality. The thin theory concerns clearly instrumental rationality, whereas the need for something more is expressed by the broad theory. The latter aims to explain the formation of beliefs and desires, though Elster's analysis mostly concerns to what extent beliefs are based on (sane) judgements and to what extent desires are autonomous. Elster shows convincingly enough that serious limitations affect the judgements and the autonomy in question, but while these considerations may help us to understand the formation and the nature of rational beliefs and desires, they do not explain them *by invoking the explanatory power* of the notion of rationality, any more than the latter *explains* why life is better than death. My point is obviously not to exclude economists from explaining the formation of beliefs, of desires or of virtues such as generosity or courage (the latter being an example considered by Elster 1983: 51, 57). My point is that either you explain the formation of such entities in an individual by reasons – related to the satisfaction of an interest, whatever it is – for deciding or for acting in a particular way, then the rationality invoked *is* instrumental. Or, you acknowledge that such explanations can hardly be acceptable, because beliefs, desires, generosity and courage are rarely the fruits of conscious decisions, as forcefully illustrated by Elster, but then you must explain the formation of these entities not by any kind of reasons that people might have for acquiring them, but by more or less uncontrolled factors which have nothing to do with the explanative power of rationality. Courage is an inner quality of certain persons, which is generally not explainable by reasons that this person could have for being courageous. Rationality has little role to play, if any, in the required *explanation*, but this does not preclude that you may perfectly claim that valuing courage positively and cowardice negatively is more rational than the opposite assessment and that considering that some beliefs and some desires are more rational than other ones is perfectly legitimate. These ethically well grounded rational evaluations have, however, nothing to do with the process through which their object was progressively shaped, which is the process that explains it.

If we exclude value-rationality and rationality associated with broad theory, which, while indisputably useful concepts, are not really explanatory, the other types of rationality typically invoked by economists are varieties of instrumental rationality. Elster (1984 [1979]: 117), for example, introduced another suitable distinction between parametric and strategic rationality. It is important indeed to be aware that problems to solve when attempting to reach a goal by choosing adequate means are not the same depending on whether the environment is parametric, which means that it is treated as a constant environment, or strategic, which means that it is 'made up of other actors' along with the considered agent (Elster 1984 [1979]: 18). However, the very explication of this distinction illustrates clearly that it concerns only instrumental rationality (the adaptation of means to ends). The same can obviously be said of the two main conceptions of rationality to which economists refer, namely maximization and consistency. Far from being the basis for appreciative judgements on the legitimacy of economic values, both are sheer magnifications of instrumental rationality: maximization implies an optimal adaptation of means to ends and consistency implies a perfect coherence in the pursuit of a preferred goal. Incidentally, the famous money pump argument, in spite of its shortcomings discussed later in this book, illustrates fairly well that, for economists who invoke it, having consistent preferences constitutes the best *means* to avoid being fouled and to get richer than inconsistent fellows. Clearly, neither of these two neoclassical conceptions of rationality supposes that when using them economists are rationally explaining why maximization and consistency are appropriate goals to pursue; it is rather decisions and actions that are explained by an elicitation of means that are instrumental for reaching a goal – the difference between them, from this point of view, being that consistency characterizes the stability of goal-oriented choices and maximization the degree of its realization.

As is well known, bounded rationality is a conception of rationality that was systematically opposed to maximization by Herbert Simon. In no way, however, should one consider it as less instrumental than maximization: its opposition to the latter bears only on agents' capacity to determine optimal means and on the fact that agents must usually content themselves with reaching their goals to a degree that is judged sufficient though not optimal. According to Simon (1976: 133, see also 140), the change in viewpoint that he is advocating implies a shift 'from concern for optimal solutions to a concern for good solutions'. Put otherwise, a decision or an action explained by bounded rationality is a decision or an action that is judged satisfactory or good enough as a means for reaching a goal. However, Simon frequently prefers to use the phrase 'procedural rationality' to designate a type of rationality that he opposes to 'substantive rationality'. 'Behavior is substantively rational when it is appropriate to the achievement of given goals within the limits imposed by given conditions and constraints' (Simon 1976: 130). This definition that 'grew up within economics' seems to correspond fairly well indeed to the notion of instrumental rationality familiar to economists; consequently, one may expect that its opposite, procedural rationality, should correspond to a non-instrumental kind of rationality. However, the definition of procedural rationality emphasizes a quite different dimension of this opposition. 'Behavior is procedurally rational when it is the outcome of appropriate deliberation. Its procedural rationality depends on the process that generated it' (Simon 1976: 131; see also Simon 1978: 9). Clearly, the opposition underscored does not concern the relation between means and ends that defines instrumental rationality, but only the process of deliberation that generates a rational response. In other words, procedural rationality is not defined by its alleged result, namely the attainment of a given goal, but by the process through which the rational individual manages to determine to what degree this goal should be attained, given the circumstances and the constraints characterizing the situation. This degree might, in principle, correspond to optimality, but if, as is usually the case, the cost of computations and other research required to determine the optimal option is judged too high to justify their implementation, or if uncertainty is such that this optimal option cannot be determined at all, decisions and actions may be sub-optimal and correspond to a bounded rationality. Nothing in this description suggests that this procedural rationality, and the bounded rationality that, in some sense, it justifies, should not be understood as instrumental: indeed, procedural rationality manifests itself by determining, through deliberation, sub-optimal but available means allowing an agent to reach a goal at least to a satisfactory degree. Put otherwise, procedural rationality determines through deliberation what is appropriate to do in order to reach what is judged good when all constraints are considered, but, in no way does it determine *what* is good.

Thus, if instrumental rationality is defined by the relation between means and goals, there is a kind of category mistake in putting the concepts discussed above on the same semantic level: they are nothing but varieties of instrumental rationality. The economist who has most specifically and eloquently defended the idea that other types of rationality must complement instrumental rationality is very probably Shaun Hargreaves Heap (1989). However, this author could not be charged with a category mistake, because he defines instrumental rationality quite differently, namely by associating it to maximization (for example, 1989: 40–41). It is clear that if instrumental rationality is more or less synonymous with rationality-maximization, other kinds of rationality are absolutely required to complete the spectrum, and I would even say required to explain most economic decisions. This is precisely why Simon invoked bounded and procedural rationality and why I even refer to a minimal rationality, which is not less instrumental for being far from maximal. Be that as it may, in spite of the fact that economic literature frequently associates instrumental and maximal, since both were traditionally the main qualifiers of economic rationality in neoclassical economics, I think that instrumental rationality has a much larger scope than maximization; a means to reach a goal such as profit, for example, is instrumental in the process of reaching this goal even if it is not optimal in the circumstances and if the profit obtained is not maximal.

Moreover, Hargreaves Heap's plea is largely based on the fact that instrumental rationality cannot explain economic phenomena alone (1989: 61, 62, 65, 69, 87, 212, etc.). On this point, he is perfectly right, but this does not mean that the rest of the required explanatory factors should be understood as other kinds of rationality. They might be unwanted consequences associated with the presence of society, natural factors such as catastrophic weather, natural selection, etc. What makes rationality an essential explanatory factor or, put in a better fashion, the basis for rational explanations, is that it determines what guides actions, which uses some means whatever they are to reach a goal; therefore rationality is involved in explanation only when actions and their consequences are concerned. Since the other explanatory factors do not concern what brings this kind of guidance to human actions – otherwise they would be typical exemplifications of instrumental rationality – they have nothing to do with rationality understood as the basis for typical explanations of economics.

Since he defines instrumental rationality by maximization, which is in fact a very specific conception of rationality, and since he claims rightly that rationality alone cannot explain it, Hargreaves Heap finds it appropriate to introduce other 'kinds' of rationality which, according to my understanding of instrumental rationality are exemplifications of the latter, but which, according to his understanding, are complementary kinds of rationality that are not instrumental. More precisely, he promotes the idea that two other kinds of rationality exist along with instrumental rationality, namely procedural rationality and expressive rationality. His analyses of these two illustrations of rationality are highly interesting not only because they offer clarifying discussions of a number of economists' theses related to these questions, but because they propose interesting philosophical considerations about various traits of the human condition related to self-respect, freedom, etc. Nevertheless, I consider that they are wrongly presented as non-instrumental kinds of rationality commanding different kinds of explanations.

As for procedural rationality, Hargreaves Heap refers to Simon's views on this notion and distances himself from them because, according to him, Simon's conception is too subordinated to instrumental rationality (understood as maximization). Simon indeed suggests that avoiding cumbersome calculations might be an optimal decision given the cost of such calculations; Hargreaves Heap aptly describes this view as 'some kind of second best optimising' (1989: 118) and adds: 'It is optimising subject to the constraint of limited computational capacity' (ibid.). Whether or not such a subordination of Simonian procedural rationality to instrumental rationality (read maximization) correctly describes Simon's famous thesis, I will not contest this view since this kind of procedural rationality, more than being subordinated to instrumental rationality, is even an exemplification of the latter as I understand it. However, Hargreaves Heap defines procedural rationality in a more positive way than Simon does. He emphasizes the fact that we live in society and maintains that this condition explains a lot of what instrumental rationality cannot explain alone. Referring explicitly to rules, whose guiding role was evoked by Simon, he claims that they should not be considered as a second best for those whose computational power is limited, but rather as the best way to guide them in this complex world. He is quite possibly right, but it is difficult to see why this construal of procedural rationality could be opposed to instrumental rationality unless we strictly define the latter as maximization. After all, the decision to follow a rule that was socially established is explained by the fact that individuals who decide to follow it estimate that this option is the best available one for reaching their goals. Of course, if the question is to explain how rules were established in the past, it is necessary to refer to various constraints, to a multitude of decisions taken throughout history and to a certain structure of society, but this illustrates nothing more than the fact that instrumental rationality cannot explain these rules alone. Nonetheless, if it was admitted that these rules were progressively established by authoritative or influential decisions of a multitude of people and if the phenomenon to be explained was the fact that the people involved decided the way they did, the explanation, if any, would be largely based on the instrumental rationality attributed to these people aiming to satisfy particular interests, but, of course, such an explanation should be completed by reference to the innumerable unwanted consequences that these decisions would have contributed to provoking and to the role of a probably significant number of non-rational factors. There is no room for a radically distinct form of rationality: when it plays a role in an explanation, procedural rationality is just a particular kind (a quite important one) of instrumental rationality.

As for expressive rationality, the third type of rationality according to Hargreaves Heap, while it undoubtedly points toward something which needs to be considered for itself, it is difficult to see why this capacity for self-affirmation and 'sense of self-management' (1989: 148) should be opposed to instrumental rationality. Hargreaves Heap is obviously right to claim that self-respect cannot be measured by utility units like common commodities can, but many other valuable things (honour, peace, health, etc.) cannot either, but this does not force us to invoke other kinds of rationality to explain the presence of these highly valuable entities. In any case, if we avoid defining instrumental rationality by maximization, the problem no longer appears, because such precise utility measurements (necessary for computing maximization) are no longer required. An explanation based on the idea that one did such and such a thing because one wanted to express one's own personality relies on instrumental rationality, just like any explanation that invokes some means (here the actions performed) in order to reach a goal (here the expression of some personal traits). For sure, one may object that this kind of explanation does not work, because usually an agent does not consciously decide to adopt an attitude corresponding to expression or to self-affirmation. This is probably quite true, but if such is the case, the behaviour adopted has to be explained either by unconscious motivations which could be construed as reasons or by other factors which could not be considered reasons to behave in a particular way. In the first case, insofar as an unconscious form of rationality would be involved, this rationality would be instrumental since it would imply that some means would be more or less unconsciously taken in order to satisfy a more or less unconscious goal. In the second case, the explanatory factors involved would have by hypothesis nothing to do with any kind of rationality. Be that as it may, let us acknowledge that the existence of personality traits – just like the existence of a rule – may be explained only marginally and indirectly by referring to instrumental rationality. Indeed, while they require an explanation, these phenomena are not actions and only actions and their consequences can be explained by invoking rationality as is the case in typical economic explanations.

To sum up, the only substantial point that I really contest in Hargreaves Heap's analyses is the identification of instrumental rationality with maximization. There is no doubt that when it comes to explaining behaviours such as rule-following decisions or self-respect, invoking rationality-maximization would be particularly pedestrian and misleading. It is much more sensible to invoke different conceptions of rationality that may be described as procedural or as expressive without any problem; such conceptions may make room for Hargreaves Heap's illuminative analyses of self-respect, but, as we have seen, they are no less instrumental for all that. Now, it is clear that for Hargreaves Heap, instrumental rationality is closely associated with rationality-maximization. This can be illustrated by any one of the examples he uses to characterize expressive rationality by contrasting it with instrumental rationality. Let us consider one of them (1989: 168), in which he discusses a case drawn from Peters and Waterman (1982). Hargreaves Heap claims that if a sales department requires more intensive work from employees, an 'instrumental management's response' would be to impose high targets which may discourage employees and hurt their self-respect, whereas 'most successful corporations actually set very low sales targets' which reinforces self-respect and generates more efficient work from employees. These considerations seem well grounded and Hargreaves Heap is surely right to emphasize the fact that economists should pay more attention to them. However, why should the inappropriately high targets be associated with instrumental rationality? Apparently, because instrumental rationality is defined by maximization and that maximization spontaneously suggests imposing the highest targets. But maximization has nothing to do with what should be understood by instrumental rationality, which might be a bounded or a minimal rationality as well. An entrepreneur who notices that enhancing employee self-respect by setting low sales targets produces results that are not necessarily maximal but much better than those obtained by imposing high targets will not be stupid enough to stick to old ideas according to which the more I impose upon employees, the more I get from them. Why should instrumental rationality require more than a behaviour of this type, which, after all, is guided by the will to take the means that are the best adapted to the realization of a goal? In fact, Hargreaves Heap is perfectly aware of possible objections suggesting that the 'expressive' rationality illustrated by his examples might be reduced to instrumental rationality (1989: 172). He answers that such objections are mistaken because '[i]t does not make sense to talk about actions as being designed to maximize self-respect because there is not the information available which would allow the calculation of optimal actions in pursuit of this objective' (ibid.: 173). Here again, he is perfectly right, but this sentence clearly illustrates that the whole debate rests on the confusing association between instrumental rationality and optimality (or quality maximization), in the absence of which Hargreaves Heap's analysis of self-respect is flawless and instrumental rationality is a perfectly appropriate description of any kind of economic rationality. Saying that the latter is instrumental is not saying that rational beings are mere instruments mechanically oriented towards the maximization of a pre-defined goal, it is saying that rationality is constantly referred to in economics not for determining what is good for people and society, but for *explaining* why people actually choose to act the way they do and why society is shaped the way it is, both in virtue and in spite of the way they act.

Explanations and laws in economics

Thus, rationality is fundamental for economics because it is the key for explanations provided by this discipline. Therefore, it is time to consider more closely the kind of explanation that is involved. However, since economists generally find it important to claim that the explanations that they propose are *scientific* explanations and not simple extensions of common-sense considerations, it is appropriate at this point to have a look at typical scientific explanations in order to check whether economic explanations can be said to be scientific in this sense. When one considers the type of explanation that is traditionally associated with natural sciences – and especially with physics, which has always exerted an uncontested leading role in these sciences – one immediately meets the concept of a law. Indeed, we are so used to hearing that such and such a phenomenon is explained by such and such a scientific law, that scientific laws seem inseparable from scientific explanations, at least if one considers the paradigmatic explanations provided by physics.

Therefore, understanding the role of rationality in economic explanations can be greatly facilitated by comparing this role with the quite different role of laws in typical scientific explanations. It is well known that what was for a long period in the mid-twentieth century considered as the standard methodological theory of scientific explanation was associated with Carl Hempel's views on the matter. In Chapter 9, I will come back to Hempel's theory and its shortcomings more thoroughly, but for now, let me just underscore and illustrate the role of laws in this theory in order to better understand the role of rationality in the explanations typical in economics. In many papers, Hempel claimed that a scientific explanation is a correct deduction of a statement asserting the occurrence of what is to be explained (the explanandum) from at least one well established law together with empirically tested statements according to which the relevant facts obtain. Later on, Hempel acknowledged that since most laws of physics are statistical laws, a strict logical deduction is not possible from such non-deterministic laws, but he claimed that in such cases, it is with the help of an induction that an almost equivalent explanation is provided by an inductive derivation from such statistical laws (together with the appropriate empirical facts). In both cases, the presence of laws is the crucial element; the essential point being that an event, however puzzling, is explained by being law-covered (once acknowledged that specific conditions or circumstances associated with the law are obtained in the relevant case). Indeed, underscoring that, according to a well established scientific law, a given event happens regularly in circumstances similar to those that characterize the situation to be explained is, at least in one sense, explaining this event. Moreover, Hempel consistently maintained that explanation and prediction are closely associated and that both are based on laws. The idea is that if I can really explain that an event occurred because, in the circumstances that obtained, such an event must, according to a law, occur necessarily or with an extremely high probability, I should have been able to predict the occurrence of this event, were the appropriate laws and circumstances well known to me.

This theory of explanation, which is often characterized as the 'standard view', is very well known, but since it has frequently been perceived as rather odd or even naive by many scientists, economists and even philosophers who tend to consider that an explanation cannot be reduced to a formal scheme of logical deduction (or induction), it seems appropriate to take a very simple example of explanation, drawn from elementary optics, that illustrates that the Hempelian scheme quite reasonably describes what a scientific explanation is. Let us suppose that an ignorant and superstitious person is puzzled by the appearance of a rainbow in the sky after a rain shower. This person might consider various ways of explaining that phenomenon: perhaps is it due to a celestial intervention with a religious meaning or to a manifestation of power by extraterrestrials or simply to a multicolour projection by a powerful lighthouse standing nearby, etc. But a physicist passing through would readily provide a much more compelling explanation with the help of a well established universal law of optics according to which light rays (sunlight in this case) passing through a transparent medium, like rain drops (present in the sky at this occasion), will be refracted in multicoloured rays. And drawing from the same set of considerations (very roughly exposed here, admittedly), this physicist could accurately predict that, by directing light rays through another transparent medium like a glass prism, a similar phenomenon can be produced. Faced with this kind of scientific explanation reinforced by an accurate prediction, the puzzled person should normally ceased to be puzzled and to look for odd or supernatural explanations: if the phenomenon is just a case of what (according to well established scientific laws) always happens in similar circumstances, why should one remain puzzled and look for supplementary explanation? On the contrary, it should be those events that would differ from what, according to the law, always happens in such circumstances that require an explanation. No doubt this example is an extremely elementary illustration of what physics can explain, but nonetheless it clearly illustrates the explanatory power of a *law that covers* the event to be explained.

One must acknowledge, however, that Hempel's views have been seriously challenged since the 1970s (see Salmon 1989). Throughout the 1970s and the 1980s, more and more philosophers of science have tended to reject the Hempelian idea that an explanation is a deduction (or, more generally, an argument whether deductive or inductive) whose conclusion is the statement to be explained. Many counterexamples have been opposed to this view and many philosophers, who claim that an explanation is *context-dependent*, would consider it senseless to reduce any explanation to the mechanical process of deriving the explanandum from a few laws presented as covering it. However, even though they consider that Hempel has clearly overemphasized this role, few of them, if any, would deny that laws (and especially causal laws) might still play a role in the process of explaining physical phenomena.

I defer the discussion of the shortcomings of this 'standard' theory of explanation and of the various attempts to replace it to Chapter 9, but I intend in the present introduction to briefly examine whether this 'covering law' approach can be applied to explanations provided by economics. However, in order to clarify this point, it seems appropriate to first discuss the question of the very existence of *economic* laws. Let us admit to start with that if this question turned on the presence of some loosely defined *regularities* described by the so-called laws in the economic world, it would be difficult to deny the existence of such laws given that it is clear that the social world does not work randomly. Since economic behaviour is, almost by definition, guided by presumably rational considerations, how could one be astonished that it manifests at least some vaguely defined regularities? In this context, economists have formulated various laws, which are based on the fact that rational people normally perform actions that aim to satisfy some of their goals. It is true that these laws are not frequently invoked in economists' research as such, but they typically find their way into textbooks of economics. One can think, for example, of Gresham's law, Engel's law, the law of decreasing marginal utility, the law of decreasing return, the iron law of wages, the law of one price and, obviously, the law of demand understood either for itself or as a component of the law of supply and demand.[3] After all, one can be reasonably sure that a significant shortage in the available quantity of a good, caused either by an increased demand or a reduced supply, will usually be followed by an increase of the price of this good. However, this well established and frequently observed fact is not sufficient to allow us to conclude that we have a *scientific* economic law, namely the 'law of supply and demand'. Indeed, such regularities have been underscored long before the birth of economic theory. Aristotle mentioned in his *Politics* (1259a: 15–18) that Thales of

Miletus was aware of the fact that the price of a good tends to rise when demand increases or when supply becomes rare due to a monopoly. We even have a clear anticipation of a version of this 'law' in *Genesis*, the first book of the Bible (chapter 41: 29–30 and 48–57 and in chapter 47: 14–16), where Joseph, the son of Jacob, draws considerable benefits from his knowledge of the fact that the demand for wheat resulting from general scarcity generates an increase in the price of this staple. It is clear that, understood in this fashion, the law of supply and demand is not a scientific law but rather a common-sense generalization.

But what have economists added to such vague generalizations? No doubt they have formulated them in a much more precise way, either with the help of geometry, algebra or other mathematical tools. They have also included these laws in more general theories allowing them to determine the nature of various factors that can influence the functioning of the laws in a relatively unsuspected way. Probably the best known textbook example of this, typically illustrated by the so-called Giffen goods, is the analysis of the way in which changes in price can affect income, which can in turn affect the demand in its own fashion, by working concurrently with prices themselves. Moreover, economists have brought another kind of improvement to the formulation of common-sense laws. Indeed, econometricians have developed ingenious models allowing them to design curves or functions that, instead of being representations based on purely theoretical postulates, fit empirical data in such a way that theoretical features of these functions, such as their elasticity, can be measured in a relatively precise way. There is little doubt that these are important contributions to the understanding of economic phenomena, but can they allow us to conclude that we really have *scientific economic laws*? This question is largely a semantic one, since it depends on the way we define both science and law, notions whose definitions have never reached a consensus among philosophers of science, especially when social sciences are considered together with natural sciences. In any case, let us see whether, once improved upon by these contributions, economic laws remain significantly different from typical laws of physics.

Let us consider the improvements brought about by econometricians. It is surely a remarkable achievement to be able to measure with some accuracy the elasticity of a demand curve that characterizes a given market at a given period, in such a way that the variations of demand provoked by fluctuations in prices on this market can be adequately described by this curve. However, according to most methodological theory about scientific laws, scientific laws are normally universal statements that do not contain dates or proper names such as geographical terms. Econometrics-based analyses of wheat supply in the 1950s in Saskatchewan or of demand for wine in London during the late 1990s might describe economic phenomena with a remarkable accuracy without being scientific laws. If the phenomenon of gravitation was such that bodies fell with a given acceleration in Paris during the past months and with a different one in Montreal at the end of the last century, physicists would surely acknowledge that there is no such thing as a *law* of gravitation, at least if we mean by this the kind of law that we presently know under this name.[4]

A law should not be understood as mostly descriptive; therefore, one should consider instead the first improvement mentioned above concerning theoretical laws that were carefully reformulated by economists. However, a law *should be* a universal statement that fits the appropriate numerical data reasonably well and, according to most philosophers of science, it should also satisfy counterfactual situations, which means roughly that it must accurately describe not only the actual situation but also situations which could obtain in other circumstances.[5] To reuse a common example, the law according to which water freezes at 0° Celsius at normal pressure is perfectly true even in the tropics as was positively tested when fridges were brought there. It is true that the law of demand, which is so central in economic theory, seems to be robust enough to be applied to quite different situations, but only if it is interpreted in a relatively vague way describing nothing more than general trends. Indeed, we can claim safely enough that an increase in price *tends to reduce* the demand for a given commodity, but it is difficult to go much further when we want to maintain the full generality of the 'law'. Put otherwise, economic 'laws' seem to be general enough to satisfy the counterfactual requirement, only by being as vague as common-sense generalizations.

It is true that one should not be too strict in requiring that scientific laws fit data. As is well known, most laws of physics, and especially those of quantum theory, are *statistical* laws; therefore, the fact that economic laws are also laws that fit a set of data not in an exact but only in a statistically acceptable fashion should not be a reason to deny their scientific character. However, this consideration neglects the fact that, for a physical law, being a statistical law means only that it is not based on the knowledge of a deterministic causal process, and *in no way* does it mean that it is only related to data in a loose fashion. Non-deterministic laws of modern physics are characterized by their remarkable precision, which allows physicists to use them for predicting phenomena with an accuracy that can be superior to what was obtained with the use of the deterministic laws of classical physics.

In fact, most economists, at least since Marshall, are perfectly aware of these limitations of economic laws. Therefore, for defending the scientific status of these laws, those who choose to devote some time to this methodological question generally adopt a strategy based on the fact that even though scientific laws must be universal statements, most of them are also *conditional* statements of the type 'if condition *Z* obtains, then all *A*s are *B*'. This conditional character of laws can be exemplified even by some laws of physics, for example, by Charles' law, which claims that '*if* its mass and its pressure are maintained constant, then the volume occupied by any gas is proportional to its absolute temperature'. Put otherwise, it is *only if* all relevant factors except volume and temperature *do not change*, that the main assertion of the law can be strictly true. It is this latter approach that was adopted regarding economic laws by Marshall when he claimed that economic laws suppose that other relevant factors do not change or, put differently, remain equal to what they were (which is what the phrase *ceteris paribus* literally means).[6] Therefore, the main debates about the status of economic laws turned around the *ceteris paribus* clauses, which are required, at least implicitly, by laws of physics as well. However, it is not an easy thing to determine what counts as an acceptable *ceteris paribus* clause, one that can legitimately transform a generalization that would be false if it was taken literally into a genuine law. For example, in spite of the microeconomic 'law' which claims the contrary, it is *not literally true* that any increase in the price of a commodity will reduce the consumption of its eventual complementary commodity, since consumers may instead buy more of a cheaper commodity that has the same complement. However, the inclusion of an appropriate *ceteris paribus* clause, one that requires that the consumption of all commodities other than the two which are involved in the alleged law remain the same, will obviously exclude this possibility and improve the chances that our generalization be considered a law. *Ceteris paribus* clauses are required by many laws of physics as well, but, in contrast with those required by economic laws, these clauses usually concern phenomena that can be controlled experimentally or that can be explained by independent laws. Since, in economics, such clauses usually cannot be controlled or explained in such a way, whereas they are still more crucially required for the validity of eventual laws, one will easily understand that the main debate about the status of economic laws turned around the legitimacy of *ceteris paribus* clauses.

This debate was reactivated during the last decades, especially by two very interesting papers by Daniel Hausman (1988; see also Hausman 1992, especially 133–142) and James Woodward (2002) respectively. The issue in question is to determine what kind of *ceteris paribus* clauses should be resorted to in order to transform a general statement that is subject to many exceptions into a scientific law. Therefore Hausman proposed four criteria (lawlikeness, reliability, refinability and excusability) that an alleged law statement (which includes *ceteris paribus* clauses) must meet to be an acceptable law (Hausman 1988: 310–311 and 1992: 139–142). This analysis undoubtedly contributed to clarifying what is required from eventual *ceteris paribus* clauses, but the problem remained of determining when these criteria can be said to be satisfied to a sufficient degree. When should we decide that a lawlike statement including *ceteris paribus* clauses is reliable enough to be considered a law? And when should we decide that introducing *ceteris paribus* clauses in order to cope with something that interferes with this kind of statement is excusable enough? More generally, is it worthwhile to grant the status of a scientific law to a generalization that satisfies these criteria to a certain point, but which remains too close to a common-sense generalization to be considered a scientific law? For example, a generalization such as the one according to which 'people who need a given good will tend to buy the cheapest among those of equal quality which are available *if* they are aware of its existence and *if* not too much effort is required to obtain it' seems to satisfy such criteria at least to a certain degree and is clearly the expression of a certain wisdom, but what do we gain by declaring that it is a law? It is the absence of compelling criteria delimiting what should count as a *ceteris paribus* clause that induced Woodward to claim that, with ingeniously chosen *ceteris paribus* clauses, any generalization whatsoever could be transformed into a scientific law. Woodward drew from this consideration a radical conclusion, which is used as the title of his paper: 'There is no such thing as a *ceteris paribus* law'. While expressing a legitimate denunciation of a too permissive use of *ceteris paribus* clauses, this conclusion however seems a bit too radical, because if it is accepted literally it would hardly make room for any law whatsoever, given that even laws of physics require implicit *ceteris paribus* conditions. Clearly some mitigation is required here since all clauses that one may invoke in order to formulate an acceptable law cannot be legitimate to the same degree. While Woodward is right to underscore the danger of voiding the meaning of a law by licensing *ceteris paribus* clauses too easily, Hausman's attempt to determine some criteria that might monitor the use of such clauses, while not perfectly conclusive, is surely justified.

In any case, it is not my intention here to decide between Hausman and Woodward's respective approaches to this question of *ceteris paribus* conditions, which may remain non-decidable. My intention was rather to summarily characterize the nature of scientific laws, before assessing whether economists can invoke them in their explanations the same way that physicists do. If one admits that the legitimacy of *ceteris paribus* conditions is a matter of degree, the very limited control that, in contrast with physicists, economists can exert over such clauses should induce one to conclude that the chance of finding compelling theoretical criteria allowing us to answer the question of the existence and the status of genuine scientific economic laws seems to be very slim. If such is the case, why not turn towards a more pragmatic approach instead of desperately looking for compelling criteria? The idea is to consider not the nature of scientific laws but the role they play in science. Why is it so important to have laws in science? Of course, it is because laws can play a significant role both in explaining and in predicting. Therefore, the relevant question to discuss is whether economic laws, if they exist at all, can play such a role in the explanations provided by economists.

What about explanations in economics?

For sure, when it comes to providing an explanation, economists can invoke common-sense generalizations, which they can even call 'laws', and proceed just like, according to Hempel, physicists do when they refer to natural laws in their own explanations. As we will see, the question is not so much whether economists can rely on such 'laws' for their explanation; it is rather what kind of premises these explanations rest on in the last resort. Let us consider an example drawn from elementary economics. Suppose that someone who is struggling looking for an apartment to rent in a given city desperately asks 'why is it so difficult to find an apartment to rent in this city?'[7] An economist could answer, if such is the situation: 'because, a few years ago, the city administration imposed a rent ceiling at a level below the prevailing price and there is *an economic law* according to which any price ceiling at a level below the prevailing price of a commodity is followed by a shortage of this commodity, therefore the house shortage was easily predictable by anyone who has acknowledged this fact along with this law'. If we assume that the law relating price ceilings and shortages is well grounded, we may judge that we hold an acceptable Hempelian explanation which is correctly deduced from this economic law together with facts that are well known about the policies recently adopted in this city. However, it is far from certain that the person looking for an apartment would be really happy with this explanation. This person may have been previously informed by a newspaper about the existence of the price ceiling and, as a would-be renter, have considered this to be particularly good news. In this situation, the explanation provided by the economist would consist only of a notification of the existence of a law-based relation between the price ceiling and the shortage. The frustrated apartment searcher might be just a little more frustrated by the explanation and say 'I know that a price ceiling that I welcomed was imposed and I know that we now face a much less welcome apartment shortage, but what I am wondering is *why* I am unable to find any one of those attractively priced apartments. How can I be happy with an answer that simply lets me know that this is a normal situation; that claims that things always happen this way? What I want to know is precisely why? Why are price ceilings always followed by apartment shortage?'

Faced with this more pressing question, the first reaction of the economist might be to claim that his previous explanation was just an application of the more fundamental law of supply and demand. When the price of a commodity is brought to a lower level, its supply is reduced and its demand increases. 'But why is it so?' our frustrated apartment searcher would still ask; 'why do suppliers not instead *increase* the supply of the cheap commodity?' The question is not as absurd as it might seem, since a lot of commodities such as ballpoints and computers have been supplied in increasingly large quantities when their prices were constantly decreasing. Certainly, the economist can easily explain the latter phenomenon, but he cannot simply present the alleged universal law according to which a decreased price is always followed by a reduced supply as an explanation of last resort. If the economist persists in invoking the authority of the venerable law of supply and demand and in claiming that things always happen this way, we may safely guess that the insistent questioner will not be impressed. How might the authority of this old law whose essential claim was known long before the time of Aristotle provide our apartment searcher with the satisfaction of holding a scientific explanation? The refusal to answer a legitimate demand for an explanation by claiming that things are what they are according to a generally respected law and closing the discussion with such a point may be an understandable expression of exasperation, but it can hardly be judged a typically scientific attitude.

There is little doubt that the person fascinated by the rainbow might have remained equally unsatisfied by the law of refraction, but the physicist could have shown that this law itself was explained with the help of more general laws concerning the very nature of light. Naturally, the explanation will not only consist of the straightforward mentioning of laws, but will necessarily consist, typically with the help of a model, of showing how many facts are involved and are interrelated in the kind of mechanism that produces the phenomenon to be explained.[8] In any case, at some limiting point in this regression towards an ultimate explanation, the physicist will have to admit that fundamental laws of physics (claiming that things always happen in a given way) have been reached despite the still possible dissatisfaction of our questioner. Nonetheless, a compelling scientific explanation has been provided if the phenomenon to be explained is presented as the thing that should be expected according to a careful analysis of the mechanism through which the consequences of some fundamental natural laws obtain. Similarly, if an astronomer provides someone who is puzzled by the planet Mars' constantly changing position in the sky with an explanation that simply consists in showing that this changing position can be deduced from the fact that Mars is a planet and that there is an empirical law according to which any planet is moving in the sky, it is quite probable that the questioner will not be more satisfied than our would-be renter and will ask: 'but why are planets moving in the sky?' The astronomer will invoke a set of interrelated empirical laws together with other empirical facts and will expose the mechanism (possibly illustrated by a physical model) that allows one to conclude that, from the place where this person was observing the sky, such a movement is just what should have been expected. Nonetheless, at some points in this explanation, the astronomer will be forced to claim that the most fundamental laws of physics have been reached and that they are what they are in such a way that one has to accept them without requiring a further explanation. However, these laws of physics are not roughly formulated pre-Aristotelian generalizations, they are members of an impressive set of interconnected regularities that are in no way related to any common-sense considerations and would even have remained totally unsuspected without the patient researches of physicists. Moreover, in contrast with economic laws, which do not make it possible to make predictions much more (if any more) accurate than those made by sensitive people who are familiar enough with the business world, the laws of physics allow physicists to make spectacular predictions that reinforce the authority of these laws. When so many phenomena observed in the world can be interrelated in a consistent fashion through the same set of fundamental laws, it is reasonable to say that these phenomena are explained, at least explained up to a very significant degree. It is only when a phenomenon stubbornly resists being covered by this set of laws that it can be said to be unexplainable. Note that my point here is not to magnify the laws of physics which, in some sense, often 'lie', as claimed by Nancy Cartwright (1983); my only claim, here, is that, in contrast with what is the case in economics, fundamental laws of physics can be reasonably and convincingly referred to in explanations designed to show that some puzzling events are nothing but what was expected to happen. It is true that what makes an explanation satisfactory is the fact that the *mechanisms* through which such an expected result obtains are exposed with clarity and precision, but this is not to deny the role of laws that are normally invoked at various points.

When it comes to answering ultimate why-questions such as the one of our apartment-searcher, the difference between physics and economics is that, in the latter case, the explanative power does not really rest on laws, even as a last resort. To answer one who seriously asks 'why do suppliers not instead increase the supply of the cheap commodity?', the economist typically will not look for more general laws. Requiring the economist to proceed like the physicist would be unfair, because human actions and their consequences cannot, normally, be reduced to strictly or even stochastically regular patterns as most physical events can. But fortunately for the economist who aims to provide a satisfactory explanation, it is not really necessary to rely on alleged universal laws. This is fortunate because economic laws would not have the authority that is granted to laws either by being tested with a compelling accuracy or by being logically related to a set of empirically tested laws. Instead, the economist may resort to the rationality principle, a principle that should not be construed as a law. As we have seen, this principle simply suggests that normally people are sensitive enough to variations in situations and are able to evaluate them in order to perform actions that they consider appropriate. Thus, suppliers are at least rational in this sense: those whose selling price (imposed by law) turns out to be lower than their cost will not continue producing; some of them will transfer their capital into more rewarding kinds of production, others will reduce this production in order to reduce their loss, and so forth. Therefore, entrepreneurs will resist building new houses since potential landlords are no longer interested in buying them.

The fact that laws are not really necessary with this kind of explanation is easily illustrated. Indeed, the economist could have quite correctly answered the initial question 'why is it so difficult to find an apartment to rent in this city?' by simply exposing the mechanism through which that result was obtained without resorting to any law. This economist had simply to recall that a few years ago, the city administration imposed a rent ceiling below the prevailing rent level. Then, it would have been sufficient to explain directly that a housing shortage was to be expected since many home owners, when seeing that the revenue they can obtain from rent tends to be lower than their cost, will not continue to rent their houses. Who would be stupid enough to offer more and more apartments to rent when the price ceiling imposed by municipal law is so low that it does not compensate the owner for the costs and trouble generated by apartment rental? Clearly, reducing the number of houses to rent was the thing to do by those home owners who are rational in the sense of being inclined to change their course of action when they estimate that it is detrimental to the attainment of their goal, which, in this specific case, is to make some profit by renting houses. These home owners simply do not see why they should keep on taking the trouble of renting houses and buying the new houses required to satisfy the increased demand generated by the attractive low price imposed by the rent ceiling if, at the ceiling price, they do not cover their expenses. Since they are (instrumentally) rational fellows, they will not lose time and money by doing so. Once these considerations are accepted, concluding that the shortage was to be expected as a normal consequence of the too low ceiling price seems inescapable. Obviously, the mechanism that is responsible for this result was totally unwanted by those who have imposed the rent ceiling, but it is easily understandable by those who accept the rationality principle or, if one prefers, the idea that people are not stupid enough to totally neglect to do what is clearly required for the satisfaction of their own goals. Since a role equivalent to the one that is played by natural laws of physics is not really required by economic explanations and since 'economic laws' would not play it very efficiently whatsoever, one can easily understand that economists became unfond of referring to economic laws in their explanations. In contrast, the explanations provided by physicists could hardly avoid referring to laws at least at some points, because, in order to ground the mechanism invoked, a physicist could obviously not allege that it is based on what is expected from rational behaviour as an economist can, but has to resort to the fact that it corresponds to *what always (or almost) happens* in similar situations, which is precisely what is stated by such laws.

Of course, economists might continue to consider the 'law of demand' or similar statements to be laws; indeed, the question here becomes purely semantic and the label 'law' is commonly used to characterize such statements whether or not they should be considered as sophisticated reformulations of common-sense generalizations. Whether 'laws' of this kind can be considered 'scientific' or not is a question that I do not consider to be really meaningful; it is more significant to observe that these laws can hardly play a role in explanations and predictions similar to the one that is played by scientific laws in physics. However, even though the 'laws' of economics do not have the qualities required to efficiently play a similar role, this fact does not seems to constitute a serious predicament for economics (which, incidentally, in its typical developments rarely grants a really significant place to its so-called laws); indeed, in its usual way of explaining based on the rationality principle, laws are not really required in the structure of relevant explanations. It is true that economists, as we will see, may also invoke evolution and selection in their explanations, but in this case as well, laws as such do not have a significant explanative role. It is not even clear that, given the nature of economic life, laws would be an appropriate instrument for making sensible predictions, but it is not useful for the present line of argumentation to push further the discussion of this last question.

The content of the book

This book is divided into four sections. The first one bears on the way the concept of rationality has evolved throughout the history of economic thought. It illustrates how far, from the classics to contemporary economists, this concept was transformed and modelled in such a way that a wider and wider gap was created between the foundational concept of rationality, whose content was rather minimal, and the notion of rationality as it was defined by marginalist and neoclassical economists. This section is divided in two chapters, which consider respectively the two main stages in this process. The first of them, after considering rationality in the classic period, analyses the progressive refinements of the maximization principle, which corresponded to the rationality principle for economists, between the 1870s and the Second World War. The second one discusses the consequences of the fact that the rationality principle was reduced to a less psychologically laden consistency principle, which economists have generally adopted as a kind of surrogate for the genuine principle since the mid-twentieth century.[9] Through discussions of topics such as revealed preferences, changing tastes, money pump and experimental economics, it will be shown that the hardly definable rationality principle, in its full generality, continues to play a fundamental role in economics, even when the use of surrogate principles seems to have almost evacuated it. These chapters will even show that interest in a more sensible, while minimal, notion of rationality is made particularly manifest each time that economic theories are seriously challenged.

The second section is devoted to a discussion of three very serious problems, which are associated with the adoption of this more sensible notion of rationality. Each of them is discussed in a particular chapter as follows. The third chapter of the book considers the fact that, in contrast with maximization and consistency that were applied in a more or less mechanical fashion, the minimal rationality that is invoked here corresponds to the rationality of an individual human being. This implies that methodological individualism must be taken seriously in spite of the fact that it was recently a favourite target of quite respectable theoreticians of economics. This chapter responds systematically to their objections and proposes a more palatable version of *methodological* individualism, which makes room for unintended consequences and must not be reduced to an indefensible reductionism. Chapter 4 raises the question of whether some room is left for irrationality when we refer to the kind of minimal rationality that, in this book, is presented as relevant for economics. Indeed, defined as the faculty of maximization, rationality does not risk being confused with irrationality, but minimal rationality cannot be so easily distinguished from sheer irrationality. This chapter reviews and discusses frequently debated approaches to the question and, while denying the existence of hard and fast criteria for identifying irrationality, it proposes a practical solution to this problem that makes some sense of Karl Popper's highly controversial view on the matter and allows us to more clearly define the kind of rationality that should be attributed to economic agents. Chapter 5 bears on a related problem, namely the problem raised by the inescapable looseness of the definition of minimal rationality. The latter, like bounded rationality, cannot be defined with great precision whereas maximal rationality (implied by the notion of maximization) seems to be rigorously defined with the help of mathematical tools. By opposing various arguments to alternative ways of fixing the meaning of such a maximum, this chapter challenges the received view according to which the concept of maximization has the advantage of allowing us to define rationality with undisputed precision.

The third section deals with the ways that economists have chosen for avoiding the difficulties and limitations that seem associated with the notion of rationality. One of them was acclaimed by economists and was even considered by many to be the standard approach. The second one is much more radical and it took various forms during the last half century. They will be discussed in turn in the two chapters of this section. Chapter 6 bears on the highly popular way of bypassing these difficulties by maintaining that assumptions such as the rationality postulate may be perfectly unrealistic insofar as the predictions of the theory are satisfactorily tested. This chapter challenges Milton Friedman's defence of this thesis with arguments somewhat different from those used by its many challengers. It proceeds mostly by showing that Friedman's three famous examples designed to illustrate his point can just as well be used to reverse Friedman's own conclusions. Equally, it will be shown that this thesis is not more acceptable when it is construed as instrumentalist, no matter what legitimacy is attributed to instrumentalism in natural sciences, which has little to do with the alleged Friedmanian instrumentalism. Chapter 7 discusses the other way of dealing with these problems that consists in relinquishing the notion of rationality altogether and in developing an economic theory that does not rely on this assumption. Starting from an analysis of the debate that was provoked by Gary Becker's heroic attempt to defend such a view, this chapter pushes the latter to its logical limit by invoking various purely mechanistic ways of reaching equilibria that economic theory normally explains with models animated by rational agents. Since more and more sophisticated automata were put forward to reach such a goal, discussions about whether pure mechanisms can produce similar results *without being rational* brings us, somewhat paradoxically, to more contemporary debates about whether such automata *might be as rational* as human beings are. This leads to discussing various challenges that cognitive sciences oppose to the use of rational explanations in economics.

The fourth section is totally devoted to analysing the specific characters of explanation in economics. The only explanations that tend to be used by economists besides rational explanations are those that are derived from natural selection. Chapter 8 will consider this kind of explanation, which, after being promoted by Armen Alchian, was referred to by Milton Friedman and Gary Becker and by many other economists thereafter. It cannot be denied that a certain kind of selection plays a role in the economic world, but, with the help of various examples and imaginary experiments, this chapter argues that rational and 'natural selection' explanations, while complementary in some sense, are exclusive in another and more fundamental sense; therefore, it explores the causes and the consequences of this situation. Chapter 9 examines rational explanations in the light of theories of scientific explanation that were developed mostly in philosophy of natural science and in philosophy of history through important debates between philosophers such as Carl Hempel, Michael Scriven, William Dray and, a little more recently, Wesley Salmon, Bas van Fraassen, Peter Achinstein, etc. Each step in this critical analysis of explanations will be illustrated by examples drawn from economic theory. The relation between concepts such as prediction and expectation will be clarified and reinterpreted, and new solutions will be proposed to long-standing problems raised by this confrontation of explanations respectively met in natural and social sciences.

The conclusion of the book relates its main theses to some specific traits of contemporary economics given that the latter can be characterized by an increasing pluralism in methodology. The fact that contemporary economics was, over the last decades, rejuvenated by approaches such as behavioural economics, game theory, and neuroeconomics will be briefly revisited in order to evaluate to what extent they might force us to reconsider our views about rationality and explanation in economics. It is because this conclusion looks at what happens to the theses of the book in the last developments of the story that I found it appropriate to call it an Epilogue.

Part I

Rationality in the history of economic thought

1 Rationality in economics before the Second World War

If the rationality principle is really the cornerstone of economic explanations, we may expect to observe its presence in economic thought as soon as the latter began to be an explanatory and not only a descriptive and normative intellectual enterprise.[1] Pretending to precisely determine a moment in time that would correspond to the birth of an explanatory type of economics would obviously be preposterous. Nonetheless, it seems reasonable to claim that somewhere in the second half of the eighteenth century, economists, influenced by the enthusiasm aroused by Newtonian science, began to devote more and more of their energy to explaining how an economy can work efficiently and, as we will see, their explanations were effectively based on the rationality principle. From this period on, throughout the whole history of economic thought, this principle has continuously animated the increasingly sophisticated explanations proposed by economists. It is true, however, that for the sake of conceptual precision economists were brought to characterize rationality in ways more and more remote from the somewhat fluid concepts associated with this fundamental rationality principle, in such a way that the exact role of the latter has almost been forgotten. Therefore, the two first chapters of this book will show why this principle has, nonetheless, remained a determinant throughout the history of economic thought, despite the fact that, in the minds of economists, it was progressively superseded by more specific views on rationality having less and less to do with what is properly called the rationality *principle*. It is in this context that the workings of the rationality principle will be analysed from its implicit adoption by eighteenth-century economists to recent debates about rationality in experimental economics and decision theory. My claim is that much of the confusion surrounding the role of rationality in economics is due to this increasing gap between the notion of rationality invoked in modern economic models and the rationality principle properly understood. It will be concluded from all these considerations that, while successive representations of the rational agent as maximizer, *homo oeconomicus* or consistent chooser have frequently been the target of devastating arguments, these criticisms have been so far from refuting the fundamental rationality principle itself that most of them have been made in the very name of this principle.

The rationality principle in classical economics

The rationality principle does not seem to have played a significant role in Aristotelian economics or in medieval economics. It is true that Aristotle depicted his heads of family as people who managed to adopt means that tended to provide the good life they wanted for their family. However, the question is not whether the analyst of economic phenomena agrees that agents behave in such a rational way, but whether the acknowledgement of this fact was determinant for the explanations provided by economic theory. Once the question is put this way, we must admit that it was not the case with Aristotle. It was ethical considerations that were decisive for him when it came to proposing some thesis about the proper amount of goods to be exchanged or the appropriateness of accumulating wealth or of imposing an interest on loans. Philosophers such as Aristotle and Aquinas, like most thinkers or their respective times, were more dedicated to exposing what people *should* do when they made economic decisions than to *explaining why* the result of their actions was such and such. Even though mercantilist thinkers were less guided than their predecessors by ethical considerations, they still devoted a large part of their writings to exposing what governments and merchants *should* do in order to insure the wealth of their nations. Naturally, it would be absurd to claim that their writings were free from explanations, but their main goal was to influence political decisions and those explanations remained limited in scope, relatively unsystematic and subordinated to this goal.

So, the question 'when did the rationality principle start to play a decisive role in economic thought?' seems to be a relevant one. Even though everyone would easily acknowledge that it is difficult to find a precise answer to this question, I suspect that most economists would probably claim that if a precise moment had to be designated, it should be associated with the marginalist revolution. After all, marginalist economists were the first to propose an explicit analysis of rational choice. But what about classical economics? It is clear that classical economists were not anxious, like marginalists were, to analyse the way individual agents make rational decisions, but the question here is not when economists started to analyse explicitly the workings of rationality by individual agents, but when the rationality principle became the key principle of economic *explanations*, irrespective of whether economists were conscious of this fact or not. Therefore, the rationality principle began to play its fundamental role when economists started to give priority to explaining the workings of economic mechanisms over determining the best way to reach economic justice or prosperity.

Given that throughout the eighteenth century more and more economists were constantly objecting to the mercantilist reliance on state management and interventions, liberal economists were forced to explain how an economy could avoid chaos when it is left to itself, or put otherwise to explain why *laissez faire* is not a disastrous kind of *laisser aller*. In order to dramatically illustrate how an economic mechanism can work, David Hume, for example, did not hesitate to claim that, thanks to free trade, the disappearance in a single night of four fifths of the entire English gold reserve would not be a real catastrophe, because the consequently reduced prices of England's output would massively attract consumers from other countries who would bring back the lost gold into England (Hume 1970 [1752]: 62–64). In spite of the various and serious objections that can be raised against this argumentation, it constituted one of the first clear analyses of the workings of an economic mechanism; and since consumers were supposed to proceed this way because taking advantage of the assumed low prices of England's output was an occasion that they were supposed to be rational enough to avoid missing, this argument was implicitly based on the rationality principle. Later, economists like Marx and Keynes, strongly hostile to this kind of liberalism, would as well analyse quite different types of mechanisms in order to explain the workings of an economy, but the circumstances specific to the eighteenth century were such that it was liberal economists who, through the analysis of a free market, provide the first full-fledged economic explanations based on the rationality principle. No doubt those explanations were still largely guided by political considerations, but they nonetheless occupied the central place in the argumentation, and this priority granted to the explanation of economic mechanisms was relatively new. Put otherwise, political arguments tended more and more to be judged by their explanative power, and no longer by their conformity to philosophical views about human nature or about the ideal of a just and prosperous society.

Let us, for example, consider Turgot who, as early as 1766, argued that a 'current price' tends to prevail in a market: 'if one [of the wine sellers] is not willing to give more than four pints for a bushel, the Proprietor of the corn will not give him his corn, when he comes to learn that someone else will give him six or eight pints for the same bushel' (Turgot 1898 [1766]: 29). This sentence contains, in a nutshell, the central intuition from which most price theories derive. Turgot's argument was clearly based on the fact that people are rational in the sense that they are far from being stupid. Who would be stupid enough to give one bushel of corn in exchange for only four pints of wine when it is well known that other wine sellers would be happy to give six or eight pints for the same bushel? Was it not legitimate to presume that (rational) economic agents prefer to get more wine rather than less and that, once informed about the possibilities available to them, will (freely) take the appropriate means to obtain what they prefer, in such a way that a single price will progressively prevail? Were a significant number of people inclined to prefer obtaining less rather than more wine for the same price or to be totally indifferent to such matters, Turgot and his successors would have been at a loss to explain that a single price tends to prevail in a market or to predict even roughly any change in price level. More generally, were a significant number of people inclined to act in a way that hardly makes sense rather than in a 'rational' fashion, the prospects for explanation by the social sciences of phenomena resulting from human actions would be reduced dramatically.[2]

It is true that Turgot had adopted a theory of value based on needs and desires which was closer to the marginalist *utility* theory of value – which is itself intimately associated with rational calculus – than was the *production cost* theory of value which classical economists such as Smith and Ricardo were committed to. This fact, however, does not imply that Smith's and Ricardo's respective theories are less indebted to the rationality principle. Here again, I do not mean that one can find an explicit acknowledgement of the crucial role of the rationality principle in the work of these economists, but rather that their theories make no sense without an implicit acknowledgement of such a role. To my knowledge, Smith never refers to the rationality principle; the passage where he comes closest to doing this is probably the one where he considers the fact that most people at least, when they refrain from considerably increasing expenses in the absence of a parallel increase in revenue, are guided by what he calls 'the principles of common prudence' which do not 'govern the conduct of every individual' but nonetheless 'always influence that of the majority of every class or order'.[3] In contrast with this rather ambiguous methodological analysis, the reliance on the fact that people are rational in the sense implied by the rationality principle occupies the central place in Smith's economic explanations as will be illustrated below.

Notice how Smith explains why market prices tend to oscillate around what he calls a 'natural price' (Smith 1937 [1776]: book I, ch. 7). In a certain sense, one can even say that the rationality principle is implied by the very idea of a natural price, which is defined as the price that is just *sufficient to bring to the market* the quantity of commodities required to satisfy normal demand. Indeed, if he did not suppose that producers are rational, how could Smith be so sure that a higher price would be operative in convincing some producers to produce more commodities and to bring more of them to the market? The role of an implicit rationality principle is even clearer when we consider the way in which Smith argues that the market price tends to be brought in line with the natural price. Indeed, in the event of a commodity supply in excess of demand, Smith confidently concludes that landowners, workers or capitalists would draw their resources away from this market when they realize that their respective revenues have fallen below their natural rates, because he postulates that people are not stupid enough to keep renting, working or investing when they are no longer paid an amount that is considered sufficient to pursue such an activity. Similarly, he can claim that such a withdrawal would be reversed as the price approaches anew its natural level, because he postulates that people are not stupid enough to indefinitely keep divesting in an activity whose returns have become increasingly consistent with what they require to practise it. And how could he know that this withdrawal would produce this happy effect for the producers if it were not because he postulates that consumers are not stupid enough to stubbornly refuse to pay a slightly higher but still reasonable price when they see that otherwise they can no longer find a sufficient amount of the commodity they need?

In Ricardo's economics, arguments based on a rationality principle become even pervasive. For example, the famous Ricardian theory of rent claims that, at given periods in the process of development of agriculture, farmers exploiting high quality land would freely comply in paying more and more significant rents to their landowner. According to Ricardo, the only reason that explains their agreeing to pay such significant amounts to landowners is that it would not make sense for them to take the trouble of moving to the lower quality lands, which turn out to be the only ones available at these periods, if their net profit by doing so would not be higher than the profit they presently obtain even after paying the required rent (Ricardo 1951 [1815] and 1951 [1817]: chapter II). But more importantly, most of Ricardo's theories postulate the equality of profit rates at each step of the argument, a postulate that is straightforwardly derived from the rationality principle associated with the postulate of the mobility of capital. Indeed, once such mobility is admitted and once sufficient information about the discrepancies between profit rates has been obtained, no capitalist is supposed to be stupid enough to leave capital in an industry which provides a smaller profit rate than another industry, instead of progressively transferring it to the latter until the equality of profit rates is reached. Why would *rational* capitalists refrain from transferring their capital in such circumstances? The same postulate also plays a crucial role in the elegant demonstration with the help of which Ricardo emphasizes the inaccuracies of the labour theory of value in situations where different labour–capital ratios prevail between industries. Indeed, in spite of his commitment to a labour theory of value, he was forced to acknowledge that capitalists could not be stupid enough to keep producing in an industry whose rate of profit, given the quantity of capital required, would fall below the rate offered by another one employing the same quantity of labour but proportionally less capital (Ricardo, 1951 [1817]: chapter I, sections IV and V). Finally, the theory of comparative advantages in international trade, which remains probably the most well known among Ricardian contributions, is based on the idea that citizens of a country are not stupid enough to keep producing a good themselves that they can obtain from another country by trading another one that they can produce at a smaller cost.

In Ricardian economics, the rationality principle already seems to take a somewhat more radical form than in Smithian analysis. The idea of an equality of profit rates suggests that capitalists would not tolerate any discrepancy between these rates. Note however that, even though this implies a perfect mobility of capital, it does not necessarily require knowledge of the evolution of profit rates everywhere in the economy since it suffices that all capitalists keep an eye on their successful neighbours and adapt their production accordingly to generate a progressive equalization process. Put otherwise, Turgot and Smith looked less ambitious in their claims, but one should not exaggerate this difference since the equalization of profit rates might be construed as something that is realized very progressively with the slow diffusion of information through the whole economy. Ricardo's agents do not need to be equipped with an exceptional computation power; they need only to be clever enough to move their capital where it is clearly more rewarding, once it has been admitted that this capital is easily transferable and that information about some discrepancies between profit rates has been obtained. Be that as it may, Ricardo did not refer to the principle of rationality as such, but he was very conscious that his own conclusions assumed a principle that implies that people were constantly searching for the most economically advantageous options and which is so fundamental that it prevails over facts attested by common sense. This is clearly illustrated in a passage found in a letter from Ricardo to Malthus: 'It would be no answer to me to say that men were ignorant of the best and cheapest mode of conducting their business and paying their debts, because that is a question of fact not of science, and might be urged against almost every proposition in Political Economy.'[4]

More directly evocative of the rationality principle is the famous passage in which John Stuart Mill describes an *economic man* as 'a being who desires to possess wealth, and who is capable of judging of the comparative efficiency of means for obtaining that end' (1948 [1836]: 137). A claim that focuses in such a way on the instrumental character of rationality remains exceptional enough within classical economics. It is even a brilliant anticipation of a view that, through J. E. Cairnes, was to find its way up to Lionel Robbins to become the standard epistemological justification of marginalist microeconomics. One must not conclude, however, that Mill's rational man is yet a sheer calculator or a maximizer as Jevons' economic man will be. While implying an aptitude to compare the efficiency of various means, rationality is still described as an affair of good judgement rather than of computation. Like Smith and Ricardo, Mill applies this kind of rationality principle in his economic works, in order to explain the workings of economic mechanisms by deriving conclusions from the fact that workers, consumers and capitalists have clearly the minimal level of good judgement required for preferring cheapest goods among those of equal quality, turning towards the most attractive jobs offered on the market, and avoiding continual loss in some ventures that are no longer profitable.

Even though it was the development of liberal economics that made the need to draw from the rationality principle evident, the importance of this principle, as suggested above, is not diminished when we turn to anti-liberal economists such as Karl Marx. When the latter revisits Ricardian analysis, as he did in his transformation theory,[5] the rationality principle still plays a crucial role in explaining why production prices must diverge from values. Just like Ricardo's, Marx's argument postulates the equality of profit rates because it seemed obvious to him that capitalists are not stupid enough to keep investing in an industry where the rate of profit does not compare with the rate prevailing in other industries. Even the most typically Marxian analysis of exploitation and of savage competition in Book One of *Capital* works on the basis of a minimal rationality principle. Otherwise, how could capitalists' compulsion to 'increase their relative surplus value' according to a so-called 'law' of capitalism be understood if it were not supposed by Marx that, once a successful innovation placed them in a favourable position, capitalists are not stupid enough to miss the opportunity to cut their prices in order to increase their profits by taking away from their competitors a greater share of a strictly limited market? (*Capital*: Book I, chapter XII). Marx's reliance on the rationality principle should not surprise us, since virtually all explanations of economic mechanisms rely on such a principle.

Summing up, classical economists, at least the most representative of them, based their theories on an implicit rationality principle which required little more than the conviction that people are not stupid enough to refrain from choosing what they *clearly see* as being favourable to the realization of their goal. While they constantly relied on such a rationality principle, they rarely, if ever, took care to characterize its content or even to draw attention to it. It is important to note, however, that, for classical economists, rationality was a much more complex affair than the mere avoidance of being fooled. Smith, in particular, had grand and complex views about what is rational for men to do (on this point, see Morgan 1997: 78–79). Nonetheless, when it comes for them to explain – and not only to describe – a phenomenon, they rely on the idea that people are rational, at least in the minimal sense of being not stupid at all, which is exactly what the rationality *principle* requires.

Modelling rationality in early marginalism

It is usual in the traditional history of economic thought to characterize the so-called marginalist revolution both by the content of the marginalist theory of value, which was based on subjective needs rather than on objective costs, and by the emphasis put on individual rational decisions whose investigation is supposed to replace the analysis of class behaviour developed by classical economics. Both considerations point correctly towards important differences between the respective views associated with these two conceptions of economics, but the wording used is misleading. Let us examine why, starting with the second consideration.

It is true that the classics were not interested in scrutinizing the subjectivity of the economic agents, but they would hardly have denied that economic agents, whether capitalists, workers, landowners, buyers or sellers, make decisions subjectively like all decisions makers do, even though these agents were supposed to be guided by economic interests that classical economists considered to be common to all members of their respective classes. As abundantly illustrated above, classical economists developed their most important economic theories by generally assuming that these economic agents make decisions according to their own interests, in agreement with their implicit version of the rationality principle.

But if decisions based on the rationality principle were so pervasive in classical economics, one may ask what was revolutionary from this point of view in the so-called 'marginalist revolution'? The answer is surely that marginalist economists required much more from the rationality principle. They were not content, as were the classical economists, with invoking an implicit rationality principle allowing them to understand the workings of the mechanism responsible for the fact that the price level (or the level of any other economic variable) is relatively determinate without being fixed by anybody. They adopted an idealized version according to which agents almost necessarily make maximizing decisions. Moreover, the first marginalist economists were directly interested in analysing such maximizing decisions through formal schemes, because they were convinced that it was only through a clear representation of the idealized principles as they were assumed to operate in the mind that they could understand the formation of value and of price levels, and more generally have a fair idea of economic mechanisms. Rationality, which, up to that point, was nothing more than the unformulated but *implicit basic principle* of economics, started to become an important part of the *subject matter* of economic analysis. As for classical economists, since they claimed that value was explained only by costs of production, such an inquiry had no particular interest for them. As economists, their quite different agenda, which essentially concerned the distribution of production's surplus between classes rather than between individuals, postulated a rationality principle as a fundamental and necessary condition of their argumentation, but did not require an *analysis of its working* as a tool for deriving their economic conclusions. The latter type of analysis, and in no way the reliance on the rationality principle, which was pervasive in classical economics, was the great innovation introduced by marginalism.

This important turn in the interpretation of the rationality principle is easy to understand in the context of the last decades of nineteenth century where hard sciences exerted such an attraction on the less prestigious social sciences. The precision that is generally required from scientific concepts implies that rationality should not be seen as a simple disposition to adopt means that are supposed to be oriented towards the satisfaction of some goals. Such a conception of rationality relies on much too vague notions. Therefore, it looked essential to marginalist economists to construe rationality as the propensity and capacity to *actually maximize* the level of an economic variable. Indeed, this approach looked more attractive, because it seemed quite possible for an economist, at least in principle, to mathematically determine the maximal level of a variable thanks to calculus. In contrast, it is not possible to precisely determine what would be the action resulting from the uncertain and possibly erratic decision of someone who is simply disposed to adopt means oriented towards the satisfaction of some goal. Consequently, for Stanley Jevons, it was not enough to suppose that agents were not stupid; it was important to analyse further what is implied by the fact that an agent manages to act in a way that *maximally* satisfies an explicit goal. And once the idea that rational agents necessarily maximize is accepted, a lot can be derived from that. In his preliminary philosophical considerations, Jevons claimed that some economic laws can be deduced from a few basic 'axioms' among which the first is that 'every person will choose the *greater* apparent good' (1957 [1871]: 18, my emphasis). Walras, for his part, when it comes to analysing the cause of value was brought to 'suppose' that, when people are trading, their object 'is to gratify the *greatest possible* sum total of wants' (1954 [1874]: 121, my emphasis). While being very different between them in almost all other regards, models built up by both of these marginalist economists were conceived in such a way that they trace the proper way to maximize for maximizing agents. Once it was agreed upon that agents systematically prefer more rather than less of economic goods (including money) which are themselves conceived of as sources of satisfaction, such agents were almost literally defined as hypothetical sources of choices that are programmed to reach a maximal point on a utility scale that is devised in such a way that it can meaningfully be maximized. The track that the alleged rational agent follows in such models, and the computations that this agent makes, are predetermined by the fact that these models are nothing but a precise description of what a rational (maximizing) behaviour *should* be. In this context, one can easily understand that a marginalist economist, who used to design economic agents as efficient utility maximizers, finds it either redundant or meaningless to insist on the fact that economic analysis is based on a principle according to which people tend to make decisions that make sense. In the realm of maximization, the fundamental version of the rationality principle is quickly forgotten, or almost.

Note that this does not mean that the rationality principle ceased to play the role that it did in classical economics. The presupposition that people are not stupid and that they make decisions that make sense with regard to their goals has continued to support the models devised by marginalist economists: it is even this presupposition that provides them with explanative power and that is responsible for the fact that these abstract models look, nonetheless, quite reasonable to us as an explanation of economic behaviour. Thus, the rationality principle has played a fundamental role in this development of economic theory, even though the economist's attention was directed more and more to models of rationality associated with strict maximization. For example, according to marginalist microeconomics, the capitalist entrepreneur should increase the level of production exactly up to the point where marginal cost equals marginal revenue, since this point corresponds to a maximum of profits. Clearly, if this model of maximizing behaviour seems sensible and almost compelling to us, it is due to the implicit role of the rationality principle. Indeed, the latter suggests that capitalists are not stupid enough either to lose the chance of making more profit by increasing production when the revenue drawn from an extra unit is larger than its cost; or, when the situation is reversed, we suppose that this entrepreneur cannot be stupid enough to keep on incurring extra costs in order to obtain a supplementary revenue inferior to these costs. Nonetheless, being a strict maximizer able to efficiently calculate a maximum value is quite different from making consciously evaluated decisions that make sense. Therefore, with this first modelling of rationality, a gap, doomed to become wider and wider, began to appear between the rationality principle itself and the picture of rationality designed by economists.[6]

Of course, Smith's capitalists cleverly managed to avoid losing chances to get profit and, from this point of view, they are akin to Jevons' agents maximizing their utility; thus, the difference between classical and marginalist economics should not be exaggerated. However, this kinship between these two approaches should not hide the fact that the principle in virtue of which Smith concluded that they do so was an implicit postulate according to which people are normally endowed with sound *judgement* allowing them to normally avoid stupid decisions and to act in a sensible way. In his paper on Adam Smith, Ronald

Coase even explicitly claimed that 'Adam Smith would not have thought it sensible to treat man as a rational utility-maximizer' (Coase 1976: 545). In contrast, for marginalist economists, it is the very content of a rational choice that has to be strictly determined by the theory in which the notion of rationality – conceived as propensity to maximize a properly reified representation of the utility provided by any good – is embodied. Thus, the rational decision-making process was reduced in those marginalist models to an almost mechanical comparison between marginal utilities, a comparison whose first application was the Jevonian rendering of the 'law' of diminishing marginal utility, which is nothing but a straightforward application of the rationality principle to a world with stable and clearly defined preferences between goods whose each successive units are associated with clearly defined (cardinal) units of utility. Indeed, in such a world, marginal utility is conceived of as necessarily diminishing, since it seems clear that an agent who is conceived of as a utility maximizer will necessarily, when it comes to using a given good, choose to satisfy a need whose satisfaction provides more utility before satisfying a need whose satisfaction provides less of it; consequently, for a rational agent *with such stable preferences*, marginal utility was conceived as necessarily diminishing.[7]

One might object to this almost mechanistic interpretation of marginalist models by recalling that marginalist theory of value was always considered to be *subjective* whereas the classical one was clearly *objective*, but this traditional way to oppose them is misleading. Once they have put the spotlight on the subjectivity of economic agents' choices, marginalist economists do not push further the analysis of the subjective idiosyncrasies of these agents; instead, they claim that those agents are guided by a mechanical process of maximization of utility, which, oddly enough, makes the behaviour of Jevons' and Walras' agents still more 'objective' (or less 'subjective') than the behaviour of Smith's potentially erratic capitalists. The latter were 'subjectively' appreciating their situation before concluding that it is time to move their capital towards a more profitable venture. Since their decisions are made in the context of their limited and imperfect knowledge, nothing excludes that some of them made bad decisions and took inappropriate actions. Otherwise, there would be, to start with, no unprofitable ventures from which 'rational' capitalists would withdraw their capital after experiencing too heavy a loss. With the marginalist maximization, this appreciation of the situation by an economic agent is replaced by a maximization function that literally defines the *homo oeconomicus* who has literally no room for being erratic. This efficient economic agent is implicitly endowed with a knowledge that – given the number of variables to take into account in a maximization process – should be close to omniscience. It is true that, in order to avoid invoking such an unrealistic postulate, one can follow Walras and suppose instead that every market choice of an agent is submitted to the control of an Auctioneer who manages to realize an equilibrium, but such a process is not much more realistic.

If the idea is simply to emphasize the fact that marginalist economists chose to base their analyses on a sophisticated interpretation of the *subjective choices* of economic agents, it makes sense to underscore the 'subjective' character of their approach. But given that this interpretation literally transforms this subjectivity into a mechanistic function, this label is deceiving. Clearly, with this kind of 'subjective' theory, there is no need for an objective one! In fact, Jevons did not even reject the cost of production theory as radically as suggested by his first methodological claims (Regarding this rejection, see Jevons' Preface to the first edition of *The Theory of Political Economy*, 1957 [1871]: v–ix). His thesis was rather that classical economists were wrong to pretend that costs of production *directly* determine value without granting the primary role to utility. In order to clarify his position, he even adds a simplified 'tabular' form of his views in his second edition:

> Cost of production determines supply;
> Supply determines final degree of utility;
> Final degree of utility determines value
> (Jevons 1957 [1871]: 165)

I do not want to deny the determinant role played by the final degree of utility in Jevons' approach, nor its dependence on consumers' needs and satisfaction, but it is nonetheless true that the indirect role accorded to cost of production provides a basis for a more objective interpretation of value and price. Far from being a kind of expression of a subjective state of mind concerning the usefulness of some good, value is a magnitude which is determined by the interaction of two factors, one (cost of production) which is strictly 'objective' and the other (final degree of utility) which is the inscription in an (objective) good of its actual efficiency in satisfying people's needs. It is this complementation of Jevons' theory by Ricardo's that Alfred Marshall emphasized in Appendix I of his *Principles*, where he compares this kind of interdependence to the two blades of a pair of scissors (Marshall 1949 [1890]: 675). In order to vindicate his interpretation, Marshall recalls Jevons' tabular form and inverts its order to obtain what he presents as a 'rather less untrue' catena:

> Utility determines the amount that has to be supplied,
> The amount that has to be supplied determines cost of production,
> Cost of production determines value.
> (Marshall 1949 [1890]: 674)

This quasi rehabilitation of an objective theory of value did not relax the objections that had been raised against the fact that the classical theory of value does not take account of utility, but it was a first step in a process that has progressively dissolved the individual agent as the subjective source of rational decisions. Determined jointly by an objective cost of production and by utility understood as an objective feature of goods, the value had no longer very much to do with rational decisions subjectively made by individual agents. However, since economists cannot avoid relying on rationality to develop their theories, it was an objective (in the sense of being no longer subjective) process of maximization that was invoked. The rationality principle, whose workings were made self-evident in the minimally rational decisions of Turgot's dealers or Smith's capitalists, was more or less forgotten and replaced by a much more mechanical process more congenial to the conceptual apparatus of developed sciences.

Marshall himself was always paying particular attention to concrete situations and he would never have accepted the reduction of human agents to sheer bearers of well behaved utility functions. According to him, it is not true that economists 'assume every action to be deliberate, and the outcome of calculation' (Marshall 1949 [1890]: 17). He acknowledged that since many actions are influenced by a habit or a custom, there might be 'no exact relation between the effort and the end which is attained by it' (ibid.: 18). He nonetheless claimed that 'habits and customs themselves' were generated by closely and carefully watching 'the advantages and disadvantages of different courses of conduct' (ibid.: 17). This way of describing the workings of a kind of rationality principle is clearly compatible with the hesitating process of reasonable people progressively discovering the proper way to act in changing circumstances. However, Marshall acknowledged that 'the side of life with which economics is specially concerned is that in which man's conduct is most deliberate, and in which he most often reckons up the advantages and disadvantages of any particular action before he enters on it' (ibid.: 17). This was just enough to license the substitution of a maximizing view of rationality over the more humble one evoked above, and to legitimate what is possibly the most acclaimed contribution of Marshall, namely his idealized transposition of the logic of the main arguments of his 700-page book in the elegant formulation of his 17-page Mathematical Appendix. In spite of Marshall's insistent advice concerning the difference of degree 'so great as practically to amount to a difference of kind' (ibid.: 700) between his mathematical discussion and his careful analysis of the 'ordinary business of life', it was the former that was really influential in the future development of microeconomics in which rationality was more and more understood as a process of maximization of a utility function. An important gain in clarity was paid for by the promotion of a maximization principle doomed to be progressively separated from its foundation in a genuine rationality principle.

This observation should not be seen, however, as a denial of the significance of the application of mathematical techniques in economics. As claimed by Bernt Stigum, mathematization and formalization of economic theories is highly important because these processes open the possibility of exposing how a mechanism works with great precision, facilitate the confrontation of theories with data and allow us to perceive either the hidden similarities or differences between two theories in such a way that brand new insights in the theory are made possible (Stigum 1990: 15–16). Thus, mathematization is essential in economics, but it should be understood in the proper way, namely Marshall's way: mathematics is nothing but a powerful instrument allowing us to understand more clearly, more easily and more fruitfully the logical relations which are involved in common language explanations. And, as we have seen, the latter can be developed by invoking only a relatively minimal degree of rationality with economic agents.

Marshall was not the only marginalist economist to offer certain resistance to the process through which the individual agents' uncertain preferences were replaced by idealized utility functions. As is well known, Carl Menger, who is traditionally associated with the so-called marginalist revolution, developed a theory quite different from those of Jevons and Walras (which are far from being identical themselves). This is not to say that Menger was closer to classical economics than his marginalist colleagues were. On the contrary, he was much more radically opposed to a theory of value based on costs of production than they were. Indeed, he does not hesitate to say that '[a]mong the most egregious of the fundamental errors that have had the most far-reaching consequences in the previous development of our science is the argument that goods attain value for us because *goods were employed in their production that had value to us*'.[8] For Menger, the value is not transmitted, as is the case with the classics, from the various kinds of goods required by production to the finished product, but, on the contrary, from the finished goods immediately used by consumers to the goods – that he calls 'goods of higher order' – which are required by the production of the consumer ones.[9] This way to put the matter excludes any kind of re-objectivization of the value theory and it establishes the individual agent as the ultimate source of economic decision by the very fact of establishing this agent's satisfaction as the ultimate source of value.

Menger's theory, which aims to explain the development of exchange, the formation of price and the nature of commodities and of money, does not refer to the phrase 'rationality principle' to describe the principle which is the motor of its essential arguments, but it is clearly the same idea that is invoked when economic agents are assumed to behave 'economically' (1976 [1871]: 205; see also 201) or to be 'economizing individuals' (ibid.: 180,191, 211, 213, 222). Even though 'economizing individuals' tend to behave in order to obtain 'the greatest possible satisfaction of their needs' (ibid.: 94; see also 95–96) in such a way that a monopolist's economic policy 'is directed to making a maximum profit from the quantity of the monopolized good available to him' (ibid.: 213), Menger refuses to construe such 'economizing individuals' as depersonalized utility functions. These individuals are rather people who 'strive to better their economic position as much as possible' (ibid.: 191). Their behaviour is described as an '*effort to satisfy their needs as completely as possible*' (ibid.: 180, Menger's emphasis). Nothing is mechanically warranted in the behaviour of people who do their best in this fashion. Menger claims that 'if economizing men must choose between the satisfaction of a need on which the maintenance of their lives depends and another on which merely a greater or less degree of well-being is dependent, they will *usually* prefer the former' (ibid.: 123, my emphasis). This leaves ample room for error and Menger, indeed, insists on the fact that even economizing individuals or, if one prefers, 'individuals whose economic activity is conducted rationally [...] are subject to error'.[10] Economic individuals can make errors because they are not omniscient and not rational to the point of being endowed with an indefectible good judgement.

When it comes to explaining the origin of exchange, Menger observes that if two farmers who own abundant quantity of the same kind of barley engage in mutually exchanging their identical crop, they would be 'regarded as insane by other economizing individuals' (ibid.: 176). But fortunately for the development of economics, most people are not insane; they are not stupid, and this is enough to explain that they will choose, for example, to buy their second or third preferred good, when they realize that they have accumulated so much of their preferred one that a new unit of the latter would provide them less satisfaction than a unit of the former. In order to develop his economic theory, Menger only needed to endow his agents with this relatively minimal but absolutely fundamental kind of rationality.

Rationality under the rug of maximization

But let us put aside Menger's quite particular legacy on Austrian economics and consider the next step in the development of what was to become 'mainstream' economics. In Jevons' scheme, rationality was reduced to maximization, but the value to be maximized, being rather clumsily modelled as an amount of cardinal utility, could still be considered as dependent on agents' preferences, whatever way these preferences are construed. Since the rationality principle implies that agents take some means – which, for Jevons, were reduced to maximizing means – in order to satisfy their still undefined goals, modelling the process in question required specifying these goals or, more precisely, specifying the preferences from which the latter are supposed to be derived. With Paretian indifference maps, corresponding to the next step in this process, preferences themselves are modelled in a way which avoids any reference to the cumbersome concept of cardinal utility and provides an idealized picture of an individual's tastes without giving up the mathematics that the concept of utility had made possible (on this point, see Hollis and Sugden 1993: 6–7). The notion of rationality is still implicitly defined through maximization, which corresponds to the attainment of the highest available indifference curve, but both the preferences and the process through which the maximum satisfaction can be attained are given a representation which made them much more convenient to analyse. As was frequently observed, an important merit of this ordinal revolution was to have de-psychologized the economic analysis and this fact can hardly be contested. It was judged essential for economics to isolate economic relations and to analyse them as such, instead of relying on doubtful psychological considerations, but this important conquest was made by still more occulting the dynamic principle on which this analysis was based. Naturally any economist knows perfectly well that the attraction exerted by the highest in a set of preference curves is explained by the fact that it represents the various combination of goods that a *rational agent* endowed with the required budget should choose, but the point is that, once reduced to this idealized and schematic mechanical process, the economic choice can be reinterpreted with the help of still more abstract models in which the rationality principle will lose any meaning and the economic agent any function.

Let us see how the following developments in this story will bring this result about. The next step in this process of occultation was associated with the concept of marginal rate of substitution. As was shown by Hicks and Allen in their classic 1934 paper, in the same way that ordinal utility replaced cardinal utility, the law of increasing marginal rate of substitution between any two goods must replace the law of diminishing marginal utility (of any good), in which Jevons and his successors had implicitly integrated the rationality principle. Indeed, just as ordinal utility designates a relative order between (cardinal) utilities, an increasing marginal rate of substitution is a ratio between (diminishing) marginal (cardinal) utilities. This economic theory clearly draws from the rationality principle the idea that such a rate must increase with the development of the transaction because if each added unit of some good *A* provides less and less utility to an individual, this individual would not be stupid enough to not require more and more of good *B* in exchange for each unit of *A* given up.[11] Since this increasing character corresponds geometrically to the convexity to the origin of indifference curves, the convexity of a standard indifference map became an expression of the preferences of individuals who care not to part with their last units of a valuable good as easily as they do when they have a large amount of the same good. Non-convexity in an indifference map is normally excluded because it would suggest that individuals (whose preferences are supposed to be stable) are prepared to behave irrationally by requiring a smaller and smaller price for successive units of an increasingly scarce good. Even though this theory is acceptable because it rests fundamentally on the idea that, after all, agents are not stupid like those who would 'behave irrationally', the alleged rational behaviour of these agents is strictly predetermined by the model, once correctly shaped preferences are given. This kind of 'rationality' looks like a logical force that, in an indifference map, attracts any agent towards the point where a budget line touches tangentially the highest of the attainable indifference curves (which are presumed to be convex to the origin). With this picture of a necessarily rational agent as their principal tool, economists had even less a need for an explicit rationality principle, which they tended to forget completely. Consequently, the gap between this geometrical picture of rationality and the rationality modestly attributed to economic agents by the rationality principle had become still more accentuated.

Among the first economists to be alarmed by this increasing gap were those who raised the lively controversies that raged in the 1940s and early 1950s over the relevance of marginalism in the analysis of the firm (see Mongin 1986a sections IV and V; Mongin 1992; Hausman and Mongin 1997 and Backhouse 2009). Those who challenged the standard marginalist approach documented their arguments principally by using surveys that showed that successful decisions taken in the business world did not correspond to the marginalist picture but were rather based on alternative principles. It is not my intention here to revisit these old debates, but I do want to underline the fact that they were quite symptomatic of the gap referred to above. In these debates, the real question was not whether the observed business practices were rational. It seems clear that the decisions taken by these firms were far from being stupid. Given the assessment of the situation in which they were taken, it is even possible to claim that they were appropriate enough. It was not the rationality principle as such which was challenged by the business surveys, but only the notion of rationality embodied in marginalist economic theory.

If we turn now to the other side of this debate, it is significant to note the different reactions of the two main defenders of the marginalist approach. On the one hand, Milton Friedman, in his acclaimed 1953 methodological essay, managed to dissolve the problem by claiming that the only tests of a theory which matter concern its predictions and not its assumptions, including the rationality assumption.[12] Whatever the legitimacy of this position, which was based largely on the alleged empirical success of economics, its considerable influence contributed significantly to pushing the already almost forgotten principle of rationality completely beyond the range of the preoccupations of economists who were discovering by this time a new concept of rationality which was, as we will see, still more distant from the fundamental principle. On the other hand, Fritz Machlup, the main defender of the marginalist approach, after distinguishing three irrelevant levels of assumption, acknowledged the special role of the 'fundamental postulates' that are included in what he called 'assumed type of action (or motivation)' (Machlup 1955: 13). Among them, according to him, the most fundamental is known under various names such as the 'maximization principle' and the 'assumption of rationality' (ibid.: 16). However, in spite of the role accorded to this assumption of rationality, he added that one 'need not worry about independent verifications' of such a principle (ibid.: 17). Indeed, who would seriously test directly whether people usually tend to act in a stupid way or not? But a few lines above, he had justified this openly rather casual attitude by observing that the type of action modelled as maximization is 'understandable' after all, and that, when human action is involved, 'understandability' is a more appropriate criterion than verification.[13] When the problem is to debunk challenges to the unrealistic modelling of rationality, the efficient strategies have been either to present the matter with Friedman in such a way that all the questions related to the nature and implications of rationality are perceived as irrelevant or to present the matter with Machlup in such a way that the unrealistically modelled rationality take advantage surreptitiously of the fact that it was, after all, derived from the quite realistic, unassailable and 'understandable' (but increasingly forgotten) rationality principle according to which people normally act in a sensible way.

However, other economists were much more worried than Friedman and Machlup were by the unrealistic character of the modelling of rationality. Herbert Simon based his life-long systematic challenge to the standard association of rationality with maximization on the idea that maximization is just 'a very particular and special form' of rationality (Simon 1978: 2). In regard to what he explicitly calls the 'principle of rationality' – a principle which, according to him, is not quantitative but structural – Simon proposes the following formulation: '*Ceteris paribus*, situations and practices will be preferred when important favorable consequences are associated with them, and avoided when important unfavorable consequences are associated with them' (Simon 1978: 7), the word 'important' being included as a subtle reminder that, for Simon, optimization is not required by rationality. In any case, what I want to underscore is that, in order to challenge the maximization (or optimization) model, Simon appeals to a more general understanding of the principle of rationality, which is nothing other than the principle according to which people normally act in a sensible rather than in a stupid way. Still more clearly than the challenges based on the actual behaviour of firms, Simon's challenge to economic orthodoxy reveals the presence of a gap between the standard modelling of rationality and the genuine principle of rationality on which his challenge was explicitly based in the last resort. Like the rationality principle that guided Turgot and Smith, Simon's fundamental 'principle of rationality' refers only to favourable (or unfavourable) consequences without specifying what should count as consequences and how one should measure the success in reaching these favourable consequences.

It is true that, in some versions of this approach, the relatively vague notions of *satisfecit* and bounded rationality have been given a more precise content with the help of certain models that make room for information and deliberation costs (See Mongin 1986b; Conlisk 1996; Lagueux 2002). Simon's agent could still be considered as a maximizer, or better, as an optimizer, once the sizable costs that are implied by the process of making the allegedly optimal decision are taken into account. But, given that this kind of meta-optimization could hardly avoid being the first step of an infinite regress,[14] it would be much more faithful to Simon's view to simply put forward the consideration that the decider is not stupid enough to incur time-consuming research, tiresome calculations, deprivation of pleasure in life, etc. in order to obtain a so-called optimal result whose advantages could hardly compensate for such a price to pay. Rather than arbitrarily attributing monetary value to these costs, it seems more reasonable to conclude that bounded rationality is the rationality of an agent who does not have the formidable capacities required to accurately determine and efficiently reach a mathematical maximum, but who has the capacity to determine what is 'good enough' with the sound judgement of a fellow endowed with only a certain degree of rationality.

2 The hardly consistent story of rationality-consistency

A few years before Simon developed his theory, economists, who are fond of the precision of mathematical language but who also enjoy having their science count among the empirical sciences, took a new step in the transformation of the notion of rationality. Although indifference curves no longer suppose any cardinal measure of utility, they still imply a comparison of preferences, which, being psychological entities, can hardly be analysed with the economist's new theoretical toolbox. In fact, such preferences were the only thing left of Turgot's implicit principle of rationality, but their subjective character excludes the possibility that the required comparisons between them be made on an empirical basis. With the next step in the modelling of rationality, taken mainly by Paul Samuelson, rational choices are no longer deduced from a comparison of preferences; it is preferences that are revealed through choices, the latter having the advantage of being observable. However, since preferences cannot be revealed by inconsistent choices, this new approach implies strictly consistent choices. Therefore, the *first axiom* of revealed preferences requires that if some good X is revealed as superior to another good Y, then Y cannot in turn be revealed as superior to X. What looked attractive with such an approach is that there was no further need to define rationality by reference to an unobservable utility maximization. It was defined rather as sheer consistency in choice making, which, after all, was easily perceived as a necessary requirement of any successful construction of a scientific economics. The shift was significant. Indeed, even though maximization is an idealization, it remains an idealization of a standard rational decision that makes sense because it corresponds to one's endeavour to satisfy one's preferences as much as possible. In contrast, consistency has nothing to do with usual rational decisions, which must be adapted only to actual conditions without being linked by previous decisions.

Rationality or consistency

Nicola Giocoli has devoted a large part of his recent book to analysing all the implications of this dramatic shift in the concept of rationality in which he sees a radical change in the fundamental image through which economists perceive their discipline. According to him, they forsake an economics understood as a system of forces to adopt an economics understood as a system of relations. While largely agreeing with this remarkably well documented analysis, I would like, for my part, to insist on the fact that these two concepts of rationality correspond to two steps in a process of occultation of the fundamental rationality principle on which economics is based. It seems important to inquire why consistency – which was invoked as a necessary condition of revelation of preferences – was immediately construed as the very expression of agents' rationality, in spite of the fact that, as we have just recalled, rationality has apparently so little to do with such a condition. One might be tempted to conclude that being consistent is a condition of maximizing as well – and to derive from this conclusion that rationality implies consistency – if one accepts the following three premises: (1) being rational is to maximize in the sense of reaching the highest degree in preference satisfaction, (2) preferences cannot be observed and measured without consistency, and (3) 'to maximize' in a way that cannot be observed and measured is not to maximize at all. This might be an acceptable derivation, but only if we accept (1) and (3). However, we have seen that (1) is an unnecessary idealization of what should be called rationality, and we may add that (3) arbitrarily excludes any maximization de facto as if a phenomenon does not exist as long as it cannot be efficiently (and elegantly) measured by those who are studying it. Nonetheless, this shows that some indirect links exist between rationality and consistency and, in this context, it is not surprising that H. S. Houthakker (1950) established, with the help of a few postulates, that this consistency approach to rationality, far from contradicting an approach based on utility maximization, is complementary to it. Thus, the links between consistency and maximization can be expressed in a formal model, but how can we relate consistency to the fundamental rationality principle? Whether or not we should conclude from these considerations that consistency in choices is a necessary condition of rationality understood in a more traditional sense, it can hardly be considered as a *sufficient* condition of rationality. Indeed, as emphasized by Amartya Sen (1987: 70), a person can do *in a perfectly consistent fashion* the exact opposite of what would be suggested by 'the goals and aims of that person'. This argument seems inescapable, but it may not be too devastating for those who would like to link rationality with consistency, since one may suppose that what is consistently chosen is what is preferred even if this might be deleterious for the choice maker. In this perspective, a consistent masochist might be considered rational from the point of view of rationality-consistency, and from the point of view of instrumental rationality as well. In any case, this formalized notion of rationality is far from the rationality principle itself and the gap between them will become more evident if we can show that consistency is not even a *necessary* condition of genuine rationality.

One might argue that the logical requirements of the first axiom seem to be so weak that the very idea that any notion of rationality could not imply it appears rather odd. After all, rationality should exclude sheer contradiction and preferring good X to good Y, and then good Y to good X is contradictory. However, the matter is far from being so simple if one considers that the concept of consistency introduces into the notion of rationality an intertemporal dimension which was absent from previous views about economic rationality – including rationality understood as maximization – and which threatens to transform its meaning dramatically. Consistency implies that rational agents, rather than being committed to maximizing their preferred objective at any moment in time, are committed to being *consistent over time with previous choices* they made in order to reach whatever objective they had. Indeed, simultaneous preferences cannot be considered since the main idea behind revealed preferences, in contrast with preferences traditionally referred to, is that choices that reveal them can be *observed*; but, to be observed and compared amongst themselves, the various choices of a single individual must be made at different points in time. Indeed, inconsistent choices simultaneously adopted by an agent would be not only contradictory but also unobservable since they could not be simultaneously actualized. But the problem with such intertemporality is that the notion of rationality-consistency can work only if change of tastes is excluded. Otherwise, the fact that someone chooses Y over X after having revealed through a previous choice a preference for X over Y might be explained by the fact that this person experienced a change of tastes which took place because either X or Y have been re-evaluated to a degree sufficient to make Y preferable to X.

But, why should we take for granted that inconsistency in choices (associated or not with a change in taste) is a symptom of irrationality? Such a way of thinking is rather odd, since rationality is usually associated with adaptability and opposed to rigidity. David Hume, who is usually credited along with Thomas Hobbes as being the first to posit rationality as the basis of a theory of action, was so far from associating changing tastes with irrationality that he did not hesitate to declare that '[r]eason is, and ought only to be the slave of the passions' (Hume 2000 [1739]: 266) and, consequently, reason had to adapt itself to serve the fluctuating whims of its master. It was apparently a similar approach that guided Gary Becker when, in his attempt to prove that some important conclusions of economics could be established even in a world in which all agents would be totally irrational, he spontaneously and quite reasonably associated such *total irrationality* with the rigid behaviour of an individual who always (very consistently) reacts the same way without considering environmental changes (Becker 1962). But what about individuals who would react with the same rigidity in the face of changing tastes, given that tastes can be considered as an aspect of one's inner environment? Would it not be for such individuals more rational to adapt any action to any change in goals resulting from the evolution of their tastes? Be that as it may, since the fact that tastes frequently change is one of the most unquestionable features of human behaviour and that stable (unchanging) tastes cannot be dissociated from consistency, it is worth pausing in our inquiry about the evolution of the notion of rationality in order to see how dealing with the problem raised by changes of taste was cumbersome for economists, for whom rationality was defined by consistency.

Economists and changing tastes

The possibility of changes in taste can hardly be denied, especially if one considers that economic agents can *learn*, which implies that previously unknown features of X or Y can be discovered and, for perfectly rational reasons, make the previous preference no longer tenable. Paradoxically enough, modern economists, who pay great attention to the phenomenon of learning, tend to minimize the significance of changes in taste. The fact that the latter phenomenon has little appeal for them is, however, easily understandable: it is difficult to analyse changes in taste with the help of a theory that is based on a concept of rationality that requires stability of taste. In such a situation, it is hardly surprising to observe that the problem of changing tastes has been described as 'troublesome' (Peleg and Yaari 1973: 391) and as a field in which 'the perils are extreme' (Marschak 1978: 386) by some of the relatively few economists who have dealt with it. Another among them, Carl Christian von Weizsäcker, does not hesitate to blame his colleagues for having pushed this problem under the rug: 'the overwhelming majority took the attitude that it is not their business to be concerned with these changes of taste'. To illustrate his point, he quotes a passage in which Milton Friedman claims that this situation is 'primarily a case of division of labour. The economist has little to say about the formation of wants; this is the province of the psychologist. The economist's task is to trace the consequences of any given set of wants' (Friedman 1962: 13, quoted by Weizsäcker 1971: 345). Weizsäcker challenges such a view on the ground that economists should have something to say about the formation of wants insofar as 'influences on tastes may depend more or less directly on certain economic variables' (Weizsäcker 1971: 345). I would add that if tastes are not stable, their changes have many *consequences* whose discussion, in contrast with questions concerning how tastes are generated, pertains unquestionably to the province of the economist. If changes of taste, either endogenous or exogenous, affect the results of economic analysis, the economist cannot flatly refuse to consider these *consequences* under the fallacious pretext that it is not his business to explain the *origin* of these changes. Nevertheless, most economists *did* flatly refuse to consider this phenomenon. In fact, the interest in changing tastes was always marginal in economic analysis, but some nineteenth-century economists – especially, but not surprisingly, those who offered some resistance to the systematic substitution of utility functions to preferences – did not hesitate to acknowledge the significance of this phenomenon. Alfred Marshall not only made room for the consequences of various changes in fashion, but he also considered widespread changes of taste, for example, among the factors which can affect the demand for meat or fish (Marshall 1949 [1890]: 308). Carl Menger, for his part, described changes of tastes and the 'capacity of human need to grow' as decisive factors affecting the very nature of a good, the satisfaction that it can produce, and therefore its subjective value and its attractiveness in the process of exchange (Menger 1976 [1871]: 65, 82, 83).

Economists using indifference curves models had at least a tool to deal with changes in taste. In cases where learning or any kind of experience was responsible for one's change in taste (or in preferences), these economists could cope with such modification in preferences without coming to the conclusion that irrationality is involved. Indeed, such a change in taste could simply be described as a move in the set of indifference curves. To be sure, complex computational problems might result, but changes in taste have little to do with irrationality when they are analysed in the context of indifference curves models. Nonetheless, it remains that changing tastes were never very welcome in economics. The so-called 'laws' of diminishing returns and of diminishing (increasing in the initial version) marginal rate of substitution required that tastes remain fixed during the time of their application since they referred at least implicitly to a succession of choices, but this just means that, as any law, they required a *ceteris paribus* clause. Thus, when discussing the law of diminishing returns, Marshall was careful enough to elucidate the 'implicit condition' requiring 'that we do not suppose time to be allowed for any alteration in the character or tastes of the man himself' (Marshall 1949 [1890]: 79). While the rationality principle was built in these laws, it was *not supposed to be identical* with the stability of preferences required by them, in the way that it is assumed to be identical with the consistency requirements of revealed preference theory. These laws were rather applications of this principle in situations overtly characterized by the absence of 'any alteration' in tastes, which was admittedly the situation that economists preferred.

The first modern economist to discuss questions related (albeit indirectly) to changes in taste is probably R. H. Strotz, who published a paper in the mid-1950s entitled 'Myopia and Inconsistency in Dynamic Utility Maximization'. More precisely, what Strotz discusses in this paper is 'the general problem of intertemporal utility maximization' (Strotz 1955–56: 166). Given that decisions concerning utility maximization may be revised through time, Strotz analysed revisions that concern the manner in which future satisfactions are discounted. When the date of such satisfactions approaches, one can re-evaluate the relative weight assigned to it and modify prior decisions accordingly. It is true that, as Strotz readily admits (ibid.: 173), such modifications do not correspond to changes in taste but rather to changes in the relation between the person who makes the decision and her environment. Since 'so many years from now' corresponds, year after year, to a brand new reality, it is normal that the evaluation does not remain the same. The important point for Strotz is that this change in the objective situation and in its subjective consequences for utility evaluation could be predicted by a sophisticated decision maker, whereas one that is myopic or naive could not. Whereas plans of the myopic decision maker are doomed to be changed constantly, the sophisticated one may decide, like Ulysses who pre-committed himself by requiring that he be tied to the mast of his ship, to be pre-committed to the plan adopted when the original decision was made or, alternatively, this sophisticated decision maker may manage to start with a plan which will remain feasible as such at any future time. After discussing these three possibilities, Strotz concludes that 'true' discount functions are 'sublimated by parental teaching and social pressure' (ibid.: 177). It is through such 'sublimation' that changes in taste occur as a result of training and education. Naturally, during the training process, a person is led to make decisions that are *inconsistent* with previous ones, but such inconsistencies do not seem to bother Strotz, who is concerned exclusively with the manner in which discounting occurs once a given level of education is reached and not with the training process as such. Thus Strotz avoids the intricacies of changing tastes by focusing on a level of education where tastes are taken as granted. Why the behaviour of people who do not make consistent decisions *within* the time period in which they are educated (and during which their tastes are changing) is deemed to be typically consistent during other periods remains an open question.

Strotz's paper has generated a significant number of papers in which the question of changing tastes is somewhat overshadowed by the discussion of various technical points.[1] Concerning these discussions, I will make only a few remarks about Peter Hammond's contribution, which aims to approach the problem on a more general level. Hammond borrows Strotz's distinction between naive and sophisticated choices and analyses the relations between these notions and situations that are respectively labelled 'essential consistency' and 'essential inconsistency' (Hammond 1976: 167). The latter notion refers to a situation that is interestingly illustrated by addiction, which changes tastes in such a way that once in it, it is no longer possible to make the choice that was formerly desired. With this example, Hammond distinguishes three possible states characterizing someone's situation: addiction, temporary consummation and abstinence. The point is that in an essentially inconsistent situation such as the one exemplified by addiction, both naive and sophisticated choices violate the weak axiom and are incoherent if they are made when the three states are available (ibid.: 161–163). The naive choice of someone who has not predicted the change in taste is incoherent because, in the end, it is the addiction that results from a choice in the presence of these three possibilities, whereas, in a choice between only addiction and abstinence, abstinence would have been chosen. But the sophisticated choice of a person who *had predicted* the change of tastes is incoherent as well: abstinence is chosen among the three possibilities, whereas, in a choice between only temporary consumption and abstinence, temporary consumption would have been chosen. In contrast, as Hammond observes (ibid.: 167–170), in an *essentially consistent* situation, neither naive nor sophisticated choices need to be incoherent, especially if they correspond to a strong ordering. While brilliantly formalized, this result is hardly surprising since an essentially consistent situation is defined in such a way that changes in taste no longer obtain.

Another contribution that I would like to briefly discuss is Weizsäcker's paper on endogenous changes of taste, which comes closer to analysing changes of tastes as such and to associating them with a rational learning process (Weizsäcker, 1971). At first glance, it seems to contradict the view developed in this chapter since Weizsäcker claims that his theory on changing tastes is formally analogous with revealed preference theory. However, it is clear that such a formal analogy does not imply that the two theories are compatible. It is true that Weizsäcker refers to a consistent (and even transitive) sequence of commodity vectors, each of them being preferred to the previously consumed vector whose consumption (which is no longer preferred in the next phase) is itself responsible for the change of tastes that brings the new set of preferences, and so on (ibid.: 357ff.). In such a process, transitivity concerns the successive choices of sets of preferences, not the choices of various goods throughout the whole period of preferences. If I choose sweet wine over dry wine in a situation where the very fact of consuming sweet wine, for any reason, contributes to my change of taste in such a way that I later choose dry wine over sweet wine, my behaviour clearly contradicts the weak axiom and the transitivity of choices. Consequently, this behaviour is totally incompatible with the application of revealed preference theory – which incidentally implies a kind of transitivity in choices requiring perfect information and what Weizsäcker calls 'perfect imaginative powers' (ibid.: 359). It is true that, once I have acquired this new preference, I may *consistently* never return to my old preference of sweet wine over dry wine. If this is the case, a transitive relation prevails throughout the succession of preferences, but only if we consider exclusively metapreferences concerning those successive states of preferences resulting themselves from successive inconsistent changes of tastes. Even though the rationality of changing tastes is ruled out by modern economists' very way of arguing, an adaptation of the formal tools of the latter to the case of various states of modified tastes is always possible, as illustrated by Weizsäcker's paper. However, this leaves the problem raised by the inconsistency between preferences pertaining to two different sets of them unsettled. The fact that the choices (guided by metapreferences) made *between these sets of preferences* as such may be revealed as transitive (and consistent in this sense) does not exclude that the preferences themselves were revealed as inconsistent between them.

The problem that changing tastes raises for economics is not more specifically discussed in those few other interesting contributions related to changing tastes; the latter focus on comparisons between different tastes or, more precisely, between different sets of preferences or different utility functions. They explicitly refer to 'metapreferences' about the compared sets of preferences. Burton Weisbrod (Weisbrod 1977) resorts to a Rawlsian indifference veil in order to conceive possible tests that aim to establish that one utility function can be judged preferable to another. T. A. Marschak (Marschak 1978) raises the problem of justifying policies that can change preferences on the basis of a gain in welfare. But since individuals whose tastes change are not considered rational by modern economists (on the ground that they violate the weak axiom), these individuals' preferences can hardly be taken as a measuring rod when it comes to evaluating the welfare import of the policy. Marshak proposes to solve this problem by comparing the preferences and expected behaviour of three *different* Crusoe-type individuals: the first being the individual before the policy is applied, the second the (otherwise same) individual after the policy is applied and the third the (otherwise same) individual in a situation in which it is assumed that the policy was not applied. With the help of some postulates and of a household-technology analysis inspired by Gary Becker's approach, Marshak concludes that, under this interpretation, the policy 'does not change this person's true tastes' (ibid.: 388). Clearly, in all these analyses of metapreferences, it is crucial to resort to ingenious artifices in order to avoid dealing with initial preferences that changing tastes have made inconsistent.

Let us conclude this brief incursion into the debate about changes in taste by considering the Beckerian approach as it was applied to changing tastes in what is probably the most oft-cited paper on the topics, namely 'De Gustibus Non Est Disputandum' written by Stigler and Becker. On the point that interests us, this paper is particularly radical: its main thesis is that tastes *are* stable and do not really change. Indeed, Stigler and Becker claim that apparently changing preferences result from rational choices made on the basis of stable 'preference functions' (Stigler and Becker 1977: 77). Choices whose variations are usually attributed to changing tastes associated with addiction, custom, advertising or fashion are as endogenously derived as any standard economic result. What is usually characterized as taste or preference is presented as an endowment of a particular type of capital. In fact, the authors explain in a very clever but not necessarily convincing fashion why demand for a commodity like drugs or music can increase or decrease, not because taste for such commodities changes, but because their prices (including all relevant but usually forgotten variables) for the person who 'consumes' them decrease or increase. There is no doubt that the acquisition of a skill in music can significantly reduce the 'price' (paid in tiresome practice) of acquiring still more skill. And if all variations in taste can be reduced to variations in price, it is the very notion of variations in taste that is voided of meaning. The fact that I steadily prefer buying a theatre ticket rather than a concert ticket, but decide to buy a concert ticket on a night where the price of the latter is significantly reduced does obviously not imply that my tastes have changed, as it would be in the case of a decision to play more music once some skill has been acquired. Thus, this radical dismissal of changes in tastes apparently provides the missing condition for a concept of rationality based on consistency. Those who choose A over B after choosing B over A would be perfectly consistent insofar as their different choices could be explained by differences in prices. However, this heroic attempt to deliver economics from the cumbersome problem raised by changing tastes did not succeed in explaining why, among people who are supposed to be endowed with the same basic tastes, some choose to turn to drugs and others to music. Apparently, the only explanation more or less explicitly suggested rests on the fact that people are accidentally exposed either to drugs or to music, but who would admit that sheer exposure to music during a given time determines various people's further demand for music in the absence of a predetermined taste for music, the existence of which is denied in the first place? And if specific tastes (or germs of them) are reintroduced at this point, the whole analysis collapses: indeed, once they are characterized as preferences for specific commodities, such tastes are subject to change since the intensity of preferences for any commodity clearly varies through time. This is probably the reason why Stigler and Becker managed to endow these tastes with still more stability by claiming not only that they do not 'change capriciously' but that they do not 'differ importantly between people' (ibid.: 76); they are nothing but 'deep-lying preferences' for very general valuables 'like nourishment and self-esteem' (McPherson 1987: 402). However, if they provide reasons to think that tastes do not change as capriciously as most people think, Stigler and Becker do not really show that these fundamental tastes do not differ importantly between people, nor do they really show why, if these tastes do not differ, specific orientations are adopted by different people. Whatever their intention from this point of view, their ingenious but non-compelling theory hardly helps to save the conception of rationality-consistency from the threat associated with the fact that changing tastes are pervasive in human behaviour. Put otherwise, it is difficult not to see the postulate of stable basic tastes shared by all people as one of the most extravagant attempts to eliminate a repeatedly denied, but nonetheless persistent, source of embarrassment for the conception of rationality that modern economists were led to adopt in order to satisfy the requirements of a certain type of modelling.

There is no doubt that these various discussions of problems related to changes of taste are illuminating from different points of view, but if their goal was to conciliate changing tastes with an economics based on consistency or, more radically, to prove the non-existence of changing tastes, they were not really successful. This fact is far from surprising since to conciliate contradictory notions and to eliminate a pervasive reality are surely not easy things to do. But it is time to come back to the implications of changing tastes for this concept of rationality.

Rationality and changing tastes

In order to avoid problems raised by changing tastes, one may always define a time period during which changes in tastes would be excluded for the sake of consistency, until some (not easily specified) changes in the parameters of the situation would reintroduce space for them. However, the degree of arbitrariness associated with such an ad hoc delimitation of a time period could hardly be accepted by proponents of formal models anxious to define their axioms without any ambiguity and with maximal precision and generality. Therefore, economists have typically preferred to forget about changing tastes by implicitly assuming that they deal with *omniscient* agents who, since they have nothing to learn, have no reason to experience changes of taste. An alternative solution was to acknowledge that they do not deal with empirical agents but only with purely formal entities totally free from the changing habits of human beings.

However, the assumption of omniscience (or of a purely formal world) is a high price to pay when the gain is nothing more than the substitution of a formally workable notion of rationality in place of the more intuitive one that describes the way people usually behave. Moreover, recent interesting developments in economics emphasizing disequilibrium, imperfect information, bounded rationality, learning, the search for information, etc. rest uncomfortably, to say the least, with the postulation of a world inhabited by omniscient or formal entities whose preferences and level of information must be kept immutable in order to avoid any possible conflict with the rigidly defined notion of consistency adopted as a surrogate for rationality.

But let us examine further the implications of this notion of rationality. Consistency was mainly associated with a few axioms among which, the weak axiom put aside, independence and transitivity are the most widely invoked. Let us consider first the axiom of independence (or more precisely, the axiom of context independence) which requires that anyone who chooses *X* from a set limited to *X* and *Y* should not choose *Y* from a larger set including *X*, *Y* and any other element like *Z*. In a paper entitled 'Why be Consistent?', Robert Sugden (1985), has clearly shown that consistency understood as context independence is not a necessary condition of rationality.[2] It seems rational, indeed, when choosing between two actions, to integrate into the evaluation the displeasure caused by regretting not having chosen another action that was feasible. Once this is admitted, Sugden carefully demonstrates that, for one who includes possible regrets into the evaluation, it might be quite rational, in spite of the axiom of context independence and in spite of consistency, to choose *X* over *Y* when only *X* and *Y* are available and to choose *Y* over *X* when additional actions are made available. Thereafter, he colourfully while convincingly illustrates his point using the following version of Gibbard's marriage game (Sugden 1985: 178–180). Bill will choose not to marry Annie if there is nobody else who would marry her, but knowing that Charlie would, Bill (who is jealous) chooses instead to marry her. Being single or married will be alternatively chosen in this case, depending on the presence of another alternative in the set of possibilities. In fact, Sugden's rejection of the necessity of consistency assumes that rationality supposes adaptability and excludes rigidity: the best choice crucially depends on the alternative possibilities available in the environment.

Note that in Sugden's example, Bill's apparently inconsistent yet instrumentally quite rational decisions still suppose that preferences are ordered and stable. No change in tastes is implied since Bill may know in advance whether Annie has a mate in the offing and his preferences can be fixed accordingly from the outset. But one can expand on Sugden's example by supposing that Bill knows nothing of the existence of Charlie (omniscience being excluded) and that, according to his assumed preferences, he decides not to marry Annie, but changes his mind when Charlie appears. In this case, one can say that, because some new information induced him to modify his preferences (or his tastes), Bill violates the context independence axiom, but this is surely not sufficient to conclude that he is irrational for all that. To exclude such a violation, one would have to suppose that Bill *has* stable preferences ranked in the fashion suggested by Sugden's example: being single is preferred to marriage with Annie which is itself preferred to the prospect of Annie marrying any unwelcome suitor. But this would suppose that Bill knows all possible states of the world, including ones that he can hardly imagine, and his preferences (including his own feelings for Annie) in the case of any of them. For example, it is quite possible that if an unknown but, in Bill's eyes, agreeable person by the name of Johnny had come along instead of Charlie, Bill would have preferred to see Annie marry this fellow rather than become engaged to her. It is quite possible indeed that Charlie but not Johnny provokes Bill's jealousy. Why would it be irrational for Bill to change his mind and to adapt his decision to this unexpected situation? Is it conceivable that preferences for states of the world that are not known and possibly not imaginable be ordered in advance in such a fashion that any such changes are precluded? Short of absolute omniscience, there is no reason for preferences to be stable and still less to be independent of the context. As we have seen, dissociating rationality from consistency is far from being counterintuitive. Even though commitment to previous decisions can be highly rational in some specific situations, the systematic adoption of commitment and consistency when context and preferences are changing is nothing but an irrational rejection of a clearly preferred alternative, based on the triumph of rigidity over adaptation. Since the gap between formalized models of rationality and the rationality principle turns out to look more and more like a kind of incompatibility, it is not surprising to see the challenges to the so-called axioms of rationality *made in the name of the rationality principle itself.*

But what about the still more respected axiom of transitivity (or of acyclicity)? This axiom requires that if *A* is revealed to be preferred to *B* and *B* to *C*, *C* cannot be revealed to be preferred to *A*. One of the most popular arguments among those who defend the idea that transitivity is just another face of rationality understood in a more traditional sense is the so-called money pump argument, which was exposed for the first time by Davidson *et al.* (1955: 146). The argument aims to show that transitivity might be taken as a necessary condition of utility maximization and even of sensible behaviour. Indeed, intransitive choices must cause impoverishment since, by hypothesis, they can bring a trader back to the same point after a succession of costly transactions aimed, in each case, at getting something which is deemed preferable. Being in possession of *C* and preferring *B* to *C*, I am ready to pay an extra amount of money to get *B* in exchange for *C*, but preferring *A* to *B*, I will do the same in order to get *A*. At this point if, due to my intransitive preferences, I also prefer *C* to *A*, I will pay again to obtain *C* and, after paying a sizable amount of money, return to exactly where I was at the beginning of the process. Since such a process should continue indefinitely according to the same logic, any amount of money will be pumped out of my pockets. Thus, this state of affairs is thought to illustrate the close connection between consistency and rationality understood in any sense.

However, this argument has frequently been challenged since it can work only if one supposes that the pumped individual is myopic to the point of being unable to consider more than one step at the same time. Indeed, how could one owning *C* be myopic (or stupid) enough to pay something in order to exchange *C* for *B*, which, in one's mind, is destined to be given up with extra cost in order to obtain *A* (since *A* is preferred to *B*) when one is aware that *C*, which is already in one's possession, is (intransitively) preferred to *A*? At the very least, one would stop being pumped after a few steps in the process.[3] In any case, from the point of view of this paper, the important point is that for those who discuss this argument, the decisive test of rationality cannot be associated with a criterion such as transitivity but rather with the fact that people cannot be stupid enough to be consciously involved in a process that clearly fools them. It is true that one might still conclude from this that the money pump argument is defeated precisely because a rational person would quickly refuse to engage in transactions associated with intransitive preferences, which amounts to saying that transitivity *is* a criterion of rationality. However, this is true only if stability of preferences is assumed. Changing preferences during a progressive learning process can be intransitive in a very rational way: I can give up *C* in order to obtain *B* and then give up *B* in order to obtain *A*, but later, after discovering the hidden merits of *C*, begin to be fed up with *A* and be happy to pay something to possess *C* anew. Indeed, I would just maximize my benefits if, by these successive exchanges which are not so costly after all, I manage to be in possession of either *C*, *B* or *A* precisely during the respective period of time in which I was enjoying each of them maximally. In such a situation, *intransitivity* seems even to be required by rationality understood as adaptive behaviour.

Note that just before exposing their argument, which was to be called the money pump argument later, Davidson *et al.* took care to reject an objection to the notion of transitivity, which might look similar to the above objection since it was based on the fact that changing taste might explain that at time *t2*, *C* may be preferred to *A* which was preferred to *C* at time *t1*. They easily replied to this objection by underscoring that 'if valuations change with time, this may be considered a change in alternatives themselves' (1955: 145): *C* at *t2* would be simply a 'different alternative' from *C* at *t1*. This response is unassailable insofar as it concerns the logical conditions of transitivity itself, which supposes that the alternatives are unchanging entities, but it would no longer work if one attempts to apply it to not necessarily stable preferences and to invoke it against the above objection. More precisely, it would tautologically prove that, were preferences to have remained unchanged, transitivity would have obtained and that when preferences are changed, transitivity is valid only either with the old or with the new preferences. However, in the above example, preferences *have* changed in a quite rational fashion; put otherwise, this response would just illustrate the absurdity of defining rationality by a concept (consistency) that is itself partly defined by transitivity, which cannot obtain when (rational) changes in preferences occur. There is no doubt that defining rationality by consistency may facilitate the development of elegant and formally rigorous models, but it is far from evident that this artificial construct made up of a few highly abstract axioms is as robust, reliable and intuitively acceptable as the rationality principle that it tends to supersede.

Why should intransitivity and inconsistency be declared so inimical to rationality? To recycle an example that Alexander Rosenberg (1992a: 119) used in a slightly different context, let us observe that it is surely not irrational to intransitively express a preference for regular coffee over milk at breakfast, milk over decaffeinated coffee at lunch, and the latter over regular coffee at dinner.

However, as Rosenberg observes, in order to save stable preferences and transitivity, economists might construct artificial bundles of goods corresponding to each kind of possible succession of preferences and assume that consistent choices are made among such more complex 'goods'. But what would happen if we pushed this kind of solution a step further after extending the example to an apparently not unreasonable preference for a life with significantly contrasted (and intransitively chosen) experiences? Should we denounce as irrational such a preference for sustained variety in life over the dull monotony of a life continuously characterized by the same (allegedly preferred) satisfactions repeated day after day, year after year? But if we declare such a preference for variety in satisfactions to be reasonable, transitivity (and stability of preferences) would be saved only by considering that a whole life full of multifarious experiences is the bundle to be chosen. But in this limiting case, the very ideas of rational choice, of revelation of preferences, and of transitivity would become totally vacuous. Indeed, a life of this kind chosen in a single shot and as a whole bundle would surely be the object of a stable preference, but it could not be compared with any other bundle in order to let one of them be revealed as the preferred one. Either one admits that preferences are not necessarily stable, and then transitivity is no longer a condition of rationality, or that preferences are artificially made stable, but, then, less and less room is left for choices and transitivity themselves.

It should be clear now that the rationality principle has little to do with the requirement of consistency. Nothing can illustrate this fact more eloquently than the elicitation of the conclusions that can be derived from a systematic adoption of rationality-consistency. Don Ross, who adopts Revealed Preference Theory as the paradigm of economic theory, and consequently consistency as the very meaning of rationality, concludes quite correctly that the best examples of rational agents are not human beings but insects, which indeed are much more consistent in their behaviour. Ross frequently emphasized this idea: '[a] good example of a prototypical economic agent is an insect' (Ross 2005: 251; see also 95, 241, 252, 253, 256, 290, 331, 377, 381 and 393). This is hardly surprising, since insects have little propensity to modify their behaviour and, consequently, to fail a consistency test. Moreover, they are good optimizers as, incidentally, Marx had noted in a famous passage of *Capital* according to which bees are capable of surpassing many architects in the construction of their cells, even though the worst architect is still superior to the best bee in being able to build a house in his or her head before building it in the real world.[4] But building in the head having little to do with rationality defined as consistency, if rationality is consistency, architects who constantly change their mind and human beings in general who so frequently follow their variable spirits cannot compete with bugs on this ground indeed. Now, it is great that Samuelson's revealed preference theory can be so conveniently applied to entomology, but if economists are interested in *human* behaviour in situations of scarcity, as they used to be, this kind of analysis is not very useful. In fact, Ross claims that his conception is based on Robbins' famous definition of economics as 'the science which studies human behavior as a relationship between ends and scarce means which have alternative uses' (Robbins 1952 [1932], quoted by Ross 2005: 87). But, three lines further, Ross adds that he must drop from this definition the word 'human', a move which allows him to conciliate Robbins' largely accepted definition of economics based on *human* rational choice with Samuelson's revealed preference theory which requires strict consistency and leaves very little room for *human* choices. Thus, economists who are more interested in human beings than in insects should be well advised not to base their conception of rationality on consistency.

Rationality under experimental scrutiny

The objections to the modern notion of rationality considered up to now were made from the point of view of economists or methodologists discussing the foundations of pure economic theory. Let us look now at the somewhat more aggressive challenges raised against the same notion of rationality made by experimental psychologists, whose arguments have drawn increasing attention from economists interested in the more and more popular field of experimental economics, which is now more or less integrated into the larger field of behavioural economics. Here again, we will notice that such challenges to rationality construed as consistency are based themselves on one version or another of the rationality principle. Amos Tversky's papers raised some of the most trenchant objections against the so-called axioms of rationality. Against models based on transitivity (even in its weak stochastic form), Tversky (1969) systematically analyses how 'consistent patterns of intransitive choices' are generated. Tversky's point is largely based on the legitimacy of deciding in accordance with a structure characterized as a 'lexicographic semiorder' and illustrated by the example of the employer who has to choose between three candidates who are ranked both by IQ and by experience. The employer can, in a quite reasonable fashion, estimate that a difference of five points or less in IQ can be considered insignificant and, in such a case, base his choice on experience. Thus, with candidates *X*, *Y* and *Z* whose IQs are respectively 120, 124 and 128 but whose experience (varying in the opposite direction) is respectively 20, 15 and 10 years, *X* will be preferred to *Y* (since their IQ being roughly the same, experience will prevail), *Y* will be preferred to *Z* (for the same reason) but *Z* will be preferred to *X* (given *Z*'s clearly superior IQ). In such a case, decisions which, at least made separately, can be said to be rational, lead to intransitive behaviour. It is true that Davidson *et al.* who consider a similar argument, conclude that 'a rational choice is one which selects an alternative to which none is preferred' (Davidson *et al.* 1955: 145), but they must add that such a context 'makes a rational choice impossible'.[5] One might conclude instead that, in such a context, it is only the decisions made separately that can be said to be rational, but this would suppose that rationality is not previously defined through transitivity. In any case, Tversky, for his part, proposes a more general and satisfactory approach to this method of choosing that is seen as an application of what he calls an 'additive difference model', a theoretic model of choice that, from the point of view of a *rational* decider, offers various advantages even if it can lead to various cases of intransitivities.[6]

In any case, what I would like to emphasize here is not the traits of the model proposed by Tversky to analyse this behaviour, but the fact that, to justify such an intransitive behaviour, Tversky invokes, as Simon did, the 'cost involved in evaluating alternatives' (Tversky 1969: 46). In challenging the received view of rationality and in saving rationality in spite of intransitivities, Tversky simply has no need to base his arguments on principles foreign to economic rationality; he simply asks us to include in the cost side of the decider's analysis, the cost of more sophisticated evaluations, just as so many economists have done ever since Stigler proposed his search theory (Stigler 1961). For Tversky, being rational does not mean being constrained by an axiom like transitivity; it means, rather, not stupidly incurring the burden of a process of evaluation whose costs would overcome the benefits from greater precision. In fact, if many economists were right, as well as Tversky, to take into consideration the 'cost involved in evaluating alternatives', it is because they reasonably think that, by avoiding incurring such costs, agents quite rationally manage to avoid 'important unfavorable consequences' to use Simon's wording, without granting significance to the violation of consistency (and even of monetary maximization) that is involved. Thus, in order to explain that an allegedly irrational behaviour was adopted, those who challenge economic models of rationality invoke nothing else than the fundamental rationality principle which for Popper (1985: 361) implies that agents behave 'in a manner appropriate to the situation', a manner that is far from being so irrational after all.[7]

In another paper, written with Daniel Kahneman, Tversky also challenges the context independence axiom by showing that, in various circumstances, people significantly choose in a way that is dependent on the 'frame' in which the situation is presented. But, the authors conclude that such dramatic 'preference reversals' which apparently betray 'errors of choice or judgment' are not 'necessarily irrational' since the incriminated behaviour can at least sometimes 'be justified by reference to the mental effort required to explore alternative frames and avoid potential inconsistencies'.[8] Here again, the authors are clearly sensitive to the cost of supplementary research and deliberation, but, this time, they propose to replace the rational choice model by one called the 'prospect model', which, among other things, accounts for differences in risk aversion in relation to the situation. It is not the place, here, to discuss this model, but I would like to draw attention to the fact that, to justify it, the authors note that 'a man could be judged irrational either because his preferences are contradictory or because his desires and aversions do not reflect his pleasures and pains' (Tversky and Kahneman 1986: 138). Thus, the allegedly irrational behaviour of those who, when facing equivalent problems, make inconsistent choices depending on the frame in which the alternatives are presented might be rational after all if we consider that they behave in such a way that their desires and aversions correctly reflect their pleasures and pains. Here again, the axioms of rationality-consistency are challenged in a way that, in contrast, makes room for the more fundamental rationality principle according to which people, who may be risk-averse, are not stupid enough to incur the heavy burden associated with unknown pathways and other kinds of risk only for the sake of being consistent with the choices they have previously made.

In recent decades, among the objections to the economic notion of rationality raised by psychologists, it is perhaps those concerning preference reversals that have aroused the most systematic attention by economists.[9] In a few joint papers, psychologists Sarah Lichtenstein and Paul Slovic[10] have established that a significant number of people who are offered the occasion to play free of charge their preferred lottery among two lotteries of comparable expected utilities dramatically reverse their preference when they are asked to bid to obtain the right to play one of those lotteries. Typically, a significant number of people among those who are ready to pay more for a lottery in which the prospect of money gain is larger than for a lottery with comparable expected utility that offers safer probabilities of gain, tend to opt for the safer one when they are invited to play one of these lotteries. Put otherwise, a vast majority of those who opt for the lottery with the larger probability of gain (called the probability bet) are paradoxically ready to pay more for the lottery which offers, with a smaller probability, the larger prospect of money gain (called the dollar bet). However, such a dramatic inversion of preferences is not observed, at least not to a significant degree, in the opposite case: those who choose to play the riskier 'dollar' lottery will rarely bid more for the safer 'probability' one. This phenomenon, which contradicts the most basic principles of rational choice theory, has been intensively discussed by psychologists and economists, who have invoked various kinds of circumstances to explain it. Lichtenstein and Slovic did not conclude that irrationality was involved but invoked, like Tversky did, the fact that the subjects adopt a strategy of approximation given the cost of 'evaluating alternative strategies' (Lichtenstein and Slovic 1971: 55).

Among the economists who discussed these questions, David Grether and Charles Plott (1979), after conducting their own set of tests, were convinced, against their own expectations, of the robustness of the observations establishing preference reversals. On the basis of this new evidence, they discussed thirteen possible explanations of this phenomenon and rejected all but one of them – admittedly not very compelling itself – which was, incidentally, incompatible with the context independence axiom of rationality. Nonetheless, they concluded that standard preference theory must be preserved since there is 'no alternative theory currently available' (ibid.: 634). Others managed to explain the phenomenon and maintained that individuals are nonetheless rational at the price of dropping some of the axioms normally associated with the consistency view of rationality. Charles Holt (1986) proposed to drop the Von Neumann-Morgenstern independence (or substitution) axiom,[11] a move which allowed him to ingeniously, albeit not very convincingly, explain preference reversals as a rational but highly complex choice involving lotteries whose prizes may be other lotteries. Graham Loomes and Robert Sugden (1983) claimed that their regret theory, with the help of a few assumptions, can predict the preference reversals phenomenon and make this phenomenon compatible with the 'presumption that individuals are rational, optimising agents' (ibid.: 431). Clearly, with the help of ingenious hypotheses, and well chosen restrictions, it is possible to obtain some results that make room for this curious phenomenon, but people who constantly take into account the painful sensation of regret that has been generated by their past decisions and might be generated by their present ones are rather poor candidates for consistency. After all, Sugden (quite consistently) did not hesitate to entitle 'Why be Consistent?' his other paper referred to above. It is with much more intuitive considerations that Charles Plott attempted to explain this erratic phenomenon when he came back to this question in 1996. Indeed, he put forward the fact that the discovery of the rational attitude associated with expected utility theory can be *progressive*. People who do not care to be attentive enough to make their choice of lottery consistent with the other one made in a different context progressively learn what makes sense in such situations when they are submitted again and again to similar experiences. However, as we have seen, this insistence on learning, which opens the door to the legitimacy of changes in taste, may reserve serious problems for a theory of rationality-consistency based on stability of preferences. Be that as it may, when facing seriously such a cumbersome phenomenon, many economists do not really care to save consistency, which is the core of the modern notion of rationality; they prefer instead to show that people subject to preference reversals manage to act in a way that, although possibly inconsistent, makes sense and is far from being stupid. It is mostly when the modern notion of rationality is challenged that it becomes clear that what is truly fundamental for economics is not the notion of consistency but the rationality principle as such.

During the 1990s, however, while the significance of preference reversals was partly diminished through new experiments allowing for the role of high incentives and learning through repetition, experimental psychologists came back to the question and drew conclusions still more radical and potentially more damaging for the very idea of rationality. Tversky *et al.* (1990) explain the phenomenon by 'scale compatibility', i.e. by the fact that greater weight is spontaneously given to data expressed in the same units.[12] Subjects are ready to pay more (in dollars) for the lottery whose prospects are expressed by a larger amount of *dollars* because they are influenced by the fact that 'dollar' is the single unit of the scale to consider in making the comparison. However, when choosing one of these lotteries to play, they opt for the safer one, because, in this case, their task does *not* essentially consist of comparing two values associated with a single dollar unit. The authors conclude that such behaviour implies the rejection of the principle of procedure invariance, which, according to them, is still more important for economists' notion of rationality than transitivity or independence. This principle stipulates that if A is preferred over B, 'the cash equivalent, or minimum selling price, of A should exceed that of B' (Tversky *et al.* 1990: 204). It seems difficult indeed to characterize economic rationality without implicitly accepting this principle.

Before briefly discussing this case, I would like to make room for more general considerations by examining the interesting debate that in 1996 opposed

Daniel Kahneman to Charles Plott. In this debate, Kahneman did not come back to the case of scale compatibility; instead, he developed his own synthesis of objections to economists' conception of rationality that can be derived from an impressive set of laboratory experiments. After underscoring the role of 'transient emotions' in the making of rather myopic decisions (Kahneman 1996a: 209), he concluded that there is 'compelling evidence that the maintenance of coherent beliefs and preferences is too demanding a task for limited minds' (ibid.: 217). When it comes to explaining these erratic decisions, he referred to his own model of behaviour according to which rather unstable preferences are constructed by the agents rather than given to start with, and claimed that, while less elegant, this model is better supported by evidence (Kahneman 1996b: 253). Plott, for his part, in order to cope with problems raised by psychologists, while maintaining the generality of economic models, introduced an admittedly somewhat philosophical but nonetheless 'observational theory' that he called 'discovered preference hypothesis'. To illustrate his point, he invoked a number of examples of situations, some of them typical of game theory, in which subjects *progressively* become sensible to incentives and learn to behave rationally. Note, however, that even though these subjects learn progressively to become more consistent, they are far from being consistent during the process of learning; but the kind of rationality which seems important for Plott is not so much consistency as the aptitude to be sensible to incentives. He even claims, '[t]he general thesis of this chapter is that rationality can be understood as a process of discovery' (Plott 1996a: 248), a view that I find quite appropriate, but which is hardly compatible with rationality-consistency. In any case, what is determinant in his objections to Kahneman's model (Plott 1996b: 223) is related to the generality of the predictions derivable from economic models in contrast with the limited 'power' that he acknowledges to the criticized model. Here, Plott partially comes back to the main argument of his paper with Grether, which was largely based on the importance of scope as a criterion for judging the success of an explanation. In fact, most economists tend to value highly this argument based on scope: disregarding philosophical questions concerning the notion of rationality, they are easily convinced that their elegant models are preferable for having the advantage of being, in principle, applicable to any type of human action.[13] Whether or not they propose a specific explanation for phenomena like preference reversals, they are easily inclined to downgrade such threatening challenges to their theory, given their firm conviction concerning its scope and the weaknesses of its rivals.

For their part, psychologists continue to pinpoint various limitations in the alleged rationality of human choices. But what kind of limitations is being referred to? Let us consider again the 'scale compatibility' hypothesis, which is so damaging for the principle of procedure invariance. It is true that gamblers who let themselves be influenced by the simple fact that one alternative is clearly expressed in the same dollar unit as the amount to bid, when facing exactly the same choice in two different situations, are acting on a largely affective rather than on a purely rational basis. If we accept the conclusions of Tversky *et al.*

(1990), saving rationality – but an extremely fragile and minimal form of rationality – would require attributing a hardly justified amount of pleasure or of security to the fact of having a price and a reward expressed in the same unit. It would be difficult to predict anything and to convincingly explain on the basis of this kind of 'rationality' but, in any case, it was already acknowledged that human beings are very far from making perfectly rational and predictable decisions all the time. What I say, however, is that almost all decisions that are significant for economic analysis are explainable – and, in the most favourable cases, predictable – if we know what information is available to agents who are assumed to be *at least minimally rational*. However, the decisions made in the laboratory experiments that provoke preference reversals are not typical economic decisions. The evaluation that is required to make the correct choice in such situations ideally implies relatively complex computations of expected utility or of an alternative measure of benefits. Such computations are rather difficult to make in the context of the quick decisions required of the subjects, and especially so if we take account of the fact that decisions to bid and decisions to play are separated in time by a number of similar but numerically different problems to solve. Saying that those subjects are nonetheless rational does not mean that they are endowed with perfect computing abilities and unaffected by any kind of emotions; it simply means that they are not stupid and that, consequently, they decide in a sensible way given their limited knowledge and abilities, and given the way they assess the various elements of the situation.

The problem faced by such subjects puts them in a situation comparable to that in which those who are submitted to the famous Allais paradox found themselves. It is well known that Leonard Savage failed to respond correctly when faced with the choice that reveals the Allais paradox, since he opted for incompatible answers contradicting his own ideas on the matter. But no one would conclude for all that that the author of *The Foundation of Statistics* is an irrational and stupid fellow. He is very far from being stupid, indeed, but when choosing relatively quickly between the options proposed, he was not in a position to evaluate and to make all the computations required. Consequently, in a situation which was probably somewhat stressful, he was influenced, as nearly everybody else would be, by the deceptive way in which the problem is set up. When making the first choice in the Allais problem, one is usually influenced by the certainty of winning a large amount whereas, in the second choice, where this certainty is absent, one is strongly tempted to decide differently even though the decision to take is strictly the same in all other respects. When facing the Allais problem or questions about lotteries raised by experimental psychologists, people look for the most appropriate solution given their goal which is in this case to provide a sane answer, but not being in position to exert very much in the way of their computational abilities, they adopt rules of thumb (associated with the prospect either of a high or of a sure gain) which in usual situations (but not in those deceptive situations that are considered here) might be tolerably reliable ways to reach an appropriate solution. Turgot and Smith's rationality principle does not really require much more than this of economic agents, but the modern axioms of rationality are quite different animals.

To be sure, one might argue that such a rationality principle is much too vague to satisfy the requirements of modern economics. However, the explanatory power of this modest principle should not be underestimated. To illustrate this, let us consider the following explanation, which admittedly rests on pure fiction. Suppose that, in order to explain the fact that, in preference reversal situations, many people are inclined to pay a higher price for a lottery that they do not choose than for the lottery that they actually choose when both are offered to them, I invoke a law according to which those who are risk-averse tend much more than the risk-lovers *to equalize everywhere* the arithmetical product obtained when the amount paid for a lottery is multiplied by the utility which they attribute to this lottery when it comes to playing it. Let us call this curious propensity the 'product equalization' compulsion. Such a theory might have interesting prospects from an empirical point of view since the reversal observed among so many who are risk-averse would be explained through the predominance among them of this 'product equalization' compulsion. Indeed, the risk-averse would play the safe (high probability) lottery because they attribute more utility to it than to the riskier (high gain) lottery and should tend normally to pay more for it; but for a significant number among them this 'normal' trend would be overcompensated by the need to pay more for the lotteries with less utility in order to make sure that the product of these two variables (the utility and the amount paid) is roughly equalized for each lottery. In contrast, risk-lovers (who would play the riskier lottery), since they are much less affected by this bizarre compulsion, would rather tend to pay more for their favourite lottery in conformity with what is empirically observed. But why would you strongly resist such a so-called 'explanation' in spite of its relative empirical success? The answer is, clearly, because *it does not make sense*. A gambler who is not stupid might be totally unable to make complex computations, might avoid tiresome deliberations for a return judged not worthwhile and might even be influenced by irrelevant variables (e.g. scale compatibility) whose irrelevance is not instantaneously seen as self-evident. But someone who is not stupid cannot be moved by a morbid compulsion to equalize arithmetical products whose equalization has no meaning at all! In other words, such a silly explanation does not comply with the rationality principle, which is the supreme criterion for any theory to be seriously considered in economics.

True, one might argue that this 'product equalization' theory is totally ad hoc and that this is a sufficient reason to reject the so-called explanation without any help from the rationality principle. But which criterion allows one to judge ad hocness in such a case? If *all* such lottery type situations can be 'explained' by this theory, the principle is not so ad hoc after all. In fact, if such a principle cannot be extended to other types of situation, it is precisely because, since it does not make sense, it is not possible to characterize the way it could be *sensibly* adapted to a situation different from the choice between lotteries. Even if, with a bit of imagination, I could show successfully that this 'product equalization' compulsion could help fit the data in other contexts, such a tentative generalization would do nothing to reduce the ad hoc-ness of the incriminated explanation, precisely because the case which would allow one to conclude that this factor has some generality *would not make more sense* than the first and, consequently, *would not count as another case* of explanation based similarly on the role of this bizarre factor. In contrast, suppose that I observe that individuals who each have at their disposal a fixed amount of money to spend on lotteries during their whole life spend the amount, from period to period, in two quite different fashions whereas it could be theoretically expected that any one of them should adopt the same optimal pattern. And suppose that I explain this phenomenon by distinguishing the risk-averse, who tend to *equalize* for each period the arithmetical product obtained by multiplying the amount spent on lotteries bought by the average utility they attributed to the lotteries chosen, from risk-lovers who do not bother with such equalization. I would have invoked an explanation that, at first glance, looks as bizarre and ad hoc as the one used above, since it seems just as oddly formulated and explains only the situations of the type described. However, this principle could not be dismissed as ad hoc because it makes some sense in such a situation: some lottery fans who are risk-averters might care to enjoy the pleasure of having exactly the same chance of winning at every period of their life rather than exhausting all of it in a short period. In such a case, the equalization of the arithmetical product of an expected utility and an amount of money might make sense, at least for some people. Indeed, this way of proceeding can be *interpreted* as a variant of a more general principle of equalization of utility over time, a principle that appears sensible for someone who eschews risk. The comparison between these two examples clearly shows that even though many different variables related to human behaviour can be arbitrarily introduced into a model in order to fit the data, only those which can be explained by a rational move, however minimally rational, have any explanative power. As was illustrated in the first two chapters of this book, most of the great economists in the last 250 years were forced to ground their theories on this fact in spite of their renewed attempts to find for their explanations more 'objective', 'positive' or 'formal' conceptual apparatuses.

Once having accomplished this short trip through the history of economic thought, the three following questions remain with us. How can we determine to what degree minimal rationality should be minimal, a question that apparently does not arise with maximal rationality, which can be defined precisely with the help of the exact concept of a maximum? How can we avoid this minimal rationality being understood in so minimal a fashion that no more room is left for irrationality? Since this minimal notion of rationality is clearly understood as the rationality of an individual agent, how to face the objections that theoreticians of economics tend more and more to oppose to methodological individualism? The next three chapters will discuss these three questions respectively, but in the reverse order.

Part II

Objections to the notion of minimal rationality

3 Can methodological individualism survive?

Methodological individualism is a methodological approach that has been traditionally associated with social sciences. For decades throughout the twentieth century, philosophers such as Karl Popper and J. W. N. Watkins, sociologists such as Max Weber and Raymond Boudon and economists such as Joseph Schumpeter and Friedrich Hayek were particularly eloquent promoters of this approach of social sciences and were frequently engaged in debates with the defenders of the opposite view. Without necessarily being involved in theoretical debates, most social scientists proceeded in ways that were illustrative either of methodological individualism or of this opposite approach, which rejected individualist postulates and was known either as methodological holism or collectivism when it was not identified with a variety of organicism. For their part, most economists, especially since the so-called marginalist revolution, were inclined to adopt more or less explicitly the individualist posture which was more consonant with their attempts to elucidate the arcane dimensions of the market economy by relating them to well understood rational behaviour of people. Be that as it may, it is not my intention in this chapter to revisit the rich history through which methodological individualism and methodological holism have progressively defined themselves. This work has been competently done by various historians of thought who devoted works specifically to this question.[1]

Instead, my task will be, after characterizing a viable conception of methodological individualism, to discuss the apparently very damaging objections that have recently been raised against the idea of maintaining this methodological approach in economics. This will be an unavoidable task because the *rationality principle*, at least in the minimal version that I have proposed, supposes an understanding of individual behaviour which is hardly distinguishable from methodological individualism properly understood. Throughout the last decade, or perhaps the last two, economists' attitudes seem to have changed to such a point that methodological individualism has become somewhat suspect to many of them. And in the last few years, methodological individualism was harshly attacked by some of the most vocal among recent contributors to the history and methodology of economics. Indeed, methodological individualism is clearly the favourite target of Don Ross' book on microexplanations (Ross 2005), which suggests grounding micro in macroeconomics rather than the other way around, and even asserts that a human being is more similar to a nation than to a straightforward agent. Moreover, methodological individualism seems to be disqualified by an eventual disintegration of the self, which is insistently underscored by Ross and which is one of John Davis' book's main themes (Davis 2003). A few months before them, Philip Mirowski devoted the first section of chapter 7 of his book on 'Cyborg science', *Machine Dreams*, to emphasizing the multiple problems met by philosophical attempts to individualize the Self (Mirowski 2002). For his part, Harold Kincaid published in 1997 a book entitled *Individualism and the Unity of Science* in which he severely denounces individualism. In this context, it seems that defending methodological individualism largely consists in rowing against a very strong current.

However, before showing why these challenges do not seriously attain a properly characterized conception of methodological individualism, it seems appropriate to identify the defendant more precisely. From this point of view, my two preliminary remarks about the meaning of the word 'methodological' will appear almost self-evident to most readers, but it might nonetheless be worthwhile to briefly formulate them. On the one hand, methodological individualism should obviously not be confused with *ethical* individualism even though in common parlance the word 'individualism' refers primarily to the ethical attitude of those whose concerns tend (selfishly) to be limited to their own interests at the expense of their fellow citizens and of societies of which they are members. It is true that many people (wrongly) estimate that *homo oeconomicus* is typically such a selfish individualist,[2] but this ethical attitude attributed to economic agents has obviously nothing to do with the epistemological attitude that is required from theoreticians who adopt methodological individualism. On the other hand, this methodological approach should not be confused with *metaphysical* or *ontological* individualism. Even if the nuances (to be underscored below) that must be brought to the definition of methodological individualism are disregarded, it should be clear that claiming that it is appropriate to explain social processes as resulting from a set of individual actions rather than the other way around does not require attributing an ontological primacy to individuals over societies. If a privilege is attributed to individual human beings, it is because human beings who are, after all, those who need to understand the social processes that are explained, will more satisfactorily understand them if they can see how these phenomena derive in some sense from their own actions. This fact concerning the meaning and the kind of explanations that are required in social sciences does not imply that the *ontological* status of human beings should be considered superior in any sense or more fundamental than the ontological status of societies, a question that, meaningful or not, bears on a totally different issue.

But how should we define methodological individualism? Defining this notion does not seem particularly difficult at first glance. For example, it does not seem very risky to adopt even a rather rough definition such as the one proposed by the French sociologist Raymond Boudon, for whom methodological individualists are those who claim that a social phenomenon must be grasped as the result of the aggregation of individual behaviours guided by (individual) motivations

(Boudon 1986: 46). However, it quickly turns out that the difficulty appears when it comes to precisely characterizing an individualist thesis in order to *clearly* distinguish it from an opposite one, whether dubbed holist, collectivist or whatever. What type of aggregation does this definition refer to? Is it a purely additive aggregation of a multitude of individual behaviours that would be gathered together to form a society? It is doubtful that any social scientist including Boudon has in mind this kind of aggregation, which would imply that a society would be nothing but a crowd. For sure, the aggregation in question is a more subtle process that takes into account the consequences of this aggregation on the social result that is obtained. But what kind of consequences are involved and to what extent might the presence of these consequences blur the apparently clear distinction between methodological individualists and those who tend to be closer to the holist or collectivist side of the picture? To have a better and possibly contrasted view of this process, let us consider the case of two important thinkers who are usually associated with this latter 'side' and rarely with the individualist one.

Are Marx and Keynes holists or individualists?

Karl Marx and John Maynard Keynes are two important economists who are usually perceived by most contemporary economists as collectivists, or at the very least as pertaining to a tradition generally opposed to methodological individualism. Nonetheless, it is unexpectedly easy to underscore individualist features in the methodology of those two alleged radical collectivist thinkers.[3] This does not mean that we must change our views on standard history of economics and claim that both of them are adepts of methodological individualism like so many of their fellow economists. Instead, it is our view of the radical opposition between methodological individualism and methodological collectivism or holism that we have to revisit. More precisely, we should question the relevance of presupposing that we have necessarily to choose between so loosely defined methodological postures.

It is true that Marx seems to be at the antipode of individualism when he explains the capitalists' compulsion to accumulate capital not by invoking a psychological attitude of individual capitalists but by a socially generated attitude that would be strictly determined by the fact that the compulsive entrepreneurs are members of the capitalist class. However, this does not mean that Marx supposes that the class efficiency in shaping capitalist behaviour is explained itself in virtue of a holistic power emanating from the very existence of collectiveness. Marx would surely have rejected such a quasi-mystical approach. What he had in mind, much more concretely, is that the constraining power of the class is explained itself by the fact that each entrepreneur is involved in a savage competition. Each of them quickly learns that refraining from the accumulation of capital would mean being excluded from the process of innovation, which is constantly going on in a competitive capitalist world and which allows competitors who innovate to slightly reduce their prices and, through this way, to win over the customers of competitors unable to face this kind of competition.[4] Put otherwise, it is individual capitalists' own decisions to get richer that generate a competition whose unwanted effect is to force each of them either to continue indefinitely to wrestle in order to accumulate more and more capital and introduce more and more lucrative innovations or to progressively lose customers and sooner or later become bankrupt. Should we characterize such an explanation as an example of methodological holism or of methodological individualism? There is no clear answer to this question.

Similarly, when Keynes rejects the neoclassical microeconomics, he seems to reject methodological individualism as well. For example, when he asserts, in the second chapter of *General Theory* (Keynes 1936), that, during an employment crisis, workers are completely unable to accept a decrease in real wages in order to increase the general level of employment, as was recommended by microeconomists of his time, he clearly seems to denounce the individualist postulates of microeconomics. But what, in more precise terms, is involved in this argument? Obviously, a single worker can easily manage to reduce his (or her) real wages, simply by accepting a decrease in monetary wages which would make this worker unable to buy as many commodities as before, if, as expected in such a case, the level of prices is not changed in the process. However, what Keynes envisaged was a *general* decrease in wages, which in a free labour market should result from more or less simultaneous decisions made by a significant number of workers to reduce wages in order to save their jobs. Indeed, more and more individual workers would accept reducing their wages in order to face the competition of those other workers who are ready to work for lower wages. But such a general decrease in wages would necessarily result for capitalists in an important reduction in costs, which, in a competitive environment, should command a proportionate reduction in prices. And this price reduction, Keynes explains, would leave the workers in position to buy as many commodities as before. Therefore, real wages (i.e. wages in the only sense that, according to Keynes, should induce employers to modify the level of employment) would not be significantly changed in spite of the prevalent view among economists of the time – and in spite of the common-sense intuition – according to which workers might accept a reduction in wages in order to increase employment. Thus, this result is explained by referring to a set of apparently rational human decisions successively made by workers and by capitalists and not to a particularly holistic power of any kind of macro-phenomena.

In this context, why should we conclude that Marx and Keynes' arguments imply a rejection of methodological individualism? It is not clear in what way such arguments differ so much from those, typically associated with methodological individualism, through which Hayek and other economists explain social processes such as the creation of money and the workings of the market. In all of these cases, it is claimed that various individuals make decisions guided by what they consider their own interest. But since, in a society, a large number of individual actions are simultaneously going on, they interfere amongst themselves in such a way that unwanted and unexpected results are generated by these normally uncoordinated and conflicting interactions.

Of course, a finer analysis might emphasize some differences between explanations that are traditionally associated with Marx's 'collectivist' approach or Keynes' macroeconomics and those associated with microeconomics like Hayek's explanation of the way the market works. There are such things as well established macroeconomic relations between rate of unemployment, rate of inflation and gross national product, as well as between rate of suicide and level of anomie, but these relations, by themselves, are not *explanative* theories. And since methodological individualism is essentially a strategy (or a methodology) for explanation, its relevance is not affected by the existence of relations that can be used in explanations but that cannot be considered as explanations themselves. True, the relative robustness of such relations can be explained, just like Marx and Keynes' explanative theories discussed above provide a way to explain the logic of similar macro-relations. However, if the required explanations involve human actions with consequences unexpectedly modified by the fact that they take place in a constraining society, there is no reason to think that they would be less compatible with methodological individualism than Marx's and Keynes' explanations considered above were. In fact, interpreting the explanations provided by these 'collectivist' thinkers in such a quasi-individualist way is legitimate, because these explanations are never of a purely holist variety, which would be based on a purely social emanation independent from individual actions. Indeed, granting to a social entity a strictly autonomous power that would be independent from any human action has generally looked too mysterious to be adopted as an explanation of last resort by economists who are eager to convince their readers with the help of rationally compelling arguments. However, as illustrated by the cases of Marx's and Keynes' arguments, the point is not to deny that social structures can considerably influence individual behaviour. No doubt it is because capitalist societies are structured in a way that allows competitiveness that Marx and Keynes can argue that people will behave in the fashion they do, but this is true of Hayek's explanations as well. The point for the relevance of methodological individualism is that the structure of society is not conceived of as primitive data in the process of explanation and that the intelligibility of social phenomena is provided, in the last resort, by the fact that they were produced by interacting human interventions.

This does not mean that individual (and rational) human interventions are the only factors explaining social events; it is clear that physical and biological factors can explain some of their features and that, as we will see in another chapter, a kind of natural selection may contribute to their genesis and their development. Indeed, the present discussion of methodological individualism does not aim to promote an imperialistic version of this methodological approach. It more modestly aims to show that, for their explanations, the social sciences may rely – and have extensively relied – on a principle, namely the rationality principle, which claims that individual people are not stupid and act in sensible fashions, in such a way that it is appropriate, as suggested by methodological individualism, to explain social processes as resulting from unwanted interferences between these rational actions. Thus, methodological individualism is not the dogmatic and imperialist methodology usually evoked by its adversary; however, concerning its true nature, there are still two more subtle sources of confusion that we have to consider before discussing the contemporary objections evoked at the beginning of this chapter.

Methodological individualism is an *anti*-constructivist methodology

Insistence on the role of individuals in explaining social processes may have induced some people to associate methodological individualism with a Cartesian methodology according to which it is possible to *reconstruct* complex phenomena (such as social entities) with the help of simple ones (in this case, individual human actions). There is no doubt that where this Cartesian method is applicable, for example in some parts of geometry and of mechanics which were fruitfully cultivated by René Descartes, it may produce remarkably intelligible explanations; but it can almost never be applied to explanations of social phenomena since, in contrast with mechanical phenomena, the latter are generated by untraceable interactions whose consequences are unpredictable. A lot of confusion on this point may have been induced by the fact that many authors of microeconomic textbooks have proposed to help understanding economic analysis by considering first how Robinson Crusoe managed on his desert island. This pedagogical device more or less explicitly suggests that in order to understand the workings of a social economy, one would be well advised to trace how the latter was built up through a step-by-step construction whose bricks and mortar would be found in Crusoe-like situations.[5] But, whether apt or misleading, this kind of pedagogy has nothing to do with methodological individualism. As we have seen, economists associated with methodological individualism do not explain social processes as if the latter were simply an aggregation, independent from the social context, of individual actions taken by rational economic agents. On the contrary, methodological individualism – especially, but not exclusively,[6] when defended by Austrian economists – has generally been closely related to the idea according to which social processes are the result of *unwanted consequences* of human actions. According to this view, social phenomena are explained by being derived from the interference of a multitude of anonymous human actions, which have the advantage of being understandable, at least in principle. Put otherwise, it is true that methodological individualists explain social processes by invoking the multiple actions of human beings, but the latter are supposed to be members of a society whose members are all continuously interacting amongst them in such a way that these interactions radically transform the consequences of their actions.[7]

This way to understand methodological individualism was defended by Menger, who refers to 'unintended results' (1985 [1883]: 130, 155, 158), and abundantly developed by Hayek in a paper whose very title claims that social processes are the results of human actions, but not of Human Design.[8] This view was not really new; Hayek acknowledges his debt on this point to Adam Ferguson and even to Bernard Mandeville's *Fable of the Bees*.[9] This view is also shared by many of those who have exposed the very meaning of methodological individualism. J. W. N. Watkins, a philosopher who, in the 1950s, devoted various writings to the promotion of methodological individualism, claims that to be a consequent individualist the point is not to deny the existence of unwanted consequences but to impute these consequences to the responses that individuals adopt to face their situation (Watkins 1957: 113). Similarly, in his entry on 'Holism and Individualism in History and Social Science' for the Edwards *Encyclopaedia of Philosophy*, William Dray (1967: 54) observes that the non-intentional character of what results from human actions, far from being antithetical to methodological individualism, is an integral part of this methodological approach.

If methodological individualists consider that social processes are explained by a set of human interactions that are not wanted by any individual – individuals being literally powerless when it comes to controlling such processes – one should not be surprised to see that the 'constructivist' idea that social entities can be understood as directly resulting from well thought and well planned human actions is severely disparaged by methodological individualists such as Friedrich Hayek (see in particular Hayek 1952 [1942–44]: chapters 4 and 6). For consistent methodological individualists who claim that social processes are explained by the clash between human actions, these entities *cannot be constructed* with the help of those human actions as if they were similar to a set of blocks. Conversely, social processes cannot be deconstructed into human actions because they were never constructed to start with. Methodological tenets promoted by individualist thinkers such as Hayek are so far from defending the idea of a conscious construction of social entities that Hayek does not hesitate to say that we may refer to such entities only 'insofar as the conscious action[s] of many men produce undesigned results, insofar as regularities are observed which are *not* the result of anybody's design' (Hayek 1952 [1942–44]: 69; emphasis added). One can even conclude that this individualist idea of *imputing* the features of social entities to individual actions whose consequences were uncontrollable is theoretically interesting mainly because it reveals in what sense social entities are social and not individual entities. But what kind of imputation is methodological individualism requiring? Does methodological individualism imply that social entities must be *reduced* to individual ones?

Methodological individualism is an *anti*-reductionist methodology

Since untraceable interactions dramatically modify the consequences of human actions and consequently the contribution of these actions to the explanation of social processes, it is difficult to see in what sense the latter could be *reduced* to human actions. Thus, in spite of the common view on this matter,[10] methodological individualism *should not* be treated as a kind of reductionism. For many observers, such an anti-reductionist individualism sounds like a contradiction or, at the very least, an inconsistency. Robert Nozick, for example, denounced methodological individualists for being reductionists when they 'reduce' social entities to individual actions without being ready to go further in this process:

> Methodological individualists are reductionists to the extent of their claim that true theories of social science are reducible to theories of social human action, but typically Austrians *oppose* other reductionist claims, e.g. that theories of human action are reducible to neurophysiology, chemistry, and physics, or that social science is reducible to these in a way which *bypasses* human action.
>
> (Nozick 1977: 353–354)

In fact, methodological individualists have no reasons to defend those claims or any other kind of reduction, because they are not reductionists at all. If we accept what was said above about the unwanted consequences of these actions, any attempt at reduction would fail for being unable to trace the exact way through which social processes 'derive' from individual actions; therefore methodological individualism properly understood cannot be a reductionism. To better understand this claim, one may, for example, look at the conditions that, according to Harold Kincaid, are required for a theory to be called reductionist. Indeed, Kincaid's second condition implies the possibility of deriving 'all the explanations in the theory to be eliminated from the more fundamental theory without at the same time presupposing any elements of the theory being eliminated'.[11] In the case that interests us, the theory to be eliminated would be a theory based on social forces and the more fundamental theory, a theory based on individual actions. But since the latter concedes a considerable role to unwanted consequences of actions – which are unwanted because the social context dramatically matters – it would not make sense to claim that nothing is presupposed from the eliminated theory; therefore methodological individualism is in no way a reductionism.

Thus, we may now understand why Nozick's observations did no damage to methodological individualism.[12] It is true that the version of methodological individualism that is promoted here – which is relatively close to the Austrian version, even though this fact does not imply the endorsement of other Austrian theses – does not recommend reducing human actions to their neurophysiological, chemical, and physical sources, but nor does it recommend *reducing* social entities to human actions either. If human actions seem to be privileged in a process of imputation of social entities whose origins are looked for in human action, it is because it is precisely their role in the formation of those social entities that needs to be understood by human beings who are both those who perform such actions and those who experience this need. Of course, human beings also need to understand the development of physical phenomena and in this case, they might find the Cartesian idea of reconstruction from elemental parts attractive, in spite of the fact that such reconstructions suppose complete reductions. Nonetheless, it would not make sense for methodological individualists to recommend *bypassing* human action in the process of imputation of social entities. Indeed, when it comes to explaining the role of human actions in the formation of social entities, it is human actions as such that are the source of intelligibility and not the more elemental constituents of human beings, which would be a possible source of intelligibility if the Cartesian methodology so fruitful for the analysis of physical phenomena was adopted. Note that this is not to say that the latter methodology and its corresponding source of intelligibility could not be applied to social and human phenomena. It simply means that the explanation of social phenomena that is provided by social sciences and especially by economics, in an overwhelming majority of cases, corresponds to this different type of methodology and of intelligibility that is based on the rationality principle and on methodological individualism.

But what is the point of methodological individualism if it is not to promote the reduction that Nozick and many others associate with it? It is to help understand social phenomena by relating them to individual actions. More precisely, it is to explain why rational human actions, which are constantly interfering amongst themselves, produce social consequences that are significantly different from those that are normally expected by people who perform these actions. Many people still today wonder a bit naively why it is not possible for rational people to build up an efficient society that could replace a capitalism that imposes its cruel and apparently irrational laws on everyone. Human beings need to understand why the consequences of their actions are typically incorporated in social structures (such as a market, a monetary system, a political structure, an economic crisis, a system of production, etc.), which escape them, fall out of their control and seem to impose their laws on them. For people who are familiar enough with the human actions that they frequently perform (buying, selling, working, etc.) but who need to understand the mystifying formation of social structures, imputations of social phenomena to such human actions are a key element in providing the required explanation. Therefore, methodological individualism is the intellectual strategy of those who, facing such social processes – whether Marxian law of accumulation, Keynesian constraint on real wages or the more or less regular workings of a market – try to explain them by analysing how the expected consequences of human actions independently taken by a multitude of people are radically modified, and modified in directions that are uncontrolled, while generally understandable, at least after the fact. One may even describe this strategy as the elicitation of the mechanisms through which consequences of individual actions are transformed into unwanted, while sometimes beneficial, social entities.

One might object that a reasonable version of methodological *holism* can hardly be defined very differently. This might be true since palatable versions of methodological individualism and of methodological holism are not so easy to disentangle. Of course, the confrontation of straw men built up by their respective opponents in order to depict either holism or individualism can easily suggest the existence of a radical opposition between these philosophical perspectives; but it is very difficult to find serious defenders of such extremist theses. Usually, those who are championing a tenable version of one of these theses take care to introduce so many nuances into the characterization of their favourite 'ism' that the distinction between the opposing views becomes more or less blurred. One may estimate that the interpretation of methodological individualism exposed above is insufficiently specific, but it is such an interpretation, and not an indefensible reductionist version, that is required by the proper workings of a minimal rationality. The latter, indeed, is the rationality of an individual whose actions, not determined by biophysical factors, contribute through their very modest capacity to the development of social structures.

Can methodological individualism survive the fragility of the self?

Understood in this fashion, methodological individualism can hardly be damaged by the traditional objections that were raised against it. However, a quite different type of argument is invoked in the recent trial to which this approach to economics was subjected. Indeed, most recent objections to methodological individualism bear on the notion of an individual as such, which, for some methodologists involved in this debate, is almost totally discredited. Were this view justified, the rug would be drawn out from under the feet of the advocates of any version of methodological individualism. How could one defend the methodological relevance of basing explanations on a fragile and almost vanishing individuality? In fact, the status granted to the notion of an individual by neoclassical economists has always been a favourite target for those who were bothered by its egoistic connotations. We have seen, however, that methodological individualists do not judge these objections to be very troublesome, precisely because the individualism that they promote is explicitly *methodological* and not ethical. However, the new charge against the individual was of another nature. It is no longer the moral connotations of individualism that were targeted, but its ontological consistency.

In fact, the trial of the individual in this context was, for a significant part, the trial of the self. The notion of a self is what better characterizes the autonomy of human beings, which are normally referred to by the notion of an individual, as used by methodological individualists. It is in order to emphasize the extreme fragility of this notion that, in *Machine Dreams*, his all-encompassing book about cyborg culture, Philip Mirowski distinguishes eight conceptions of the Self and addresses each of them with sharp and colourful arguments.[13] I am surely not ready to endorse each of these arguments, but it is not my intention to discuss them here. My claim is rather that, even if we were to accept them, the thus acknowledged fragility of the Self would not very seriously affect methodological individualism, as I understand it. In order to substantiate this claim, I think that it is worthwhile to consider each of these conceptions of the Self. According to Mirowski's categorization, the first of them is based on the atomic model; the second is associated with the nature of human body; the third emphasizes its pretension to be the centre of causal agency; the fourth links the

Self to consciousness and intentionality; the fifth reveals its serious instability; the sixth is implied by the Kantian approach emphasizing autonomy and freedom; the seventh supposes that the Self is the 'storehouse of memory' and the eighth associates it with consistency. It is possibly a bit tedious to discuss each of them, but I think it is important to briefly do so, given the attention granted to the status of the Self in recent philosophical and even economic literature and the dramatic impact on economic methodology that an eventual dismissal of methodological individualism would have if it were to result from the weakening of the Self.

The first conception of the Self that Mirowski considers is based on the indivisibility attributed to atoms seen as paradigms of individuality. Mirowski is right to claim that modern physics has since long relegated this view to the history of science, but since the Self that is referred to by methodological individualism owes nothing to this quasi-mythical view of atoms, this conception does not really need to be discussed further. Moreover, as more or less implied by Mirowski's discussion (2002: 443), the appropriate way of explaining social phenomena is perfectly indifferent to the degree to which physicists are successful in their attempt to penetrate further and further the subcomponents of matter.

Concerning his second paradigm, the 'somatic self' ending 'at one's skin', Mirowski raised troublesome philosophical questions generated by the possibility that bioengineering makes somatic identity rather problematic. No doubt that these considerations are based on well grounded data, but why should we conclude that they are fatal for methodological individualism? If human beings, sustained by all their prostheses, are still able to act (such prostheses being supposed to amplify the capacities of those who benefit from them), their actions would normally interfere as well as before and generate unwanted social consequences that should still be usefully explained by an analysis of the way they derive from this set of interactions according to what methodological individualism suggests. Naturally, if the development of such prostheses were to result in the creation of robotic entities that would take over prosthetic human beings by controlling their behaviour as well as the consequences of the latter, the rules of the game would be changed and methodological individualism would lose its very object, but we are still very far from there. In any case, my point is not that methodological individualism would survive any conceivable change in human nature and human society; it is that it can survive in a sound theory of the present economic and social changes that affect humanity.

According to the fourth approach considered by Mirowski (I will come back to the third one later), the Self would be 'the seat of human consciousness and intentionality' (ibid.: 445), but, Mirowski argues, this is more and more contested, given the development of the computer to which consciousness and intentionality might well be acknowledged. This raises formidable problems that I will not discuss here. But if we admit that computers are endowed with intentional capacities, and even if we go as far as some theoreticians in eventually attributing consciousness to computers (what Mirowski does not seem really ready to do, see ibid.: 445), this does not really affect methodological individualism as such.

Indeed, if these conscious computers *need to understand* like human beings do, and if, still like human beings, they *enjoy satisfaction* when a compelling explanation of a phenomenon such as the equilibrium eventually observed on a computer-animated market is provided to them, the only question concerning the status of methodological individualism would be whether such computers would *appreciate* better (and find more compelling) an explanation based on the unwanted results of their robotic actions than an explanation based on the holistic power emanating immediately from the socialization of the robotic society. If such robots are really human-like, the first alternative seems to be the most probable. One may find a bit far-fetched the attribution of such an unnatural scope to methodological individualism, but one must recall that the latter is essentially a *methodological* approach, which concerns the best strategy of explanation, but in no way the ontological status hypothetically attributed to the agents or to the receptors of the explanation. But if we suppose that, while conscious like human beings, the robots are structured in such a different and superior way that their essential epistemic features have little in common with us, it would be appropriate to let them define the epistemology corresponding to their eventual type of knowledge. And since it seems reasonable to think that such an eventuality might not be actualized before a sizable period of time, it might be wise in the remaining time during which the standard kind of humanity is still in command to stick to the more prosaic epistemology corresponding to our actual way of knowing. Put otherwise, given the actual state of our knowledge on these matters, it may still be appropriate for a certain amount of time to 'wait and see'.

In fact, the two latter conceptions of the Self that I have just discussed were largely generated by speculation, a quite legitimate and potentially fruitful speculation, which however has relatively little to do with epistemology and methodology of sciences. Let us consider now the third 'incarnation of selfhood' discussed by Mirowski, which is somewhat more closely related to the question concerning the status of methodological individualism. It is introduced by the following question: should the Self be understood as 'the only real center of causal agency in a world where all other activity may or may not be properly understood as the resultant of similar kinds of agency, animate or inanimate' (ibid.: 439)? It seems clear that no exclusivity on real causal agency can be granted to the Self, but it is not clear that this lacking exclusivity is essential to avoid the dismissal of methodological individualism. In any case, even though, as Mirowski reminds us, 'the putatively imperturbable conception of the self' is seriously 'shaken' by the existence of mental disorders such as anosognosia (ibid.: 444), the causal agency of the Self is a phenomenological datum of our common experience. Therefore, if one claims that this experience of causal agency is a pure illusion, one should have to assume the onus of the proof. But is it a pure illusion? When Philip Mirowski writes a highly original book, which has a considerable influence on economic community, can we really say that attributing any causal agency to Mirowski and considering that he is entitled to be the author of this book would be due to a pure illusion? In fact, even though attributing authorship to a being to whom any kind of causal agency is denied seems contradictory, no one will contest Mirowski's authorship. In this context, what does it mean exactly to deny him and other authors, as well as buyers and sellers, some significant degree of causal agency? Note that the point here is not whether this agency is or is not influenced itself and even made possible by neurological or sociological factors. Of course, it is. The question is whether human beings who require explanations have serious reasons to think that they are causal agents to some degree and whether the analysis of their interacting interventions can be particularly insightful when it comes to understanding the formation of social structures. One can even say that, insofar as the only question at stake is the relevance of methodological individualism as an appropriate strategy for explanation, this approach might survive even if the autonomy of actions is an illusion. Indeed, how can one deny the explanative value of an analysis of the process through which – if such were really the case – market equilibrium would result from the interactions, necessarily unwanted, between such pseudo-autonomous actions naively assumed as theirs by individuals? Were this the case, rational explanations would have to be reconsidered, but *methodological* individualism as such might remain an appropriate strategy for explanation. Be that as it may, it is far from clear that autonomy of any kind must be denied to human actions.

The fifth view of the Self that Mirowski discussed concerns its stability and identity through time which was already contested by David Hume and which, as Mirowski underscores, is much less evident with the increasing place granted to biological evolution in scientific explanations. Since I will have to come back to this question later in this chapter, I reserve for then my discussion of the consequences of these considerations on methodological individualism. The sixth version of the Self, based on Kant's view on autonomy and freedom, is made implausible, according to Mirowski, by the development of cyborgs to which Kantian categories are clearly not applicable. Note that this is apparently due to the fact that, in spite of arguments so frequently expressed by many cyborg people, computers and humans are not so similar after all. Moreover, as Mirowski aptly observes,

> the more that decision theorists and philosophers jump on the cognitive science bandwagon, and fall all over themselves to portray the rational agents as an automaton of various levels of computational capacity coupled to an arbitrary aggregation of genetic material, then the less likely it becomes that the Self will earn its spurs by learning to exercise its inviolable Selfhood.
>
> (Mirowski 2002: 446)

As I have argued in the first two chapters of this book, it is precisely economists' ungrounded urge to portray rational agents almost as automata that is the source of their problems with the notions of rationality, agency and individualism. This remark, incidentally, is still more directly applicable to the eighth, and last, Self considered by Mirowski, which derives from the massive endorsement by economists of the Samuelsonian portraying of rational agents as consistent choosers.

Before discussing more specifically the problems raised by this last type of Self – which, as well as the fifth one, is referred to, still more systematically than by Mirowski, in challenges to methodological individualism raised by Davis and Ross – I have to say a few words about the seventh Self presented in *Machine Dream* as the 'only reliable storehouse of memory'. Mirowski is obviously right in emphasizing poor reliability, 'weaknesses and instabilities of human memory' (ibid.: 447) when compared to computers' memory. But, once again, and for the same reason, the non-disputed unattractiveness of this conception of the Self has very little to do with the status of methodological individualism as a strategy of explanation. More generally, as we have seen above, methodological individualism is not dependent on the status of human beings, insofar as the human need to understand is preserved. Indeed, methodological individualism concerns exclusively the strategy for making social processes understandable by human beings, irrespective of the ontological qualities of the latter and of their interventions.

The proliferation of selves in economics

Whatever repercussions it might have on methodological individualism, Mirowski's discussion of the Self is not based on considerations directly related to economics and to its methodological strategy. In contrast, John Davis and Don Ross directly criticize methodological individualism as most economists understand it. Both of them consider that Samuelson's postulates associated with revealed preference theory dominate neoclassical economics, at least when it comes to defining rationality and agency. In other words, they agree that economists have massively adopted Mirowski's eighth type of Self that is associated with consistent choice. But since human agents are notoriously inconsistent – as illustrated by experimental economics (see Mirowski 2002: 546–551 and Ross 2005: 177–189) and as expected from the importance of continuous learning in their evolution – the idea that, in adopting consistency as the criterion of rationality, neoclassical economics does not provide an adequate conception of the Self was inescapable. Given this situation, Ross fully endorses the view on selfhood and agency that is associated with neoclassicism, but is forced to conclude that human beings are not straightforward agents. For his part, Davis, who finds it essential to base economics on a satisfactory theory of the self, denounces an approach such as Samuelson's for its sheer behaviourism and its formalist indifference to the question of the individual's status (Davis 2003: 93–94); therefore, he chooses to turn away from mainstream economics, and finds in the 'socially embedded individual conception' (ibid.: 117) developed in heterodox economics a more satisfactory approach to the question. However, both object to methodological individualism understood as the principle which brings orthodox neoclassicism to ground microeconomic explanations on individuals' decisions and actions. Ross cannot accept the central place that, in virtue of its commitment to individualism, orthodox neoclassical economics continues to grant *human* agents, and Davis cannot accept the reductionist and formalist definition of individual agents that, in virtue of its conception of individualism, the neoclassical *orthodoxy* has adopted.

In fact, Davis' view on methodological individualism is more complex. He distinguishes within orthodox economics 'between neoclassical economics and contemporary mainstream economics' (Davis 2003: 16), the latter being a development of the former. According to him, if methodological individualism as defended by neoclassical economics were reductionist (ibid.: 36), it is no longer the case with mainstream economics, which 'remains individualist, though on fundamentally different terms than was neoclassical economics' (ibid.: 42). Thus Davis acknowledges that (methodological) individualism is not necessarily reductionist since he attributes a non-reductionist methodological individualism to contemporary mainstream economics, but he still objects to this kind of individualism, not so much because it is individualist, but because 'this new basis for individuating agents has no essential connections to human beings' (ibid.: 42).

This is not the place to discuss Davis' book which is devoted to the individual (and the self) in economics, and which is only indirectly a critique of methodological individualism. Indeed, according to Davis, the latter has little chance of finding any room in contemporary economics: indeed, one can summarize his position on this matter by saying that, in orthodox neoclassical economics, methodological individualism is associated with a reductionism that has progressively lost its *terminus ad quem* given the vanishing status of the self; in contemporary mainstream economics, it is divorced from the *fons et origo* of its meaning, which are human beings; and, in heterodox economics, it is *persona non grata* given that more or less genuinely holistic values are central to this approach.

It is true that adjusting the notion of rationality (together with the notion of agency) to the needs of formal analysis – as economists have progressively done by defining rationality successively by maximization and by consistency – was damaging for the self and the individual that consequently have lost any kind of identity in corresponding economic models. Indeed, once defined by a utility function, the individual no longer has any specific identity. As put by Davis, there is 'no essential connection between a set of preferences and the particular individual to whom these preferences belonged' (ibid.: 57). And, as he adds, no reidentification is possible over time, since there is no reason to find in the future what is excluded, on principle, from the present time. Of course, this might be a serious problem for one who looks to economics for a satisfactory analysis of the day-to-day behaviour of human beings in their social economic relations. It is also true that this may endanger the relevance of methodological individualism, not because its strategic efficiency in allowing human beings to understand social phenomena unwillingly generated by their actions is contested, but because mainstream economics has introduced a gulf between human beings who need to understand and the formally defined agents from whom 'human' behaviour is supposed to originate. But why should the epistemic status of methodological individualism – understood as an appropriate approach in understanding why social processes unexpectedly result from intertwined actions of a multitude of real human beings – be made dependent on the theoretical needs, or even elegant vagaries, of mathematical economists?

Rejecting the authority of economics in defining the self through its way of defining preferences disposes of problems associated with Mirowski's eighth Self (the Samuelsonian one), but the self that for Davis is a disappointing candidate for the animation of individuals is related to both Mirowski's fifth and eighth selves. In Davis' book, the self, who is ever changing and even multiplies through time, is always there to make its stability still more implausible. The same agent may indeed experience a multiplicity of selves. The idea that agency and selfhood may not coincide, invoked by Mirowski, Davis and Ross in their respective challenges to methodological individualism, is not new. As is well known, it must go back at least to Hume, as recalled by Mirowski (2002: 445) and by Davis (2003: 52). In a less distant past, Jon Elster edited a book entitled *The multiple self,*[14] gathering papers that gave a fair idea of the state of the question in mid-1980s. However, in his introduction to the book, Elster insists on the fact that most of these tensions inside a person do not literally imply the duplication of selves.[15] Indeed, the metaphoric use of the idea of multiple selves is frequent, just like the use of the expression 'in a previous life', which is commonly used to refer to a period in one's life that was dominated by quite different interests or convictions. And, for sure, such evolving selves should not be perceived as sets of literally different selves. In any case, for Davis, the way neoclassical economics conceives individuation implicitly suggests to us that individuals might be constituted as a community of selves. The kind of communities to which this view refers are typically households and firms, which must 'be made up of individuals, so human individuals would also be made up of individuals, or are multiple selves' (Davis 2003: 79).

Here again, it would be the schematizations introduced by economists that would be responsible for this dissolution of the individual. In any case, it is not my point to decide whether this methodological stand of neoclassical economics has ontological implications, and neither is it my intention here to discuss the problem raised by this alleged proliferation of selves (to which I will nonetheless briefly come back later in this chapter). My point concerns rather its eventual consequences for methodological individualism. Even if we accept the most radical and literal version of this thesis (which is clearly not adopted by Davis, apparently not by Mirowski and probably not by Ross), namely that an individual life is made of a succession of selves totally foreign to one another (whatever the way the experience of memory of one's past and of one's responsibility over this past is explained), it is far from clear that methodological individualism would be disqualified for all that. Indeed, if the various actions of those foreign selves of a given individual interfere with each other *and* with actions of the selves of other 'individuals', and if those complex interactions generate social consequences that are satisfactorily explained through the analysis of these interactions, methodological individualism would be vindicated. One must admit that, by hypothesis, 'individuals' could no longer attribute a significant part of 'their' past actions to 'themselves', but this would simply multiply the population of independent actors (which was already huge) responsible for the unwanted consequences that materialize into social phenomena. There is no clear reason to think that methodological individualism understood as a strategy of explanation of such phenomena would be made obsolete even if we accept this improbable interpretation of the proliferation of selves. And, unless the latter lose their status as agents, the rationality principle could still be invoked for explaining their economic behaviour.

A more radical challenge to methodological individualism

Davis' opposition to methodological individualism is indirect in the sense that it is based on the fact that methodological individualism is closely associated with neoclassical economics – which he criticizes for reasons not immediately related to this epistemic principle – and is generally disparaged by heterodox economics that he endorses for somewhat different reasons. In contrast, Ross takes a stand directly opposed to methodological individualism, not only by denying that human beings are straightforward agents, but also by not hesitating to put social entities like nations on the same footing as human beings when it comes to characterizing their respective capacities as agents. If we agree with Ross, the two most popular arguments (which, in fact, are complementary) in favour of methodological individualism are neutralized: (1) there are no longer any reasons to privilege human beings as the source of intentional actions and (2) when it comes to explaining decisions of firms and nations, it is no longer necessary to attribute them to individuals in positions of command in these societies. Given the radical character of these stands and their eventual consequences for methodological individualism, it is worthwhile to pay attention to Ross' argumentation even though it leads us for a moment outside the ground on which methodology of economics is usually cultivated.

Let us recall, to start with, that, for a large part, Ross' radical conclusions are based on his decision to adopt Samuelson's revealed preference theory as the criterion for deciding what is a straightforward agent. Once it is admitted that any straightforward agent must strictly respect the Samuelsonian axioms, which imply consistency, it is clear that human beings are disqualified, given their lack of consistency clearly manifested in experimental economics. But where can we find agents if human beings are such poor candidates for this title? There is apparently a crowd of other candidates, and among them, as we have seen in the previous chapter, Ross seems to privilege insects, whose paradigmatic quality as agents he has so frequently referred to.

According to Ross, however, what is important for agency is not the capacity for representation but rather 'the central locus of control' (2005: 381), which is present in bugs, but not in humans, according to Ross, as will be underscored below. It is not clear on what ground one can rely on this central control to generate the consistency and the maximization which is required by revealed preference theory, but it seems that insects are successful from this point of view. In any case, there is no doubt that some electronic devices can be modelled with the capacity to satisfy the criterion, and, a little more unexpectedly, neurons and modules (organized groups of neurons) constitute another type of candidate for being straightforward agents that Ross considers carefully. On this point, Ross mainly refers to Paul Glimcher's research program called 'neuroeconomics', which consists of the application of economic analysis to neural behaviour (Glimcher 2003). Ross explains that functional analyses of the behaviour of neurons proposed by Glimcher 'implicitly assign utility functions' to these neurons (Ross 2005: 324–325). But since it is out of the question to suppose that these tiny parts of organisms 'have utility functions based on internally represented preferences', Ross concludes that 'the economics in question must obviously be Samuelsonian' (ibid.: 325), which means that these 'preferences' must be revealed but not investigated. Thus, brains would be 'an ideal site for Samuelsonian microeconomics' where the agents are neurons[16] and perhaps modules (ibid.: 334) such as the visuomotor cortex, which, according to Ross is 'a straightforward economic agent, just like an insect' (ibid.: 331).

Ross acknowledges that *intentional* states cannot be attributed to straightforward subpersonal agents such as neurons and modules. In contrast, an irreducible intentionality is attributed to 'the various long-, medium- or short-term interests', which were analysed, equally with economic tools, by the psychiatrist George Ainslie in his *Picoeconomics* (1992; cf. Ross 2005: 336–337). So much so that those *interests* as such are considered to be 'as clever as a person' in such a way that 'their strategic cunning will tend to unravel all equilibria' (ibid.: 345), at least in some types of games. Now, the idea that human beings are constantly divided between opposite trends, and that they consequently draw their decisions in various directions, is an old one, which goes back at least to Augustine. According to Ross, however, this tension is explained by the fact that a typical human is constituted by a 'colony of agents' which 'emerge under analysis as a complex assembly of buglike homunculi' (ibid.: 252). This leads us to what Ross designates as 'this book's central thesis'. Since one must recall that his book bears on microexplanations in both economic theory *and cognitive science*, one should not be too surprised to note that this central thesis does not directly concern economics – at least as it is traditionally understood – but rather the very nature of a person, which is defined as 'a set of basically compatible long-range interests that have co-opted a sufficient army of short-range interests into their coalition to maintain stable equilibrium' (ibid.: 351).

It is in consequence of all these considerations that Ross maintains that 'selves aren't straightforward economic agents' (ibid.: 290). However, since people do perform actions, they should be agents in some sense; in contrast with straightforward agents, they are 'agents-by-extension' (ibid.: 256). From this point of view, they are put on the same footing as nations, which, according to Ross, can perform actions just as well. Thus, 'they are more like nations than insects' (ibid.: 290). Consequently, '[t]he application of economics to people will thus have to follow the same methods, and meet the same ontological and epistemological demands, as the application of economics to countries and corporations' (ibid.: 257). Since they are no more unified than nations, it is not surprising, Ross argues, that, when treated as agents, humans 'show ubiquitous preference reversal and time inconsistencies' (ibid.: 253). Thus, if we agree with this view, human beings have no advantages over nations as sources of decisions and actions. Consequently, it would no longer make sense to claim that an essential merit of methodological individualism is to avoid the attribution of decisions to nations themselves. Indeed, there would no longer be reasons to claim that alleged decisions of nations should necessarily be attributed to human beings who are in position to make decisions in the name of nations.

It is true that human beings are inconsistent in their decisions and that, from this point of view, their record is not much better than that of a nation. However, instead of choosing to follow Samuelson in defining agency through consistency and concluding on this basis, as Ross does, that humans are *not* prototypical agents, one may acknowledge that human agents, who were always prototypical agents, were never very consistent and that, accordingly, their rationality as agents cannot realistically be characterized by consistency. I do not want to dispute the proper definition of the word 'agent' since it may depend on the chosen programme of research, but insofar as we are interested, as economists used to be, to analyse the economic activities of *human* beings, it seems appropriate to admit that the latter are guided in their decisions by a type of rationality that has little to do with Samuelson's axioms. If saying that human beings are not straightforward agents simply means that they do not respect these axioms and that their central control of decisions is far from being absolute since they are submitted to various trends and interests, then it is clear that their agency is not straightforward in this sense. But if we reject Samuelson's conception of rationality and accept instead to turn our attention towards actual human beings who are not consistent but who are nonetheless rational, at least to a degree that while minimal is quite sufficient to allow economists to develop a fruitful economic analysis, we would no longer have to look towards bugs or neurons to exemplify our view of agency. And if we aim to develop a conception of rationality and agency in order to apply it to human beings who are the only agents who really need to understand the consequences of their actions and to whom explanations put forward by economists are provided, this move seems to be the appropriate one to make.

But what about methodological individualism in this context? Here is not the place to discuss Ross' ontological views for themselves, but I will examine what happens to methodological individualism in both of the extreme ways we can interpret these views. On the one hand, if they simply mean that, even if it is admitted that they differ from other agents by being the only ones who *need* to understand, human beings are the least internally unified and consequently the most erratic and inconsistent deciders among the set of possible kinds of agents (with the probable exception of social groups like nations and firms), then we are not very far from an acceptable view of methodological individualism. At the very most, a slight (while a bit odd) change in vocabulary would have been introduced: instead of using the word 'agents', one should use the phrase 'non-straightforward agents' and if one has to refer to the bearers of almost mechanically consistent and maximizing behaviour, one should refer to 'agents'. On the other hand, if Ross' views mean that human beings corresponds to just a member of the set of different types of agents including robotic computers, internal interests and possibly neurons and insects,[17] and that all of them would act intentionally and would *even* need to understand what happened to their intentional actions, then methodological individualism could become the strategy according to which social processes resulting from interactions between the various interventions of all these 'agents' might be satisfactorily explained by an analysis of the unwanted consequences of these interventions. I suspect that Ross would not be prepared to go so far as endorsing as such the second interpretation, but would unhesitatingly reject the first one in order to go much further. Whatever may be the proper interpretation of Ross' views, the level of capacities attributed to these individual and subindividual entities could hardly affect methodological individualism considered as the strategy of explanation described above.

Naturally, if social groups and nations are counted among agents and put on the same footing as others, methodological individualism will lose its very meaning. Thus, the survival of methodological individualism as a strategy of explanation would be seriously threatened not so much by an eventual multiplication of types of agents, but by the quasi-blurring of the distinction between individual entities and social groups through the view according to which nations are entities that are not less individualized and not less centrally controlled than human beings.[18] However, the least that we can say is that if it is construed not as an inoffensive metaphor but as an ontological statement about societies such as nations, the latter view remains a boldly refreshing but still unsubstantiated theory. Indeed, how could one grant such an ontological identity to nations which are intermingled between themselves, vaguely circumscribed and constantly redefined according to people's sensibilities and ideologies? For example, the question whether Canada is a nation is still debated almost a century and a half after the foundation of the country; as for Quebec, it has been recently declared a nation, which many consider autonomous, whereas others locate this national entity inside the Canadian nation; for others, it is French Canada that is the true nation scattered throughout Canada, just as Acadia is another one whose core lies in Eastern Canada with diasporas in various parts of the United States; meanwhile, Canadian Amerindians claimed that they have constituted over a much longer period a number of nations; this does not exclude the fact that various ethnic groups, mostly based in Western Canada, such as Ukrainians, consider themselves a nation, as well as the Jews whose religious based nation is not contained by any frontier, etc. Of course, one might claim that each of these more or less vaguely circumscribed nations would be non-straightforward agents whose decisions would result from decisions made by human beings that constitute them, just like the decisions of the latter – who, as we have seen, may also be ill circumscribed – might result from decisions made by the neuronal straightforward agents evoked by Ross. But, even though it is far from clear that the role of neurons in human decision making is the same as the role of human decisions in the making of nations' decisions, the point of methodological individualism is not to contest the indisputable role of neurons; it is to explain societies such as nations and their decisions through the interfering decisions and actions of human beings, something which seems to be inescapable.

In spite of its apparently increasing unpopularity among economists, one can say that it is only by association that methodological individualism was condemned to be relatively ignored. This condemnation results either from interpreting it abusively as a quasi ontological thesis that denies the obvious role of society and that promotes an implausible reductionism, or from associating its destiny with that of a much too static conception of the individual and of the self. The present chapter is an invitation to reconsider a verdict that might have been too hastily delivered. The survival of an appropriate version of methodological individualism is a condition for the survival of the interpretation of the rationality principle defended in this book. It would be absurd to claim that people do what they do because it makes sense for them, because they have reasons to do it, and that their doing so can play a decisive role in social sciences, if it was established that it is, on the contrary, social structures that are explanative and that individuals, whether human or post-human,[19] have no influence on them. If the arguments presented in this chapter can successfully challenge the plea that was conducive to the dismissal of methodological individualism, we should still be in position to claim that *individuals* perform actions that are rationally motivated and whose consequences play a decisive role in the explanations provided by social sciences.

Does this imply that human actions can always be said to be rational? If such were the case, the very meaning of a rational action might be diluted by the absence of irrational actions in contrast to which such an action might be judged rational in a meaningful sense. Indeed, if any action is rational, saying that an action is rational is saying that it is an action, and nothing else! Maximization and consistency have the advantage of being such demanding criteria that there is little chance of confusing irrational actions with rational ones that must satisfy the high level of requirements that is associated with these conceptions of rationality. Conversely, it seems much easier to define rationality with precision by the satisfaction of these requirements than by invoking just the presence of an indeterminate level of a few traits such as purposefulness or adaptability. Before discussing this eventual definitional advantage of more demanding conceptions of rationality, I will consider in the next chapter the problem raised by the fact that, in the absence of the latter, rationality might be attributed too generously to any human action in such a way that irrational actions could no longer be identified as such.

4 Is still some room left for irrationality?

If rationality is defined by maximization, optimality or consistency, there are plenty of actions that can be characterized as irrational because they are clearly non-maximizing, sub-optimal or inconsistent. However, the price to pay for those who adopt this position and attempt to apply it to actual human societies is the quasi-necessity of concluding that most decisions and actions of actual people are *irrational*. Few among the adepts of such a view of rationality will draw such an embarrassing conclusion; they will rather avoid raising the question and develop a theory that can describe with remarkable precision, as suggested by Ross, the behaviour of insects or of some robots, but only in a distortedly idealized fashion the behaviour of human beings, who are poor maximizers and inconsistent choosers. Moreover, as we have seen, they refer to a very counterintuitive notion of rationality since rationality should instead be characterized by constant adaptation rather than by mechanical implementation of predetermined solutions. In contrast, characterizing rational actions by the simple claim that such actions are purposeful and make sense is much more intuitive and much closer to the actual behaviour of human beings; however, a consequence of this approach is that it becomes much more difficult to clearly characterize rational actions by contrasting them with irrational ones since, by placing the bar so low for being considered rational, it becomes difficult to even find convincing examples of irrational actions.[1]

Can any action whatsoever be rational?

For certain economists – Ludwig von Mises being the most representative among them – the problem of determining under what conditions human actions can be said to be rational is literally dissolved. Indeed, according to them, any action whatsoever, by the very fact that it is an action and not an uncontrolled mechanical reaction, is rational a priori. It is true that when they refer to rationality, economists have in mind instrumental rationality, which implies that an end is satisfied with the help of any means (in contrast with a conception of rationality that implies an evaluation of this end). However, Mises not only adopts this instrumental view but defines action as a 'conscious behavior' which, by the very fact of being conscious, is oriented towards an end that is understood as *nothing more* than the 'removing or alleviating' of a 'state of dissatisfaction' (Mises 1976: 23–24). But if an action is by definition a conscious attempt to alleviate a state of dissatisfaction, it is necessarily the implementation of an instrument essentially oriented towards *this* end, a fact that, according to Mises, is sufficient to allow us to characterize any action as rational. Therefore Mises does not hesitate to claim that 'action' and 'rational action' are strictly equivalent (Mises 1976: 23). For example, when I buy something, I am reaching a new state that I perceive as more satisfactory than the earlier state. According to Mises, such a more satisfactory state counts as the end of the action taken; therefore, reaching this end through the means used (buying) is necessarily rational because I clearly have reasons to prefer being in the second state, since otherwise I would not have taken this action. Mises even concludes: 'as far as there is scarcity of means, man behaves rationally, i.e., he acts. So far there is no room left for "irrationality"' (Mises 1944: 544). But if such is the case, how could any action be irrational?

This ambiguity in determining what should be considered as the end of an action (the more satisfactory state immediately obtained by the action or the final result that is expected from performing it) has sometimes been exploited by authors of comedies. For example, George Dandin, the main character of one of Molière's comedies, makes a decision that looks particularly erratic and mistaken from an economic point of view. He decides to sacrifice his entire fortune to marry a lady of the nobility, but discovers soon after his wedding that the fact of being known henceforth by an appreciably longer name, 'Monsieur de la Dandinière', did not provide him the consideration he was looking for. But in a Misesian perspective, to conclude that Dandin's marriage was irrational because it had not permitted him to attain his goal (being a highly respected person) is confusing the immediate end of an action with the goal of a whole strategy. Becoming a respected personage was the real goal of Dandin as well as of many people. However, while Dandin's very expensive marriage was indeed a quite appropriate means towards his immediate end of being associated with the nobility, it nevertheless failed to help him attain his more fundamental goal of being respected. Nonetheless, since the immediate end of a specific action must be a member of the set of *available* ends such as 'having his name changed for a longer one associated with nobility', which is a situation that Dandin prefers over his previous status of a rich money-holder, Mises would have said that Dandin's action was rational. Indeed, the latter was clearly motivated by an end (having a noble name) that was actually reached by performing it, in spite of the fact that this successful action was far from being followed by its expected consequences. But if any action is rational whatsoever, including those that look particularly stupid, what does it specifically mean for an action to be rational?

Mises' views on rationality were harshly rejected by most economists, at least in the second half of the twentieth century,[2] due to the close association of these views with his apriorist approach to economics, but it was not so easy to get rid of the problem illustrated by his analysis. Indeed, against those who are offended by the neoclassical conception of rationality, because it treats rational human beings as mere *homini oeconomici* motivated only by monetary gains, the standard argument – popularized by Lionel Robbins' very influential book[3] – was that the notion of rationality required by marginalist analysis implies nothing about the nature of the ends as such. Thus, if a lady philanthropist gives her whole fortune to poor people instead of profitably investing it, because she feels – at least when the donation takes place – happier as a generous donor than as a mean investor (otherwise the donation would not occur), this philanthropist would be a perfectly rational utility maximizer whose actions can be theoretically analysed with the tools of economics. But, if we accept such a way of thinking, Dandin's 'transaction' can also be characterized as perfectly rational since it is oriented towards the satisfaction of bearing a name associated with nobility, which was – at least on his wedding day – greater for him than the satisfaction of being a rich money-holder. But given such a conception, how could anyone be irrational at all, and consequently what does it mean for an action to be *rational*?

Ulysses and Horatius

Jon Elster is probably the methodologist who has devoted the most significant part of his work to solving this cumbersome problem. Like Mises, Elster considers that the rationality principle concerns intentional human action whose ends are not of a predetermined specific type. However, in contrast with Mises, he considers (1) that there is ample room for irrationality in human behaviour and (2) that rationality concerns not only efficiency in the means of reaching the immediate ends of action but also the assessment of the ultimate goals that are adopted and that are supposed to guide the action. According to him, it does not make sense to refuse to assess ultimate goals when discussing the rationality of human action; as we have seen in the Introduction of this book, this task should be done by developing what he calls a 'broad theory' of rationality (Elster 1983: section I). It is no doubt quite sensible to claim that not all ultimate goals are equally rational and that assessing the rationality of those goals is an important philosophical task. However, it is also clear that the rationality principle, on which economics and other social sciences are based, does not refer to this ultimate and normative kind of rationality and has to be defined only in terms of the adaptation of means to a given end. This does not mean that what I call the ultimate goal cannot be the end considered when assessing the rationality of an action; the crucial point is that the type of rationality required by explanations in the social sciences is the one that concerns the appropriateness of some means to a given end, whether this end is ultimate or not.

In any case, Jon Elster also contributed to a 'thinner' discussion of rationality, even though he relates means and ends in a somewhat larger framework and attempts to develop a more satisfactory way to characterize irrational behaviour. An important dimension of Elster's strategy for solving the problem of distinguishing rationality from irrationality is to introduce degrees in the assessment of rationality. This strategy allows him to define a paradigmatic model of rationality which is associated with maximization or optimality. However, since rational behaviour is characterized as an *intentional* behaviour, it cannot be associated with the almost mechanical behaviour of an omniscient *homo oeconomicus*. Rather, it is typified as the behaviour of angels, which are allegedly perfect but *intentional* decision makers. Human beings, by contrast, are 'neither angels (i.e. fully rational) nor animals (i.e. essentially myopic); they are imperfectly rational creatures able to deal strategically with their own myopia' (Elster 1984 [1979]: 86). Choosing *perfect* rationality as an illustration of the notion of rationality forces us to conclude that an imperfectly rational behaviour is one that is, at the very least, partially irrational, which implies that elements of irrationality are pervasive in human behaviour. Put otherwise, the germs of irrationality are diagnosed wherever a behaviour does not maximize anything. For Elster, agents have general goals that should be reached in an optimal way, eventually through strategic behaviour, and they express their intentions to reach such goals. Thus, if a perfectly rational agent is an 'angel' who, having a goal in view, acts in an optimal way, we may contrast such an agent with the imperfectly rational human agents who tend not to persist in their determination to reach their goals and who tend consequently to adopt behaviours, which, from various points of view, are irrational in the sense of being sub-optimal. In this perspective, human irrationality is a matter of the *limits* of information and of intelligence, and even more a matter of weakness of the will (the *akrasia* of Aristotle),[4] which is so frequent in human behaviour. However, even though this approach makes ample room for irrationality, one who wants to characterize the latter along these lines might face somewhat paradoxical situations.

At some point in his analysis of weakness of the will, Elster discusses the stratagems that can be used to overcome such a limitation to rational behaviour. As a paradigm of such strategic behaviour, he proposes the case of Ulysses binding himself to his mast to be able to hear the sound of the Sirens without being seduced by them.[5] Ulysses is clearly not an angel and he knows that his will is too weak to resist the seductive Sirens' song. Being insufficiently 'rational' to overcome directly what he perceives as an obstacle to the attainment of his goal (going back home), he uses the stratagem of being bound and decides to temporarily reduce his options in order to avoid a fatal threat to his ultimate goal. But why does Elster consider that it is less *rational* to use such a stratagem than to directly face the danger and triumphantly overcome it? This last course of action is possibly more glorious and more honourable, but is it more rational? Rationality is not sheer virtue; it is the ability to take the proper means to reach a given end. After all, the rational entrepreneur is not necessarily a paragon of either virtue or honour. He is, rather, a paragon of skill in efficiently reaching a given goal. Entrepreneurs who are successful thanks to the use of stratagems, could hardly be characterized as *less rational* than those who are equally successful but have proceeded in a more straightforward way as determined either by sheer chance or by purely intuitive moves as response to changes in the economic situation. The entrepreneur whose success and straightforward way of acting rely on such intuitions will tend to be characterized as a lucky or bold player but surely not as a model of *rationality*. In contrast, Ulysses had such a good self-knowledge that he knew that he was totally unable to resist the Sirens' song, and, as such, this self-knowledge is surely a plus. Thus, to reach his goal, two ways were open to him: to become temporarily deaf by filling his ears with wax (a strategy he reserved to the members of his crew) or to be bound to his mast with the help of his crew. If Ulysses chose the second option, it was because it permitted him to *maximize* his satisfaction, since a secondary goal (experiencing the sound of the Sirens' song) could be reached in this way without sacrificing the first (going back home). How could anyone discount the rationality of such behaviour?[6]

In fact, self-binding is just one type of stratagem among other *indirect* stratagems. Let us consider the case of Horatius who, in a battle between two families that was to determine the destiny of Rome, succeeded alone (after the death of his two brothers) in killing the three Curiatius brothers by resorting to a stratagem which, while in no way implying self-binding, was still less glorious but surely as rational as that of Ulysses. Horatius' knowledge was remarkably precise. He knew that he was able to beat each of the Curiatius brothers separately (each of them having been wounded in the first assault) but unable to beat them together. He knew enough about the gravity of each of the brothers' wounds to be able to conclude correctly that they would run after him at respectively different speeds. Finally, he knew their respective psychologies so well that he was able to conclude correctly that the less seriously wounded brothers would not adopt the slower speed of the more heavily wounded. Horatius, at the (calculated) risk of looking like a coward, wagered a temporary reduction of his capital of honour against the gain both for Rome and for his future personal honour and decided to simulate flight, in order to be in position to kill each of the three Curiatius brothers separately. Is this not a remarkable example of rationally calculated behaviour? In this case, the indirect stratagem was adopted to compensate for physical weakness rather than for weakness of the will, but it nevertheless illustrates fairly well that a high level of rationality can allow one to use indirect means as a substitute for direct ones. In any case, a strong will is just as much an endowment as strong arms or intuitive ability. Since nobody would argue that one who cleverly invents an ingenious system of pulleys to raise a weight is less rational than the colossus who easily raises it by the sheer strength of his arms, why should Horatius be considered less *rational* than the powerful colossus who would have killed the three Curiatius brothers together? Why should Ulysses be considered less *rational* than the virtuous and angelic captain whose will would have been strong enough to remain almost unaffected by the Sirens' song?

For Elster, the point seems to be that if rationality is the capacity to use the proper means to reach a goal, *full* rationality is the capacity to reach this goal *directly* by more immediate means (like remaining imperturbable while hearing the Sirens' song). However, if generalized, such a view of rationality would imply a negation of any constraint, since a limitation of the will could be considered a constraint, just like a limitation of physical strength or a limitation of material resources or of wealth. The typical rational entrepreneur who accumulated his fortune painfully in spite of various constraints should, by such a view, be considered less rational than the one who was so rich to start with that he could adopt, without significant budgetary constraints, any course of action he found appropriate. Who would accept such a conclusion?

Inverting entomology's lessons and indulging in a pleasant activity

This is not to say that there are no degrees in rationality, but rather that straightforwardness and absence of constraints are mistaken or, at the very least, too ambiguous measures of such degrees. Moreover, this emphasis on degrees in rationality does not by itself tell us what an irrational action is. In other sections of his many writings on this topic, Elster attacks this question more directly and considers cases that are more immediately associated with irrationality. These cases are usually related to weakness of the will. A remarkable one among them concerns time preferences. Note, incidentally, that if the straightforwardness approach discussed above was understood as deriving from a maximization conception of rationality, the one associated with time preferences is understood as deriving from a *consistency* conception of rationality.[7] According to Elster, 'a rational actor on the standard definition is simply one who has consistent and complete preferences *at any given point of time*' (Elster 1984 [1979]: 65, Elster's emphasis). Once this definition of rationality is admitted, it seems easy to point out where irrationality is to be found: 'It is widely, but far from universally, agreed that for an individual the very fact of having time preferences, over and above what is justified by the fact that we are mortal, is irrational and perhaps immoral as well' (ibid.: 66). For sure, when making decisions about allocation for an uncertain future, rational individuals should apply an appropriate discount rate; however, the presence of this discount rate being immaterial for the following argument, let us admit, in order to simplify the matter, that a rational fellow would tend to distribute his consumption equally over his lifespan. I would like to illustrate my point with the help of Jean de La Fontaine's famous fable that suggests that the grasshopper that does not make reserves is less rational than the ant that does. The ant's behaviour would look still more rational if it wisely managed to consume its entire resources in equal amounts each day of its life. Applied to this example, Elster's thesis would be that the grasshopper-type of discounting the future is *in itself* irrational. Indeed, people who quickly spend a large portion of a fortune and complain thereafter of being left with too few resources for the remainder of their lives would look rather irrational.

However, the trouble with such a view is that it supposes a *value judgement* in order to uphold that the adoption of a particular goal (the ant's goal) is more rational than the adoption of another one (the grasshopper's goal). Suppose that for someone the very fact of saving is enough to spoil any pleasure in life; why would it be so irrational for this person to spend heavily now for full enjoyment in life and to add later to this unspoiled pleasure the extra unspoiled satisfaction that the meagre resources left available can provide? Naturally, I do not want to recommend this far-fetched grasshopper-like behaviour; my point is only that the frontier between what is rational and what is irrational cannot be determined as if it were a matter of fact. As for time preferences cases of irrationality, they are detected and denounced simply because rationality was associated with consistency – an association which is counterintuitive and arbitrary as we have seen in a previous chapter – and because irrationality was diagnosed through departure from a particular scheme of consistency in time preferences, which is deemed to be consistent with rationality-consistency.

Elster has invoked other cases of irrationality that, at first glance, seem more compelling. In order to pinpoint a case of weakness of the will that is hardly contestable, he refers to the standard example of the alcoholic who wants to stop drinking but who, by weakness of the will, takes another drink. It seems clear that the alcoholic is less rational than he would have been had he resisted the temptation. The ultimate goal of the alcoholic is clearly to stop drinking, and it seems reasonable to say that an action that contradicts an ultimate goal can unequivocally be said to be irrational. However, the matter is not that simple, because one must determine *what counts as an ultimate goal.* Is the ultimate goal the one that people *present* as their ultimate goal? That solution would make the criterion of rationality too dependent on an unreliable self-appreciation. Should it be a *long-term* goal in opposition to short-term temptations? But how long should the term be? Suppose you want to become one of the most prolific economists of your generation and that you are convinced that constant work is a necessary condition to reach such a goal. Suppose further that you are also a zealous movie fan. Since seeing a movie is always a very pleasant and easy experience and working on a paper in economics is a very painful one, one might think that deciding to see an extra movie instead of working is just like the alcoholic's having another drink. Given your ultimate goal, it clearly seems that it would be much more rational not to attend an extra movie and to continue working on a paper. However, at the very moment you decide to see this extra movie, you think that, after all, you have no serious chance of reaching your excessively ambitious goal and that it is more sensible to see this movie, which will not only be a source of pleasure and beneficial rest, but a source of culture and general background knowledge as well. If, after some time, you realize that your chance of reaching your ambitious goal has dwindled considerably, largely because you have seen too many movies, one may consider that this was due to weakness of your will, but before concluding that another course of action would have been more rational, one has to make sure that this goal was really your *ultimate* goal. But suppose that, in the wisdom of a more advanced age, you reconsider the whole thing and you conclude that life is too short and that, given your own limits, your ambitious goal was by far too pretentious and that you were right when you decided to indulge in the pleasures of life and improve your general culture by attending more and more movies. On what grounds would one characterize as irrational your past decisions to see these movies? It is true that an objection to this line of argument could be that, at the very moment that you decided to go to the movie, 'to become a prolific economist' was then your *main* goal, whether or not this goal turned out to be your ultimate goal. But on what grounds is it possible to concede such priority to this one among all your goals at the precise instant when this priority seemed to be, at least temporarily, rejected? Why would it be unacceptable to say, rather, that it was the goal (doomed to be perceived as an ultimate goal in your late wisdom) that was taking shape in this very instant and that it was *not irrational* to act in a way commanded by this emergent ultimate goal?

There is no doubt that it is, nonetheless, quite reasonable to consider that being a prolific author is more meritorious than just being a person who got a lot out of movies and that, for someone who seriously adopts the former as an ultimate goal, it is more rational to work to its realization than to forget it and devote one's time to indulging in satisfying a less meritorius goal. Here again, my point is simply that such assessment cannot be presented as establishing a hard and fast line between rationality and irrationality. In some sense, this problem corresponds to the one of establishing a hard and fast line between an ultimate goal and a dream. Suppose that, in fact, becoming an internationally respected author is a somewhat fantastic dream instead of being an ultimate goal, is it irrational to choose to go to the movies instead of nurturing your dream? Similarly, becoming a sober citizen might be a dream for the alcoholic who chooses to enjoy another drink when negatively assessing the accessibility of such a dream. One may blame this alcoholic for not transforming that dream into an ultimate goal, but if he sincerely considers this unfeasible given his present situation, just as he considers that he is unable to climb Mount Everest given his physical condition, one might consider that he is mistaken or not courageous enough, but should we declare this person *irrational* because of that?

But irrationality exists!

Should we conclude from these examples that any action is rational? Of course, we can't. Who would doubt that plenty of irrational actions occur in human behaviour? The only thing that the cases discussed above proves is that it is not possible to declare an action irrational on the basis of its material description. It is always possible to interpret it as a rational action because it is always possible to suppose that the reasons that have motivated the action were those that the agent estimated to be the best ones when the action was taken. Therefore, in spite of the fact that experimental economics have clearly revealed that frequently adopted behaviours are sub-optimal and inconsistent, these behaviours are usually explained or justified, as we have seen, by invoking reasons such as avoiding tiring computations and relying on rules of thumb that are judged sufficiently rewarding. If we admit that these reasons really correspond to what the subjects consider the best thing to do in the circumstance, they allow us to conclude that the actions taken were not really irrational. In order to exclude the generalization of such interpretations and restore the verdict of irrationality, the description of the action must stipulate that the action was motivated by a reason that contradicts what the agent considers to be the best. In other words, the description has to specify that the action intentionally contradicts a principle which, at the moment it is taken, is unequivocally considered by the agent as the one that should guide the action in question. Such a specification, however, seems to be literally equivalent to a specification that the action *is* irrational! Since an irrational action can be defined as an action that contradicts what the agent, when taking it, considers the rational thing to do, we must conclude that in order to illustrate the fact that an action can be irrational, one has to admit and to invite one's audience to admit that the action chosen as an example must be interpreted as corresponding to what the definition of irrationality requires and not otherwise. Should we conclude that this is requiring too much? In any case, such a situation is obviously a source of embarrassment for a methodologist of economics who wants to empirically prove that Mises is wrong by *showing* that there are irrational actions.

But why should the onus of proof be only on the side of those who refuse to accept that all actions are rational? After all, invoking secret reasons in some of the cases discussed above may be judged a little too far-fetched. When you decide to go to the cinema instead of working on your paper, is it necessarily because you grasp intuitively at this very moment the idea that, all things considered, a life full of pleasant and cultural movies is better than your long cherished goal of being a prolific economist? It is possibly because you do something that, even from your own point of view, is frankly irrational. For sure, if this is the case, a psychologist could not explain your behaviour by invoking the rationality principle, but there is no need to claim that all human actions *can* be explained on this basis. It seems quite sufficient to say that it is the case for most actions and that those that are significant for the explanation of economic processes overwhelmingly satisfy the requirements of this principle, a point to which I will come back later in this chapter.

Be that as it may, philosophers who have discussed the question of irrationality were not generally interested in *proving* that irrational actions exist; instead, given their conviction, shared by most people, that cases of sheer irrationality cannot be denied, they were comitting themselves to explaining how such actions are possible. Explaining how they are possible is far from simple. For Donald Davidson, a philosopher who directly attacked this question, there are even such things as 'paradoxes of irrationality' that render an explanation of them particularly delicate:

> if we explain it [irrationality] too well, we turn it into a concealed form of rationality; while if we assign incoherence too glibly, we merely compromise our ability to diagnose irrationality by withdrawing the background of rationality needed to justify any diagnosis at all.
>
> (Davidson 1982: 303)

However, for Davidson, in spite of this state of affairs, irrationality is a fact that needs to be explained. Thus, the problem is clearly not to trace an implausible line between rationality and irrationality, but to *explain* irrationality, which, by its very nature, resists being explained. For Davidson as well as for Elster, who has analysed this phenomenon in his essay entitled *Sour grapes*, wishful thinking constitutes 'a model for the simplest kind of irrationality' (ibid.: 298). To illustrate this kind of irrationality, Davidson refers to a young man who literally *wants* to have a belief that provides him some pleasure. 'But if the entire explanation of his holding the belief is that he wanted to believe it, then his holding the belief is irrational. For the wish to have a belief is not evidence for the truth of the belief, nor does it give it rational support in any other way' (ibid.). Davidson, who had previously defended the idea that mental entities such as reasons can *cause* actions (Davidson 1963), suggests that, in cases of irrationality,

> there is a mental cause that is not a reason for what it causes. So in wishful thinking, a desire causes a belief. But the judgment that a state of affairs is, or would be, desirable, is not a reason to believe that it exists.
>
> (Davidson 1982: 298)

One may accept that a reason can cause an action, but it remains to be seen how a mental event can be a cause *without* being a reason. According to Davidson, who draws from Freud, this is possible only if the mind is divided into independent parts (ibid.: 303). If such is the case, a mental event in one part can cause a mental event in another part of the mind without being a reason for that event. Such a thing is possible, just like causality of a mind over another mind is possible in social intercourse, even though this causal influence is not based on the presence of a reason (ibid.: 300ff.). This does not mean, however, – Davidson insists on this point – that these parts of the mind should be understood 'as independent agents' (ibid.: 304). For him, the important point is just that one part of the mind can have some causal impact on another of its parts through a mode of causality that has nothing to do with giving a reason. Thus, a desire experienced in one part of the mind would cause a pleasant belief in another part of the mind without being a reason for this belief.

Along a similar line of argument, Davidson holds that cases of weakness of the will involving incontinent actions – which contradict the consciously accepted principle that one ought to act on what one 'holds to be the best, everything considered' (ibid.: 297) – would be explained by such interferences between different parts of the mind. Now, the interventions of independent parts in the mind may contribute to explaining the contradictory states of mind that characterize irrational behaviour, but Davidson does not explain clearly in this paper, which is relatively short for attacking such a huge problem, what such parts of the minds that are not agents but are independent and have power to influence the intentional state of other parts of the mind are. Neither has he very clearly explained how a belief can, without the help of a reason, be generated by a cause residing in another part of the mind.

Among philosophers, the question of explaining irrationality has raised many debates that do not have to be reviewed here, but I will still consider the way Alfred Mele has taken over Davidson's problem in a book entitled *Irrationality,*

An Essay on Akrasia, Self-Deception, and Self-Control. Mele, who is not convinced by Davidson's solution, is, nonetheless, ready to accept the Davidsonian idea according to which it is necessary to invoke 'mental causes that are not reasons for mental items that they cause' (Mele 1987: 76). However, he estimates that this does not imply that such causes should be located in autonomous parts of the mind separated from other parts where they have a causal impact. He defends this claim by arguing that mental causes that are not reasons for mental events that they cause happen frequently inside a normally unified mind. To illustrate his point, Mele proposes a few examples such as mnemonic mental techniques that provoke the remembering of forgotten words, and self-control techniques, including mental concentration, which can efficiently reduce the desire to smoke (ibid.: 77–78). In both of these examples, a mental activity that has nothing to do with a reason causes a desired state of mind, and these examples do not postulate a partitioning of the mind.

In order to explain the incontinent action of one who does something when being fully conscious that one's best action is contradicted by what is done, Mele invokes a set of considerations – one of them being borrowed from George Ainslie and another from Amelie Rorty – that taken together might satisfactorily explain irrational behaviour such as incontinence. The proximity of the rewards associated with the incontinent action, the respective levels of motivation to perform either the incontinent or the rational action, the failure to make an attempt at self-control and the degree of attention granted to the rewards associated with alternative actions are invoked together to reinforce, through their interaction, the motivation to opt for the incontinent action (ibid.: 84–95).

You may or may not be convinced by Mele's, Davidson's or any other explanation of such phenomena, but my point is not to find an acceptable explanation of irrationality. If I referred, while perhaps too briefly to do full justice to them, to these attempts to explain irrational actions, it was only in order to show that the latter may exist and might be explained despite the absence of a borderline between rationality and irrationality. Note that this kind of explanation does not imply that there is such a borderline. Even wishful thinking, which is possibly the most irrational among the various kinds of irrational behaviour, might be *interpreted* as rational, while by stretching to the extreme limit the possibilities of such interpretations. Suppose that a woman who is totally desperate about life and close to committing suicide succeeds in convincing herself that she is an exceptionally beautiful and coveted person, which becomes a source of pleasure sufficient to provide her with a reason to keep living. Even if this person is aware of the fact that the content of this belief is a pure desire without realistic foundations, one might claim, insofar that such an atypical description of the situation is correct, that such a behaviour is rational since it would be consciously chosen in order to keep living. Thus, irrational actions cannot be separated from rational ones on the basis of their material description, unless this description excludes any interpretation that would make them rational, but this is not a reason to deny that irrationality exists in human behaviour, nor that it can potentially be explained. However, as implied by Davidson's and Mele's views, irrational actions could hardly be explained by reasons, given that it is another action, namely the action that corresponds to what the agent considers to be the best thing to do that would have been rationally expected. Therefore, since an explanation based on the rationality principle always concerns actions motivated by reasons corresponding to what the agent considers to be the best thing to do, actions which, according to their description, are motivated by reasons that contradict what the agent considers to be the best thing to do *cannot* be explained with the help of the rationality principle; philosophers and psychologists must find other ways to explain them.

Karl Popper and the rationality principle

What becomes of the rationality principle if we are convinced that human behaviour can be irrational? That is precisely the question that Karl Popper has discussed in his highly controversial – while certainly underestimated – paper entitled 'The Rationality Principle'.[8] Let us briefly consider and discuss his analysis in order to see whether a paper that was scornfully rejected by so many commentators can deliver a few illuminative elements for the question at hand. Popper unambiguously considers that the rationality principle is the fundamental principle upon which all the social sciences are based. For him, this principle is so fundamental that, paradoxically, he recommends not rejecting it, even though he considers that it is clearly false. The fact that he recommends not rejecting a principle whose falsity is acknowledged seems to clash dramatically with falsificationism, the epistemological thesis that he has promoted throughout his career; and this is the main reason why his thesis on the rationality principle was harshly denounced in certain papers (for example, Hands 1985). I have attempted elsewhere to explain in some detail why Popper's view is less contradictory and more sensible than it appears (Lagueux 1993b and 2006b), but I would like to focus here on Popper's contribution to the understanding of the rationality principle.

Popper, who is strongly opposed to Mises' apriorism, estimates that the rationality principle is far from being a priori since it is indisputably false. According to him this principle can be defined in the following basic terms: 'agents always act in a manner appropriate to the situation in which they find themselves' (Popper 1985: 361). Since inappropriate actions are frequent in human societies, concluding that such a principle is false and, consequently, anything but a priori seems inescapable indeed. However, in order to emphasize the scope of the principle, Popper recalls that a version of this principle is what Sigmund Freud and other psychologists use when they explain various cases of neurosis. However, one must acknowledge that this version is a significantly different one since typical responses of neurotic individuals are described as appropriate to the situation *'as they see it'* (ibid.: 363). The important modification introduced with this new version of the principle was underscored, in particular by Nadeau (1993), who concluded that, in spite of Popper's emphatic rejection of apriorism, a principle construed as this new version is can no longer be said to be false and, consequently, can no longer be free from being considered to be a priori, just like Ludwig von Mises' version of the rationality principle.

Long before writing the passage in which the Freudian version is invoked, Popper clearly had in mind such an objection. Indeed, in a footnote to a paragraph added to the text of an earlier lecture on a similar topic,[9] he acknowledges without the least bit of hesitation that he refers successively to two versions of the principle and even to a third intermediate version of the same principle (Popper 1994: 183). However, even though he was fully aware of the fact that the implications of the principle differ significantly according to the version adopted, Popper formally denies that any of his three versions make the principle a priori. On the contrary, he claims that each of them is false by being contradicted by some cases of irrational behaviour. In order to show not only that his basic one but even the Freudian version of the principle can be contradicted by some counterexamples, Popper invokes his famous example of the flustered driver who, by trying stupidly to park his car in evidently too small a space, *manifestly does not act in a manner which is appropriate to the situation in which he finds himself.* According to Popper, the driver behaves in a manner that is *inappropriate* to the situation *even as he himself sees it*, since it is supposed that this driver knows perfectly well that parking there is literally impossible. In contrast, Popper observes, the pedestrian who throws himself in the way of an oncoming cyclist in order to avoid being hit by a car acts in a way that is *appropriate* to the situation *as he himself sees it*, even if, with a better view, this pedestrian could have avoided both accidents.

It is true that, while fortunately being atypical, this driver's behaviour is of a kind that cannot be excluded. Similar exasperated behaviours have been observed or even experienced by most of us. Such behaviours can surely be said to be irrational and Davidson could explain it by invoking conflicting semi-autonomous parts in the driver's brain and Mele by the fact that an excessive attention, joined to a failure to make an attempt at self-control, was granted to the too proximate satisfaction of expressing rage, motivated by the quasi-desperate situation of one looking for a parking place. However this does not mean that we have found the dividing line between rationality and irrationality. Indeed, if we base our judgment *on the description alone*, we cannot be sure that the flustered driver's action is really irrational. Are we certain that he does not *see* the situation in a way that renders his behaviour relatively appropriate? This driver may, for example, derive satisfaction from the fact that his conduct demonstrates to the surrounding population, in full conformity with his political convictions, that a city in which it is impossible to park one's car is a city badly administered. After all, if Freud has explained neurotic action with the help of the rationality principle, why would it be impossible to explain the driver's behaviour in a similar fashion? One who admits this might conclude that this example is not the most convincing illustration of irrational behaviour and look for a better one. However, it seems that the search for a better example should unavoidably lead one to the conclusion that no such example can do the job, precisely because arbitrarily imagined examples can always be arbitrarily construed in such a way as to associate the behaviour involved with a relatively appropriate reason. The point is that, depending on the analyst's perception, the same behaviour can be interpreted as irrational and potentially be explained by invoking conflicting parts of the mind or by the set of factors invoked by Mele, but it can also be interpreted as a relatively appropriate answer to the situation *as the agent sees it*, and, in the latter case, explained with the help of the rationality principle. The debates surrounding the nature of incontinent actions clearly illustrate the fact that deciding whether an action is irrational is largely a matter of interpretation; indeed, the verdict of irrationality depends on postulates about hardly observable mental events such as the presence of a genuine *intention*, the *adherence* to a second order principle claiming that one ought to act on what one holds to be best, and the *unconditional* character of the judgment about what is best.

The meaning of rationality: Popper versus Mises

Now, claiming that human actions can potentially be explained by referring to the rationality principle and claiming that this principle cannot be declared false simply because it is apparently falsified by an alleged counterexample *does not imply* that this principle is a priori true. Such a principle might even be declared false, because it is non-sense to attribute rationality to any actions, regardless of their apparent degree of stupidity, simply because it is theoretically possible to systematically interpret them in a way that provides them with a rationale. The opposite view would risk relying as a last resort on the hardly justified a priori claim that all actions are rational. In some marginal cases of particularly bizarre actions, it may appear so grotesque to construe them in a way that would make them apparently rational that it seems more sensible to renounce such an interpretation, to declare such actions irrational and to explain them without referring to rationality, if they can be explained at all. Therefore, the point is not to find a better example of irrationality, but to decide at a more general level whether it makes sense to claim, as Ludwig von Mises did, that all actions are a priori rational, simply because they necessarily correspond to a way of satisfying an immediate purpose whatever it is. When the question is raised in this fashion, almost all contemporary philosophers and economists find it extravagant and unacceptable to admit that any action is rational simply because it can always be construed as purposeful by simply alleging that the purpose consists in reaching whatever is reached by its performance.

Let us try to illustrate this point with the help of a thought experiment. In order to eliminate any alleged a priori knowledge based on introspection (or internal experience), let us consider inhabitants of an outer world who are perfectly capable of deduction and induction but unable to experience the need to satisfy a specific goal or to act purposefully. Arriving on planet Earth, these newcomers would be unable to conclude through a priori reasoning that (1) human beings are constituted in such a way that, depending on the way they see their situation, they can determine a main goal or have a purpose and that (2) they systematically tend to adapt their actions in order to satisfy such a purpose. At first glance, the newcomers might think that human beings are absolutely irrational (or rather non-rational) organisms in a way similar to how plants and most animals appear to us. However, through careful observation of the regularities in human behaviour, they could *arrive at the empirical conclusion* that this behaviour is not mechanically commanded but more or less systematically oriented towards an apparently conscious realization of something (which in our language is associated with a purpose that follows an evaluation), and from this fact they could induce that human beings are 'rational'. With still more careful observation, they could even observe that, very often, human beings *see their situation in an erratic way* and that, in these circumstances, their behaviour is, nonetheless, adapted accordingly and, in such cases, the newcomers might still conclude that human beings are rational. Occasionally, however, they would consider too far-fetched any rational interpretation of a given action. In such marginal cases, they would have no other choice but to acknowledge that such a human behaviour appears irremediably stupid and to explain it, if they can, without referring to rationality. Given these conclusions, they might, if their aim were to understand usual manifestations of human behaviour, *empirically* adopt a rationality principle even if experience has convinced them of the fact that this principle is approximately but not universally true. Such is the kind of principle that, according to Popper, is required by any model designed by social scientists.

It is, however, by a somewhat different approach that Popper saves the rationality principle. He observes first that testing a theory is testing a theory as a whole in such a way that it is always possible to conclude that any alleged refutation of rationality does not directly refute this principle, but only a theory consisting of *a model plus the rationality principle* (Popper 1985: 359–364). If this is true, modifying the model itself (for example, including in it the will to denounce the city administration at any price) may be sufficient to save the rationality principle. Assuredly, Popper would have insisted on choosing a different example illustrating the required modification of such models, but I apply his views to his favourite counterexample in order to illustrate, once again, that there is no hard and fast line between cases of rationality and of irrationality. Be that as it may, Popper's argument is that we are losing our time in challenging the rationality principle: the fact that we already know that it is false (given that this universal principle is not universally true) implies that such a challenge will not teach us anything. According to Popper, it is much more fruitful for the development of science to improve our models in such a way that an explanation based on the rationality principle can work – except, as more or less implicitly implied, in the very rare cases of sheer irrationality.

For Popper, the rationality principle, while empirical and fundamental for all theories in social science, has a content that tends to be minimal to the point of being 'almost empty' (ibid.: 359). Indeed, this principle need not have a very specific content since, as Popper explains, it is the refinements in model making – and the fact that models include more and more detailed pictures of mechanisms involved – that is responsible for progress in social sciences. True, the rationality principle is necessary for 'animating' such models, to use Popper's wording (ibid.: 358), but, to do this job, what is required is that this principle imports the idea that agents actually agree with what is clearly presented as the appropriate thing to do into this kind of model. This interpretation of Popper's view is legitimate because it is clear that, for Popper, the rationality principle, as such, need not include more than this, since all other relevant aspects of the situation (whether physical or psychological) are preferably taken over by the model itself. In economics, for example, sophisticated models define parameters, variables and relations in such a way that the appropriate thing to do, whether corresponding to an equilibrium point, a maximal gain or a minimal cost, is logically determined by the model itself. In such a model, the role of the rationality principle is nothing more than insuring that the agents are sensible enough to make the choice suggested by the model. To illustrate this point with a simple but telling example, let me recall the way I have described the role of the rationality principle in the famous marginalist theory according to which capitalists increase the level of production exactly up to the point where marginal cost equals marginal revenue, a point corresponding to a maximum of profits. The model involved might be conceived of as a set of hypotheses which are embodied in the curves or in equivalent equations that may be interpreted as informing the agent in the following fashion: 'here is the situation: if you produce a few units more, you will gain such extra amount, but you will have to pay such extra amount as costs'. In a model construed in such a way, it is simply required that the entrepreneur, as I put it in Chapter 1, is 'not stupid enough' either 'to lose the chance of making more profit by increasing production when the revenue drawn from an extra unit is larger than its cost' or 'to keep on incurring extra costs in order to obtain a supplementary revenue inferior to these costs'. The rationality principle that 'animates' such a model does not imply that agents are omniscient calculators who can determine maximum points thanks to their powerful capacities; it simply means that they are not stupid and that they are able to act in ways which are clearly designated as appropriate by the model. Of course, one could object that, in actual life, entrepreneurs do not have such clear and precise indicators at hand, but the point here is to characterize the role of the rationality principle in the explanatory models designed by economists and not to propose a principle that could serve as an instrument allowing entrepreneurs to be correctly guided in the difficult decisions they have to make.

The role of a minimal rationality principle

We have seen that we should forget the idea of clearly isolating irrational actions in order to more easily characterize rational ones. Any dividing line that one would like to see between them would be too dependent on various interpretations to be traced in an objective way. But happily for social scientists, and especially for economists, it is not really necessary to be in a position to clearly discriminate between rationality and irrationality. The fact that some people indulge in wishful thinking or that they do not perform actions that they consider the best for themselves raises a problem for philosophers and psychologists who want to explain such relatively atypical behaviour, but it hardly raises a problem for economists who want to explain general economic phenomena, such as movements in price. Obviously, if a significant number of people were inclined to do what contradicts their best judgements, for example if they tended to systematically buy more of a good when the price of this good increases, when they are aware that their best interest is to buy less, or at least to avoid buying more, of this good in such a circumstance, economic theories would be seriously in trouble. If such a bizarre situation was the case, we would be forced to conclude that prices and other economic variables could not be explained in the way they are explained presently, because it would no longer be possible to rely on a rationality principle that would be so often contradicted by such irrational behaviours. For sure, we could not a priori deny that other kinds of explanations relying on totally different bases, which are not easily conceivable in our relatively rational social world, could be developed and satisfactorily explain such behaviours; we can only claim that our usual theories could not work in such a world because their animating principle would be radically false to the point of being practically useless.

In any case, the rationality principle is precisely based on the denial that such an irrational behaviour is typical in human societies, and even on the fact, as Popper suggests, that it is very exceptional, since people normally act in such a way that makes sense, at least from their own point of view. There is no doubt that people make a lot of mistakes and rarely make the *best* decision, but their sub-optimal behaviour can generally be explained by various reasons that make sense for one who understands the way they see the situation. It is true, even in economic matters, that they rarely maximize *stricto sensu* and that they are frequently inconsistent, but their behaviour is nonetheless usually guided by what they quite sensibly consider to be the best thing to do *in their situation*, and this is the case frequently enough to make the construction of meaningful economic models and theories possible. It seems reasonable indeed to say that people are very rarely stupid enough to perform actions that go against *what they consider* to be the best thing to do in typical economic situations. And, in most situations typical of ordinary economic life, the best or a 'second best' thing to do is not something that is exceedingly difficult to determine. Indeed, one can rely on the fact that people generally tend to act rationally enough and to make *relatively* unambiguous decisions that make sense for economists: for example, they massively prefer a job that pays more to an equally attractive one that pays less; and they massively prefer to pay less than to pay more for a given good whose qualities are well known. This simple fact illustrates fairly well what the rationality principle conveys and, as we have seen in the first chapters of this book, this principle, even in a not too demanding version, was sufficient to allow economists to develop instructive and clarifying theories throughout the history of economic thought. There is no need to determine with precision the degree of rationality required to animate these theories; it is normally sufficient to require that agents not be thoughtless to the point of resisting adopting the choice that the model presents as the most advantageous. This may appear to be too banal a content for the fundamental principle of social sciences, but this content is dictated by a state of affairs that does not prevail in the physical sciences and that partially compensates for the methodological limitations of the social sciences.

Most economists would find that this relatively minimal conception of rationality is too loosely defined to occupy the central place in their discipline and they generally prefer to define rationality in a more rigorous way with the help of concepts like maximization and consistency. But it is not so clear that the latter concepts are preferable from this point of view. We have seen how problematic the notion of consistency is when we define it in the 'rigorous way' that makes rationality oddly inimical to adaptation and learning. Even though the notion of *maximization* does not seem to raise the same problems in spite of the fact that it is understood as closely related to the notion of consistency, it will be the purpose of the following chapter to examine whether rationality can really be unambiguously defined with the help of notions such as maximization and consistency.

5 Minimal *and* maximal rationality

Loosely defined concepts?

Everyone will agree that an *economic* agent is, before all, a *rational* agent, but disagreements appear when it comes to characterizing the rationality involved.[1] Among economists, it is common enough to refer to an ideal agent, of which *homo oeconomicus* is supposed to be the paradigm insofar as this agent is presumed to be capable, thanks to appropriate calculations, of maximizing whatever the value that is at stake and, consequently, of making optimal decisions. However, more and more objections have been raised against this way of conceiving of an economic agent, since it does not account for important traits of actual rational decisions. Therefore, various models of rational agents that avoid this kind of idealization have been proposed. Among them, the model developed by Herbert Simon in his life-long work on 'bounded rationality' is no doubt the most well known example. It is interesting to note that Simon's conception places an emphasis on previously almost unexplored aspects of the rationality of agents. It is with the help of concepts such as 'satisfactory pay-offs' (Simon 1957: 245–252) and 'aspiration level' (ibid.: 254) that Simon manages to account, in a novel fashion, for subtle relations between preferences, beliefs and inferences. Other models of agents with limited rationality have been proposed, for example, by the psychologist Daniel Kahneman whose model P (as designated in Kahneman 1996b: 252–254) reduces in an even more radical fashion the traditional features attributed to the rational agent by economists. Indeed, in this model, rules and attitudes count among the components of rational behaviour. Kahneman's explicit aim in devising this model was to explain any behaviour, whether strictly rational or 'less rational', with the help of the same mechanism, which can operate differently in different circumstances.

It is also suitable in this context to consider the view of the philosopher Christopher Cherniak, for whom the rationality of the agent can be perfectly well described as 'minimal'. According to Cherniak, the fundamental condition of minimal rationality can be formulated in the following way: 'If *A* has a particular belief-desire set, *A* would undertake *some, but not necessarily all*, of those actions that are apparently appropriate' (Cherniak 1986: 9; my emphasis). Note that the word 'apparently' is important here, because as minimal rationality does not imply that the beliefs are true, the actions suggested by an inference correctly drawn from false beliefs could be revealed as inappropriate while being minimally rational. According to Cherniak, minimal rationality requires a (minimal) condition of consistency as well: 'If *A* has a particular belief-desire set, then if any inconsistencies arose in the belief set, *A* would sometimes eliminate some of them' (ibid.: 16). Even though they might appear somewhat restrictive and vague, these propositions are sufficient to highlight the fact that we are dealing with a form of rationality, since beliefs and desires are assumed to be related to the actions undertaken in an appropriate fashion, and since the few eliminated inconsistencies are eliminated precisely because their presence within the ensemble of desires and beliefs ends up being intolerable. Furthermore, as Cherniak suggests (ibid.: 19), the rather vague character of laws and principles of action that rest on such a minimal rationality would in no way deprive them of their predictive power.

It is also a kind of minimal rationality that I am referring to when I claim that it is sufficient and less deceiving to simply assume that economic agents are not stupid and that they usually make decisions that are normally guided by reasons that they judge suitable for themselves. For sure, many economists will not like this somewhat informal way of characterizing rationality and agency and will claim that an economic science must be based on a much more precise definition of *homo oeconomicus*. Therefore, in order to vindicate the notion of minimal rationality, which risks being contested on this ground, I would like first to challenge an argument that seems to be a central tool in the arsenal of the defenders of the idealized model of the economic agent. Even though the rejection of this argument will not guarantee that resorting to a relatively minimal model of rationality in economics is well founded, it should contribute to assuring the degree of credibility that was denied to this approach by the argument in question. But first let us establish what this argument consists in.

An argument in favour of the idealization of rationality

The debate between proponents of idealized and formalized models and proponents of more realistic models of rational agents has been pursued in various forms throughout the twentieth century, but most often it concerned the importance of requiring that rational agents be represented in a realistic fashion in economic models, whereas most model makers assume that they must only retain the truly essential traits of the involved agents. We must acknowledge, to start with, that even the most radical defenders of the idealized models would easily admit that flesh and blood consumers and entrepreneurs in competitive environments frequently make choices whose rationality is far from corresponding to the idealized rationality of their models. In spite of this, they would not conclude that realism should necessarily be the last word when judging the relevance of the model invoked. After all, science has always been developed with the help of highly abstract theories that have allowed for the construction of models whose precision, generality and explanatory power we admire. For example, in constructing many of these powerful explanatory models, physicists were not hampered by the existence of friction and other analogous contingencies.

My point here is not to take sides in the debate regarding the epistemological merits of realism in economics; I will return to this question in the next chapter. For now, I wish solely to discuss the argument that draws from the virtues of abstract theory a justification for idealizing the notion of rationality and disqualifying softer notions like bounded or minimal rationality. In the same way, so the argument goes, as physicists' models must be based on precisely defined concepts, explanative models in economics must refer to an idealized notion of rational agents that has the advantage of precision and generality, and this is exactly what the notion of maximization provides the concept of rationality. In contrast, models that attribute only a reduced level of rationality to agents seem to be condemned to rely on imprecise definitions expressed in a vague language. And this imprecision becomes still more apparent when it comes to determining the level of rationality that is referred to. Indeed, it seems legitimate to ask what this *lower level* of rationality is and how to determine whether or not it should still be considered rational. If we refer to *minimal* rationality, how do we determine the level than can meaningfully be called minimal and resist flattening out all that remains of rationality? It seems that defenders of models based on maximization are fully justified in finding it intolerable that what should be judged satisfactory (while less than optimal) is vaguely determined by an agent endowed with only a limited degree of rationality. What is deemed to be rational in the behaviour of an agent to whom nothing more than a minimal degree of rationality is attributed may appear to vanish.

In contrast, as they do not fail to observe, a maximal degree of rationality can in principle be precisely determined insofar as a maximum corresponds to a definite point on a curve, which is normally a unique point. The eventual non-existence or non-singularity of such a point constitutes, as we know, a problem to which economists have long been deeply concerned with finding a solution, and this concern is related to the importance of defining, without the slightest ambiguity, what should be meant by a strictly rational agent. Rather than seeking to identify the vague and uncertain traits of actual agents, economists generally prefer to refer to agents who do not really exist as such but of whom one knows exactly of what they consist.

It is true that the evocation of a maximizing agent so cavalierly indifferent to the limitations of real individuals frequently caused some embarrassment to economists. Physicists may neglect to account for friction, but they do so in cases where the latter does not play any role in the mechanism that they seek to shed light on, and they *do* take it into account when they pursue the analysis in contexts where the effects of friction become significant. Therefore what defenders of more realistic models of economic agents find intolerable in the adverse position is that the rationality of economic agents, to whom is so incautiously attributed a capacity to strictly maximize, is precisely the element that plays the essential role in the mechanisms that the economists undertake to explain. It strikes them as all the more shocking that, despite this fact and in contrast with physicists, many economists did not seem to find it particularly important to push the analysis further with the idea of analysing the role of the 'contingent' factors that are not accounted for in models where ideal agents bear so little resemblance to real agents. Thus engaged, or almost, in a dialogue of deaf persons, neoclassical economists tend to justify their idealized model of rational agents by the fact that no other model of economic agents is available to be substituted for the one they have adopted. By which is meant, of course, no other model that would be defined with a precision sufficient for making possible the elaboration of a theory whose conclusions could be systematically derived in a formalized manner. Since a bounded rationality, and a 'minimal' rationality, can hardly be characterized in a very precise fashion, it has seemed advisable to the majority of economists to turn instead to a maximal rationality that corresponds to rationality's plenitude. It seems indeed that the merit of a model idealizing the agent in this way is that it is possible to draw exact conclusions regarding actions this agent is liable to engage in, conclusions that are crucial for the development of an economic theory. Thus, if a scientific discipline must above all be established on a precise and non-fluctuating base, when it comes to characterizing economic agents, it seems normal, at least at first glance, that economists have a clear preference for equipping them with a maximal rationality.

But when is rationality maximal?

But is this notion of the maximally rational agent so clearly defined? Does it suffice to refer to a maximum in order to know exactly what we are talking about? If it were found that the idealized agent to which we refer, to whom we are granting an aptitude for maximization, is in fact no more than an imprecise and fluctuating construction, which might even contain some contradictions, then the advantage that is assumed to be gained from an idealized representation as opposed to a more realistic one might be found to be seriously weakened. If this were to be the case, the weighty argument that denounces the imprecise nature of a bounded rationality or of a minimal rationality would lose much of its impact indeed. It is necessary, then, to examine more closely that which constitutes an agent to whom we so generously grant an aptitude to maximize or optimize. But let us first ask what is meant by the term 'agent' before examining what such an ideal agent is supposed to be.

An agent is, by definition, an acting subject whose actions must be motivated by beliefs and desires, being admitted that an action is essentially guided by a set of beliefs and oriented towards the satisfaction of desires. If no belief plays a part – for instance, when a windfall event has the result of satisfying a desire – this has nothing to do with an action. If no desire plays a part – as would be the case if one's beliefs generated a physical movement of the body that was not consciously oriented towards the satisfaction of a desire – no action would have been performed. This view, which is generally accepted, obviously implies that an action differs somehow from other behaviours, such as reflexes, that are conceived of as immediately subordinate to the type of determinism that governs natural phenomena. Without entering into a metaphysical debate about free will, we can at least admit that an action should not be interpreted as a 'reaction' *necessarily* and mechanically provoked by certain beliefs and certain desires being held by a given person. If such was the case, it could not even be said that the agent 'acts', since, in spite of the role of beliefs and desires, it would not be a matter of action but of a movement similar to a pure reflex. If, for example, the belief that dogs are dangerous *irresistibly* compels individuals wanting to protect themselves to flee at the sight of a dog, unable in any way to avoid or delay such a flight, it would be difficult to speak of actions in order to characterize this strictly uncontrollable movement of fleeing. In such a situation, the fleeing would obviously be predictable, but when it comes to a genuine action, in order to predict it, one cannot rely on the same kind of mechanism, because an action cannot be conceived of as having been brought about by a strictly irresistible force.

Nonetheless, many actions can be predicted successfully with a fair degree of precision, for although an action cannot be the necessary result of a process, it cannot be mistaken for an *arbitrary* movement. If actions were the result of a random process, it would not be possible to predict that they would take place, since it is a question here of predicting individual actions and not a stochastic tendency concerning a vast set of actions to which the law of large numbers could apply. In contrast, recognizing that economic agents are rational is acknowledging that they tend to act in an appropriate fashion or, using Cherniak's wording, to act in such a way that, given the content of their beliefs, their actions tend to satisfy at least one of their desires. However, rationality is an extremely complex notion. To determine what is appropriate, a rational agent must proceed to certain inferences from his beliefs and so must be endowed with a certain power of deduction. In addition, because the number of one's beliefs is necessarily considerable – given that they bear on each of the multiple objects of knowledge that are accessible to one's consciousness – and that the number of inferences that are possible is, consequently, virtually unlimited, a rational agent must have the capacity to retain, from the possible inferences regarding a given situation, only those that are really appropriate. On top of that, because the rational agent who has multiple beliefs can also have a very large number of desires, a certain degree of consistency both between beliefs and between desires is required. It would be difficult indeed to qualify as rational an individual who believes simultaneously that the stock market is steadily progressing and that it is silly to invest at this moment in the risky ventures associated with the stock exchange, or an individual who desires at the same time to increase his wealth as much as possible and to live, like Francis Assisi, in a situation of poverty that is considered sanctifying and regenerating. In summary, it can be affirmed that economic agents are presumed rational insofar as they can make some correct and appropriate inferences from a relatively consistent set of beliefs in order to engage in an action capable of satisfying a given desire belonging to a relatively consistent set of desires. It can equally be affirmed that, by relying on the rationality principle, it is possible, in principle, to predict with a certain amount of success actions of this type, even though those actions result from a free choice. But it is time to ask how these various components of the definition of an agent should be understood when the agent is assumed to be an *idealized* and *maximizing* one. What kind of fellows should *homines oeconomici* be once they are considered to be maximally rational economic agents or, to use a more explicit parlance, economic agents that ideally fulfil the conditions for deciding and acting according to maximal rationality?

Idealized agency and rationality-maximization

It is self-evident that the characterization of a *maximally rational* agent must exclude approximate or ambiguous formulations that would make it impossible to construct a precise representation of the kind of rationality involved. Now, the feature of such an agent that can most unequivocally be given an idealized representation is certainly the power of deduction. Complex inferences depend upon recourse to logical calculations that are not accessible to all; therefore it is usual to consider an individual to be more rational than another insofar as his capacity to carry out such logical calculations is clearly superior to the latter's. Thus, it is advisable to endow our maximally rational economic agent with an unlimited capacity when it comes to such logical calculations. But since calculations of this sort *normally* require a certain amount of time, and since the number of calculations to be performed might be practically infinite, truly maximal rationality must imply that our idealized economic agent be able to perform all such calculations instantaneously and, consequently, able to perceive in the blink of an eye all the possible consequences that can be derived from any kinds of beliefs. If we agree with such a maximal endowment, the problem of determining the appropriate inferences to make will vanish, since such agents would instantly perceive *all* the consequences that could be drawn from the totality of their beliefs. It may seem reasonable to claim that agents of this kind who could outperform any computer with respect to inferences are maximally rational.

However, matters are not so simple, since even though such agents have no need to choose among inferences to make, since all possible inferences are immediately made by them, it remains to be determined which of the consequences drawn are relevant for guiding the action to be undertaken. Therefore, in order to talk of maximal rationality, we must also endow our agents with the capacity to select, from the many consequences derived from beliefs, those that are most appropriate in light of the desire that is to be satisfied. Yet this cannot be achieved unless all these beliefs are true. To illustrate this point, imagine a farmer, let us call him Peter, whose beliefs can be summarized by firm adherence to the five following propositions: (1) burning his corn crop will reduce it to ashes, (2) the corn ashes have a higher value at market than the corn itself, (3) the act of pouring gasoline on the corn would cause it to burn more efficiently, (4) throwing a lit torch on the gasoline-soaked corn would be sufficient to start a fire, (5) a fire in the corn crop carries the risk of spreading to the rest of his land where other crops are being cultivated. Suppose now that Peter legitimately desires to increase his income and that his deductive powers are flawless. On the one hand, he deduces from (1), (2), (3) and (4) that the use of gasoline and torch in the described fashion would have the effect of increasing his income, since he could then sell his corn in the form of ashes. But, on the other hand, he deduces from (3), (4) and (5) that this course of action runs the risk of reducing his income since he could lose the income that the other crops could bring him. Therefore, Peter cannot act in a maximally rational fashion without determining which of the two consequences correctly derived from his beliefs is more likely to satisfy his desire. Yet he can only do so by comparing the loss of his other crops with the amount to be gained by selling his corn crop as ashes rather than as normal corn. However, how can he do so without taking into account the real costs and earnings that are at stake, which implies that he recognizes first that proposition (2) is manifestly false? If we extend the argument to all the possible beliefs and if we acknowledge that knowing that *A* is false means having a true belief concerning non-*A*, we are obliged to conclude that a maximally rational agent can only have true beliefs.

To be sure, ignorance of particular facts as such cannot be considered a symptom of irrationality. For example, Peter might not have belief (5), or might be convinced that the loss that it threatens is less important than the earnings promised by belief (2) and then the decision to fire his corn crop could be qualified as rational since it resulted from a correct deduction about the best course of action to take given his beliefs. But when we speak of a *maximally* rational agent, the situation is different, because this agent is capable of deducing all the possible consequences of multiple beliefs; yet if certain of these are false, this ideal agent would deduce from them consequences that could suggest an action contrary to that which would maximize the degree of realization of a preference that could be estimated to be the highest one (for example, maximizing net income or, in more general terms, attaining an optimal position). It would be absurd to use the phrase 'maximally rational agent' to designate an agent whose capacity to achieve an objective, thanks to unlimited deductive powers, could be constantly neutralized by the fact that this agent maintains false beliefs. Therefore, it is necessary to make our idealized agent absolutely impermeable to any false beliefs, without which it would be pointless to depend on the services of such an allegedly maximally rational but still unreliable agent in the construction of a theory that is assumed to not make room for approximate conceptions.

Should we lengthen this list of qualities that are to be attributed to our maximally rational agent and presume that desires themselves (or preferences, to use the parlance of economists) necessarily conform to the requirements of an ideal rationality? Can maximal rationality impose its constraints on desires as well as beliefs? We may be tempted to respond negatively, for if there is a sense in which beliefs can be said to be objectively true, it cannot be the case that desires could similarly be judged to be objectively valid. Most economists agree with Lionel Robbins (1952 [1932]: chapter II), that the economist need not be concerned with ends as such, which seems to imply that our maximally rational agent need only be able to determine the best means of achieving an end (or a desire), whatever it may be. However, this matter too is not so simple. Let us suppose that an entrepreneur endowed with maximal deductive power and holding only perfectly true beliefs desires to attain profit maximization as soon as possible. Since a profit is a net income, we might discuss the ambiguities associated with the notion of a net income, which complicate the precise determination of this entrepreneur's desire (or preference). Indeed, the determination of a net income supposes knowledge of the costs associated with the realization of the gross income from which this net income is derived. But the determination of the various costs involved (production costs, communication costs, transportation costs, information costs, deliberation costs, transaction costs...) is a tricky matter that would have to be reinterpreted to be used for determining the meaning of the maximum profit that corresponds to the preference attributed to our maximally rational agent, for whom some costs such as information costs, but not all costs, would be reduced to zero. But let us put aside this source of ambiguity in order to concentrate on the main problem. Our entrepreneur may rationally choose to dismiss some highly paid while particularly skilled employees, to use only relatively cheap materials and to resort to various economizing measures that undermine credibility, all these decisions being possibly the most suited to easily and quickly maximize profit in the short term. However, as expected, through such a course of actions, this entrepreneur loses any chance to maximize profits in the long term and risks being bankrupted sooner or later. By referring to what is implied by instrumental rationality, we can maintain that the entrepreneur's behaviour is 'rational' to the extent that it was efficiently oriented towards profit maximization in the short term, an objective that, with no regard for future consequences, might be justified by personal reasons that we have not to judge.

However, we must recognize at the same time that it would be odd to qualify such an economic agent as maximally rational insofar as such behaviours, as we have seen in the previous chapter, are normally associated with intellectual myopia or with weakness of the will, two traits that are generally considered to be typical symptoms of irrationality. Therefore economists usually admit that if the monetary profit is the value that an individual intends to maximize, rationality demands that this value not be simply maximized in the short term. And if we raise the question of the duration of time considered to be the long term, the determination of the maximally rational action to undertake becomes still more complex. Is it the life expectancy of the entrepreneur or of the enterprise or still another time period that is the appropriate term to consider? Also, while it is true that rationality does not exert as direct a constraint on desires as it exerts on beliefs, since we can not judge the objectivity of desires in the way we can judge the objectivity of beliefs, it is nonetheless true that it would not make sense to describe as maximally rational economic agents who let themselves be guided by idiosyncratic desires that are clearly contrary to the idea we have of rationality. But if such is the case, the virtually unsolvable problem of determining what the preferences that should be considered rational are can hardly be avoided. All these problems are very familiar to economists but, in the present context, my point is that, when it comes to characterizing the preferences of rational agents, resorting to an idealization established by pushing qualities involved to their maximal level helps still less than when it came to characterizing their powers and their beliefs. Whether we consider one or another of these aspects of the representation of an agent, maximal rationality does not seem to correspond to a much more precise concept than minimal rationality.

Idealized agency and rationality-consistency

It is in a significantly different way that the notion of consistency – which, for most contemporary economists, is literally that which defines rationality – imposes a kind of constraint on the preferences of a maximally rational economic agent. At first sight, the idea of 'revealed preference', which is directly associated with the notion of rationality-consistency, seems not to be highly constraining, since *any* preference can be recognized as such insofar as it is revealed in a choice. However, nothing would be 'revealed' if new choices could freely contradict a previously expressed preference. Therefore, it is important, from this perspective, that a rational individual who, for example, has chosen *A* rather than *B* at time *t1* cannot choose *B* rather than *A* at time *t2*. Moreover, various arguments, among which the money pump argument is the most popular, aim to show that transitivity in choices, which is an axiomatic condition of consistency, is strictly required for not being fouled like an irrational trader can be. Without questioning the negative conclusions reached in Chapter 2 of the present book about the value of such arguments with respect to their claims concerning the relation between rationality and transitivity when applied to the behaviour of people, it seems reasonable to admit that a *maximally* rational economic agent, endowed with an unlimited deductive power and resistant to any false beliefs, must be perfectly consistent when it comes to revealing preferences. It seems obvious that a maximally rational agent's preferences cannot be progressively discovered in a way that might generate inconsistency. Indeed, to say that one *discovers* one's own preferences little by little is the same as saying that one's degree of knowledge and consequently of rationality is limited. An individual whose rationality is limited – we might have in mind 'bounded rationality' in the sense analysed by Simon – may resolve to act only when discovering a quite new possibility that reveals itself as clearly preferable when compared to the situation accepted until then, whose *unsatisfactory* character is revealed by this very fact. In contrast, a maximally rational agent must have perfectly clear preferences to the point of being capable of instantaneously arranging them in a succession of indifference curves, which is what economists implicitly suppose. To accept that an agent, who has such perfectly self-conscious and immutable preferences and beliefs could be revealed to be inconsistent by choosing *B* rather than *A* after having chosen *A* rather than *B*, would render meaningless the very notion of maximal rationality. And if such an eventual inconsistency was tentatively explained by the fact that the agent in question *falsely believes* at *t1* that *A* is preferable to *B* or *falsely believes* at *t2* that *B* is preferable to *A*, we would be even further removed from an idealized view of this agent. Thus, let us admit that a maximally rational agent, in contrast with ordinary human beings, should be perfectly consistent.

But this implies that our ideal agent is incapable of undergoing changes of taste. As we have seen in Chapter 2, economists generally tend to avoid analysing the consequences of changes of taste and to assume that preferences are stable. But the preferences of human beings frequently change, not only because tastes can change more or less spontaneously but also because these changes can result from learning. It is surely rational to adjust our preferences when experiencing a source of satisfaction that was previously unknown or even unsuspected by us. It is indeed a stubborn refusal to adapt our preferences to such discoveries that would be fundamentally irrational. Nonetheless, this rational aptitude for adaptation cannot be granted to our maximally rational agent, since it cannot be reconciled with strict consistency. As the notion of consistency would risk collapsing under the pressure of subtle and progressive changes in taste, it is advisable to admit instead the fact that we face an incompatibility and to attribute to our maximally rational agent a more absolute and less fragile consistency. Thus, maximal rationality will not include the faculty of adaptation that is so closely related to what we usually mean by rationality, but this should not be too much of a problem if we admit that a maximally rational agent never has an occasion to adapt to any new situations. And this is warranted by the fact that this rational agent never has an occasion to experience changes in taste, neither whimsical changes nor changes due to the acquisition of new knowledge, because there are no such things as previously unknown situations for a maximally rational agent.

When economists speak of consistency, they refer generally to the consistency of preferences (or desires), but such a consistency implies the consistency of beliefs, since otherwise an inconsistent shift from one preference to another could be provoked by an inconsistent shift in beliefs about the attributes of the objects towards which these preferences are directed. Yet learning implies that a progressive change in beliefs takes place and that new objects of desire (with the potential to modify an order of preferences) could be discovered; thus, from this point of view, our maximally rational agent could definitely never learn. And we gain nothing by stipulating that the beliefs of this rational agent remain consistent between two successive periods of learning, since it is the very notion of learning or of the search for truth that are unacceptable when we are dealing with an agent whose perfect rationality implies perfect consistency and complete knowledge. This incompatibility between all forms of learning and the notion of a maximal rationality is reinforced by what is called the 'paradox of the Preface'.[2] The idea is as follows: if you accept that there exists a strict consistency between your beliefs, you cannot believe that any particular one of your beliefs could be false: indeed, if *A* is one of your beliefs, believing that *A* might be false is manifestly inconsistent with believing *A*. Yet, since the same argument can be applied to each of anyone's beliefs, we must conclude that accepting that there is a strict consistency between one's beliefs leaves no room for the idea that any one among one's beliefs might be subject to the slightest doubt. Yet, to be engaged in a process of learning is to recognize the possible falsity of certain beliefs that might be abandoned in this process, and it is to hold as true the new beliefs that are being acquired, all while recognizing that the latter could theoretically be judged false in their turn if a subsequent process of learning would have the effect of showing their falseness. Therefore, all forms of learning are incompatible with a strict consistency of beliefs and with the notion of the maximally rational economic agent whose beliefs cannot leave room for the slightest doubt regarding their consistency and their truth.

All these considerations force us to conclude that a maximally rational economic agent must be rigorously *omniscient* in such a way that this agent, having nothing to learn, cannot experience the slightest change in taste that would result from the emergence of new beliefs. And such an omniscience must include the science of all that the future holds; otherwise all the problems that have just been discussed could resurface. An agent who ignores whatever may occur in the future is an agent who might acquire new knowledge in the future, in such a way that preferences (tastes) of this agent might be modified accordingly. In particular, such an agent might discover that certain actions that were rationally based on that which seemed to be the best possible evaluation of their future consequences would be revealed as less beneficial than other actions given their actual consequences revealed by the passage of time. It might even be discovered that objectives pursued with the greatest conviction would turn out to be much less desirable compared to other ones whose attractiveness was unsuspected. How could an agent whose decisions would be based on uncertain and potentially false beliefs about the future – beliefs that are no more likely to hold true than those of any of us – be declared a maximally rational economic agent? Such decisions might be revealed to be inappropriate and the beliefs on which they were based revealed to be inconsistent with the new beliefs (unsuspected by hypothesis) that future times are probable to generate. Clearly, only omniscience, including knowledge of the future, can make an agent worthy of being considered a maximally rational agent.

So, without being able to instantly infer all the consequences that could be deduced from a rigorously true and strictly consistent set of beliefs with respect to the whole of reality including future events, and this in order to satisfy, with the help of appropriate actions, a set of consistent desires formulated in the light of necessarily true beliefs, an agent cannot legitimately be qualified as a maximally rational economic agent. For the sake of illustrating that the maximum looked for can hardly be associated with a particular degree of rationality, one might even push the idea to its extreme limit and claim that maximal rationality should imply perfect knowledge of all constituents of the world at all levels including atomic and subatomic ones up to the most elementary ones. Otherwise, the limit of this agent's allegedly perfect knowledge would be fixed at an arbitrary point. But an agent endowed with such knowledge and with absolute deductive power might, like Laplace's demon, be able on this basis alone to instantaneously predict the future, which he (or she) was supposed to know perfectly well in any case. But what about an agent who could, hypothetically, respond to such extraordinary requirements? Such an agent would be an atemporal 'agent', in the sense of being necessarily outside the course of time in order to be able to contemplate the future as well as the past and to choose in a *single choice* optimal strategies to adopt, taking into account any states of the world that would be instantaneously apprehended. This agent who would know all the consequences of this unique choice of strategies in the very instant of making it would necessarily be a kind of immutable god or, if we prefer, a Parmenidean pseudo-agent. The latter would be motionless insofar as this so-called agent would have nothing to decide other than that which would have been decided once and for all in a uniquely determined choice, somehow outside of history, or before the beginning of historical time within which the consequences of this choice have only to be actualised. This ahistorical 'agent' would not, properly speaking, *act*, and even less so in that he would have no new desires to satisfy. We can conclude, then, that the notion of the maximally rational agent is a *self-contradicting* notion by the fact that the agent in question would be incapable of action as soon as we push the idea of maximal rationality and perfect consistency to the limit.

The 'moderately' rational agents of economic models

Given that agents whom economists refer to are normally called upon to make choices that are rational but costly in a world characterized by scarcity and uncertainty, it is clear that such agents have little to do with the godlike and atemporal agent that I have tried to describe above. But, precisely for this reason, the economic agent that they invoke in their models cannot be unequivocally characterized as being a maximally rational agent. To appeal in an economic model to an agent whose decisions are presumed to be perfectly rational because, hypothetically, this agent maximizes a particular value and respects the axioms associated with consistency, is to attribute, more or less arbitrarily, a certain degree of rationality to that agent, such that there is no sense in pretending that this particular degree of rationality corresponds to the *maximum* of rationality. One might object that the latter should not be seriously considered since it is unattainable by a human being, but this objection does not work because perfect maximization and strict consistency are also unattainable. Taken literally, the idea of a strictly maximal rationality leads us to a self-contradictory situation, as we have just seen. Therefore, the decision to stop at a certain point in the idealization of a rational agent is certainly well advised, but it does not avoid the arbitrary character of all decisions of this kind. Although such an idealization has an undeniable heuristic value, the hope that pushing the notion of rationality to its maximal limit may allow us to avoid any kind of arbitrariness in the determination of the degree of rationality to be granted to *homo oeconomicus* – the paradigmatic economic agent to which economists implicitly refer – turns out to be an illusion. Even though it is declared minimal or maximal in order to roughly characterize what is involved, rationality is never either strictly minimal, in which case it would tend towards irrationality, or really maximal, in which case it would tend towards an infinity where it would lose its very meaning. Beyond these formulations, the point is to grant a representative agent the degree of rationality that is required either, in the case of bounded or of minimal rationality, to explain the workings of the actual economy, or, in the case of maximal rationality, to comply with what is required to construct models that work smoothly and elegantly.

Whether characterizing their rational agents by maximization or by consistency, economists idealize the representation of this agent just enough to render more convincing and elegant the solution to the problem being resolved. But if all ways of representing a rational agent contain an arbitrary element, and if the unavoidable delimitation of the rationality of this agent depends on the problems that designers of the models want to resolve, it is time to revise our assessment of those representations of rational agency that do not aim to portray an idealized functioning of economy but that seek to account for the actual economy resulting from interactions of human beings who make rational decisions, but who rarely maximize and are frequently inconsistent. These latter conceptions of rational agency should not be disqualified hastily simply because they cannot be circumscribed in as precise a way as those proposed by supporters of rationality-maximization or of rationality-coherence. If my analysis is correct, there cannot be such a thing as a maximally rational economic agent. All the representations of such an agent correspond instead to a sort of compromise between various traits that are associated with rationality when it comes to deciding and acting (validity and intelligibility of beliefs, attention to desires and preferences, power of deduction, coherence of beliefs and desires, aptitude to confront incertitude, capacity to anticipate and predict, adaptability, etc.). This is why various representations of rationality differ between themselves with respect to the weight given to each of these traits. Pushing one of these traits to the maximal limit can simplify somewhat the definition we give to a rational agent and facilitate the determination of the latter's actions in an appropriately designed model, but it does not really contribute to granting a more definitive and universal character to the representation of rationality. Put in a nutshell, there is no such a thing as a paradigmatic and well circumscribed notion of a rational agent which should be judged superior to softer notions that better capture actual agents' behaviour but must pay a price for this in term of conceptual precision.

If such is the case, 'softer' conceptions of rationality such as Simon's bounded rationality, Kahneman's rationality that makes room for rules and attitudes, and minimal rationality, whatever way it is characterized, should not be excluded a priori. It is surely not absurd to invoke a minimal or strongly limited rationality, rather than to have recourse to an idealized rationality, when it is a question of predicting the behaviour of human beings whose rationality *is* in fact limited and even rather 'minimal' – in the sense that we can simply say of them that they are far from being stupid and that they take, when the time comes, certain measures in order to ameliorate their situation. The word 'minimal' may look excessively reductive as a description of human rationality, but measured *on the scale* established by the requirements of maximal rationality analysed above, the label 'minimal' attributed to rationality seems, rather, to give a reasonably fair idea of the degree of rationality of typical human beings. Be that as it may, if economic models make sense for us, it is because they are based on a principle according to which people are guided by this kind of rationality. As we have seen in the first chapters of this book, in spite of the formalization brought forth by economists, it is this kind of rationality that can be invoked in the last resort to support the results of economic analysis since the middle of the eighteenth century up to the recent debates on rational choice and on experimental economics.

As we have seen, it is not even clear that neoclassical models should necessarily be interpreted as requiring agents conceived of as powerful calculators rather than as minimally rational fellows. It depends on whether the model is construed as a picture of the decision processes of agents or as a picture of an economic situation. In the first construal, agents themselves are supposed to be able to derive an optimal solution with the help of sophisticated calculation and then decide to act in the way suggested by this calculation. Such a view is obviously highly unrealistic and somewhat cumbersome because it is clear that flesh and blood agents are far from being so calculating. However, with the second construal whose legitimacy was argued for in the previous chapter, it is the optimal solution itself that, with the help of curves or equations, the model presents as maximally attractive for the agent. The only thing that is required from this agent is to accept the solution suggested by the model. The degree of rationality required to make an appropriate decision of this type is quite minimal indeed. By hypothesis, the agent does not have to maximize through calculation: models so construed include within themselves the results of appropriate calculation; everything is conceived of as precalculated. However, this interpretation of the model is not more realistic, because actual economic situations never 'speak' so clearly.

This dual fashion of interpreting economic models is particularly well illustrated by the way Léon Walras developed his general equilibrium model. If his model is interpreted as picturing individual processes of decision making, it would require that agents be endowed with extremely powerful computational capacities. Indeed, they would have to determine what prices to enter in a number of transactions concerning a multitude of goods desired at various degrees by an indefinite number of potential buyers and sellers. They should even have the capacity to figure out the intimate propensity of each of them to buy and to sell. Probably because he was aware of the totally unrealistic character of such a requirement, Walras preferred to present his model otherwise by invoking the role of an Auctioneer exercising an absolute monitoring control over the market and managing it in such a way that agents are not allowed to enter into transactions before the calling of an equilibrium price. Controlled by such a frame of reference, agents do not need to be particularly efficient maximizers in order to materialize the equilibrium situation; they simply have to be guided by a minimal rationality that incites them to buy or sell at the called equilibrium price, according to their desires for various goods. In such a construal, the requirements for optimization are taken up in the description of the situation that is personified by the Auctioneer. Naturally this construal is not more realistic than the previous one, since even though agents are more realistically described, the same thing cannot be said of the hypothetical auction situation: there is no auctioneer in typical markets and nothing can prevent agents from buying when they like and at any price, however far this price may be from equilibrium.

This illustrates fairly well what Popper meant when saying that when a theory does not work, it is recommended to try to improve the model rather than blaming the rationality principle. To someone disappointed by the fact that a model of general equilibrium does not give a fair picture of actual economic markets, Popper would surely have recommended looking for a better adapted model, rather than explaining the failure by the fact that human beings do not act rationally enough. The latter are only minimally rational indeed, but in order to satisfactorily account for what is going on in *actual* markets, one would have to design a model that can work reasonably well even with minimally rational agents. As we have just seen, various neoclassical models can be construed as manageable by minimally rational agents, but this is possible only because they include more or less unrealistic components (whether they be auctioneers, smooth curves or equivalent equations) that constitute a framework that efficiently guides agents' decisions but which is absent from actual markets.

Incidentally, it is interesting to note that, whereas typical economic models can be construed as *frameworks* guiding minimally rational agents toward optimal solutions, in many experiments put forward in experimental economics, it is, in contrast, a deceiving framework that is designed in such a way that agents are frequently trapped and led to adopt a solution that may be economic and rational from their point of view, but whose clearly sub-optimal character discloses the relatively minimal level of their rationality. We have even seen that the famous Allais paradox rests on such a deceiving framework that can constitute a trap even for people endowed with much more than minimal (but far from maximal) rationality.

Though economists may prefer to develop their models in a (moderately) idealized world where they can more easily rely on powerful mathematical instruments, they should recognize that the model of rationality that they use to this end can in no way be considered a kind of paradigm of which the less idealized notions of rationality would only be less interesting avatars. Note that it is not a question here of denying the importance of idealized models that have the advantage of making possible analyses developed in a language whose remarkable precision can be highly fruitful. It is certain that, even though the way neoclassical economists associate rationality with maximization is somewhat arbitrary and can hardly be used in testable explanations of actual situations, it allows them to analyse economic trends in a language much more precise than the one that less idealized notions of rationality would allow. However, nothing authorizes us to conclude from that that the conceptual precision associated with such an idealization makes possible a more accurate account of what happens in the economic world. And, we can conclude from the present chapter that, if sacrificing realism in order to attain this conceptual precision is perhaps justified by some interesting theoretical results made possible by such an idealization, it would be a pure illusion to think that it is justified by the avoidance of arbitrariness in determining what exactly constitutes the rationality of an economic agent. Put otherwise, concepts such as bounded or minimal rationality should not be disqualified solely on the basis of the relative imprecision of their definition, since the idealized models of maximal rationality that we oppose to them are more precisely defined only by the fact that their authors arbitrarily chose to stabilize the process of idealization at the point that appears the most convenient for the role they choose to attribute to rationality. If it is legitimate to ask what degree of minimalism we can legitimately push the notion of minimal rationality to, it is also legitimate to inquire about the degree of maximization that economists have chosen to stabilize the notion of maximal rationality.

In any case, many economists who easily admit that one cannot seriously maintain that human beings are efficient maximizers or consistent deciders would not accept a notion of rationality that remains vaguely defined. Therefore, especially in the mid-twentieth century, the avoidance of any dependence on the notion of rationality looked particularly attractive to them. Since they refused to refer to an imperfectly defined notion, there were only two possibilities left open: either they can argue that rationality-maximization can play a perfectly legitimate role in a scientific enterprise in spite of its admitted lack of realisticness, or they can argue that it is possible to dispense with the notion of rationality altogether without real damage to scientific analysis. The next two chapters will discuss these two ways of avoiding the cumbersome situation associated with the concept of rationality in turn.

Part III

But is rationality really necessary in economics?

6 Why unrealism of assumptions remains a predicament

One must admit that methodological papers rarely have a considerable and immediate impact on the practices of economists, but if we are looking for an exception to this rule, the example that comes to mind is surely Milton Friedman's famous 1953 essay (Friedman 1953), which, apparently, was enthusiastically perceived of as a liberating piece by most economists. This enthusiasm is understandable: this paper written by a respected economist proposed relatively sophisticated arguments in favour of the legitimacy of the neoclassical practice consisting in assuming that people are rational in the sense of being maximizers, in spite of the admittedly unrealistic character of such an assumption. And the fact that these arguments were based on suggestive comparisons with the practice attributed to natural scientists was in itself powerfully reassuring for economists who did not want to put aside their secret ambition of being perceived as genuine scientists, in spite of their relatively weak propensity to base their analyses on factual inquiries and their clear preference for speculations bearing on the highly idealized world of rationality-maximization and rationality-consistency.

However, Friedman's paper was also the subject of unending and rarely very sympathetic discussion emerging from methodologists of economics and frequently enough from fellow economists as well. A significant number of papers were devoted to analysing this essay usually described as brilliant but misleading, somewhat confused and written by an author who was not too familiar with important developments in philosophy of sciences. In fact, discussions on this paper have occupied such a place in methodological debates that many methodologists became literally fed up with such discussions. Thus, readers who are in this situation and who are familiar with most objections that have been raised against Friedman's thesis might skip this chapter without incurring too much damage for the understanding of the whole book. I think, nonetheless, that it might be worthwhile to pay attention to this chapter, which proposes some arguments that significantly differ from those that are usually opposed to Friedman's approach.[1]

Let us note to start with that it is not my purpose here, far from it, to refer disparagingly to Friedman's methodological essay. Even its most negative critics easily acknowledge that it is full of bold and fresh ideas – some of them quite original and even ahead of their time – that are formulated in an exceptionally ingenious and attractive fashion.[2] It is nonetheless important to show why the reassuring conclusions of this essay cannot be accepted so easily and also why it became the source of such an almost emotional debate that has divided methodologists of economics for more than half a century. In order to understand why the question was so passionately debated, one must realize that what was at stake in this long debate was not a simple technical point, but the very possibility of treating economics as a positive science, just like the natural sciences. After a relatively standard discussion of what allows us to characterize a science as positive, Friedman develops an argumentation against those who objected to the positive character of economics. This argumentation was exposed in a few provocative general considerations aiming to show that it is totally inappropriate to require that assumptions of a science be realistic. This thesis was then illustrated with the help of three colourful examples devised to show that their admittedly unrealistic assumptions do not contribute to making economics less 'positive' than any other science. It seems very probable that these examples were mostly responsible for the essay's enduring influence over economists, but it is the general considerations that were at the core of the debate. These considerations quickly became the target of most commentators whose objections were frequently rather harsh; other commentators, however, maintain that Friedman's views were the expression of a more palatable philosophical language, especially by presenting Friedman's essay as a particularly clever 'instrumentalist'[3] response to the damaging consequences that a too demanding realist approach can have on the practice of economics as well as on the practice of any science.[4]

In order to reduce the confusion around this unending debate, without pretending to propose a definitive interpretation of the many ambiguous passages that have provoked it, my claims will be the three following:

1 Friedman's most influential thesis seems to confuse a fundamental assumption with some consequences derived from it, in such a way that when he rightly claims that a fundamental assumption does not need to be tested other than by its implications, he wrongly considers that it is mistaken to check whether something which is *implied* by such an assumption obtains;
2 Friedman's main thesis in this paper is in no way substantiated by his three famous examples: these examples could even be used to establish radically opposite conclusions;
3 instrumentalism as a philosophy of the physical sciences is quite different from the 'instrumentalism'[5] that was associated with Friedman's views,[6] which raises different and even more serious problems.

Consequently, to clarify what is really at stake in the debate between realism and 'instrumentalism' in economics, it is useful to introduce a kind of middle way between these two positions frequently and unduly presented in too extreme a fashion.

A controversial thesis

Let us first recall what Friedman's 'most influential thesis' was. More precisely, which one of its not particularly consistent theses was at the core of the debate that interests us? Put in a nutshell, this thesis stipulates that to the question which serves as a sub-title for the third part of the essay 'Can a hypothesis be tested by the realism of its assumptions?', one must answer negatively. It should be clear, however, that this question does not have to be understood too literally, for it is obvious that the realism of assumptions is not sufficient by itself to *test* a hypothesis (or a theory, to employ a more usual parlance).[7] Therefore, it is more appropriate to read this question negatively in the following way: 'can a hypothesis be falsified by the unrealistic character of its assumptions?' A still better way to read it (in order to avoid interference with any eventual objection to the possibility of falsification which would be unrelated to the question of the realism of assumptions) would be: 'should we be concerned with the unrealistic character of the assumptions of a hypothesis which seems to have fairly well tested implications?' This interpretation is clearly suggested by the way the argument is developed in the preceding section of the essay. In this section, Friedman acknowledges that, in social sciences, it is difficult to find 'new evidence' for 'the class of phenomena the hypothesis is designed to explain' – which means evidence that differs from what these phenomena constitute themselves – and to judge whether such evidence really corresponds to the implications of the theory to be tested. This acknowledgment is surely well grounded, but, as Friedman continues, this acknowledged difficulty

> makes it tempting to suppose that other, more readily available, evidence is equally relevant to the validity of the hypothesis – to suppose that hypotheses have not only 'implications' but also 'assumptions' and that the conformity of these 'assumptions' to 'reality' is a test of the validity of the hypothesis *different from* or *additional to* the test by implications.
>
> (Friedman 1953: 14)

Thus, Friedman's thesis on the 'positive' character of a science based on unrealistic assumptions rests on a sharp distinction between assumptions (abstract statements on which the hypothesis is based) and implications (factual statements which derive from the hypothesis) and on the strong contention that empirical tests should bear on implications but not assumptions.[8] According to Friedman, testing 'the validity of the hypothesis' is testing 'by implications', and any attempt to test the so-called assumptions of the hypothesis directly is based on a 'misunderstanding':

> This widely held view is fundamentally wrong and productive of much mischief. Far from providing an easier means for sifting valid from invalid hypotheses, it only confuses the issue, promotes misunderstanding about the significance of empirical evidence for economic theory, produces a

> misdirection of much intellectual effort devoted to the development of positive economics, and impedes the attainment of consensus on tentative hypotheses in positive economics.[9]
>
> (14)

Thus, it is the will to test hypotheses (or theories) by the realism of their assumptions that is responsible for so much 'mischief' and for a 'misdirection of [. . .] intellectual effort'. Hence, Friedman concludes that it does not make sense to be worried about the unrealistic character of the assumptions of a hypothesis that seems to have fairly well tested implications. Consequently, he claims that it would be wise to avoid spending 'much intellectual effort' in attempts to find hypotheses based on more realistic assumptions.

However, the most significant question to be raised in this context is 'what counts either as an assumption or as an implication?' The answer to this question is important because if one can arbitrarily confer the status of an 'assumption' that is not directly testable on an easily falsified 'implication', then what looks like a sound principle might become a dangerous incitement to remain unconcerned with falsifications that should otherwise be disturbing. In fact, by referring to 'the class of phenomena the hypothesis is designed to explain', Friedman explicitly assumes that the set of phenomena that could be considered to be implications can be strictly circumscribed. For example, a theory designed to explain prices and the quantity of goods produced may *assume* profit maximization and have for *implications* that prices and quantity of goods must be such and such. Of course, that the neoclassical price theory was not *designed* to explain the behaviour of entrepreneurs can hardly be contested, but no theoretical conclusion can be derived from this historical fact. And Friedman could hardly contest that, whatever the intentions of its designer, a theory whose *implications* would be contradicted by observable facts would be in trouble.

It is true that philosophers of science sometimes refer to the 'domain of a theory'. For example, it is the case of Alan Musgrave (1981: 380–382) who makes the meaning of restrictions associated with 'domain assumptions' very clear. What Musgrave calls the 'domain of a theory' corresponds exactly to what Karl Popper described as the 'range of application of a theory', which, according to him, defines 'the limits of its applicability'. Thus, in spite of his refutationism, Popper does not hesitate to claim that '[for] instrumental purposes of practical application a theory may continue to be used *even after its refutation*, within the limits of its applicability' (Popper 1963: 113, Popper's emphasis). There is obviously no reason to interdict a scientist from using such a refuted theory to efficiently predict or even explain some phenomena in a particular domain, but this does not allow us to claim that analysing the data that have refuted it is misguided. Musgrave's and Popper's point is obviously not to arbitrarily exclude some of the implications of such a theory from being analysed and tested; it is to *restrict* its useful application to the (possibly rare) situations that it can effectively predict. If physicists found it necessary to exclude the fact that bodies fall to the ground from the domain of a fundamental theory that could predict and explain the motion of the planets, they surely would not consider it misdirection of intellectual effort to investigate why falling bodies would behave so oddly. Why should not economists do the same concerning the behaviour of entrepreneurs, if they really have good reasons to exclude it from the domain of their theory? In fact, it is such an investigation of entrepreneurs' and other economic agents' behaviour that behavioural economists are massively doing today, without being disturbed by Friedman's injunction to avoid such misdirection of intellectual effort.

Before discussing Friedman's position further, it is important to distinguish *contingent* assumptions that limit the generality of a theory, and allow us to see whether this theory is applicable in particular circumstances, from *fundamental* assumptions that play a dynamic role in the theory – that literally 'animate' it, to use Popper's wording (Popper 1985: 358) – such as gravitation in Newton's theory or rationality in economics.[10] To be sure, if 'testing by the realism of assumptions' is interpreted as meaning that, in order to vindicate a theory, one must test whether each of the relatively *contingent* assumptions exactly corresponds to what is going on in the real world, Friedman's position is quite sound, since such tests, useful to determine the applicability of a theory, have little to do with its validity. It is also true that if it means that the *fundamental* assumption of a theory must be independently tested with the help of tests specifically designed for testing it as an assumption, Friedman would be right as well, because any attempt to test such a fundamental assumption will necessarily consist in checking the soundness of at least one of its implications.

There is little doubt indeed that an attempt to *directly* test profit maximization (by directly checking whether entrepreneurs, by the very fact of being entrepreneurs, are endowed with such a fundamental disposition and a fundamental capacity) would be a 'misdirection of intellectual effort'; but if the assumption of profit maximization *implies* that, on the average at least, entrepreneurs should behave in a way that is compatible with maximization, on what ground could one object to testing this kind of *implication*, given that this behaviour is easily observable after all?[11]

Thus, the true question is whether the alleged maximizing behaviour of entrepreneurs should be considered as an implication of the fundamental assumption of rationality-maximization or as the very content of the assumption itself. No doubt Friedman would maintain that the latter option is the correct one, which means that the maximizing behaviour of entrepreneurs is precisely what is assumed. But this is, rather, Friedman's (legitimate) hypothesis and not a fundamental assumption. Similarly, the fact that bodies fall to the ground is not Newton's fundamental assumption, which is gravitation (the fact that, on principle, bodies attract themselves, according to a particular law). If it might be a waste of time to try testing a principle adopted as a fundamental assumption otherwise than by its implications, the same thing can obviously not be said of immediate implications (the free-fall of bodies towards the Earth, and the average behaviour of entrepreneurs) of such a fundamental assumption. It is true that the test of the latter may not affect the application of the hypothesis that Friedman recommends, but it can surely not be discredited by this application, whether successful or not.

In any case, if Friedman means that an alleged principle according to which *actual entrepreneurs* are maximizers can be declared as such a fundamental assumption, which, therefore, would not be directly testable, his position would hardly be defensible. Since it was empirically observed that entrepreneurs are not very efficient maximizers, the question becomes whether it is sensible to assume that what is blatantly contradicted by observable facts were true and to freely grant to such an admittedly false assumption the *foundational* role in a theory. If it is sensible to say that a fundamental assumption cannot be tested other than by its implications, it is tautologically because such an assumption is formulated in such a way that the only way to test it is to look at its implications. An eventual assumption according to which actual entrepreneurs are maximizers *can* be tested *directly* and has already been tested directly but negatively. Assuming this would be like assuming that iron bars float on water and claiming on this basis that this assumption cannot be falsified by the fact that no iron bar can float since an assumption should been tested only by its implications! In fact an implication of such a non-fundamental (and absurd) assumption is that iron bars should float, just as an implication about an eventual assumption claiming that actual entrepreneurs maximize is that entrepreneurs maximize! In both cases, these direct but appropriate tests defeat the assumption of the involved theory in spite of its (unfounded) pretension of being fundamental. Therefore, raising an already empirically falsified claim to the level of a fundamental assumption could no longer draw on the fact that it is only through its implications that it is possible to test a *genuine* fundamental assumption of a theory (such as rationality-maximization or, better, rationality as such), from which everything derives. Now, if we put aside the frequently criticized relation that he establishes between the fruitfulness of a theory and its unrealistic character, which largely rests on a conflation of abstraction and falsity,[12] Friedman does not provide any theoretical argument in support of his apology for assumptions that are, in his own words, 'wildly inaccurate descriptive representations of reality' (Friedman 1953: 14), an apology that is as crucial for him as it is controversial for his commentators. He does not propose any argument to support the idea that empirically contradicted hypotheses, however 'inaccurate' they are as 'representations of reality', could be freely declared *fundamental* assumptions and therefore be free from direct testing, simply because it would be possible with their help to explain 'much by little'.

If the main thesis of this essay has nonetheless been so readily accepted among economists, it is clearly because its three memorable examples strongly suggested that this apparently strange methodological view corresponds more or less to what is going on in the most respected sciences. So, it is time to turn to these three famous examples whose suggestive power was largely responsible for the astonishing influence exerted by Friedman's thesis.

Three examples too quickly celebrated

The first example: the law of falling bodies

The first of Friedman's examples put forward in support of his thesis concerns the physical law of falling bodies. Even though it assumes that the atmosphere is a vacuum, this law is quite satisfactorily applied in many situations where this assumption is contradicted, for example when a stone is falling through the air and not in a vacuum. Indeed, the hypothesis of a vacuum does not correspond to what is actually the case.[13] Therefore, a comparison with the case of perfect competition in economics appears attractive. If, in analysing a situation where competition is imperfect, an economist obtains interesting predictions with the help of a theory that assumes perfect competition, this economist is apparently in a position similar to that of the physicist who uses the law of falling bodies to predict the movement of a falling stone. Thus, Friedman's example was designed to show that a theory (or 'a hypothesis' to use his own wording) might be applied more or less successfully, depending (to a variable degree) on how well the *conditions* are fulfilled. Thus we may safely conclude that a *slightly unrealistic* assumption is not necessarily fatal to a theory's predictions. Seen in this fashion, Friedman's example shows convincingly that we should not reject the theory and its assumptions simply because the latter do not describe the conditions prevailing in the real world in a perfectly realistic fashion. This can easily be admitted, but what challengers maintain is that, from the analysis of this example, it *cannot* be concluded that it is a 'misdirection of intellectual effort' to test how far from perfect competition the real markets are. Indeed, this comparison with the law of falling bodies suggests just the opposite of what Friedman draws from it. Just as testing the air pressure allowed physicists to develop useful knowledge about effects of friction on various falling bodies, which is non-negligible after all, it might be very useful to get more information about the way imperfect competition might modify the predictions of economists regarding prices and quantities.[14]

In any case, the question at stake in the debate raised by Friedman's essay *is* the validity of microeconomic price theory and, typically, the assumption that the debaters usually referred to was not perfect competition as such, but profit maximization. Hence, when the issue at stake is the realism of a fundamental assumption like profit maximization, this example cannot be instructive, because the vacuum is just an antecedent condition and not a *fundamental* assumption of the theory,[15] as many authors have already pointed out (Archibald 1959: 64–65; Nagel 1963: 212; Melitz 1965: 42; Rosenberg 1976: 161–162). Indeed, in contrast with gravitation, the vacuum does not play a dynamic role in the gravitation theory; manifestly, it does not significantly contribute to *explaining* the falling of bodies. Since profit maximization is considered to be a 'fundamental postulate' of neoclassical economic theory, Friedman's example should be adapted to this context. A corresponding example involving falling bodies would have to refer not to a contingent condition like a vacuum, but to a fundamental assumption like universal gravitation. It is true that physicists try to test the law of gravitation by its predictable consequences without being concerned with any allegation about its apparent lack of realism. So, at first glance, Friedman's thesis seems to be vindicated. But suppose that physicists observe that some bodies do not fall to the ground when released at a non-excessive distance from the Earth. As mentioned above, there is no doubt that they *would be concerned* with such a phenomenon, for the law of gravitation entails that, in normal conditions, bodies *have* to fall to the ground. Consequently, they would try to find unusual circumstances (air pressure, centrifugal force, magnetic fields, etc.) that could explain this cumbersome 'exception' to the law of gravitation. They would certainly not be content to conclude that there is no need to worry about it, since the theory satisfactorily predicts phenomena like the tides and the motion of the planets that constitute 'the class of phenomena the hypothesis is designed to explain'. The point is that the movement of unsupported bodies to the ground counts as a banal but necessary *prediction* of the theory; it is not, as such, the fundamental assumption of this theory, since fundamental assumptions must be formulated in much more general terms. Thus, physicists test their theories by their predictions only, but they do not exclude from the class of phenomena to be explained and predicted the most immediate ones like the free-fall of bodies. For them, it would be anti-scientific and arbitrary to ignore these immediate consequences of the theory and be concerned only with a group of so-called predictable and testable implications that they would have determined in advance. If some consequences concerning the tides, the planets, etc. are considered as members of a different class, it is because they were more difficult to explain and more interesting from a theoretical standpoint, and not because they would be the only ones relevant to the validity of the theory at stake.

Revenue maximization is usually considered to be the fundamental postulate of microeconomics. Of course, this theory has to be tested by its consequences rather than by the realism of this assumption; but, *among these consequences*, it seems reasonable to include the fact that, on the average, entrepreneurs should de facto make decisions that reflect their alleged commitment to revenue maximization. If an inquiry reveals that this is not the case, economists cannot simply ignore this fact.[16] How could they justify such a stance? Simply by alleging that their theory was designed to predict only the level of prices and quantities produced? Given that the degree of precision of those predictions can hardly be characterized as highly impressive, this line of defence does not seem very convincing. In any case, physicists do not consider only the tides and the motion of the planets but also the motion of mere falling bodies; why should economists allow themselves to include prices and quantities only and not the average behaviour of entrepreneurs in the set of *testable and significant consequences of their theory?* Even though Friedman does not use this argument, one might answer that the sharp distinction made between changes in prices and behaviour of entrepreneurs could be based on the well known positivist distinction between observable and theoretical terms, but it would be odd to argue that testing the behaviour of entrepreneurs would systematically involve more *theoretical* terms than testing the level of prices.[17] Thus, no matter how this comparison between physics and economics is construed, it clearly shows that, in similar situations, physicists opt for a position which suggests that it is far from being a 'misdirection of intellectual effort' to test *any* aspect of a theory (or to explain with precision any observed discrepancies with it) whenever it is possible.

Naturally, Friedman is perfectly aware of physicists' analysis of the role of factors such as air pressure, but he considers that a theory that includes these factors is a more general but complex one from which the above evoked simple theory of falling bodies is a particular case. He concludes that it is a wasting of time and energy to use the more complex theory if we are happy with the result offered by the simpler one. If such is the case, he is right to say that 'the question under what circumstances the simpler theory works "well enough", as he rightly says, remains important' (Friedman 1953: 18). Indeed, one who is satisfied by the results obtained by neoclassical microeconomics when predicting prices and quantities exchanged going on in the actual economic world may agree with Friedman's recommendation to avoid wasting more time on this problem. But one who considers that it is the aim of any science to improve predictions that are not particularly precise would hardly reject the idea that it *makes sense* to be concerned with the unrealistic character of what Friedman calls the 'assumptions' of a hypothesis, especially when the tests of its acknowledged implications are not that impressive.

The second example: the density of leaves around a tree

Friedman's second example involves 'the density of leaves around a tree'. The argument supposes that this density can be predicted with accuracy with the help of the unrealistic 'hypothesis that the leaves are positioned as if each leaf deliberately sought to maximize the amount of sunlight it receives, given the position of its neighbors' (Friedman 1953: 19). No one would deny that this example illustrates the fact that good predictions may be derived from false assumptions. However, this point had been well illustrated for a long time by the example of various rejected scientific theories that nonetheless allowed scientists to make relatively good predictions, the paradigmatic example of them being Ptolemaic astronomy whose remarkably accurate predictions were based on a false but sophisticated theory (see Kuhn 1957: especially 64–73). In any case, Friedman's example in no way suggests that one who adopts the hypothesis that leaves deliberately sought to maximize the amount of sunlight they receive should not be concerned with the overwhelming evidence according to which leaves cannot 'deliberately seek to maximize'. Otherwise, there would have been no reason for Copernicans to be concerned with the evidence that the Earth was not at the centre of the Universe given that Ptolemaic theory made it possible to derive good predictions with the help of a geocentric postulate.[18]

In any case, Friedman uses his example in a different way and claims that there is no need to postulate that leaves 'deliberately' seek to maximize anything, because we have in fact a 'more attractive' alternative theory. This superior theory explains by a mechanism, which is not unrelated to natural selection,[19] that the surviving leaves have to be precisely those which grow, by pure chance, in the areas which are most exposed to sunlight, which contributes to their expansion. More or less implicitly, it is suggested that a 'more attractive' way to explain the results predicted by economic theory would be to suppose similarly that the surviving entrepreneurs have to be those who, by pure chance, happen to choose a course of action which tends to maximize profits.

Why should this theory be considered superior to the other one that implies 'deliberate maximization'? Friedman's answer is the following:

> This alternative hypothesis is more attractive than the constructed hypothesis not because its 'assumptions' are more 'realistic' but rather because it is part of a more general theory that applies to a wider variety of phenomena, of which the position of leaves around a tree is a special case, has more implications capable of being contradicted, and has failed to be contradicted under a wider variety of circumstances.
>
> (Friedman 1953: 20)

One may think that the essential point for Friedman is that the natural selection theory explains more phenomena (the evolution of species being obviously the most important among them) than the theory of deliberate maximization and is therefore preferable. But, since the theory of maximization also explains a large number of social phenomena (cf. decision theory in economic, but also in military, engineering and even political contexts), it is not clear, at this level of generality, which theory has the larger scope. But why are we nonetheless convinced that a theory based on selection is a more satisfactory theory than deliberate maximization when it comes to explaining the position of leaves around a tree? No doubt it is the fact that, irrespective of the exact number of other phenomena explained by each of these theories, natural selection is compatible with more phenomena related to the phenomenon that is to be explained, namely the position of the leaves around a tree. But, in this example, both theories predict exactly the same facts concerning this position itself, with the exception of those (compatible only with the idea of selection) concerning the fact that leaves *behave* in a totally passive way: indeed, they manifest no sign of being conscious and they have neither a brain nor a reasonably developed nervous system. To use Friedman's pleasant wording, they 'have not been to school and learned the relevant laws of science or the mathematics required to calculate the "optimum" position, and cannot move from position to position' (ibid.: 20). Consequently, were this example taken literally, the superior scope of the theory based on selection over deliberate maximization would be based *strictly on its capacity to account convincingly for the way the leaves actually behave.*

Since the publication of Friedman's paper, many technical objections have been raised against this type of application of the natural selection argument to economic matters.[20] Let us, however, forget these objections for the time being, and consider only what is implied by Friedman's example when it is applied to economics. In this application of natural selection, entrepreneurs succeed in surviving because they have been, by pure chance, actual maximizers in spite of their incapacity and probably their unwillingness to make their decisions by applying maximizing estimations. Instead of consciously maximizing, many of them are rather guided by what Marx and Keynes, after Descartes, characterized as 'animal spirits' or refrain from taking drastic actions required by maximization. Nonetheless, it progressively happens that only those who have turned out to be maximizers in any fashion avoid bankruptcy and actually survive. Since agents will actually maximize according to both a theory based on rationality-maximization and one based on natural selection, the question at stake when it comes to determining which theory is superior is not whether maximization and its consequences for prices occur or not but *why* this maximization obtains. If, as Friedman notes, leaf density is better explained by a theory based on selection than by conscious maximization, it is because the former explains this density without supposing that leaves can do mathematical computations. Similarly, if natural selection is presumed to be a superior theory in economics as well, it is because it explains why people maximize *in spite of* the fact that they are generally unable to take adequate measures to do so, in which it is clearly more satisfactory than a theory such as one based on rationality-maximization that supposes that people maximize when it is admitted that *they are far from doing so*. Thus, it would make sense to regard a theory of natural selection as superior to a theory of deliberate maximization because it would be compatible *not only* with prices and quantities equalizing marginal costs and marginal revenue, *but also* with the actual (more or less erratic) behaviour of most entrepreneurs. Therefore we must conclude that the *behavioural implications*[21] of our assumptions *matter*, and consequently, that it makes sense for someone who has to choose between two theories or between two ways of interpreting a theory, *to be concerned* with what Friedman calls the lack of 'realism of the assumptions' of these theories. If the density of leaves example illustrates anything at all, it illustrates that testing the behavioural implications of a theory can hardly be considered a 'misdirection of intellectual effort'. Indeed, such a test may be the only way to vindicate a potentially more satisfactory theory – such as a 'natural selection' theory that would explain why surviving entrepreneurs are de facto maximizers in spite of their relatively careless behaviour. Thus, concern about an apparent contradiction between entrepreneurs' behaviour and the implications of a theory based on maximization could definitely contribute to advancement in science.[22]

We will see in Chapter 8 that this application of natural selection cannot be so easily accepted as an explanation of microeconomic phenomena, but it might be interesting to see that a more significant example of the importance of being concerned with the lack of realism of the assumptions of a theory can be found in the development of modern genetics. This science proposed a theory that superseded the Mendelian version of heredity theory even though the latter gave fairly good predictions of the statistical phenotype of empirical populations. Mendelian theory, however, assumed the existence of unobservable and apparently non-localizable entities, which are now called genes. Since one may expect that these postulated entities manifest themselves somewhere in the organism, many biologists became concerned with this assumption's lack of realism. It is true that we know now, *ex post*, that Mendelian theory was vindicated by the discovery of chromosomes (where genes have been finally localized) and that, consequently, its postulated entities were not unrealistic; but *ex ante*, they looked almost as unrealistic (while not yet contradicted) as the calculations made by the leaves and the maximizing rationality of economic agents. Moreover, for a number of years after Mendel's theory was proposed, there was no alternative better theory on offer. Thus, had they been convinced by Friedman's injunction against 'misdirection of intellectual effort', modern biologists would have consistently chosen to push aside the putatively unrealistic character of a theory that, after all, permitted predictions far more spectacular than those obtained by contemporary economists. But, *they were concerned* by the lack of realism of these assumptions and thus the discovery of the genetic function of chromosomes and DNA was made possible.

As a last resort, Friedman tends to argue that, in economics, we are still waiting for an alternative theory that could be judged 'superior', and that until we have one, it makes sense to rely on the performance of the standard theory.[23] But obviously, those who are looking for a more satisfactory theory, as modern geneticists did, can never rely on another theory that would be already superior to the one whose shortcomings are bothering them. In any case, if Friedman's idea is that neoclassical economics should not be rejected in the absence of a better theory, he is surely right; but the point is not to reject neoclassical theory, which is a quite valuable instrument for understanding many economic mechanisms, but whether it makes sense to devote much 'intellectual effort' towards looking for an alternative theory that would not be handicapped by the lack of realism of the behavioural *implications* of its fundamental assumption. It is only in this sense that the lack of realism, not of 'assumptions' but of some of their immediate implications, really *matters*. It matters because it concerns a class of implications – related to the behaviour of leaves on a tree, actual actions of average entrepreneurs, localization of genes in the organism, etc. – which in fact might only be predicted by a superior theory. Naturally, the implications, including behavioural implications, of a theory (with a larger scope) could not correspond sufficiently well to what is going on in the actual world without being derived from a somewhat different fundamental assumption. An assumption such as rationality-maximization would have to be replaced by a more 'realistic' one, but this does not imply that it should be subjected to the kind of *direct* 'test of assumptions' that Friedman is right to condemn. This point is illustrated by the case of modern genetics, whose assumptions are somewhat different from those of Mendel's theory, and even by the case of the hypothetical application to economics of natural selection that Friedman presents as a superior theory, but which is also more realistic than maximization. In both cases, indeed, it becomes more and more possible to predict not only the phenomena that were more or less arbitrarily included in the class that 'the hypothesis is designed to explain', but equally *all* those that derive from the reformulated fundamental assumptions of these theories.

The third example: the expert billiard player

Let us now turn to Friedman's last example, the one in which he discusses the behaviour of an expert billiard player:

> It seems not at all unreasonable that excellent predictions would be yielded by the hypothesis that the billiard player made his shots as if he knew the complicated mathematical formulas that would give the optimum directions of travel, could estimate accurately by eye the angles, etc., describing the location of the balls, could make lightning calculations from the formulas, and could then make the balls travel in the direction indicated by the formulas.
>
> (Friedman 1953: 21)

In contrast with the example of the falling body, this example refers to a fundamental assumption of a 'theory' (the 'lightning calculations' of billiards players being understood as an optimization principle that cannot be derived from anything else); and, in contrast with the example of the leaves, it is not a pure fiction concocted in order to be compared to a superior theory. Indeed, it seems reasonable to assume that billiards players let their decisions be guided by at least some intuitively understood mathematical principles.

In any case, there are two obvious differences between the situation of billiards players and the one of economic agents such as entrepreneurs. (1) While the typical entrepreneur might refrain from *profit* maximizing because he might give more importance to some other goals (for example, good relations with employees or customers, desire to have an easy life, etc.), an expert billiard player would never make a decision that is not strictly guided by a maximization objective. Indeed, in contrast with the entrepreneur, it is difficult to see what other objective could overwhelm the latter when he is playing an important game. (2) By insisting on the fact that the billiards player is an 'expert', Friedman chooses not to consider amateur billiards players whose shots might be more difficult to predict by way of a theory based on 'lightning calculations' of 'mathematical formulas'. This is worth mentioning because, as the economy is the result of the actions of all entrepreneurs, not just those who are the most successful, exclusive attention to the expert billiards players might introduce a bias into the comparison.

It is true that the example is only supposed to show that the inability of expert players to use complicated mathematics does not have to be a source of trouble for a theoretician who claims that, *if* the expert's shot is to reach its goal, this player has to hit the ball precisely at the point he would have chosen had he been consciously applying some specific mathematical laws. In itself, however, while quite true, such a claim is almost tautological and totally without consequence, just like the claim made by a physicist that a cannonball follows precisely the path it would have followed, *had it* consciously determined its own path by strictly applying the physical laws about cannonballs! Clearly, the point lies elsewhere. Unlike cannonballs, billiards players and entrepreneurs have goals and they may or may not succeed in reaching them. To claim that expert billiards players maximize in the sense that they are *actually hitting* the ball in the *best* way so as to reach a pocket, we have to rely on a hypothesis, more or less akin to 'natural selection', implying that unsuccessful players (those who do not maximize) are driven away from the pool tables. Similarly, in order to claim that entrepreneurs maximize in this sense, once again we have to rely on a process that is related to 'natural selection' and to admit that it implies that unsuccessful entrepreneurs (those who, more or less unconsciously, fail to take the appropriate actions to maximize) are driven through bankruptcy out of the marketplace.

If we keep in mind that the issue at stake is whether or not it makes sense to be concerned with apparent discrepancies between assumptions and the observed behaviour of entrepreneurs, then our problem is not to decide whether entrepreneurs actually maximize or not. The point is, rather, that the example of the billiards player shows that such concern *makes* sense anyway. Let us illustrate this by considering the two following explanations (depending on the situation observed) that can be invoked to account for the fact that maximization can obtain in spite of non-maximizing behaviour.

Let us first suppose that entrepreneurs are (deliberately or by virtue of 'natural selection') maximizing *just like expert players*; if such is the case we can, thanks to the marginalist theory, expect some success in predicting prices. But why, then, could we not predict the optimal behaviour of the players as well as their optimal results? And how could we not be concerned about our theory if, on the average, a far from optimal behaviour were regularly associated with the optimal results, which were not expected from it? Therefore, if we apply to economics the expert billiards player example, we must conclude that surviving entrepreneurs behave in such a way that prices are predictable *precisely insofar as* their behaviour is equally predictable.

The second possibility is that a large portion of entrepreneurs either do not aim to maximize profits or, like amateur billiards players, do not succeed in maximizing them; then there would be no particular reason to expect better results in predicting prices when assuming rationality-maximization than in tentatively predicting the erratic billiards shooting of amateurs when assuming that they optimally apply mathematical formulas. If, nonetheless, predictions are not seriously affected by the lack of realism of such a maximizing assumption, it might possibly be thanks to statistical compensations or to the workings of a kind of 'natural selection'. On the one hand, one may think that, given a large number of decision makers, mistaken decisions compensate for each other in such a way that average prices (or the pool balls' average positions) can be fairly well predicted. But, if we are right to grant such an efficiency to that statistical compensatory effect, it should not be too difficult to predict the *average* behaviour of entrepreneurs (or of billiards players) as well. But were this average behaviour predictable in this fashion, should one not be concerned by significant discrepancies between the actual and the predicted average behaviour of entrepreneurs (or of billiards players)? On the other hand, if the effect of natural selection is that the unsuccessful decision makers are pushed out of the market (or out of the pool halls), the survivors can be described as (unconscious) *maximizers*. In the case of billiards players, this hypothesis makes it legitimate to expect some success in predicting the final positions of the balls successfully directed in pockets, but, for the same reason, it should be possible to correctly predict the *actual behaviour* of the surviving billiards players and not only the result of their shots. Thus, if predictors observed that a significant number of 'surviving' billiards players were not behaving in the expected way but were hitting the balls in an erratic fashion, they *would have* serious reasons to be concerned by such an unexpected observation. Similarly in economics, with the help of the 'natural selection' hypothesis that implies that non-maximizers will hardly survive, it would be legitimate, according to the neoclassical theory, to expect some success in predicting prices and quantities produced, but why would it be not appropriate to test another *implication* of such an hypothesis as well, which is that most of the entrepreneurs who keep going into competition *do* behave in a maximizing way? And how could we not be concerned about our theory if their observed behaviour sharply contradicted what is expected from this theory? Indeed, applying to economics what is suggested by the import of the expert billiards player example is admitting that surviving entrepreneurs behave in such a way that prices are predictable *precisely because* their behaviour is predictable as well.

Thus, if we use the phrase 'lack of realism' to characterize a discrepancy between the observed behaviour of most entrepreneurs and the implications concerning entrepreneurial behaviour of the fundamental assumption of neoclassical microeconomics, then each of Friedman's examples, when properly reformulated, suggests that we *should be* seriously concerned by such a 'lack of realism'.

Was Friedman an instrumentalist?

If Friedman's essay remained a kind of basic tenet of economic analysis for so long, this was partially due to the fact that it was perceived of as a ticket for freely constructing elegant models unhampered by requirements of realistic assumptions. For many economists of the last half century, a too realist approach of science appeared almost as a threat to this intellectual freedom whose limitation risked reducing economic analysis to an uninspiring descriptive work. Therefore, the idea of rejecting a too demanding realism was well received by them. And, as we have seen, the fact that it was presented by Friedman as congenial to what was done in natural science made it still more welcome. In this context, it is not surprising that, while acknowledging some forgivable clumsiness in Friedman's essay, some participants in the debate, who were more familiar than Friedman with the philosophy of science, were brought to conclude that a rewording of his thesis along 'instrumentalist' lines could vindicate it.[24] Instrumentalism as a methodological approach clearly constitutes an alternative to realism, but in what does it consist? Basically, instrumentalists claim that a scientific theory is an instrument for prediction, but if this approach amounted to that claim only, then all methodologists including realists would probably consider themselves to be instrumentalists. So, one must be more precise and add that only those for whom a scientific theory is *nothing but* an instrument for prediction may be properly considered to be instrumentalists.[25] With this in mind, since it is in debates about physics that instrumentalism is opposed to realism, it will be clarifying to consider the respective attitude of theoreticians of each family when faced with unobservable entities such as those that abound in physics (electrons or neutrinos for example). While sharing with instrumentalists the conviction that these particles play the central role in predicting a large number of phenomena, realists would conclude that, for this very reason (and possibly others), they surely exist in the real world. By contrast, instrumentalists would hold that there is no reason to grant an ontological status to such hypothetical constructs, which can, nevertheless, be referred to as long as it is possible to derive successfully tested predictions merely by proceeding *as if* they exist. Daniel Hausman, who analyses this opposition in more detail (1998: 187–192) cautiously avoids radicalizing it too much, but maintains that the place granted to truth is a key element in distinguishing these views. Therefore, after describing the instrumentalist attitude, he asserts: 'Scientific realists, in contrast, defend a realist thesis about the goal of science – science aims at truth' (ibid.: 190).

Where physics is concerned, this debate about truth divides the two camps mostly when it comes to characterizing the status of the numerous unobservable entities (such as particles, waves, etc.) that are crucially referred to by physicists. Can we say that sentences referring to such entities are true? Realists maintain that they must be true to save the cognitive value of theories, whereas instrumentalists consider that, efficiency rather than truth being the goal of science, they do not need to bother with the requirements of true knowledge. From this point of view, these positions seem radically opposed in such a way that some room is left for an intermediary approach that was introduced by Bas van Fraassen under the name of 'constructive empiricism' (van Fraassen 1980: chapters 1–4). My intention is not to analyse the relation of van Fraassen's type of empiricism with other trends in the philosophy of science, nor is it to extol its virtues, which has been the target of various criticisms[26] that cannot be systematically discussed here. Instead, I want to characterize this position in order to better illustrate the difference between the debate that is going on in physics and the one that Friedman's essay has generated in economics. Concerning the unobservable entities, van Fraassen adopts an agnostic view, which makes his position not easily distinguishable from the one of instrumentalists: according to him, it is not possible nor useful to take a stand on the ontological status of these entities. But concerning the goals of science, while adopting an anti-realist position, he shares with realists the idea that developing correct explanations of phenomena is fundamental in science; therefore, in his view, it is absolutely essential to 'save the phenomena'. Indeed, according to van Fraassen, science should 'save' *all* phenomena – i.e. 'correctly describe what is observable' (ibid.: 4) – and hence account for all of them, at least in principle: a scientist cannot tolerate that some phenomena be systematically betrayed even if it were to increase predictive efficiency.

In spite of Friedman's alleged 'instrumentalism', this description of the debate regarding physics, which involves realists, instrumentalists and constructive empiricists can hardly be directly transposed into the debate generated by Friedman's essay, because it is far from clear that unobservable entities exist in economics.[27] Hausman, who cautiously discusses this question (1998: 196–202), considers the case of preferences and expectations, but observes that, while unobservable in a sense, these entities are not 'new' entities such as those postulated by physics; they are not really different from common-sense entities and, at the most, presented as either preference rankings or subjective probabilities, they are 'merely idealized variations on familiar notions of desire and belief' (ibid.: 199). He then examines a few other candidates such as 'labour value', 'human capital' and 'attributes' and concludes that they are not important enough in economics to justify that an issue parallel to the one involving realism and instrumentalism in physics occupy a significant place in this discipline.

For my part, when I discussed the same issue (Lagueux 1994: 161–162), I considered cases such as a demand function, but it is clear that a demand function, which is essentially a *relation* between potential prices and potential demand, is not an *entity* in the same way that physicists' particles are entities. It might be compared, for example, to a relation defining, at a given moment in time, the gravitational force between two planets. Just as planets are the entities underlying this gravitational force, the agents whose demand is analysed are the entity behind demand functions. Similar considerations can be applied to the case of other functions. While a purely philosophical question could be raised about the existence of functions, a more appropriate candidate might be the stable utility function that Stigler and Becker postulate to explain phenomena like addiction (Stigler and Becker 1977), but this would be a still more marginal and controversial case than those that Hausman proposes.

Thus, it seems almost impossible to find unobservable entities that economists refer to as physicists refer to unobservable particles, but this does not preclude that a corresponding debate takes place in economics with a slightly modified object. A strategy better adapted to a discipline such as economics might look for unobservable *properties* instead of looking for unobservable entities like philosophers of physics do. If this is admitted, there would be room for a dispute between, on the one hand, realists who would maintain that demand or utility functions are real properties existing in some fashion in the brains of consumers and, on the other hand, instrumentalists who would argue that it is a pure waste of time to indulge in such speculations about the existence of these properties, even though they allow us to make accurate predictions of prices or of output level. This is what a potential debate concerning the status of properties in economics would look like, *had it paralleled the debate concerning the status of entities in physics.* On the one hand, realists would defend the real existence of properties associated with any function referred to by economists; on the other hand, instrumentalists would maintain that such commitments are beyond the scope of a science whose essential role is to predict efficiently and to facilitate interventions.

Although debates of this type might occasionally occur among economists, it is doubtful that such an issue could have been judged so intellectually exciting that, more than half a century after being launched in 1953, it is the single object of a book to which some of the most gifted methodologists and historians of economics have contributed (Mäki 2009a). The status of particles may be a question with major implications for subatomic physics, because the precise content of theories in this field depends, to some extent, on the ontological status of entities like electrons. In contrast, one can hardly see how the status of the economic properties evoked above might be so important for economics since it is much more difficult to figure out how the instrumentalist and the realist positions differ when the question at stake is the *ontological status* of the properties of functions such as demand functions. Indeed, it is difficult to see what kind of *existence* a realist would require over and above what would be readily admitted by an instrumentalist, since both of them consider that these functions *correctly describe the relation in question.* In this context, it is so difficult to characterize an instrumentalist stand that clearly differs from the realist one that it seems reasonable to conclude with Hausman that 'there is no anti-realist school of economic methodology' (1998: 208) and that 'every economist is a realist of one kind or another' (ibid.: 209).

Since the debate between realists and instrumentalists, construed as it is when it concerns physics, has so little substance when it concerns economics, one easily suspects that the debate Friedman was engaged in was a very different animal. Let us note first that in the debates considered up to now, whether related to physics or to economics, both sides agree about the usefulness of the *role* played by the unobservable entities or properties, whether particles or functions, in the scientific development involved. Between them, the issue at stake (which is more important for physics than for economics) is the *existence* of the relevant entity (or property). However, in the case of the *actual* debate concerning 'realism' and 'instrumentalism' in economics, the situation is totally different. As is well known, Friedman, who is allegedly the paradigmatic figure of 'instrumentalism' in economics, invoked the views defended in his essay for denouncing most participants of the famous controversies over the marginalist theory of the firm, which were going on in the 1940s (Friedman 1953: 15–16). While these views were somewhat ambiguous, since he did not really take sides in the debate, it became clear to most analysts of the latter that his main target was Lester's radical critique of profit maximization (Lester 1946). According to Lester, the marginalist theoretical apparatus implying profit maximization was incompatible with the result of inquiries about the behaviour of a significant sample of entrepreneurs (for a detailed analysis of this debate, see Mongin 1986a, section IV and V; Mongin 1992; Hausman and Mongin 1997 and Backhouse 2009). While typically being perceived of as the 'realist' counterpart of Friedman's alleged 'instrumentalism', Lester could surely not be called a 'realist' for promoting a realistic interpretation of any entity (or property) used by microeconomists in their analysis. On the contrary, if he is at all a 'realist', this is because he flatly rejects the *relevance* of the use of such theoretical concepts. We have seen that in order to reject the idea that the existence of preferences, expectations or other mental structures such as functions was contested by members of an alleged instrumentalist school in economics, Hausman invoked the fact that these notions do not really differ from common-sense entities. Indeed, only radical physicalists or eliminativists really contest the existence of such entities, but even if some economists were defenders of these views, they would hardly be characterized as 'instrumentalists' in the sense that is supposed to characterize Friedman's approach. In any case, it is clearly common sense that guided Lester – whose approach obviously need not be endorsed for the present argument to be valid – in his contestation of the *relevance* of maintaining the theoretical apparatus associated with marginalism, which was blatantly unable to give a realistic picture of the way prices and output depend on the behaviour of economic agents. In contrast, 'instrumentalists' inspired by Friedman are those who claim that this theoretical apparatus, in spite of its blatant lack of realism, is perfectly relevant insofar as it helps in making useful predictions. As we have seen, Friedman would not deny the lack of realism of this theoretical apparatus, since he has readily admitted that 'important and significant hypotheses will be found to have "assumptions" that are wildly inaccurate descriptive representations of reality' (Friedman 1953: 14). That does not mean, however, that he would be inclined to contest the *existence* of any economic entity or property. From this point of view, Uskali Mäki is surely right to present him as a realist (Mäki 2009c).

Nonetheless, the divide between Friedman's and Lester's respective positions is large and it should not just be forgotten. Thus, it might be useful to introduce a middle position between them that can save what seems acceptable and could hardly be rejected in each of their views, just like van Fraassen's constructive empiricism has proposed a way to save what was judged acceptable and worthwhile to maintain in the respective theses of realists and instrumentalists in physics. Whatever name should be given to such a middle position, it should share with constructive empiricism an absolute commitment to save all phenomena. This does not mean that it would require establishing the whole truth regarding these phenomena, but it would require considering all those that are of some consequence for economics, and – to use Mäki's phrases (2009c: 97–99) – to make sure to say 'nothing but the truth', while not the 'whole truth', about them. Defenders of this middle position *would* be concerned with the discrepancy between the behaviour of the entrepreneurs and the assumptions of the theory, or, if one prefers, by what Friedman dubs the lack of 'realism' of these assumptions. Thus, from this point of view, such a position is undoubtedly close to a realist one. However, this middle position shares with Friedmanian 'instrumentalism', not an agnosticism about entities or properties, since this has nothing to do with this type of 'instrumentalism', but, rather, a firm conviction regarding the appropriateness of using *unrealistic* theoretical apparatuses that are useful either as instruments for prediction or as heuristic devices. While being far from considering attempts to directly analyse the behaviour of entrepreneurs as a 'misdirection of … intellectual effort', its adepts would, nonetheless, agree with Friedmanians on the *relevance* of developing a useful theory that is based on assumptions whose implications might be contradicted by the observed behaviour of economic agents, at least until a superior theory can be developed. On this point, this middle position may part with van Fraassen's constructive empiricism, which would not make room for a theory that contradicts some observable phenomena so easily. However, it is in order to adapt itself to the debate going on in economics and to the limitations of economic theory building that this middle position acknowledges the heuristic virtues associated with Friedmanian 'instrumentalism'.

Thus this middle position is not a simple application of constructive empiricism to economics, but in order to better distinguish it from both Lesterian realism and Friedmanian 'instrumentalism', it might be useful to take the reverse way and to illustrate how it can itself be applied to a situation pertaining to physical sciences. This situation will be purely imaginary since it must be designed in such a way that it reflects exactly what is involved in the situation that has generated the debate between realism and 'instrumentalism' in economics, instead of reflecting an actual debate regarding physics. Suppose the only known way of precisely predicting the observed motion of the planets is by constructing a theoretical model according to which the planet 'Earth' is totally composed of magnetized iron. In such a situation, the significant question would not be the one concerning the *existence* of such an iron-entity, which has little to do with the actual Earth, because this issue would not be at stake given that no one, and the realists less than anyone else, would be prepared to defend the existence of this magnetized iron ball to which the Earth is supposed to be reduced. It would be, instead, the methodological question of knowing whether it is *relevant* to proceed just *'as if'* modelling the Earth by way of an imaginary iron-entity were fully justified, in such a way that any concern raised by the lack of realism of such a model is 'misdirected'. To this question, Friedmanian 'instrumentalists' would answer 'yes', after claiming that it would be a sheer waste of time to question and discuss the existence of such an entity as long as the model is the best available instrument for predicting the motion of the planets. In contrast, realists of all types would readily answer 'no' and would be shocked by the absence of concern for lack of realism. As for the adepts of the middle position, they would say – just like constructive empiricists would – that resorting to such an entity is not acceptable because it obviously implies that this theory is incapable of saving phenomena such as the chemical heterogeneity and the relatively weak electromagnetic field of the Earth. That is why their position would differ from that of the Friedmanian 'instrumentalists'. However, they would agree with the latter on the *relevance* of accepting the theory in question only for predicting the position of planets and for its possible heuristics advantages. By taking this position, they would not remain faithful to constructive empiricism as they would if the only available (hypothetical) theory had invoked mysterious unobservable and undetectable particles surrounding the planets. In this case, indeed, constructive empiricists would have had no more problem than the adepts of this middle position in accepting such a theory insofar as it saved all the (observable) phenomena, even though they would have remained agnostic with regards to the existence of these particles.

What will probably help us to understand the meaning of what I called the middle position much more than this fanciful story about fictional physics is the fact that this position was adopted by economists who are involved in the 'behavioural economics' programme. These economists are particularly reluctant to accept Friedman's injunction to avoid wasting their time in analysing entrepreneurs' and other economic agents' behaviour. Those who have developed experimental economics and their successors who have generalized a programme devoted to analysing all aspects of economic behaviour do not hesitate to acknowledge and document the fact that the rationality of economic agents is far from the rationality-maximization or rationality-consistency of neoclassical models. However, many (possibly most) of them continue to respect these models as useful heuristic instruments that may help them to make predictions – maybe not as accurately as Friedman's essay suggests – and, still more, to understand the (idealised) mechanisms involved in economic activity.

What should we conclude?

It is true that Friedman's paper is rich enough in suggestive ideas to have been interpreted in a great number of inconsistent fashions. It is even true that some of these interpretations might be considered much closer to the middle position whose merits I have emphasized. I readily admit that, in the present analysis of Friedman's contribution, I have possibly overemphasized the passages about the 'misdirection of intellectual effort' and the alleged virtues of 'wildly inaccurate' assumptions. But the point of this discussion was not to propose, after so many predecessors, a more correct interpretation of Friedman's thought, but rather to explain why a debate about an issue as important as the fundamental assumption of economics – namely the rationality principle, whatever way it is understood – was so confusing and inconclusive. In fact, I emphasized these passages because this debate focused spontaneously on the most *provocative* aspect of Friedman's ideas that has frequently been presented more or less in the following way: 'false assumptions being potentially fruitful for science, concern about their falsity is a misdirection of intellectual effort'. Economics being a science whose respectability is constantly endangered, this extreme form of Friedman's thesis was particularly welcomed among economists because it was seen as providing a complete safeguard against the multiple objections that raise doubts about the seriousness of a science whose assumptions' behavioural implications have been repeatedly falsified. Since the methodology of economics has constantly been developed with an eye to the methodology of physics, Friedman's approach was, somewhat equivocally, associated with the instrumentalism as understood in philosophy of physics, and it gained a temporary credibility by being confused with an instrumentalism whose case against realism seemed to be better grounded. Given the place occupied by this confusing association, I found it worthwhile to pay some attention to the somewhat artificial debate opposing 'instrumentalism' to realism in economics.

Of course, a more generous reading of Friedman's ambivalent essay (and of his followers' papers) was possible, but it is doubtful that more palatable versions of its main thesis would have been received with the same enthusiasm by the economic community. Indeed, a more generous and better-equilibrated interpretation should present as essential to the development of a scientific enterprise both a complete freedom in constructing theoretical entities *and* a commitment to save all the phenomena. It was the will to save all the phenomena that induced realists like Lester to challenge a bit awkwardly, a boldly constructive economic theory. It was the will to protect the rights of theory from such a challenge that induced Friedman and most of his followers to literally discourage theoretical attempts to 'save' *behavioural* phenomena. If this methodological debate has lasted for so long – with repeated suggestions for construing each thesis in a manner which alleviates their mutual opposition – it is apparently because economists, while convinced of the necessity of being both theoretically constructive and empirically devoted to save all phenomena, have not yet found a satisfactory way to simultaneously fulfil these two scientific goals.

In any case, the net effect of privileging such a more generous reading would be, by forgetting Friedman's apparent objections to this move, to stimulate research aiming to test these behavioural implications, as behavioural economists have systematically done for a few decades in spite of the limited enthusiasm of certain economists towards experimentations in which the influence of psychologists is too manifest. And more importantly, this move would require, in order to be consistent with this reorientation, a reformulation of assumptions in a more appropriate wording. Since most developments in economic analysis assume one form or another of the rationality principle, it seems reasonable to maintain rationality as the fundamental assumption, but to forget the idealization of this notion in which it is a mechanical maximization or an inflexible consistency that stands for human rationality. Why not, instead, assume that people are rational, not in the sense of being maximizing machines, but in the sense of having just the level of rationality that is required to animate an economic model? As we have seen, even if we maintain the role of economic models, this level is relatively minimal; it corresponds, for example, to the degree of rationality required to induce people to usually choose obtaining more rather than less revenue (or any good) when all costs involved clearly seem to be smaller than the gains realised by such a choice.

Note that relinquishing the notion of maximal rationality would not exclude the development of formalistic models with the help of tools such as calculus and matrix algebra, whose heuristic value is indisputable. While not particularly realistic, these models allow us, nonetheless, to clearly figure out the main features and the principal forces involved in actual economic phenomena. Those who designed general equilibrium models, for example, were not pretending to give an exact picture of an equilibrium that would be realized in typical markets. They contented themselves with revealing with great precision the workings of a mechanism capable in principle of generating an equilibrium and with determining the proper way of fully analysing it.

However, if economists aim, like Friedman did, to construct a really 'positive' science, then they cannot disregard a contradiction between the actual behaviour of economic agents and the behavioural implications of their theory, any more than physicists can disregard an eventual contradiction between the 'behaviour' of falling bodies and the implications of their theory, whatever success they might have in predicting tides and the motion of the planets. In this context, invoking minimal or moderate instead of maximal rationality, while possibly making the matter a little more complicated, would make possible the development of a theory whose *implications*, including the behavioural ones, would be compatible with observed facts. With a theory based on such an understanding of rationality, all phenomena including entrepreneurs' behaviour might be saved, in such a way that usual allegations of incompatibility between observed behaviour of economic agents and behavioural implications of the theory would no longer have any object. Nonetheless, with such an approach, free model construction of economic conditions would remain perfectly legitimate since minimally rational agents can easily do the job that they usually have to do in economic models. Thus, Friedman's justified opposition to the paralysing consequences of a stubbornly 'realistic' rejection of bold theoretical construction would be without object as well. Moreover, the foolish idea of designing *specific tests* for directly testing fundamental assumptions as such should also be forgotten. Indeed, it would be preposterous to look for ways of testing whether people are moderately rational other than by checking *implications* of this assumption in specific conditions, such as the fact that entrepreneurs generally behave in a particular fashion *or* that prices tend to move in pre-determinate ways, just as it would be preposterous to look for ways of testing universal gravitation other than by checking implications of this assumption in specific conditions, such as the fact that bodies generally fall with a given acceleration *or* that planets tend to move in pre-determinate ways.

Moreover, such an economic theory would be perfectly adapted to most explanations of past economic situations provided by economists, since when it comes to explaining – necessarily after the fact – something that happened in the actual world, economists never refer to maximal rationality or to perfect consistency. Rather, they refer to the fact that economic agents act rationally, but according to their own (non-optimal) view of what is appropriate to do in a given circumstance (for example selling stocks in a context of panic after a sharp fall in stock prices or selling a good as soon as its price starts to rise). Such is the kind of rationality that should be assumed if it is true that economic theory can hardly be developed without relying on the rationality principle. But is it really necessary to assume rationality at all? This is the question that will be discussed in the next chapter.

7 Explaining in the absence of rationality

For most economists, sociologists and political scientists, the name Gary Becker is closely associated with a bold and highly controversial generalization of an approach typical of neoclassical economists to every field of the social sciences. The fact that this approach was clearly based on the principle of *rationality* possibly explains that Becker's provocative 1962 paper published in the *Journal of Political Economy* under the title 'Irrational Behavior and Economic Theory' (Becker 1962) has been relatively neglected by economists and nearly forgotten a short time after publication. Yet, this paper proposed a very unusual and ingenious approach to the most fundamental questions concerning the very status of microeconomic theory. Some methodological implications of Becker's answers to these questions were discussed by Israel Kirzner in a strongly critical response published a few months later in the same journal (Kirzner 1962). Unconvinced by Kirzner's arguments, Becker issued a short reply (Becker 1963), which was matched by Kirzner's rejoinder (Kirzner 1963). These new contributions allowed both authors to clarify their respective positions, but the two were still totally at variance with one another when the debate seemed to come to an abrupt end.[1] Fourteen years later, when Becker reprinted his original paper in his *Economic Approach to Human Behavior* (Becker 1976: 153–168), he did not judge it worthwhile to mention this earlier (inconclusive) controversy, nor to explain how this apology for irrationality found its place in a book devoted to applying an analysis based on rationality to almost every kind of human behaviour.

In the present chapter, after recalling the essential elements of this debate, I attempt to show that even though the debate seemed to bear on a rather technical question, namely the possibility of substituting irrationality for rationality in equilibrium theory,[2] it actually concerned the meaning, the status and the role of the concept of rationality in economics, and consequently the very foundations of economic theory. I do not intent to analyse this debate for itself, but I consider that it is worthwhile to follow the main lines of each protagonist's arguments, and even a few intricacies involved in them, because the clarification of this controversy constitutes an excellent point of departure for an analysis of the more general questions evoked above. Incidentally, the analysis of the equivocal nature of this debate should also help us to understand why it had to be aborted.

An atypical debate quickly aborted

Like Milton Friedman, his fellow economist at the University of Chicago, Becker aimed to contribute through his intervention to neutralizing objections frequently raised against the role of rationality understood as maximization in neoclassical microeconomic theory (Becker 1962: 13). According to Becker's paper, objections of those who rejected as unrealistic and arbitrary the economists' way of relying on an idealized rationality were far from being as damaging as their authors believed for microeconomic theory because the most important theorems of the latter can be demonstrated even if one supposed agents to behave in totally *irrational* ways. To establish this point, Becker first characterized irrational behaviour as either 'impulsive' or 'inert', depending respectively on whether (irrational) agents were typically making decisions at *random* or always mechanically making the *same* decisions no matter how the parameters of the situation might change. If both types of behaviour are said to be 'irrational', it is obviously because they are totally unresponsive to changes in the situation. Next, Becker claimed that constraints imposed by their budget line will restrict such impulsive or inert consumers' choices to those that are possible in the context of the new opportunity set made available to them after any change in price. With the help of the usual tools of economic analysis, he maintained that this fact implies that 'regardless of the decision rule used' the average behaviour of these consumers must be reflected in a negatively sloped demand curve. Indeed, if the price of a good significantly increases, some irrational consumers might no longer have the opportunity to buy as much of this good as they could when the price was lower. They will be forced to buy less of it and, on the average, to turn towards less expensive goods that are still in their opportunity set, a move whose consequence is that the demand curve for this good will still be downward sloping in spite of the irrationality of these consumers.[3] By following a similar line of argument, Becker also established that other theorems of economics would hold without any reference to rationality. For example, in a monopoly situation, impulsive or inert entrepreneurs will be forced to reduce their output, just as rational entrepreneurs would, according to the standard theory (Becker 1962: 11).

Kirzner did not directly object to Becker's ingenious model, but he unequivocally contested its significance. According to Kirzner, 'the important theorems of economics [in his mind, the theorems explaining market prices] cannot be extracted without first introducing some assumptions of rationality in an essential way' (Kirzner 1962: 380). For Kirzner, demand curves are of little interest if they do not help to solve the problem of market prices. But, according to him, market prices result from *'the systematic way in which plan revisions are made as a consequence of the disappointment of earlier plans'* (ibid.: 381, Kirzner's emphasis). Because such disappointments and plan revisions are excluded when we refer to impulsive or inert consumers, there is no reason to think that a disequilibrium price will be corrected by irrational agents.

In his short reply to Kirzner, Becker answered this objection by slightly rephrasing his earlier argument (Becker 1963: 83). Concerning the producers, for example, this argument was based on the idea that the (irrational) suppliers would be price-setters, and that, whatever the prices decided by them, they would *sooner or later* be put on the right track by a force comparable to the one budget lines exert on irrational consumers. Indeed, their choices would be constrained by what Becker calls a 'production opportunity set', which corresponds to the 'region of non-negative profits', the idea being that these irrational producers are forced to set prices corresponding to this region because otherwise they would not survive since 'all the resources at their disposal would be used up' (Becker 1962: 10).

In his rejoinder, Kirzner restated his essential objection and claimed that by being unable to experience disappointment, irrational consumers or producers would have, strictly, no reasons to modify their decisions (Kirzner 1963: 85). Now, Kirzner was surely right to say that nothing can bring irrational agents to modify their way of deciding, whatever happens to these opportunity sets, but Becker's approach was crucially based on the 'distinction between group or market and individual responses' (Becker 1962: 13). The group response being an *average* response, if the opportunity set is displaced, due either to a 'change in cost or demand conditions' or to 'cartelization' (ibid.: 11), more suppliers, on the average, will be forced by the conditions for survival to set their output level and their prices inside the limits of this moving opportunity set, just like rational suppliers would do (Becker 1962: 10–11 and 1963: 83). Thus, Becker's argument significantly relies on the 'survival argument' (Becker 1962: 10) that was invoked previously by Armen Alchian (1950) and by Milton Friedman (1953) in order to suggest that a selection mechanism can generate a situation very similar to that which would normally have resulted from rational decisions. In Becker's construal of it, only the decisions that fit the requirements of the opportunity set will tend to influence the average price level; indeed, by virtue of the definition of this opportunity set, the decisions that do not fit its requirements would generate negative profits and ultimately provoke the bankruptcy of the suppliers who make them, in such a way that, after some time, such decisions would no longer be implemented. Consequently, on the average, the prices set by the surviving firms will tend to be closer to the equilibrium level, no matter how irrational their price-setting decisions would be.

As was sometimes underscored, an essential proviso to this argument concerns the long run. Biologists know that the natural selection argument is only valid in the very long run, and while bankruptcies are probably more frequent than extinctions of animal species, they too require a considerable length of time before significantly influencing the overall situation. Because a market equilibrium price is normally considered a short-term phenomenon, this proviso seems very damaging to Becker's argument. If we are interested in a short-term phenomenon, why should we care about an equilibrium price that could only be attained in a very artificial situation in which conditions of production and other relevant parameters are rigidly fixed over a long enough period to let a significant number of firms go bankrupt? If Kirzner did not give serious attention to Becker's survival argument, it was precisely because he interpreted this argument not as an actual way of eliminating wrong-headed price-setters in the long run, but as a simple threat that would force these price-setters in the short run to adopt more appropriate prices (cf. Kirzner 1963: 85). Insofar as such a course of action is not open to Becker's impulsive or inert fellows, who are indifferent to threat, Kirzner flatly denied the relevance of a survival argument. According to Kirzner, Becker's model would fail because the assumption of irrationality does not allow agents to revise today's plans, as rational fellows would do after having been 'chastened by yesterday's grim market experience' (ibid.: 85). Becker thinks that the effect of the survival mechanism is to systematically discount any irrational decisions too dissimilar to those that would have been rationally taken by someone chastened in such a way, but this might be true only in the long run. Therefore Kirzner observes that in Becker's model nothing permits us to think that today's decisions need be systematically different from those of yesterday. Given that 'in the long run we are all dead' to recycle Keynes' famous dictum, one may legitimately be tempted to disqualify a model that works efficiently only in the long run, and to conclude that there is no need to push the discussion any further.

From another point of view, however, it can be argued that the proviso about the long run does not so seriously weaken Becker's argument. In a theory attempting to show that we can dispense with the fundamental postulate of economics when it comes to establishing some of its fundamental theorems, it is surely not extravagant to ask that we suppose also that the length of time does not matter. Indeed, no one would expect irrational agents unintentionally to reach a particular result as quickly as rational agents. The question is not who would normally win a race between rational and irrational competitors, but whether any trend exists which systematically will tend to push irrational agents in the same direction that rational agents would normally take. It is true that Becker's argument supposes the parameters of the situation to remain stable over an unrealistically long period, but this was also the case for some strictly logical arguments developed by Ricardo, Walras and by many other pure theoreticians. In any case, my point is not to counter the many well founded objections to the usefulness of such 'long run' models but, for the sake of pure theory, to understand the nature of Becker's argument before discussing it for what it is.

Can Becker's 'survival argument' survive?

But is Becker's argument logically acceptable even in the long run? In his brief but thoughtful considerations about this debate, Richard Langlois (1986: 237–240) maintains that Becker's argument suffers from serious difficulties, even if we take it to be applied over a sufficiently long period. Langlois refers to two problems. The first concerns what is implied by a bankruptcy, a notion that must be reinterpreted when it concerns the venture of irrational entrepreneurs. Langlois observes that since a bankruptcy supposes various rational moves on the part of creditors, stockholders, etc., one may conclude that the rationality which is eliminated from entrepreneurial behaviour in Becker's model is pushed 'back one stage into the process of bankruptcy' (ibid.: 239, n. 13). Of course, a complete Beckerian argument would suppose a careful discussion of financial behaviour to show how impulsive and inert decisions on the part of creditors and stockholders would also push towards bankruptcy those creditors (or stockholders) who inertly or randomly lend to (or invest in) firms which themselves set prices too high or too low. But since the present considerations aim to question the relevance of Becker's argument for economics even if it worked perfectly, we may suppose for the sake of simplicity that we are in a world without credit and that all firms are completely owned by their managers. Moreover, we may suppose that, for these totally irrational people, going bankrupt means nothing more than no longer having enough money to make the deals which might turn out to be profitable, and therefore being forced to stop playing the market game. For example, a firm would go bankrupt in the sense that it must shut down because, due to its incapacity to sell at an appropriate price, it can no longer get the financial resources to buy what is required for continuing production.

The second difficulty underlined by Langlois might be more damaging. It implies that Becker's argument would collapse in the case of impulsive firms. In fact, Langlois' objection is exposed in little more than one single line of a footnote: 'if the behavior of the firm is truly random, there will be no systematic tendency for the pricier firms to go bankrupt first' (ibid.: 239, n. 13). It might be useful, however, to present the important distinction made here between the respective cases of inert and impulsive price setters in a slightly different way. It is true that Becker's discussion of a situation in which the price was set too high is more easily handled in the case of inert firms than in the case of impulsive ones. In the former case, the pricier firms will continue to set prices too high indefinitely and will be doomed to be the first to go bankrupt, leaving on the market only those firms that happen to stick to more realistic prices. In the latter case, in which prices are set at random, the situation is different because the future pricing decisions of the firms which have randomly made wrong decisions could randomly turn out to be safer. It is not totally true, however, that there would be 'no systematic tendency for the pricier firms to go bankrupt first'. Indeed, if by 'pricier firms' we refer in this case to the firms that had randomly maintained a record of overpricing in the past, it may make sense to say that they would have suffered heavier losses up to now. Thus, they *would be* more threatened with bankruptcy, even though this would not be inevitable since more reasonable prices might randomly turn out to prevail. Moreover, even though it is true that we cannot say that firms that have randomly set their prices either too high or too low will tend to go bankrupt first, it is sufficient to vindicate Becker's claim that firms that, by pure chance, usually set prices which turn out to be more appropriate (as made manifest *ex post*) stay in business longer.

Thus Langlois' objection cannot be taken literally. Nonetheless, the problem for Becker's argument is that if natural selection rewards the firms that have the most realistic pricing record, the rewarded firms are *not* more likely (as evaluated *ex ante*) than the eliminated ones would have been to price realistically in the next round. If the decision is 'truly random' as Langlois insists, each round is independent and there is *no relation at all* between the decisions to be taken in the future and the decisions that have been taken in the past by a given firm. Thus, the elimination of the most erratic firms will be of no help, *even in the long run*, if the point is to arrive at more realistic prices, meaning at prices approaching an equilibrium price. Natural selection would not improve anything when it comes to the impulsive deciders. The latter being totally unable to learn from their 'grim market experience' to use Kirzner's phrase, it seems that Langlois is correct in his assertion that Becker's model would not work at least in the case of impulsive behaviour.

Although such a conclusion is well grounded, it is not as damaging to what Becker aimed to show as might be thought. The problem with Becker's impulsive price setters lies in the fact that a random model will never meet the requirements of natural selection. In biological organisms, mutations occur randomly, but once they have occurred, the genetic configuration they have produced tends to remain stable in successive generations. Otherwise, there would be no particular feature of a population to be selected by natural selection. This means that natural selection requires some stability, even though it obviously does not require rationality. Thus, since Becker's thesis is that the postulate of rationality is not required to obtain an equilibrium price, I suggest slightly modifying his model in a way that will not make it more reliant on rational behaviour. When modelling irrational agents, Becker chose to describe them as impulsive or inert because these types correspond to the two extremes of a continuous spectrum in which intermediates were expected to be the most frequent cases. Thus, as acknowledged by Becker himself (1962: 5), the set of irrational agents is not made up of two well defined types, but is rather a mixture of inert, impulsive and intermediate cases. In a model modified in an appropriate way, natural selection might operate and select those price setters who *inertly* stick to a *randomly* chosen price that turns out to reduce the chances of bankruptcy because it would by pure chance be close enough to a profit maximizing price and consequently to an equilibrium level.

It must be admitted however that such a model would be valid only in a still longer time frame, since enough time has to be allowed not only for the bankruptcy of those who inertly maintain inappropriate prices but also for the bankruptcy of those who impulsively set prices which too often turn out to be equally inappropriate. Bankruptcy would normally take more time to occur in the latter cases, because non-adapted prices might be randomly followed by better-adapted ones frequently enough to significantly delay its occurrence. But such a mixed model would have to face a still more difficult problem involving, this time, more specifically the inert behaviour. As has been forcefully argued by Sydney Winter (Winter 1964: 240), the problem with such a model based on selection is that it describes a process that, through the expansion of successful firms and extinction of some other ones, constantly modifies the economic environment and consequently the frontiers of the Beckerian opportunity set. Thus, there is no reason to think that a maximizing behaviour at time t, which is indefinitely repeated by its surviving 'inert' initiator, would still be a maximizing behaviour at time t + n. Nevertheless, the situation is not hopeless for Becker's thesis if one admits that the essential question is to check whether an equilibrium-clearing price could be obtained or at least approached. Indeed, if we assume that all clearly erratic price setters have plenty of time to disappear from the market and if the process continues thereafter with inert survivors and, moreover, if we assume that the latter, given their inertness, contribute little to modifying the economic environment and finally that such modifications are no longer caused by bankruptcies which, by hypothesis, no longer occur, it becomes conceivable that the mechanical trading of inert survivors mimics to a closer and closer degree what might be a clearing price. Of course, we may suppose that new irrational firms might enter the market during this period and modify the economic environment in this fashion. However, if we consider that they would replace sets including only the erratically pricing firms that have gone bankrupt, one can think that the successive sets of firms on the market, which includes both surviving and new firms, will comprise less and less erratic firms. If such is the case, trading being less erratic on the average, the wide changes in economic environments resulting from erratic moves and bankruptcies might be more and more overweight by the steady working of the inert survivors and might generate prices moving closer and closer to some equilibrium point.

It is true that these somewhat extravagant assumptions and considerations bring us further and further from a realistic analysis of an actual economic behaviour, but the point is not whether Becker's model can correctly describe a human economy; the point is whether the irrational automata (having, in fact, relatively little in common with human beings) that are freely created in order to mechanically animate this model can produce a result relatively similar to the one that is assumed to be reached in a model animated by rational *homines oeconomici.* It would in itself be a theoretically interesting result to establish that, in a closed economic world, if certain parameters are kept fixed over an unrealistically long period of time, a trend towards an equilibrium price might possibly obtain, even if all agents behaved in totally irrational ways. It is doubtful whether Becker wanted to prove much more than this. It would be odd, indeed, to maintain that his intention was to describe the actual behaviour of a human society. Such an intention was apparently so far from Becker's real objective that, in his *Economic Approach to Human Behavior*, this theoretical exercise on the implications of irrationality was reprinted amidst a number of chapters that emphasize the crucial role of rationality in a generalization of the economic mode of explanation for any type of human behaviour. Thus, Becker's argument is not as irrelevant as Kirzner, Langlois and Winter seems to suggest; it is rather a purely theoretical discussion referring to a highly artificial long run situation which has very little to do with actual economic societies, but whose content, after all, is no more artificial than many other ones that are required by less instructive theoretical models devised by economists.

The real debate: rationality *versus* mechanism

But in what sense should we consider it particularly interesting that, *however it may work*, a model of behaviour was designed without requiring any postulate of rationality? Perhaps the answer can be obtained by considering the domain in which a selection mechanism has permitted scientists to eliminate all references to teleological considerations. Darwin's argument based on natural selection allowed him to explain species evolution without invoking finality or intentionality. Likewise, applying a similar mechanism to an economy allows Becker to explain the (unrealistic) genesis of a relatively stable equilibrium without invoking the notions of finality and intentionality, which rationality implies. However, even if we took it for granted that the mechanism works as efficiently in economics as in biology, the essential question is whether it is really advantageous to avoid references to finality or to intentionality in such a way. It was clearly so in biology because any *intentional* explanation of evolution implies a reference to a Creator's intentions, whereas, in contrast with theology, science claims to account for natural phenomena without resort 'to this hypothesis', to use Laplace's parlance. But, as was sometimes pointed out by Hayek, even though the elimination of any reference to God's intentions clearly improves the scientific understanding of biological evolution, it is far from clear that an analogous elimination of references to *human* intentions improves our understanding of *human* behaviour. After all, whereas so many people deny the very existence of a Creator acting intentionally, very few, if any, deny the existence of human beings acting intentionally. It is true that the highly unrealistic assumptions of rationality-maximization or of rationality-consistency were the target of harsh objections, but, as we have seen, intentional action invoked in explanations of economic phenomena requires no more than moderate or even minimal rationality. Thus, it is reasonable to ask: what is gained by claiming or even establishing that there is no need to refer to the 'hypothesis' that human beings can act rationally, at least in the realistic sense which does not imply exceptional human powers?

As an explanation of markets involving *human* beings, Becker's model is needlessly complicated, since it painfully manages to eliminate an essential and perfectly acceptable component (rationality) of the phenomenon to be explained. Moreover, it is unrealistic since it explains only in the very long run what is essentially a short run phenomenon and treats as relatively static what is essentially a dynamic phenomenon. Thus, Becker's model is merely the interesting result of an exercise in mechanical simulation of human behaviour. Just as Irving Fisher, Kenneth Boulding and A.W. Phillips devised hydraulics models of economic phenomena,[4] so Becker devised a model of such phenomena that involves only irrational agents whose 'actions' could, without any loss, be replaced by the motions of a machine working either repetitively or randomly. When the issue is recast in this manner, the fact that Becker's model works only in the long run is not very damaging for it since time does not really count with such mechanical apparatuses. Or, more exactly, time can be stretched or contracted almost at will.

When a computer simulates human action, we regard it as immaterial that it has to pass through an 'unrealistic' number of operations before reaching a very simple result, since the time required to do these operations is regularly and dramatically reduced by technology from decade to decade. So a physical version of Becker's model could surely be constructed with repetitive or random buying mechanisms and price-setting machines. This apparatus might be designed with a structure such that price-setting machines would collapse when, after too frequent input–output deficits, their reserve of a money simulacrum became empty. There is no reason to rule out the possibility that such a complex apparatus, properly designed, would tend towards an 'equilibrium price'. Once rationality (with the finality and the intentionality that it implies) is totally excluded from a model in which allegedly human agents are involved, this model cannot be distinguished from a purely physical model, whether using the resources of hydraulics, standard mechanics, electricity or electronics. Understandably enough, mechanization is the price that must be paid for successfully eliminating the non-mechanical components of human behaviour! The question of whether such a mechanical model really can be a useful element in the *explanation* of human behaviour is another issue and, I suggest, the real issue that divides Kirzner and Becker.

In fact, Becker does not pretend to have 'shown that all the market implications of rational behavior would be reproduced by all or most irrational behavior' (Becker 1963: 83). And Kirzner underscores that his argument 'does not, in any way affect Becker's demonstrations' concerning the possibility for 'a market of irrational buyers' to react systematically to price changes, and for 'the cartelization of a group of irrational producers' to reduce output systematically (Kirzner 1963: 85, n. 5). It is not even clear that Kirzner contests that a stable equilibrium is possible when agents behave in impulsive or inert ways. Like most Austrian economists, Kirzner never found the idea of equilibrium very seductive, and he explicitly reproached Becker for interpreting his comment 'as being concerned with the *stability of equilibrium*' (Kirzner 1963: 84, n. 3; Kirzner's emphasis). The real debate between them rather bears on the importance when it comes to developing a price theory of relying on the possibility for those who participate in markets (that are *not* in equilibrium) of systematically revising their plans in the name of rationality. Put otherwise, the real debate between them concerns the question of whether rationality is eliminable from the explanation of the most essential dimension of economic agents' behaviour. For Becker, the essential component of rationality is clearly the responsiveness to new information. Consequently, he assumes that his irrational agents are irrational for *not* responding to new information (either they blindly continue to act like they do before obtaining this new information or they act in random ways that are not absolutely dependent on it). Apparently, Kirzner does not disagree with this characterization of rationality and irrationality, since he argues that the problem with irrational individuals is that, when 'chastened by yesterday's grim market experience', they do not care to 'revise their plans' accordingly. However, the notion of revising one's plan after being chastened introduces an intentional component that is not present in all kinds of responsiveness. And in Kirzner's conception of rationality, this component plays an essential role.

Now, as we have seen in previous chapters, the faculty of adaptation, or what I just called responsiveness, is a feature that characterizes rationality much more aptly than consistency. However, this does not mean that any kind of responsiveness should be identified with rationality. Some apparently irresponsive attitudes might be said rational in certain conditions and many highly responsive apparatuses could hardly be said to be rational. Before illustrating this, let us see why Becker was, nonetheless, right to characterize as irrational individuals who act either repetitively or randomly irrespective of eventual changes in the situation. The point is that such individuals, in contrast with normal human beings, are not really adapting themselves to new situations. Even though Becker claims that the final result might be roughly the same thanks to a kind of natural selection mechanism, irrational individuals whose relatively well adapted final behaviour is explained by a mechanism based on natural selection were not *intentionally* adapting themselves to the situation. In fact, this is precisely what makes Darwin's discovery of natural selection so revolutionary.[5] According to natural selection, giraffes do not have to intentionally adapt the length of their neck to the height of food in branches. And, as Friedman correctly noted, leaves did not learn mathematics and consequently they cannot intentionally determine by calculation the best position in which to grow. Similarly, Becker's inert and random deciders cannot intentionally choose a behaviour that can generate maximum profit and equilibrium price.

We will discuss in the next chapter whether the same can be said of actual entrepreneurs, but for the time being, let us simply conclude that the general adoption by Becker's irrational individuals of the behaviour eventually conducive to an equilibrium price in the long term was achieved non-intentionally. This fact, readily admitted by Becker, explains why Kirzner was not impressed by this theoretical achievement. For him, it is intentionality that characterizes rationality and that explains human aptitude not so much to reach an equilibrium but to reach 'determinate movements in market prices, starting from given non-equilibrium conditions' (ibid.: 84, n. 3). According to him, these 'determinate movements' are possible only if the alleged irrational consumers, in violation of Becker's description, 'reluctantly *rein in* their impulses, confine themselves *carefully* within the bounds of their opportunity sets, and *revise* prices downward – exactly as traditional theory describes' (ibid.: 85; emphasis added). In this perspective, the essential thing is not to know where these movements will lead us, but to know *why* and *how* they are initiated. According to Kirzner, who is concerned with the meaning or with the *rationale* of such movements, the latter are initiated because it is meaningful for economic agents to revise their plans when facing disappointing results. Thus, rationality would be even more a matter of purposefulness than a matter of efficiency in responding to a situation.

Let us see now why some apparently irresponsive attitudes might be called rational in certain situations or, put otherwise, why responsiveness is not a *necessary* condition of rationality. It is true that revising a plan after being chastened by a grim experience is clearly a form of responsiveness, but the essential issue is not whether plans are *automatically* revised on such occasion; it is whether this revision is provoked by disappointment because, if such is the case, the re-evaluation is done with a *purpose* in mind. And one consequence of placing the emphasis on a purposeful re-evaluation is that Becker's inert and impulsive consumers need no longer be considered irrational if they defend their attitude as a well thought out intentional strategy. For example, Becker's inert consumers could freely reinterpret the Hayekian thesis according to which traditions are usually a more reliable guide than most allegedly rational computations. Guided by this view, these individuals, instead of attempting a risky response to each new piece of information obtained about their situation and their environment, may have purposefully decided to continuously stick to the same behaviour whose not too unsuccessful record seems to be warranted by a long tradition. Similarly, though without invoking the authority of any economist, impulsive consumers could say: 'We want to reach happiness with the help of our limited resources, but we think that random decisions are the most promising ones for reaching such a goal, for two good reasons. First, they avoid troublesome computations and second, on the average at least, they tend to reduce the occurrence of extreme situations and consequently allow us to avoid the tensions associated with such situations, which look to us the most inimical to happiness. Given the very limited state of our knowledge, we think that making decisions at random is still the wisest position to hold.' One may find it difficult to agree with this kind of wisdom, but insofar as it is based on an argumentation that draws possible consequences from a set of assumptions and of preferences however bizarre they are, it is difficult to declare this kind of 'wisdom' irrational. An example more familiar to an economist might be the use of mixed strategies in game theory that Elster (1984 [1979]: 140) evoked in order to illustrate that there are some cases 'where the agent deliberately acts randomly'; however, in contrast with the cases described above, mixed strategies are normally responses to specific situations.

Agents justifying themselves in such a way might, at least in principle, be disappointed by the results of their bizarre principle of action and adjust their behaviour in consequence. Indeed, their behaviour was adopted because they judged that it was the most appropriate thing to do given their incapacity to cope more actively with any kind of situation, but nothing forces them to maintain this judgement if they learn from an eventual grim experience that another way of proceeding is preferable. Therefore, actions of those who would justify their adherence to repetitive or random decisions with the help of such an argumentation should not be said to be irrational too quickly, even though they are based on a doubtful rule, which, if not corrected by learning, could generate undesired results such as bankruptcy. After all, there is no reason to link rationality with profit, at least as long as we refer, as most economists pretend to do, to an *instrumental* conception of rationality. Indeed, the latter does not depend on any specific goal, in contrast with a normative one according to which, for example, monetary profit might be judged more valuable than tranquillity. If impulsive and inert consumers looked irrational, it was either because they did not care to modify a behaviour that generates losses when Becker had implicitly postulated that avoiding losses and making profit was more valuable for them than any alternative result, or because their behaviour was purely mechanical and not based on any kind of evaluation.

Thus, strictly speaking, responsiveness to changes in the environment is not a necessary condition of rationality. I would like to show now that neither is it a *sufficient* condition. Suppose that instead of relying like Becker on a survival mechanism, we invoke a slightly more complex type of irrational behaviour that I will call a 'quasi-responsive' behaviour. For example, price setters can be 'irrational' in a combined impulsive and inert way. Irrational agents of this type choose to continuously and mechanically repeat the same behaviour until the level of losses generated by their apparently unresponsive behaviour becomes significant and upsetting enough to provoke an increase in their level of adrenaline which induces them to randomly set a new price for their product. Once this satisfaction is obtained, they again start to maintain this new price in an inert way until the next time their wealth undergoes a comparable drop. Since any inappropriate price would not be maintained indefinitely, such behaviour might produce a sequence of adjustments that might be conducive to a viable equilibrium. But, even though this behaviour is clearly more responsive to changes in the situation than genuine impulsive or inert behaviour, it can hardly be characterized as more 'rational' than the latter, since being hormonally induced to indulge in the satisfaction of letting oneself be guided at random in the event of a decline in wealth can hardly be said to be rational.

Alternatively, let us consider a computer algorithm based on a feedback mechanism and let us assume that the computer tends to systematically maximize a variable associated with monetary gains. It is not clear that the highly complex sequence of events in the computer makes its basic algorithm radically different from the algorithm describing the 'quasi-responsive' behaviour seen above. In both cases, multiple detours (involving important costs) are taken to obtain the result. Anyone slightly familiar with programming knows that there are normally many different ways to obtain a given result with a computer. The difference between these ways concerns mainly the degree of complexity, the speed and the various costs. It is difficult to see why we should consider any one of these alternative ways of obtaining the same result more 'rational' than another. If one of them acquires the common result by maximizing the winning variable much more directly than the others, which reach it through more or less complex detours, the former cannot be said to be more rational for all that. More precisely, to characterize any one of these alternative routes as more rational would clearly depend on the particular values attached to convenience, cost, speed, and so forth, by the human beings who are programming or using this computer.

Thus, all these algorithms (the impulsive and the inert behaviour submitted to a 'survival constraint', the 'quasi-responsive' behaviour based on adrenaline level and the various feedback programs maximizing a variable) are samples in a set of mechanisms permitting a given result (namely, in the case that interests us, a behaviour conducive to an equilibrium price) to be attained under certain circumstances. None of them seems to have a special connection with rationality, at least if the crucial element for characterizing a behaviour as rational is not maximization of a variable or consistency of choices, nor even responsiveness as such, but the presence of valuations which are intentional and purposeful and which are subject to being disappointed by unsatisfactory results. A computer maximizing a variable is never disappointed; the idea that it *conceives* plans that it eventually *revises* later *due to disappointment* would be highly questionable. From this point of view, a computer does not seem to be more rational than Becker's impulsive or inert consumers, even though it can be said to be much more efficient. Naturally, it is possible to program a robot in such a way that it will progress in a given direction as long as the level of a regularly checked variable (associated with monetary losses) has a negative value, but will systematically change this direction as soon as this variable acquires a positive value. One might say metaphorically that the computer was disappointed with those losses, and that it consequently decided to revise its plan, but this type of programmed 'plan revision' cannot be what characterize rationality. Indeed, if the behaviour of a robot of this type were to be explained through rationality, it would be the rationality of the programmer that would be involved. If such a mechanical adjustment could count as a rational plan revision, it would be legitimate to say the same of Becker's society of *irrational* price setters if it is taken as a whole and considered as a gigantic mechanism. Indeed, it could be said of this irrational society that it checks the level of its losses by counting the number of bankruptcies among its membership, and, if 'disappointed' by the amount of these losses, decides to revise its plan regarding the level of the average price of its product. But here again, it is difficult not to think that 'disappointment' and 'plan revision' would in this context be mere phrases used metaphorically to describe a mechanical process in an anthropomorphic way. I characterize these two uses of intentional language as purely metaphorical because, in both cases, the causal efficiency of the level-checking mechanism upon the reorientation of behaviour was designed by a programmer or an engineer and has nothing to do with an intentional evaluation process which could have provoked the painful sentiment of being disappointed in a meaningful sense of the word.

Why this charge against rationality?

But is it really so? The most sophisticated computers, for example those that can efficiently play chess and frequently win against expert human chess players, are not simply applying a plan preconceived by their human programmers. These computers learn by being fed back in the course of their successive games. The very fact of being involved in situations or patterns that were not explicitly expected allows these machines to use what they have learnt from more or less accidental moves in previous games in the solutions to future problems. Since these problems and their efficient solutions were not – at least not directly –

conceived by the programmer, one may say that such computers literally learn new ways to solve problems. And it is thanks to what was learnt this way that they can outdo human beings in realizing astonishingly complex performances. The spectacular development of cognitive sciences and artificial intelligence combined with the parallel development of neuroscience since the mid-twentieth century has opened unlimited perspectives to those whose ambition was to construct robots able to realize, as well or even better than humans, virtually any of the characteristic performance of the latter, including autonomously thinking and deciding. This possibility has fascinated some of the most gifted economists of the twentieth century, such as John von Neumann and Herbert Simon, who, through very different approaches, were pioneering the idea that developing such thinking machines was the key to a better understanding of socio-economic phenomena (see Mirowski 2002: 94–152 and 452–479). We have seen why Becker's attempt to dispense with rationality in explaining the formation of economic equilibrium remained somewhat ambiguous. But were artificial intelligence developed to the point of endowing robots with the capacity of judging and deciding in a fully autonomous way, these robots might qualify as efficient economic agents and Becker's attempt to replace rational human beings with mechanically acting agents would apparently be vindicated, whatever degree of rationality should be granted to these robots.

However, even though we cannot exclude this possibility for the future, robots with this capacity have not yet been designed. What is missing from the best machines presently on the market? Surely not the capacity to compute or to maximize a result; computers have long surpassed human beings on this ground. Nor the capacity to make quick decision in complex situations; humans rely so often on computers to decide in their place what the proper moment to make crucial moves is, especially in complex situations, that claiming the contrary would be ridiculous. In fact, what is missing is precisely what makes human beings less reliable than machines; it is the full autonomy that allows them to have changing beliefs and desires, to evaluate a situation according to their own values and their own purposes, and consequently to be disappointed or encouraged by the result of this evaluation, to regret their own decisions or to be stimulated by them, to be revolted by attitudes of their fellow citizens or enthusiastic about their actions, etc. This is much more difficult to implement in a machine because all these attitudes suppose intentionality or, if one prefers, they suppose that the agent's state of mind bears on a statement that must be interpreted in order to be meaningful. But interpretation is subjective: it can differ with different agents and the same interpretation can correspond to differently labelled statements.[6]

In any case, such is the way human thought proceeds by developing (intentional) beliefs in such an intentional context. Thus, after maintaining that intentionality and not only '*symbol* manipulations' are required for thinking, John Searle (1980: 422) answers the question 'Could a machine think?' by claiming that '*only* a machine could think, and indeed very special kinds of machines, namely brains and machines that had the same causal powers as brains' (ibid.:

424). Other philosophers might not be ready to define thinking machines by referring to human brains, but it nonetheless sounds a bit paradoxical that an inquiry about the possibility that economic equilibrium be mechanically generated *without the help of rationality* brings us to wonder whether the required automata should be endowed with the kind of rationality that characterizes human beings. If 'thinking machines' must clone human beings and, consequently predict and explain social phenomena by invoking rational behaviour, as human beings presently do, the wish to predict and explain such phenomena in a mechanical fashion, without relying on loose notions such as rationality, seems to be circular or self-contradicting.

This fact however is not so paradoxical. Indeed, the very act of constructing a machine that could think the way human beings are thinking would be a fantastic accomplishment for those who are not satisfied with social sciences based on rationality and on intentional states such as beliefs and desires. Since human rationality is based on beliefs and desires (a rational response tends to satisfy a desire through ways suggested by a set of beliefs), the perspective of showing that beliefs and desires are working like certain components of a machine might change the very meaning of rationality, in such a way that it would no longer be true that social phenomena are explained by something as evasive as *human* rationality. That would mean that the genesis of intentional states, thinking and consciousness being in principle explained with the help of an appropriate arrangement of the physical components of the machine, the unity of science would be warranted or, at least, warranted in principle. The embarrassing gap between social and physical sciences would be largely overcome. But we are not there. Robots can accomplish many tasks much better than human beings, but there is currently no compelling reason to attribute intentional states and consciousness to them. They are far from being able to do a large part of what is rationally done by human beings such as preferring a world with more equality, being revolted or disappointed, admiring cultural events with enthusiasm, signing a check with the sense of fulfilling a duty, etc. Obviously, one cannot authoritatively exclude the possibility that sophisticated robots will be empowered with such capacities in a distant future, but between acknowledging such a possibility and thinking as though it were actualized, there is an important gap.

At this point, the question at issue is 'why is it so important to look to natural selection, artificial intelligence and neuroscience for finding ways to explain economic phenomena without relying on the rationality principle?'[7] The answer lies in a malaise afflicting economic theory, which has been particularly well diagnosed by Alexander Rosenberg throughout his various publications (for example, 1988a: 15–20; 1992a: 129–131 and 148–151; 1994: 217). Rosenberg complains that, in spite of the fact that it was born more than two centuries ago, economics did not manifest the type of progress in the accuracy of predictions that is expected from a genuine science. According to him, the predicament is due to the fact that concepts like 'beliefs' and 'desires' (or 'expectations' and 'preferences' as economists prefer to say) do not 'describe "natural kinds", which Rosenberg describes as 'sets of items that behave in the same way, that share the same manageably small set of causes and effects' (1994: 224). Concepts used by economists, being based on what is described as a folk psychology, cannot be integrated in compelling causal generalizations that could allow improvement of predictions and consequently applications in the 'control of human actions' (ibid.: 224). In contrast with concepts like 'gene' and 'acid', Rosenberg explains, they have not been 'carved' by a rigorous scientific analysis. Inherited from a popular way of speaking – he gives, as an example, the concept of 'fish' – such concepts are useful in common life but not in scientific analysis. Consequently, the terms of theories built with them 'do not correlate in a manageable way with the vocabulary of other successful scientific theories' (ibid.: 224). While Rosenberg and other critics of folk psychology acknowledge the latter's remarkable efficiency in predicting with a sometimes astonishing accuracy many decisions and actions typical of the daily life of human beings (Rosenberg 1988a: 15–16; Dennett 1991b: 29, 42, 43; Churchland 1984: 58–59), they nonetheless maintain that these predictions did not progress like scientific ones should.

An increasing number of philosophers and economists are confident that it should be possible to avoid relying on folk psychology concepts judged inappropriate for scientific investigation. This confidence is largely based on the fact that folk concepts that characterized the first stages of more matured sciences such as astronomy and biology were progressively replaced by scientific concepts. Ancient astronomers believed that the sun and the whole sky turned around the Earth, but this folk view was replaced by a scientific one according to which it is rather the Earth that is turning around the sun. Similarly, folk biologists considered that a Creator or an Intelligent Designer was necessarily required to explain the remarkable adaptation of most organisms and of specialized organs, such as the eyes and the heart, but this view was replaced (while not yet in every circle) by a scientific theory based on natural selection. So, why would folk concepts used by economists not be replaced in turn by concepts developed by scientific psychology or, still better, by neuroscience?

One might think that the appropriate way to proceed towards this radical reorientation of economics was to eliminate any references to these folk concepts by challenging the very existence of their objects, and this is roughly the view defended by those who were called 'eliminativists'. Paul Churchland, for example, claims that he does not have to bother further with intentional states and consciousness if his materialist 'bottom up' methodology does not reveal their eventual objective existence: 'If the thumb-worn categories of folk psychology (belief, desire, consciousness, and so on) really do possess objective integrity, then the bottom up approach will eventually lead us back to them' (Churchland 1984: 97). But is it reasonable to assume that phenomena experienced by everybody like beliefs, desires and consciousness may be forgotten and a priori reputed non-existent if they do not happen to be rediscovered by a particular type of materialist analysis? In fact, the phenomena that were unsatisfactorily explained by folk astronomy and folk biology were not eliminated by the development of modern science, they were explained in a much more satisfactory way. The diurnal movement of the sun and the whole sky from east to west is still experienced by us as it was by Ancient Greeks, but it was explained by Copernicus and modern astronomers in a much more satisfactory fashion than by the Ancients. Similarly, the functional adaptation of living organisms continues to amaze us long after Darwin, but it is explained in a much more compelling fashion by natural selection than it was previously. Therefore, it would be ill advised to drastically eliminate concepts like expectation and preference from economics simply because their prospect as scientific concepts is rather poor. They refer to intentional states which are constantly experienced by human beings and that could not be simply declared non-existent, even if it is judged essential to develop an alternative and more scientific explanation of them.

One may claim that a satisfactory explanation of such experienced intentional states should be based on neuroscience, but it seems reasonable to require that this explanation (1) 'save' the phenomena that we used to characterize as intentional and (2) be really compelling as an explanation of their occurrence, whether as manifestations of brain activity, persisting illusions, epiphenomena or whatever. It is for having provided such compelling explanations of what was experienced by everyone that Copernican astronomy and natural selection have respectively replaced folk astronomy and folk biology. Had Copernicus and Darwin been content to complain that traditional explanations did not fit well with the methodology that they judged appropriate for scientific inquiries without proposing more satisfactory explanations, the learned community would surely not have been massively persuaded to reject folk astronomy and folk biology. Therefore, even though such generally experienced phenomena desperately need to be explained in a scientifically more acceptable way, the onus of proof lies on those who want to dislodge folk theories. In fact, various theoreticians have concluded that attempts to eliminate all references to intentional states is a deadlock and turned instead towards researching a scientific explanation of intentional states and of consciousness based on an analysis of the brain and on the environmental conditions of its development. Among them, Daniel Dennett is probably the one who is the most influential in economic circles. This is especially the case since Don Ross has devoted many works to integrating Dennett's views into his own critical analysis of economics. Dennett and Ross have rejected eliminativist theses such as Churchland's (Ross 2005: 51–52). And since they propose a new way of explaining these intentional states, which are so closely related to the notion of rationality, it is surely worthwhile to pay particular attention to the way they rescue these states from elimination and to the ontological status that they grant them. A detour by a careful examination of their views on this matter seems to be crucial in assessing whether it is possible to dismiss the rationality principle from the social sciences.

Intentional states and intentional stance

It is with the help of the notion of 'intentional stance' that Dennett and Ross account for the fact that people *have* intentional states such as beliefs and desires. But what is meant by an intentional stance? For them, it is an intellectual attitude corresponding to a strategy of interpretation that presupposes that an object (not necessarily a person) has intentions and acts rationally in such a way that it becomes possible to predict its behaviour.[8] At first glance, the notion seems to be a quite familiar one since it describes what we are so frequently doing when we say, for example, that our computer wrongly *believes* that we ask it to do an operation which, in fact, is not the one we have in mind, or that it stubbornly does not *want* to do something, or when we explain to a child that a frog *believes* that a fly is good to eat and *wants* to eat it. We may be convinced that such a parlance is metaphorical, but, for Dennett and Ross, it is not really so. While admitting that the metaphorical view is 'immensely persuasive', Dennett rejects this interpretation as deceptive in favour of his own position according to which 'there is *nothing more* to *our* having beliefs and desires than our being voluminously predictable (like the frog, but more so) from the intentional stance' (Dennett 1989 [1987]: 108), first emphasis added, second one is Dennett's). Taking an intentional stance towards human beings – which means postulating that they have beliefs and desires – allows us, indeed, to voluminously predict their behaviour. But the behaviour of a computer or of a frog can be predicted as well when we grant them these intentional states by taking an intentional stance; therefore Dennett concludes that the difference between them and us turns out to be a simple matter of degree.

Now, the intentional stance is not the only way we have of predicting the behaviour of what Dennett and Ross call a 'system' (either a human being, a frog or another animal, a computer or another machine). One may take a design stance, which consists in treating the system the way we are used to considering a machine that has been designed by an engineer. People unfamiliar with mechanics are frequently inclined to take an intentional stance towards their car which does not 'want' to work properly, but, in this case, it would be more appropriate to take a design stance and predict or explain the behaviour of the car by taking into account the functions that the engineer has reserved for its various parts. Dennett adds that a third stance must be distinguished from these first two, namely the physical stance, the one we take when we predict or explain the behaviour of a physical body with the help of the causal laws of physics without assuming the intervention of any designer.[9] For example, in order to predict or explain the behaviour of a thermostat, one may take either a physical stance, looking at the causal laws affecting its material parts, a design stance, looking at the functional parts put into interrelation by engineers or an intentional stance looking at the thermostat as believing (rightly or wrongly) that the temperature is at such a level and wanting to avoid further heating. Dennett insists on the fact that, while the physical stance remains the most fundamental one, each of these three stances allows us to understand many phenomena that would be inaccessible from the other stance. This might be illustrated by an example of a kind familiar to economists. A Martian familiar with physics and mechanics trying to understand what is going on in an economic exchange by observing the physical movements of commodities and of pieces of money involved in the process would totally miss the economic exchange itself.

Consequently, this Martian could hardly predict the developments of the phenomenon, in contrast with economists who quite appropriately take the intentional stance (they grant beliefs and desires to the traders) in order to explain it.

Nothing in these considerations should be a source of annoyance for traditional economists, except, maybe, for the idea according to which there is nothing to beliefs and desires other than the fact that an intentional stance is taken towards the one who is reputed to have such intentional states. Note however that this view does not mean that every time one takes an intentional stance towards something, let us say a car for example, one is committed to admitting that the car actually has beliefs and desires. To avoid this misinterpretation, Dennett and Ross insistently claim that beliefs and desires should be attributed to a system when an intentional stance is taken toward it only when the intentional stance is the *only way* to predict or explain the behaviour of this system. This proviso about intentional stances may sound a little odd, but the idea is the following. As illustrated by the example of the Martian, it is not possible to capture what is involved in an event such as an economic exchange without taking an intentional stance. Yet, no one will deny that an economic exchange really exists; it is a *real pattern* that must be explained like anything else. Dennett and Ross maintain that it is precisely because the seller's and the buyer's actions cannot be predicted (and explained) other than by granting them beliefs and desires that their beliefs and desires can be said to be real. This is not the case with my car since granting intentional states to it does not help me to predict its behaviour which I can predict much better by taking a design stance toward it or by taking an intentional stance toward myself, the driver. In contrast, if the moves of a sophisticated chess-playing computer cannot be predicted other than by taking an intentional stance towards it, Dennett and Ross will say that this computer *really* has beliefs and desires.

Indeed, Ross claims: 'What it is to have intentional states – real ones, in the only sense of "real" that attaches to any intentional states – is to exhibit behavioural patterns that can't be predicted or explained without recognition of the patterns indexed by the intentional states in question' (Ross 2005: 63). According to him, this view is even the 'core thesis' of intentional-stance functionalism, which is the name he gives to Dennett's philosophical approach that he equally adopts.[10] As seen above, Dennett, for his part, presents an equivalent thesis in the following terms: 'there is nothing more to *our* having beliefs and desires than our being voluminously predictable [...] from the intentional stance' (Dennett 1989 [1987]: 108). But what is the exact meaning of this sentence? It surely does not simply mean that the existence of specific beliefs and desires can be inferred from the fact that we can predict someone's behaviour with their help, since this view would hardly be distinguishable from the traditional one. Indeed, economists and historians who rely on folk psychology do not pretend to directly experience beliefs and desires of agents they are studying; they assume that these agents have particular beliefs and desires and, since they can predict or explain their behaviour on this basis, they conclude that their assumption was well grounded. To fully appreciate the originality of intentional-stance functionalism, one has to take the words 'nothing more' in Dennett's sentence seriously, and construe the latter as denying that *the existence of beliefs and desires means anything more* than the fact that they are a necessary condition for predicting a particular behaviour.

One may be impressed by this elegant non-mentalist attempt to 'save' intentional phenomena from being purely eliminated, but remain bothered by a self-evident objection concerning the capacities of the 'systems' that take such intentional stances. Who takes intentional stances? Clearly human beings can take them, whether or not other systems also can. But if human beings have the capacity to take intentional stances, which means to interpret the behaviour of something by attributing it intentional states such as beliefs and desires, it is apparently because they *already have* beliefs and desires themselves (they desire to predict a behaviour and they believe that taking the intentional stance is the proper way of satisfying this goal). Now the point of invoking intentional stances was precisely to solve the problem raised by the questionable existence of beliefs and desires. Explaining beliefs and desires by the fact that an intentional stance was taken towards the person who has them and explaining the capacity to take this intentional stance by beliefs and desires of the intentional-stance taker clearly looks like a circular kind of explanation.[11]

Ross, however, rejects such an objection since he does not consider that taking an intentional stance requires intentional states. He, rather, maintained (in a personal communication) that such an operation 'is manifested in "behavior" not, in the first place, in beliefs'. Moreover, for him, beliefs and desires, when referred to in the context of intentional stances, should not be understood as 'internal states of people' but rather 'as descriptions of relationships between patterns in their behaviour and external circumstances' (Ross 2008: 56). As an attempt to grasp the exact meaning of this claim, let us recall the text where Ross associates having real intentional states to exhibiting 'behavioural patterns that can't be predicted or explained without recognition of the patterns indexed by the intentional states in question' (Ross 2005: 63). For example, one might be tempted to claim that the traders observed by the Martian clearly exhibit behavioural patterns that can't be predicted or explained without recognition of their intentional states, namely their beliefs and desires. But this might be interpreted as suggesting that intentional states have something to do with 'internal states of people'. In order to avoid 'logical conundrums' (Ross 2008: 56) associated with this way of thinking, Ross invites us to acknowledge that intentional states refer to nothing other than a set of relations to 'external circumstances', and that, according to the other passage quoted above, their role is to index some other patterns that would allow us to predict and explain the behavioural patterns exhibited. The status of the former patterns, which are not behavioural but explanative, is not easy to characterize. They are indexed, whatever this means, by intentional states, which should themselves be perceived as describing the 'relationships between patterns in their behaviour and external circumstances'. The way such relationships (or their description) can 'index' some undefined patterns is not very clear. Moreover, if intentional states can really be reduced to 'descriptions of relationships between patterns in their behaviour and external circumstances', claiming that they really exist only when it is not possible to predict or explain these behavioural patterns without invoking such 'descriptions of relationships' sounds a bit curious. Any time such descriptions play an essential role in prediction or explanation, one would be committed to acknowledging that intentional states really exist, in contradiction to Ross and Dennett's thesis explained above. Should the fact that some behaviours of my car cannot be predicted or explained without taking into account the description of its relationships with the poor state of the road, the strong wind and the heavy rain commit me to acknowledging that intentional states really exist in the car and are essential to understanding this behaviour, even though taking a design stance or even a physical stance could allow us to understand the phenomenon in a much more satisfactory fashion? I am aware that these tentative characterizations of intentional states should not be taken too literally, but the apparent ambiguity in the way Ross discusses their status – which contrasts so much with the usual clarity of his analyses – probably illustrates the fact that characterizing intentional states that would be totally free from any trace of their traditional construal as 'internal states of people' is not an easy task!

Be that as it may, the important point is whether this approach can save and compellingly explain the phenomena that are experienced by everyone and associated (perhaps wrongly?) with intentional states and consciousness. Ross does not deny the existence of such phenomena insofar as they are construed as resulting from intentional stances. Thus, he maintains that the main difference 'between existing chess-playing machines and human chess-players is that the latter do, and the former don't, take the intentional stance toward *themselves*' (Ross 2005: 63). Ross, who believes with Dennett that taking the intentional stance towards oneself has much to do with consciousness, is fully aware of the fact that such a view does not come without serious difficulties. Indeed, since the subject that takes this kind of reflexive intentional stance cannot be 'a *part* of the system' the 'most immediate and vicious sort of circularity thus seems to threaten' (ibid.: 286). To avoid being trapped in this threatening circle, Ross turns towards the thesis that Dennett developed in *Consciousness Explained*. Whereas in *The Intentional Stance*, Dennett was inclined to rely mostly on natural selection to explain features of the human mind, in this other book, it is not natural but *cultural* selection that is the key factor in accounting for human specific capacities and especially for consciousness (Dennett 1991a: 199–207). More precisely, while he still maintains, like other theoreticians, that natural selection has designed the brain as a remarkably efficient hardware, it is cultural factors that he invokes to explain the development of the required software, namely intentionality and consciousness. Consciousness should be seen as 'a product of cultural evolution that gets imparted to brain in early training' (ibid.: 219; see also Ross 2005: 160). Thus, it is through a resolutely *externalist* approach emphasizing cultural and social factors and not by developments internal to the human brain that intentional-stance functionalism proposes to account for consciousness.

According to Dennett, consciousness must not be conceived as a solidly unified entity monitoring the activity of a person. It would be, rather, the result of multiple drafts (the word 'draft' being understood here as the successive drafts of a paper written by a perfectionist author) that can successively operate, each at one point in time. There would be no particular privilege for an eventual final draft, which should not be exclusively associated with 'the moment of consciousness' (Dennett 1991a: 126; see also 113 and 125–126). The progressive development of these drafts would be generated and stimulated by social intercourse and the use of public language.[12] Now, few persons will deny the decisive role of society and of public language in the formation of human beings, both as a species and as individuals, but Dennett and Ross go much further. Public language is described by Ross, who makes explicit one of Dennett's suggestion, as '*the* scaffold that makes humans so strikingly different in their ecology from other intelligent animals' (Ross 2005: 286–287, Ross' emphasis). Indeed, Dennett even claims that the difference between human beings, the 'most prodigious intentional systems on the planet' and the poor intentional systems exemplified by frogs is largely explained by the fact that the former are 'bathed in words' that allow them to 'assert, deny, request, command and promise' (Dennett 1989 [1987]: 112ff.). One may remain unconvinced that this bathing in a relatively uncontrolled use of public language may ultimately generate the capacity for human beings to take intentional stances towards themselves, even though one cannot help admiring Dennett's great ingenuity made manifest in chapter 8 of *Consciousness Explained*.

One would like to know more about the mechanism through which such a highly sophisticated software, namely consciousness – about which Dennett even suggests that, insofar as it is nothing but a software, a computer program, it can 'in principle survive' the destruction of the brain (Dennett 1991a: 430; see also 368) – has been designed, not by a wise engineer working in Artificial Intelligence, not even by natural selection, but by the virtue of the progressive use of a public language learned by cultural interaction. In any case, were Dennett and Ross claiming that social intercourse and public language can really endow people with the capacity and the autonomy required to take intentional stances towards themselves (a capacity that Ross had described as the privilege of consciousness) their thesis, according to which intentional states *depend* in some way on being the object of an intentional stance, would be seriously endangered. Indeed, if natural and cultural selection jointly provide human beings with all the intentional states required to take intentional stances, why should they have to wait to be the object of an intentional stance in order to be able to experience beliefs and desires?

Clearly, the answer would be that behaviourist and externalist components of the discussed thesis must be interpreted in a more radical fashion in order to ensure a role to intentional stances within the very process of cultural selection. However, this move raises new questions about the nature of an intentional stance behaviourally taken. Let us admit that, before being able to believe or to desire anything, it is possible to take an intentional stance simply by behaving in a specific way, and let us try to imagine such behaviour. For example, a primitive human being who has neither special 'desire' to avoid potential enemies nor 'beliefs' about the efficiency of stepping back when facing them is nonetheless afraid and steps back, in a strictly behavioural manner, when facing a stranger with a threatening frown and predicts an aggressive behaviour on this basis. In fact, it is far from clear that no intentional states would be involved in such a behaviour, especially if we remember that Dennett showed how it is complicated to decide whether frogs really have beliefs and desires or not (Dennett 1989 [1987]: 106–110). Let us admit, however, that the only intentional states involved are nothing but a set of relationships between a behaviour (the stranger's threatening frown) and external circumstances (the encounter of two strangers). Should we say that the step back provoked by the threatening frown is a behaviour that corresponds to an intentional stance granting aggressive 'intentions' to the stranger and allowing the primitive man to predict his aggressive behaviour? And should we conclude that the aggressive 'intentions' of the stranger are 'nothing more' than what was implied by the step back (understood as a behavioural intentional stance)? I do not deny that more appropriate examples of behavioural attitudes corresponding to a purely behavioural intentional stance might be found, but the problem remains of characterizing an intentional stance when intentional states, with the help of which this notion was very clearly defined, are no longer there or, at least, must no longer be understood in the way that gave these states a specific meaning.

In any case, the purely behavioural intentional stance described above might have been taken by most animals as well as by primitive human beings. One may wonder why this behavioural exercise was developed by human beings but not by other animals to the point of allowing them to take intentional stances towards themselves in a way that corresponds to full consciousness. Ross would surely recall that, in contrast with other animals, human beings were bathed in words. However, his externalist approach goes much further than emphasizing the role of public language: it implies that propositional attitudes such as beliefs and desires should be considered real 'not as descriptions of patterns in brains, but as descriptions in patterns of social communication' (Ross 2005: 61). Since this view is related to the one about behavioural intentional stances, it may be appropriate at this point to recapitulate. Purely behavioural intentional stances might have been *socially* taken in a meaningful sense in a society of pre-human individuals that have neither beliefs nor desires in the usual sense, but who are bathed with words. Such intentional stances would have generated 'intentional states' understood as relationships between some behaviours and external circumstances. Insofar as taking this kind of intentional stances is the only way to (voluminously) predict behaviours, these intentional states can be said to be real and not a purely metaphorical description. Finally, the fact that taking intentional stances is presented as a social process is more easily understood if we remember that, for Ross, societies themselves are considered to be agents as well as individuals. Admitting this set of unintuitive and non-empirically grounded points seems to be the price to pay for conciliating the role of intentional stances with cultural evolution based on public language.

If it is difficult to be convinced by this attempt at conciliation, it is obviously not because one should deny the fact that intentionality and consciousness have evolved throughout the long history of humanity – an important development was no doubt going on between the consciousness of our three-million-year-old ancestors and the consciousness of contemporary Nobel prize winners – it is because the notion of individual stance that is perfectly clear when it is attributed to human beings equipped with intentional states, becomes less and less clear when, in order to make the theory consistent, it is attributed to stance takers that have almost nothing in common with them. Moreover, if one accepts the idea that any new theory must compellingly explain and save the phenomena, one must conclude that, in this approach, the latter are far from being saved and that their explanation, for reasons exposed above, can hardly be deemed compelling. If modern astronomers explain the experience of diurnal movement much better and much more precisely than the Ancients, Ross' theory utterly refuses to save beliefs and desires as they are experienced by each of us, and the way they are accounted for radically substitutes such experienced phenomena for sets of relationships that have little to do with this experience.

A methodological divide

If I have devoted a relatively large amount of attention to Dennett's and Ross' sophisticated attempt to reduce intentional states to this kind of external relationships, it is because the acceptance of this theory would be more damaging than any other that I know to the view according to which explanations of social phenomena are normally based on the rationality principle. For Ross, it is perfectly meaningful to say that intentional stances can be *socially* taken and socially developed with the help of public language because he estimates that societies are agents as well as human beings. As we have seen in Chapter 3, both, however, are characterized as *not* straightforward agents but only 'agents-by-extension' (Ross 2005: 256), and none of them has an advantage over the other from the point of view of agency. According to Ross, societies can be said to be agents as much as human beings are supposed to be, because if a multitude of neurons, which are straightforward agents, were working in human brains, each human being is literally constituted by a 'colony of agents' or 'a complex assembly of buglike homunculi' (ibid.: 252). In fact, Ross arrives at this conclusion by adopting and construing the concept of rationality-consistency *ontologically*, whereas this concept is only adopted *methodologically* by most contemporary economists when they construct their models. Instead of acknowledging that human beings, who used to be considered straightforward agents, are only moderately rational in the sense that they are poor maximizers and inconsistent choosers, he links agency to maximal rationality conceptually and concludes that human beings, in contrast with insects, neurons and sophisticated robots are not straightforward agents. However, if one considers that an agent is, by definition, a source of action and resists the idea according to which genuine actions can be attributed to insects, neurons and robots, one may simply deny that agency must be associated with the kind of maximal rationality that only these entities can satisfy in some sense, and maintain that economic activities developed in *human* societies are explained with the help of the non-maximizing and inconsistent kind of rationality that characterizes human beings. Thus, human beings could still be recognized perfectly well as straightforward agents insofar as the moderate or even minimal character of their rationality is acknowledged.

Nonetheless, one may estimate with Ross and Rosenberg that the latter view is built up with concepts much too remote from the typically scientific ones. And one may conclude from this that even though the theories such as Dennett and Ross' that aim to explain intentionality and consciousness scientifically still suffer from important shortcomings, it is worthwhile turning in this direction from which future developments in social analysis might come. One may also think that, in spite of the important differences – especially concerning attitudes associated with intentionality and consciousness – that remain between human beings and the most sophisticated products derived from Artificial Intelligence studies, similarities between them are such that it is a joint analysis of the working of both robots and human brain that is the most promising avenue for understanding not only human behaviour but human societies. Those who have acquired these convictions may forget traditional approaches to economics and turn, like Don Ross did, towards an inclusive science in which neuroscience, Artificial Intelligence, biology, psychology and a few other disciplines are mobilized in order to attempt an explanation of the workings of any kind of 'system', including human beings and their societies (eventually understood as systems themselves). And, in such an approach, they might usefully recycle the notion of rationality-consistency, which can be applied much more naturally to the workings of some of these systems than to human behaviour.

While it is not the place nor my intention to discuss this point, I have no doubt that such a science may and will produce quite interesting results, yet not necessarily directly related to economics as understood by economists. However, in spite of the formidable progress realized by Artificial Intelligence and contemporary neuroscience, considering the limits still met when these results are theoretically or practically applied to the analysis and explanation of human action and human societies, one may have good reasons, in the absence of more conclusive evidence (that will possibly come in future time, who knows?), to remain unconvinced that this inclusive science is the most fruitful way to improve our understanding of the specific questions raised in economics. Therefore, those who aim to account for them, unless they aim to develop a unified science of systems, may quite legitimately continue to rely on explanations based on the rationality principle. In the last chapter of this book, we will see whether such explanations can be considered to be respectable components of a scientific analysis. However, one can hardly deny that, as emphasized by Alchian, Friedman and Becker, and much more radically by Dennett and Ross, some kind of selection plays a significant role in economic explanation. It is this role that I will discuss in the next and penultimate chapter.

Part IV

Regarding economic explanations

8 Rationality and natural selection in economics

We have seen that explanations provided by economics largely rest on a fundamental postulate that is generally known as the rationality principle and that used to be interpreted by most economists as the principle in virtue of which entrepreneurs tend to make decisions that *maximize* their profits in the context of the constraints to which they are subjected. Yet, throughout the history of economic thought, this principle, thus interpreted, has been one of the favourite targets of opponents of mainstream economics. How can it be claimed that entrepreneurs are so systematically oriented towards profit maximization when it has often been observed that many of them let themselves be guided by entirely different considerations (prestige, maintaining good relationships, avoiding exhausting and costly calculations that are not sufficiently rewarding, etc.), which moreover are frequently based on emotive states? It is difficult, in effect, to believe that actual entrepreneurs resemble these maximizing machines that are readily resorted to by the designers of economic models.

A highly contested while influential argument

Various responses have been made to objections of this kind. Among these, the one proposed by Armen Alchian in 1950 stands out and is known by many economists as the 'survival argument', which is explicitly inspired by the Darwinian theory of natural selection. We have seen that Friedman and Becker used this argument in specific contexts, but let us now consider Alchian's version of it and some of the many discussions and reinterpretations that it has generated. Alchian's argument can be summarized in the following way. Whatever the determination with which entrepreneurs set about maximizing their profits, they must make their decisions in the context of such uncertainty that they have very little chance of realizing their objectives. However, only those who de facto will have made decisions that are not too far removed from those that would have maximized their profits will find themselves in a financial situation capable, in a competitive market, of assuring their economic survival. Those, on the other hand, who de facto have made choices furthest from those that would permit them such a maximization, risk being irremediably condemned to bankruptcy. Now since in the actual markets that economists analyse, there would only be entrepreneurs who have known how to avoid bankruptcy in one way or another, these entrepreneurs would, as a whole, have taken decisions that were not too far from those that maximize profits. Thus the gist of Alchian's argument is that when an economist claims that entrepreneurs are profit maximizers, it is not necessary for this economist to know the intentions of each entrepreneur; it is sufficient that for any reason entrepreneurs have de facto maximized these profits, at least approximately. It is true that in order to avoid bankruptcy, entrepreneurs do not really need to maximize profits *strictu senso*, since what is important for them is only to avoid incurring too significant losses. However, one year after the publication of Alchian's article, Stephen Enke (1951) proposed a more radical interpretation of the same argument. He reminded us that neoclassical theory claims that in a perfectly competitive market, businesses must be satisfied with a zero profit which, once all costs have been calculated, indeed corresponds with the maximum profit, and he concluded that, unless effectively maximizing such profits, these businesses incur heavy losses and are sooner or later doomed to bankruptcy (see also Enke 1953). Whether the argument is radicalized in this way or not, Alchian and Enke believed that it constitutes a legitimate application of Darwin's argumentation to economics.

As we have seen in the last chapter, Gary Becker's version of this argument was subjected to various objections that were mostly related to the fact that the behaviours of his agents were uncompromisingly irrational. The meaningfulness of Becker's argument was partially vindicated, but only by introducing a succession of wildly unrealistic assumptions into it, which could hardly be applied to the analysis of a human economy. In any case, Becker's interpretation was far from being faithful to Alchian, who never excluded rationality from his model (Alchian 1950: 214, 217). However, it was, in an important sense, more Darwinian than Alchian's was since, in contrast with the latter, it excluded any trace of intentionality and consequently of finality.

Other economists were more faithful to Alchian's paper, either in a negative or a positive assessment. Among rather critical discussions of this paper, let us consider briefly those of Edith Penrose (1952 and 1953) and of Alexander Rosenberg (1992b). In a rather harsh assessment of Alchian's contribution, Penrose denounced any attempts to model economics on biology because such attempts tend to eliminate the role of motivation. In a sense, she forced Alchian to claim, in his comment on her paper, that his 'biological analogy was merely expository' and 'designed to clarify the ideas in the theory' (Alchian 1953: 601). Given Alchian's insistence on the Darwinian theory of natural selection, she nonetheless maintained that the problem with the application of this theory to economics is that it supposes an intense competition, which obtains in the animal world continuously struggling for survival, but which does not obtain in a world where entrepreneurs are supposed to make decisions more or less randomly due to the quasi-impossibility of identifying appropriate decisions in a world characterized by uncertainty. It is difficult to see indeed why people who are reduced to relying on random processes for making decisions would be engaged in a significantly intense competition. However, it is clear that, for Alchian, economic competition is going on between his entrepreneurs who, according to him, are *fully motivated*; therefore Penrose's objection, which would be quite damaging to Becker's interpretation of natural selection working in a world of totally irrational people, is not very convincing here, precisely because Alchian does not maintain that people act randomly. There is no need for him to maintain this since people can obviously be motivated at least as much as animals are, which are not randomly guided when they attack their prey. After all, it is not the behaviour of individuals (motivated or not) that is randomly determined in natural selection, it is the mutation of genes, which are transmitted with the more or less successful adaptations that they may favour.

Alchian's idea is simply that the firms which turn out to be profitable or maximizing (in the sense that is analysed by economic theory) might have succeeded in reaching this position by chance, not because they acted randomly, but because the prevailing uncertainty made their highly motivated decisions not much more adapted than random decisions would have been. However, it is true that, in spite of his acknowledgement of the role of motivations, Alchian so strongly insists on radical uncertainty and on the virtues of natural selection that Penrose (1953: 603) has good reason to present the passage where he says that his 'approach embodies the principles of biological evolution and natural selection' (Alchian 1950: 211) as representative of his views. Consequently, she has also good reason to think that Alchian's biological analogy was far from being 'merely expository'. One may even think with Geoffrey Hodgson that Alchian's argument 'clearly downgrades the theoretical status of the concept of purposeful behaviour, making it irrelevant to the explanation of the competitive process' (Hodgson 1993: 217). In any case, one of the most pernicious suggestions of the biological analogy, according to Penrose, is the gulf that is created between the knowledge attributed to business people and to economists respectively. Her point is sensible enough since if it makes sense to say that biologists have a lot of knowledge that animals do not, it is far from clear, in spite of what the analogy suggests, that economists have much more knowledge than business people about the economic conditions that are developing and the type of enterprise that has the greatest chances for survival. It is true that Alchian did not exclude the fact that entrepreneurs may make wise decisions, but once this fact is emphasized, it is the role of natural selection in explaining the development of economic societies that becomes less clear. Penrose went even further, and probably too far: 'Once motivation is introduced the usefulness of the model becomes even more questionable' (1952: 813). As we have seen, natural selection does not exclude motivated behaviour, but its application to economics excludes reliance on wise decisions when it comes to explaining success or survival. Therefore, at some point, economists must choose between explanations based on natural selection and those based on rationality; I will come back to this point, but let us first consider other assessments of Alchian's thesis.

Alexander Rosenberg revisited the latter in his critical discussion of 'appeals to Darwinian theory as a rationalization for orthodoxy in economic theorizing' (1992b: 174). In this paper, he maintains that the theory of natural selection 'shares few of its strengths and most of its weaknesses with neoclassical theory' (ibid.: 174) and concludes that 'the attractions of an evolutionary theory for economists must be very limited indeed' (ibid.: 178). While he acknowledges that Alchian's construal of the Darwinian theory is quite acceptable for the essentials (ibid.: 176–177), he does not see any advantages to its application to economics. An economic theory based on natural selection is not more promising than a biological one for predicting 'the course of behaviour of the individual economic agent' (ibid.: 177) – a point which was readily admitted by Alchian – and when it comes to making predictions about an eventual equilibrium situation, the interesting possibilities offered in biology are not applicable to economics. According to Rosenberg, such a conclusion rests on various considerations: in economics, there is no 'independent evidence that there is a stable equilibrium to be explained' and, in contrast with what is going on with organisms, the 'adaptiveness' of an agent's behaviour depends on what other agents do, which considerably complicates the matter by making the problem strategic and not parametric (ibid.: 181). Moreover, as emphasized by Rosenberg, the usual assumptions of such theories raised problems in economics: indeed, (1) because gene-frequencies can 'track every environmentally significant biologically possible adaptation and maladaptation' (ibid.: 182), the genome can be said to be 'in the long run omniscient', but this state of things is hardly matched when it comes to economic agents; and (2) the 'long run', which is required by an effective adaptation, may correspond to the 'geological epochs' in which biological evolution took place, but could only correspond to an artificially lengthened period in economics whose irrelevance was underscored by Keynes' famous dictum (ibid.: 182).

Commentators more sympathetic to Alchian's enterprise were Richard Nelson and Sidney Winter (1982)[1] who present Alchian as a 'direct intellectual antecedent' of their work (1982: 41). As we have seen, Winter himself had severely criticized Becker's interpretation of Alchian's view, but his critiques were essentially linked to the fact that Becker's agents were supposed to be totally irrational. Since this is not the case with Alchian, who attributed intelligent motivations to his agents, Winter's objections no longer applied. A problem which nonetheless plagues any attempts to apply natural selection to economics is the identification of what can play the role that genes play in a theory based on natural selection: what entity is supposed to be well adapted to a given environment and therefore selected? To this question, Nelson and Winter answer that a routine is such an entity and a significant part of their book is devoted to analysing in detail what a routine in a firm may consist of (1982: chapters 3–5). The idea is that most of what is done in a firm is not based on fresh choices: routines that were progressively developed are more or less mechanically applied by managers and workers who become familiar with them. When such routines turn out to be successful and more viable, they are progressively imitated by other firms in such a way that it makes sense to say that these viable routines are selected for, in a process that is not unrelated to what is going on in natural selection. In fact, this is precisely the process that Alchian had in mind when he referred to imitation (Alchian 1950: 28), a circumstance that explains that the problem of identifying the selected entity was only implicitly or indirectly raised against his views.

However, resorting to routines to solve this problem is far from being typically Darwinian and is better described as Lamarckian. Relying on imitation to insure that routines are transmitted from one 'generation' to another is not relying on the unconscious and non-teleological process that characterizes natural selection. If, for a Darwinian, acquired traits cannot be transmitted in contrast with genetic markers, routines that were developed and acquired by ingenious entrepreneurs are, according to Alchian as well as Nelson and Winter, transmitted by imitation, which implies that those acquired traits can fully be transmitted in a Lamarckian way to successive 'generations' of firms. Therefore, in spite of Alchian's conviction that his approach was Darwinian, Nelson and Winter did not hesitate to claim that their 'theory is unabashedly Lamarckian' and to refer, a few lines further, to their 'espousal of Lamarckianism' (Nelson and Winter 1982: 11). Once this is admitted, an evolutionary theory of economics may avoid most of the difficulties associated with the application of natural selection to economics much more easily. Now, if Nelson and Winter may be considered to be heterodox economists, it is surely due, as underscored by Hodgson (1998: 165), to their insistence on an evolutionary approach that makes room for novelties and changes, but possibly still more, due to their uncompromisingly institutionalist approach and to their rejection of the role of profit maximization (Nelson and Winter 1982: 66). According to them, people are rational, but boundedly – and I would even say minimally – rational. Indeed, even though imitating a successful competitor may require great technical ingenuity on the part of the imitator (ibid.: 119), the properly economic decision to imitate this competitor instead of sticking to a way of proceeding that has generated losses year after year requires being rational but in no way to be a powerful calculator and a maximizer. Thus, an evolutionary economics that is *not* based on natural selection can be quite compatible with rationality, and especially with minimal rationality.[2]

In fact, if we put aside Enke's refinement, which is not free of difficulties related to its optimal approach to natural selection as well as to its literal interpretation of the neoclassical theory of zero profit, which will not be discussed here, it is difficult not to acknowledge some logical force in a selection argument that makes room for this kind of rationality. Entrepreneurs who are actually doing business on a market might be there by pure chance; they might even make decisions almost randomly in many circumstances. However, in order to have been able to stay in business until now – and by staying in business I mean still being in a position to make some relatively profitable transactions – they must, at least on the average, by chance or otherwise, have usually made decisions not necessarily optimal but sufficiently far from the worst possible ones since, by hypothesis, they managed to avoid bankruptcy. This is far from being a vindication of maximization: even if one adopts Nelson and Winter's evolutionary economics theory based on routinized behaviour, one must admit with Hodgson (1991: 523), that 'there is no reason to assume that such routinized behavior will generally be on an optimal track', any more than this approach allows us to treat 'its results as predictable' as repeatedly acknowledged by Nelson and Winter (1982: 133). At the most, but this is already quite a lot, this argument may vindicate a kind of bias in favour of a relative equilibrium of the market, which is observed only *ex post.* Such an equilibrium would simply imply that participants in this market, since they are still there, have made satisfactory enough decisions which were possibly, but not necessarily, due to their rational attempts to maximize. This positive but modest conclusion is not unfaithful to Alchian who, after painfully defending the very challengeable idea that economists, in contrast with business people, 'can state what types of firms or behavior relative to other possible types will be more viable', maintained on a safer ground that if 'explanation of past results rather than prediction is the task, the economist can diagnose the particular attributes which were critical in facilitating survival, even though individual participants were not aware of them' (Alchian 1950: 216). Indeed, business people may be better predictors than economists, but when it comes to analysing past economic situations, it is reasonable to think that economists are better equipped than them. In any case, it is true that explaining past events by attributing them to a selection bias is safer than risking a prediction in a context characterized by uncertainty, but, if such is the case, predictions must be forgotten and Rosenberg, who refers to this passage (Rosenberg 1992b: 178), would still have reasons to complain about disappointing results of applying natural selection to economics.

If Alchian's survival argument works only if some room is left for motivated action and rational decisions, it becomes important to decide which is its key element, either a kind of natural selection or the skill and the rationality of agents. Not all economists would admit that determining this key element is really important. For example, Satz and Ferejohn (1994: 78–79 and 86–87) do not find any problem with closely associating these elements; according to them, 'rational-choice theory' relies on a 'structural theory of interests' that is illustrated by Alchian's idea according to which in 'a competitive market, only firms that act to maximize profits will survive'.[3] However, there are too many contradictory views on these questions to avoid reconsidering the matter. In fact, evolutionary theories are full of nuances and subtleties, which many recent developments, both in biology and in economics, have emphasized. According to Hodgson, even the phrase 'evolutionary economics' would be 'put to a number of varied and even contradictory uses' (Hodgson 1998: 161). It would not be a question here, however, of taking up the debate about all these various senses referred to by Hodgson, who has considerably contributed to clarifying this issue through works that encompass the whole history of economic thought. My goal is more limited. It consists in clarifying different interpretations of the notions of selection and competition in order to propose an answer to the two following questions: (1) Are Alchian's argument and arguments derived from it typically Darwinian, or put otherwise, are they really based on a mechanism of natural selection? And if this is not the case, what does one mean exactly when one says that arguments of this kind applied to economic behaviour are more

Lamarckian than Darwinian? (2) Could explanations that would be properly Darwinian be compatible (in the sense of complementary) with explanations based on the rationality principle, which is typically utilized by economists? And what about a 'Lamarckian' argument from this point of view?

Invisible hand and natural selection

In order to answer these questions, a useful first step is to compare Darwin's natural selection argument to the 'invisible hand' argument, as usually put forward by post-Smithian liberal economists who have reinterpreted and generalized the meaning that this famous metaphor had for Adam Smith who used it in a quite restricted context.[4] The former explains the fact that living species are remarkably adapted to their environments and the latter that market economies succeed relatively well in satisfying the needs of people living in societies where they are implemented. These two arguments bear on quite different domains and resort to quite different explanative forces, but some similarities between them are worth being mentioned. Robert Nozick has even straightforwardly included among what he calls 'Invisible hand explanations' both Darwin's evolutionary theory of natural selection and Alchian's application of the latter to economics (Nozick 1974: 20–21). The main similarities between these theories can be underscored with the help of the four following notions: competition, non-centralism, relative adaptation and selection.

1 In both domains to be explained, an intense competition is going on: plants and animals are competing for survival with the help of the limited resources available to them; similarly, entrepreneurs are competing for conquering shares of the markets which allow them to make profits and avoid losses (and eventually bankruptcy).
2 In both domains, this competition is not controlled by any central authority or central planning: the gist of Darwin's approach lies precisely in the fact that the explanation, which even allows random processes to determine key events in the transformation to be explained, does not rely on the kind of central planning that was previously attributed to God; the confident reliance on markets, which is associated with the metaphor of the invisible hand, similarly implies that markets are free from any kind of planning and coordination, if we exclude the minimal control of its basic rules that only the authority of the State can warrant.
3 In both cases, an astonishing adaptation is nonetheless observed: organisms are adapted to their environments in a way which cannot be said to be optimal but which is so remarkable that before Darwin people tended to attribute it to a divine planner, since it was excluded that random processes could perform so well; in a comparable fashion, the allocation of resources generated by free markets, while being far from optimal, is remarkably adapted in the sense that output produced by firms corresponds relatively well to the demand of consumers, whereas many people would

spontaneously be convinced that uncontrolled markets animated by egoistic firms would generate a catastrophic disequilibrium between the self-interests of the latter and consumer's needs.

4 Finally, a certain type of selection is going on in both cases: only the best adapted species have some chances of generating a significant number of descendents and surviving (to be selected); more or less similarly, only the firms that manage to adapt themselves reasonably well to changing economic environments have a chance of surviving (to remain selected) over a long period of time.

However, between these two types of explanation, important differences remain, which – in spite of Nozick's suggestion – makes it unacceptable to include those based on natural selection among invisible hand explanations. In order to illustrate these differences, let us first consider the argument associated with the metaphor of the invisible hand. It is normally applied to an economic world in which entrepreneurs are in competition, in the sense that shares of the market controlled by one of them cannot be controlled by another; that the extra profits of an entrepreneur are most often made at the expense of others; and that failures in attempting to gain a sufficient share of a necessarily limited market risk, in a more or less long term, resulting in bankruptcy, and consequently in extinction, of the unsuccessful enterprise. In such a context, entrepreneurs are obliged to make crucial decisions, since they must, according to the circumstances, invest or disinvest some portion of their assets, raise or lower their level of production, lay off certain employees or hire new ones, set the prices for their products, determine the quantity and the source of their stock, etc. It is true that a large part of these decisions are taken in a more or less routinized fashion as claimed by Nelson and Winter, but this is not to say that they are randomly taken. Were this the case, we would have serious doubts about the efficiency of such a market. Let us admit, however, that markets de facto work in an acceptably efficient manner, in the sense that the goods most able to respond to the needs of potential consumers are generally produced in sufficient quantities and in a sufficiently rational manner, with respect to the available resources. It is normal then to require an explanation of the fact that, even though no overall direction is exerted on the market as such, the latter, in which each individual pursues his own interest without particular inclination to cooperate, brings about results that are very far from the economic chaos that would dominate that world – at least so we might well suppose – if all these decisions were taken randomly.

The explanation provided by traditional economic theory explicitly calls upon the intentions of agents and the ends that they pursue. It postulates that entrepreneurs are far from leaving decisions to chance, and that, guided by their desire to increase their revenue, they strive, thanks to their skills (or their business sense), to make the decisions that favour their chances of getting more profits and avoiding those that could generate useless costs. It is true that these skills do not need to be particularly impressive, since what is important is that average entrepreneurs choose to do what seems to be the most rewarding. And since this theory supposes quite reasonably that more profits will be made by firms whose output corresponds relatively well to what is required by consumers' demand, it is no longer mysterious that the supply turns out to be relatively well adapted to the demand of those consumers in spite of the total absence of planning. In the present context, what is important to note is that this theory postulates intentional behaviour on the part of entrepreneurs, and also that such behaviour makes sense only in a thoroughly competitive market where inevitably there are winners and losers. In this sense, this theory supposes that the losers might be excluded from the market since they are threatened with bankruptcy. Therefore, it is legitimate to say that this theory also supposes the working of a certain selection in virtue of which, out of all the participants in this highly competitive game, those who remain in business for a significant period of time are those who have succeeded in making a viable amount of profit by adapting their output to what consumers required relatively well.

At this point, it should be hardly disputable that an argument such as Alchian's – *if interpreted* as referring to a selection of the kind just described – has much less to do with Darwin's argument as Alchian claimed. To make this clear, one should first determine what gives so much power to the Darwinian argument accounting for the evolution of species. It is well known that Darwin was not the first to maintain that the genesis of biological species must be understood as resulting from a phylogenetic evolution; many others, such as Lamarck, came to this conclusion before he did. If, however, the theory of natural selection occupies the place it does in the history of evolutionary theories, it is because it allows us to account for the formation of remarkably well adapted species, without relying on any type of finality for all that. From a scientific point of view, it would be just as unacceptable to resort to a Creator whose ends and plans would explain the formation of species, as it would be to attribute ends to inferior species, which would allow us to account, in a somewhat circular fashion, for the genesis of species, whose superiority, to a great extent, lies precisely in their capacity to have such ends. It is because a theory such as natural selection has succeeded in excluding all forms of teleology that it constitutes a formidable advance in scientific thought, which accounts for Darwin's exceptional place in the history of science.

Various types of selection

To bring out the originality of the selection mechanism put forward by Darwin and to show that one should avoid applying it to any kind of selection, let us consider the following situation. Suppose that various candidates interested in a few positions that have been opened in a prestigious university undergo a highly complex exam imposed by the selection committee that has been put in place at this university. Suppose as well that all of the candidates obtain remarkable results, but that the scarce positions are finally only given to the candidates who obtained the best results. Imagine now that an exterior observer appears and that, after being amazed by the fact that the people chosen to occupy the positions are of an intellectual level that is highly superior to the average intellectual level of the population, demands an explanation for the fact that such a happy circumstance – and such a statistically improbable one – was obtained. No doubt it would be explained to this inquirer that the candidates were far from being chosen at random, since on the one hand those who showed up for the examination made considerable efforts to optimize their intellectual performances, and, on the other hand, the selection committee intentionally chose from this group those whose performances were most impressive. In this process, there is therefore a competition to 'survive' and a selection of the most gifted (the fittest for the job), but it would evidently be absurd to maintain that only recourse to natural selection would allow us to explain this phenomenon, as though, without Darwin's genial idea, it would have been impossible to explain this result! Anyone can see that the selection at work in this example manifestly has nothing Darwinian about it, since it is of an explicitly teleological nature, and is so at two levels. On the one hand, at the level of the individual candidates, only those who aimed at obtaining the best result and who have taken the necessary measures to do so were engaged in the contest; and on the other hand, at the level of the overall process, the members of the selection committee who aimed at accepting only the most qualified have made the choices necessary for reaching this objective. Such a system of double-level selection may be said to be more or less akin to what would be going on in a highly idealized planned economy in which people would compete to increase their production in a context where central planners would choose the best arrangements for increasing this production. As for theories that pretend to explain the origin of the species, it seems that creationism is the one that is closest to the selection process just considered; indeed, it is solely in this type of explanation that we find a selection that, at the level of the overall process, is carried out intentionally, in this case by God who creates among all possible species some of those that are perfectly well adapted to their environment. However, it is true that this theory does not correspond exactly to the model of double-level selection illustrated above since creationism does not attribute significant roles to individual organisms when it comes to explaining their remarkable adaptation.

Let us turn now to the explanation of the efficiency of the market proposed by economic theory. This explanation is fundamentally different from the one that allows us to account for the favourable choices of our selection committee, because, *at the overall level*, the economic theory involved does not resort to any kind of finality or intentional decision. It is only *at the level of individuals* that finality plays an essential role. An entrepreneur decides, for example, to invest part of his resources in the production of cheese, rather than investing in the production of another product or saving it as a liquid asset in anticipation of more favourable occasions, because he judges it to be a decision that promises a highly interesting yield. But this entrepreneur is only one player amongst others in a competitive game where success is guaranteed to no one. The economic theory simply maintains that, notwithstanding the fact that they are made without any special care granted to the harmonious functioning of the market, the various decisions of these entrepreneurs, nevertheless, produce this result, a bit like if an 'invisible hand' had coordinated the whole process. Yet what this metaphor highlights is that, in spite of the self-interested character of the ends pursued by the agents, a totally uncontrolled social mechanism assures, *at the overall level* of the market, a result almost as well adapted as if God – who is invoked here only metaphorically – had intentionally implemented its realization. It is on this type of explanation that economists rely to account for the efficiency of the market, but such an argument, as we have seen, implies a process of selection. If such a harmonious result is obtained, it is because entrepreneurs who decide to produce cheese at a moment where the demand doesn't justify a growth in the supply of this type of food risk suffering losses that might dissuade them from indefinitely investing their resources where the latter are not required. Indeed, in this game of trial and error, if others make the most appropriate choices, they risk being forced to leave room to the latter through their own bankruptcy, which ultimately contributes to the smooth functioning of the mechanism evoked by the metaphor of the 'invisible hand'. The result of this process is that the most successful entrepreneurs, namely those who, whether by skill or by chance, have made choices well adapted to the needs of consumers, tend to be the typical participants in the market. Neoclassical theory, as Enke's argument reminds us, has even radicalized this view, since it claims that in the long run maximum profit tends to be equal to zero in such a way that bankruptcy is practically promised to those who are not maximizers. Whether or not we introduce this rather debatable refinement into the picture, it remains true that economic theory postulates that the behaviour of individuals is explained by their choices (guided by their goals), while maintaining that, at the overall level, the result obtained is unintentional and explained instead through the kind of selection just described, which operates in the context of a merciless competition. But this is not to say that the explanatory power of this selection is of a Darwinian type for all that.

Indeed, if we are interested in finding a theory of biological evolution that comes close to the economic analysis associated with the invisible hand metaphor, it seems much more sensible to turn not to Darwin's but to Lamarck's theory, as Nelson and Winter did. On the one hand, at the *overall level*, with Lamarck, just as with Darwin, there is nothing corresponding to an overall intentional selection of species such as the one referred to by creationism. If there is some sense in saying that only certain species are finally selected, this is due to features of a changing environment that reward species whose members have successfully sought to improve their adaptation to this environment. In this theory, teleological considerations concern only the individuals' behaviour. On the other hand indeed, at the *level of individuals*, it is the efforts of the latter, perhaps not intentional but at least goal-directed, that explain the progressive adaptation of organisms to their environment. According to Lamarck, the ancestors of giraffes instinctively tried to stretch their necks to better reach the fruit available on the highest branches, and, since Lamarck mistakenly believed that the acquired characteristics were hereditary, he thought it possible to explain the length of contemporary giraffes' necks in this way. Even though he intended to explain evolution by this mechanism of adaptation and transmission, Lamarck of course could not ignore the fact that it was not all the potential descendants of animals engaged in such processes that were destined to survive; also, since he supposed that the stretching of their necks was determinant for their feeding, he was aware that the giraffes that managed to stretch their necks most effectively benefited from an appreciable advantage over the others in a jungle where all animals are constantly in a struggle for survival. As we can see, Lamarck's theory of evolution is akin to the 'invisible hand' theory of the market's relative equilibrium. Entrepreneurs aim to adapt their decisions to their environment, just like Lamarck's giraffes do, but since they must, like the latter, make these decisions in a highly competitive context, the result is far from being guaranteed. There is a selection of the most successful among them, but this selection, which is due in large part to their constant attempts to adapt to their environments, is no more a natural selection in the Darwinian sense than the one which is implicitly at work in the evolutionary mechanism resorted to by Lamarck.[5]

What is it, then, that characterizes a properly Darwinian mechanism? It is, as we have seen, the absence of recourse to teleology, whether at the level of individuals or the overall level. For Darwin, the efforts deployed by giraffes to stretch their necks contribute nothing to the evolution of their species. If any given giraffe could have episodically played a determining role in this evolution, it could only be, in his eyes, in virtue of accidental circumstances – in virtue of genetic mutations, as the neo-Darwinians put it – that, at least in the typical explanations provided by this theory, have nothing to do with goals or deployed efforts. Of course, this accident can contribute to the evolution of the species, only if it turns out to be advantageous for survival and procreation, but the important thing here is that this result can be explained without appealing to the aims or the goal-directed efforts of individuals, whose results, in any case, could not be transmitted from one generation to another.

In economics, whose object results from a multitude of human actions, the fact of referring to behaviour that is clearly intentional and rational obviously does not constitute the kind of unacceptable trickery for which biologists would be blamed if they were tempted to use the same strategy for explaining the evolution of species. Also, it is not surprising that, with very few exceptions, economists' explanations did not question the role allotted to behaviour presumed to be rational. Alchian himself, while fully convinced that his argument was of a Darwinian character, does not really question the rational character of the behaviour of entrepreneurs. Gary Becker's paper, which proposes a model founded on totally irrational behaviour (Becker 1962), was an exception to this rule, but it was voluntarily designed as a bold intellectual experience and not as a rejection of this way of explaining. In any case, Becker's paper has generated rather sceptical or ambiguous reactions, but if it had been satisfactory, the view that it proposes would constitute an explanation of economic phenomena that, much more than Alchian's, could have been said to be *Darwinian*. In effect, this explanation would, like the one proposed by Darwin, permit us to account for a remarkably organized phenomenon (respectively, a free market which function in a relatively efficient manner and a species astonishingly well-adapted to their environments) without calling upon any form of intentionality, *neither at the level of individuals nor at the overall level.*

Billiards experts and sunbathing leaves

To better illustrate the difference between these various types of explanation, it could be useful to consider two of the picturesque examples – whose ambiguous character was highlighted in Chapter 6 of this book – that Milton Friedman proposes in his celebrated 1953 methodological intervention. Let us first look at the one that deals with experts at billiards. While not explicitly related to Alchian's argument, this example refers directly to 'natural selection' (Friedman 1953: 21, n. 16 and 22), Let us suppose, with Friedman, that there exists a complex mathematical formula – for example, of a trigonometric nature – that would make it possible to determine the exact trajectory of a billiard ball which must strike another one in an optimal way, and suppose that experts at this game are totally incapable of mastering this mathematical formula whose very existence they are totally ignorant of. This obviously does not mean that these players are reduced to merely hitting the ball randomly. Just like the most skilful entrepreneurs, they make the best use they can of their limited knowledge and expertise to achieve their goal. Naturally, certain players have more success than others, but only those that, *in one way or another*, manage to achieve a result that is close enough to the one predicted by the mathematical formula merit being qualified as expert players. If Friedman, according to me, was wrong to think that this example could allow us to conclude that the realism of assumptions matters little, he was justified in thinking that it illustrates the way in which neoclassical economic theory claims to account for the working of the market reasonably well. Neoclassical economic theory, just like the mathematical theory in the game of billiards, aims to describe what takes place when agents intentionally attempt to achieve their respective goals in a highly competitive game. Success evidently cannot be guaranteed to all agents, but the theory suggests that those among them whose efforts will be *in one way or another* met with success will have de facto acted in a manner the logic of which is analysed by the theory. In both cases, the argument supposes that the agents who will have performed in a way that is too different from what is required by the theory will be excluded from that competitive game. This is what economists have in mind when they say that an entrepreneur *cannot* sell at such or such a price since selling at this price would be producing at a loss; indeed, these economists do not claim that the entrepreneur is not free to sell at this price, but hold only that continuing to do so for a certain amount of time would sooner or later result in a bankruptcy and consequently in the exclusion of this entrepreneur from the market. In competitive games such as billiards and the market economy, there are inevitably winners and losers, which means that there is selection. But as it results simply from the fact that in a fight for success (whether in billiards or in business), in which a certain number of individuals engage with the firm intention of winning, this selection has little to do with the explanatory mechanism resorted to by Darwin. Indeed, referring to selection is simply a way of describing *ex post* what has resulted from a competition between agents who are motivated and rational.

Without straying too far from this example, it is possible to illustrate what might be a mechanism closer to a Darwinian one by replacing the 'standard' game of billiards evoked until now by what I call a 'labyrinthine' game of billiards. In this game, which would no doubt appear very bizarre and not very appealing, we suppose that the table is transformed into an extremely complex labyrinth, to the point that the most expert players claim to be totally indifferent to pushing the balls in one direction or another, since these balls will inevitably take trajectories that are totally impossible for them to predict. Let us assume nonetheless that this game is competitive, in the sense that the players who don't succeed in adequately directing the balls into the pockets that serve as the targets are eliminated. In these conditions, we may suppose that each player adopts the (mixed) strategy of always hitting the ball in the same way, once the first shot was randomly determined. If after a long period of time, we observe that the surviving players hit the balls in a successful way frequently enough and in a way that ultimately turns out to be in keeping with the requirements of the mathematical theory that the inventor of this game would have developed, an explanation of this unexpected phenomenon would be required. Only a kind of natural selection might explain the apparently impossible success of the survival players.

According to this hypothesis, it would be the visceral conservatism of the players (including the successful ones) that would have led to the transmission, from one shot to another and from one game to another, of ways of playing which, by pure chance, would have turned out to be relatively well adapted. If the structure of the labyrinthine billiards were to change and thus required somewhat different shots, it would be possible to suppose that, in an accidental and exceptional manner, a hit would, from time to time, be determined at random before being imitated again in a long series of successive shots, in such a way that the surviving players would be those whose accidentally reoriented shots were by pure chance adapted to the new demands of the game. In short, it is a sort of natural selection that would bring out a group of 'expert players', albeit not a very glorious group.

The situation would be quite different, however, if some particularly astute players imagined a way to outsmart the designer of the game and succeeded, with the help of a few wise tricks, in determining an efficient way to play. In the case where the players were submitted to chance, only natural selection could permit us to explain the relative effectiveness of the players who were not even able to have preferences for any kind of shot whatsoever. In the case where certain players find a way to outsmart the designer of the game and to show themselves to be more efficient than those who play randomly – otherwise outsmarting would not mean anything – their effectiveness could no longer be explained by natural selection; it would be explained by the fact that they *intentionally* and *rationally* found the appropriate means for reaching their goal. Far from having their remarkable success explained by natural selection, the winners in this game could attribute their success to their expertise *only insofar as* they knew how to surpass the results that would have been possible through natural selection.

Let us now consider Friedman's other example concerning the density of leaves around a tree. This one is explicitly associated by its author with an example used by Alchian (Friedman 1953: 19, n. 14). In Friedman's version, the fact (held as hypothetically true) that the leaves are positioned around this tree 'as if each leaf deliberately sought to maximize the amount of sunlight it receives' (ibid.: 19) is explained without calling upon an intentional process of maximization that, in this case, would appear rather incongruous. Let us recall how Friedman presents the matter:

> We are inclined to 'explain' its validity on the ground that sunlight contributes to the growth of leaves and that hence leaves will grow denser or more putative leaves survive where there is more sun, so the result achieved by purely passive adaptation to external circumstances is the same as the result that would be achieved by deliberate accommodation to them.
>
> (Friedman 1953: 20)

Are we dealing here with a properly 'Darwinian' explanation, or instead with an explanation that is closer to the one proposed by Lamarck? The response to this question is not that simple. On the one hand, the notion of 'adaptation to external circumstances' evokes, at first glance, the approach of Lamarck, but in the case of the latter, adaptation is not 'purely passive'. On the other hand, according to Darwin, adaptation does not take place in such a simple way, but by the intervention of a mechanism that is not explicitly evoked by Friedman. A properly Darwinian argument would consist, for example, in accounting for the existence of types of trees on which the leaves would be distributed in such a way as to capture the maximum amount of solar light. To provide a Darwinian explanation of this phenomenon, we must, however, call upon not simply a passive adaptation, but certain accidental variations, the result of which, by pure chance, would turn out to be favourable and would be fully transmitted, with increased chance of survival, from generation to generation. Therefore, the fact that certain explanations (whether of appropriate positions of leaves, success in labyrinthine billiard or relative equilibrium of a market animated by irrational agents) must rely on accidentally favourable but rigorously transmitted random alterations, and not on intentional interventions, is essential to allow us to claim that they are akin to Darwinian explanations.

In short, what makes Darwin's argumentation so exceptionally significant is not that it explains a fact such as the more or less passive accumulation of leaves on the sunny side of trees. Anyone who intends, for example, to explain the unquestionable fact that wheat is found in much greater quantity in soil rich in nutrients than in rocky soil does not have to rely on Darwin's natural selection theory to accomplish this task. It is sufficient to point to the fact – as was implicitly but clearly already done in a well known parable related by Mark's Gospel (4: 3–9) – that the wheat cannot survive in the soils of the second type, precisely due to the absence of nutritious elements. In the same way, it was surely possible to understand well before Darwin that there are more leaves on the sunny side of a tree than on its shaded side. There is no need indeed to call upon the logic of Darwin's ideas to explain that leaves develop themselves more effectively on the side which is favourable to their growth, just as if they had intentionally chosen this position in spite of their incapacity to do scientific calculations; it is sufficient to acknowledge that leaves grow in greater abundance where they can benefit from the light provided by the sun.

If we want to use the example of the leaves of a tree to illustrate the mechanism at work in an economic market, we must then choose between two different ways of interpreting the adaptation, which constitutes its key element. Either we are dealing with a goal-oriented process (the leaves manage to grow as much as possible wherever they can grow efficiently) in which case we are closer to Lamarckianism than to Darwinism; or else we are faced with a strictly non-teleological process (some trees are accidentally equipped with the characteristic of having more leaves on sun side, which proves to be, not necessarily optimal, but advantageous enough to favour the systematic development of this kind of tree) and it is mostly this process that would make the explanation properly Darwinian. If we come back to the economy, the first interpretation (the Lamarckian one) would correspond to a situation in which entrepreneurs actively seek to adapt to their environment with the goal of increasing their profits, so that those who have the most success at this game find themselves in a relatively advantageous position whose neoclassical theory provides the idealized picture. In the second interpretation (closer to a Darwinian one), we acknowledge that entrepreneurs, given the context of total uncertainty in which they move, cannot contribute more than totally irrational fellows to improving their situation, but, thanks to an argument of the type used by Becker, enriched with largely unrealistic assumptions, it can nonetheless be maintained that the entrepreneurs who will have the chance to survive in a given market would find themselves in a position that would be not too far from what is described by economic theory.

With the help of Table 8.1, it is possible to characterize the various types of arguments considered here. The proposed categorization by no means aims at establishing watertight distinctions between biological theories, nor at proposing strict parallels between the latter and economic theories; rather, it summarizes a way of distinguishing between various types of explanation frequently used by economists and modes of argumentation that theories of biological evolution have largely contributed to characterizing.

Incompatible modes of explanation?

The remaining question to answer is whether explanations associated with (natural) selection and those based on rationality are compatible with each other and eventually complementary. The answer depends largely on the meaning attributed to selection. If it is understood as Nelson and Winter understood it in a Lamarckian context, it is difficult to deny that both approaches are compatible as

Table 8.1

Intentional (or goal-oriented) behaviour		*Economic theory*	*Fictional examples*	*Biological examples*
Individual level	*Overall level*			
Yes	Yes	Economic planning	Committee of selection for a position	
	Yes			Creationism
Yes	No	Economic theory of the firm in a competitive market (invisible hand)	Billiards Experts (Friedman ex.) Leaves growing in sunshine (Friedman ex.)	Lamarckism
No	No	Economic model with irrational agents (Becker example)	Labyrinthine Billiards Kind of tree with leaves facing sunshine (genetically)	Darwinism

these authors acknowledge. It is especially so when rationality is understood in a relatively minimal fashion. The fact that rational decisions are frequently suggested by routinized behaviour and that they sometimes consist in introducing new routines when a need for change is felt strongly enough does not exclude the fact that entrepreneurs strive to make the decisions that, in a context of relative uncertainty, have most chances to allow them to survive in a satisfactory fashion. They must be wise enough to change routines when it is really necessary and to manage in such a way that a truce, which is a key element according to Nelson and Winter, is maintained between all those who work in the firm. It is true that something seems to be closely akin to natural selection when we consider that some firms inherit successful routines whose managers were efficient enough to avoid bankruptcy. Nonetheless, explaining the fact that the most well adapted firms tend to survive in this context is not fundamentally different from explaining, in the manner suggested by standard economics, the fact that only the firms that satisfy the needs of consumers have chances to survive for long in a competitive market.

If, as I suggest, we abandon the strictly maximizing conception of rationality, which is not compatible with the tradition originating with Alchian and developed by Nelson and Winter, these two ways of explaining become hardly distinguishable. It is true that the latter insists on the transmission (through imitation) of routines, which are even put in parallel with genes (Nelson and Winter 1982: 134–136), but the parallelism works only when we refer to the units of content transmitted, but not to the accidental, unconscious and non-teleological character of mutations. Since the origin and modification of routines depends largely, as carefully illustrated by these authors (ibid.: 72–130), on the skill and ingenuity of various people, it would sound preposterous to claim that these phenomena are purely accidental. As for the fact that it is only *ex post* that the participants in the market are revealed to have been relatively efficient, it characterizes an invisible hand explanation as well as analyses of economics derived from Alchian's paper.

Natural selection has little to do with the approach according to which entrepreneurs, who do what they judge appropriate to profitably satisfy the demand of consumers in a more or less routinized way, are those who have a better chance of surviving, whereas those who, by lack of skill or by mischance, do not succeed in profitably selling commodities risk being progressively forced to quit the market. The crucial question is that of deciding whether that which is explained does or does not exceed that which a non-intentional mechanism permits us to account for. For example, in the game of labyrinthine billiards imagined above, the question is of deciding whether certain players can or cannot, as a result of cleverness or cunning, find a way to arrive more quickly at the desired results than those who allow themselves to be guided by chance. If we respond to this question in the affirmative, then we simply have a matter of game of skill in which, however, the performances required are much more difficult to carry out than those that are normally associated with the game of billiards. In this new game, experts, if any, would be progressively recognized as in any game. At most, they would sometimes risk sharing the top ranks with others who are less skilled but who, on certain occasions, have had a fair amount of luck. Nonetheless, given the exceptional performances of these experts, it could hardly make sense to pretend that their quality is due to the blind mechanism that explains any performance whatever it is. If, on the other hand, we are forced to respond to the question in the negative, in estimating that in this game it is impossible to do better than random, then there is no reason to expect to observe particularly effective performances; however, if an astonishingly adequate result is nonetheless observed after a long period, it might be appropriate to attempt to explain this with the help of a kind of natural selection argument. In effect, it would not be possible to attribute an explanatory role to the intentional decisions of the players in this case since, according to our hypothesis, they have no impact to the point that the players are totally indifferent to pushing balls in one direction rather than another.

In short, these two types of explanations (rational individuals entering into competition and natural selection) are intended to respectively explain different phenomena and it is in this sense and in this sense only that, as explanations of a specific phenomenon, they are incompatible with each other. On the one hand, if the phenomenon to be explained is an astonishing equilibrium that, hypothetically, would result from totally irrational actions of entrepreneurs acting in a context of total uncertainty where no estimate could hold whatsoever, then only a natural selection mechanism akin to those that were resorted to when discussing Becker's model, might do the job. On the other hand, if the point is to explain that a free economy, animated by entrepreneurs who make self-interested decisions, generates markets relatively well equilibrated in a way that is judged far superior (measured by the precision and the rapidity of the adaptation required) to anything that natural selection might eventually generate, then it is the rationality (in spite of its limitations) of the decision makers that should be called in to explain the phenomenon. Put otherwise, if entrepreneurs cannot do better than what can be obtained by acting randomly, only natural selection might explain any unexpected result that would be obtained; and if they can do better, there is no point in attempting to explain through natural selection what, by hypothesis, it cannot explain. Therefore, appealing to both explanations together does not make sense.

One might object however that the picture is more complex since an economic society is a highly complex entity in which we encounter entrepreneurs that are highly skilful and very eager to increase their profits, and others more erratic and often less motivated. Couldn't the success of the first group be explained by an argument resting on the rationality of their choices, while at the same time the survival of the second group could be explained by an application of natural selection to the economy? Put otherwise, why can't both kinds of explanation be complementary in the sense that natural selection would explain the efficiency of markets in general, whereas the highly rational behaviour of some entrepreneurs would explain that it would be them rather than their less rational colleagues who are the most successful? The problem posed by this kind of eclecticism is due to the fact that, in principle, all these entrepreneurs are in competition in the *same* market and face more or less similar conditions. If it is found that the most motivated and most astute entrepreneurs of the first group, thanks to these qualities, tend to do better than those of the second group, who up to now avoid bankruptcy in spite of their poor performances, then the type of selection that takes place *between these two groups* is exactly the one that is assumed by the economic theory of the competitive market, and does not rest on a mechanism of natural selection. Indeed, resorting to natural selection as the exclusive way of explaining the survival of the members of the second group (the more erratic one) would be rather odd: since this kind of explanation is supposed to explain the survival of the *fittest*, how could we argue that it might explain the survival only of the less fitted among the survivors? It should primarily explain the survival of the most successful entrepreneurs, but if we agree, by hypothesis, that this phenomenon is explained by the relatively appropriate choices of the latter, the performance of their somewhat less successful competitors should be explained by the fact that their choices turn out to be somewhat less appropriate, while nonetheless more so than those of the entrepreneurs who did not avoid bankruptcy. Why should natural selection enter into the picture? After all, this kind of argument is normally utilized only when rational explanations cannot be applied when it comes to explaining a phenomenon (like the origin of well adapted species or the hypothetical equilibrium of a market animated by totally irrational traders) that looks like the result of an intentional selection but cannot be attributed to any kind of intentionality in a scientific explanation. In contrast, if entrepreneurs can make some profits and be selected as survivors by making rational decisions and doing the best they can, their survival can hardly be attributed to natural selection, even though they are less successful than some colleagues and more than others.

In more general terms, relying concurrently on both natural selection and rational explanations to account for the same aspect of the phenomenon does not work, because it would imply either subordinating one kind of explanation to the other, neutralizing one in favour of the other or, reinterpreting one in the terms of the other. For example, admitting than the entrepreneurs rationally take appropriate means to reach a goal that would be obtained to the same degree and in an equal period of time thanks to natural selection (if we want to suppose for a moment that such a thing makes sense) would not be to bring about two complementary explanations for the same phenomenon, it would be to dissolve the very meaning of the former and reinterpret it in the terms of the latter. While having the impression that they are making rational choices, the entrepreneurs, objectively, would hardly have done anything other than to make random choices, since all possible choices would have been, by hypothesis, rigorously equivalent from the point of view of the expected result.

Let me illustrate this kind of overdetermination of explanation with the help of a very simple example. Suppose that a group of archers succeed with astonishing success in reaching a target that is far away. We normally explain this fact by emphasizing their determination, their skill and the rational means that they have taken in order to realize such performances. If, however, we discover later that an extremely powerful magnet was hidden behind the centre of the target and that it is strong enough to easily attract any arrow flying in the area, then the astonishing phenomenon is fully explained by the powerful magnetic field associated with the magnet and nothing is left to be explained by the skill and the rationality of the archers. Since the direction towards which the arrows are fired has absolutely no impact on their final position, it is clear that the skill of the archers cannot be the explanation of the astonishing result observed. The point here is not to explain a remarkable performance of expert archers since these archers do not have to achieve anything more than the most unskilled individual who would have thrown an arrow anywhere under the same conditions. Of course, if the power of the magnet turns out to vanish, the arrows fired by the experts might still reach the centre of the target and an explanation of this fact would rely on the skill and the intentions of the archers, but the phenomenon to be explained would be a totally new one, namely the fact that the arrows fired by the experts systematically reach a point that arrows thrown by most other people almost never reach.

To summarize, when a general mechanism (whether related to a magnetic field or to natural selection) can explain a situation, it does not make sense to resort to rational explanations in order to account for it. If an individual decides to commit suicide and jumps from the summit of a high building, a rational explanation (not necessarily compelling) is required to explain such a decision and the fatal action that follows. However, if, throughout the fall, this individual does everything possible to realize his goal of quickly and fatally contacting the ground, there is no need to invoke such a bizarre endeavour for explaining the fact, rapidly verified, that the lethal goal is reached, given that universal gravitation constitutes a sufficient explanation for this fact. It is only when such general mechanisms cannot fully explain an intentional phenomenon that it makes sense to appeal to a rational explanation (referring to the determination of skilful archers or entrepreneurs, to despair and convictions of the suicidal person, etc.) to account for this phenomenon. It is because social sciences and especially economics study mostly such phenomena resulting from intentional interventions that rational explanations occupy the central place in these sciences. Of course, we must turn towards natural selection when it comes to explaining the genesis of the brain through which these interventions are initiated, but explaining the development of the brain is not explaining the social consequences of the interactions of a multitude of people, which is what economists aim to do. Explaining the genesis of the brain is not explaining the genesis of markets and of money.

No doubt many economists, eager to vindicate the scientific character of their discipline, would prefer that another type of explanation, more akin to those which are typical of natural sciences, also be available. This may possibly explain the popularity of arguments based on natural selection among many of them, even though such arguments are frequently understood in the Lamarckian version put forward by Nelson and Winter (and even by Alchian) and then do not differ so much from the rational explanations of traditional economics. However, before concluding that economics has no kind of scientific value, because the phenomena typical of this field cannot be accounted for through explanations similar to those of natural sciences, it is worth looking at how rational explanations can hold water when they are assessed by the theories of scientific explanation that have been developed with the help of examples mostly drawn from natural sciences. This will be my task in the next and last chapter.

9 Theories of explanation applied to economics

Explanations in economics and explanations in physics

As we have seen, if the rationality principle is so important for social sciences, and especially for economics, it is because it plays a crucial role in most explanations – and, to a lesser degree, in many predictions – provided by these sciences. If the latter were not oriented towards providing explanations, economists and other social scientists could almost dispense with the rationality principle. Let us try to figure out what economic explanations would look like without the rationality principle and, consequently, without its most typical explanations. Economists would be able, with a reasonable degree of precision, to describe facts such as variations in prices, demand, interest rates or money exchange rates, etc. without involving themselves in questions concerning *why* prices, demand or rates increase or decrease in such or such a fashion. Moreover, economists would be able to make predictions, but only those based on observed regularities or, if one prefers, on 'laws' that express the relatively loose regularities referred to in the Introduction of this book. These laws could even be used to provide a certain kind of explanation. For example, an economist could explain an increase in the price of good X by invoking the stability of X's supply in addition to an observed increase in demand, together with a law according to which if the demand for a good whose supply is fixed increases, then the price of this good will increase. This law might be based on statistical analysis of data concerning supply, demand and prices. Measuring the stability of supply and variations in prices would be relatively straightforward, whereas measuring demand would be based on more or less sophisticated inquiries or experimental devices. People could be asked how much they would buy of such or such a good were it sold at such or such a price, or alternatively, their reaction to various prices could be tested in various experimental situations. However, if one were to examine *why* people tend to buy more when prices are low or *why* sellers tend to raise their prices when demand increases, no possible answers could satisfy these legitimate questions. Buying more of a good when its price increases and buying more of it when its price decreases would have to be considered as two strictly equivalent possibilities, and the fact that we tend to privilege the latter alternative would have to be imputed only to the unexplained fact that, according to observation, it is the one that prevails. Economists would supposedly be unable to experience the motivations of people, nor could economists have access to an intimate experience of a preference for having more goods since such an experience would be too suggestive of the rationality principle. In fact, economists would have absolutely no reason to be puzzled if ever it was established that human beings buy more when the price is higher than when the price is lower. Naturally, if economists observe that people always buy more of cheaper goods, the fact that one individual does the contrary would be puzzling because it seems important to explain why this particular individual does not behave like others and does not respect the 'law' of demand, which is assumed to be relatively well established given the behaviour generally observed. But if it were observed that people quite generally buy more of more expensive goods than they buy cheaper ones, economists would have absolutely no reason to be surprised by this observation. The law of demand would have simply to be represented by an increasing curve. An economist's a priori preference for a decreasing curve would be an unjustified and unscientific subjective preference. It would be similar to a Newtonian physicist's *preference* for a law of universal attraction over a law of universal repulsion of bodies in a world where general repulsion would be systematically observed. The fact that, in the economic world, it is the decreasing demand curve that prevails would have to be registered as a fact that has no reason to be considered more normal than its contrary or to be considered more easily explainable than the latter. Similarly, it would be odd to a priori maintain that a physical world in which bodies were attracted to one another looks more normal and more easily explainable than a physical world in which systematically bodies were mutually repulsing.

The comparison with Newtonian physics shows that this kind of situation is quite normal in natural sciences, where laws are exclusively based (directly or indirectly) on such regularities. However, this fact does not seem to reduce the scope of the explanations that natural scientists provide. Thanks especially to physics, we understand a number of phenomena, but the laws involved in those explanations are founded on regularities and consistencies and have evidently nothing to do with any kind of rationality attributed to natural entities. Phenomena must happen in some determinate way because they obey such or such laws in full consistency with other laws involved in similar phenomena. Why should we expect something else to happen in such situations? What happens is precisely what is expected according to well established laws of nature. Thus, what actually happens is explained; why look for more explanations? Asking why bodies are attracted to rather than repulsed by other bodies is a silly question unless one envisages a still more general hypothesis according to which this fundamental assumption of Newtonian physics becomes a particular case deducible in particular circumstances from the assumptions of this eventual more general hypothesis. Similarly, the question as to why a body keeps its velocity in the absence of a specific force (whose effect would be to reduce it) is considered a silly question.[1] At any moment in time, a few fundamental facts are considered as given and, in the absence of a scientific revolution, questions about them are perceived either as silly or as purely metaphysical, similar to the venerable question 'Why is there something rather than nothing?'

One cannot a priori exclude the possibility for social scientists and for economists in particular to proceed as physicists do. Why do consumers tend to buy less of a good when its price increases? What kind of forces keep them from buying as much of this good as before in such circumstances? One might answer that consumers are forced to keep their money in such a way that they are enabled to buy more of other advantageously cheaper goods; but this only pushes the problem a step further, because the point is precisely to explain why people tend to obtain more of a good when it is cheaper and refrain from buying it when its price is higher. One cannot invoke, here, the fact that it is clearly in their interest to pay less for a given good and to get, in this way, both the good and part of the money which would otherwise be paid in order to obtain it, because such an answer would introduce the notion of self-interest, which is precisely the kind of notion that must be avoided if our explanation must be modelled on explanations provided in physics and exclude reliance on the rationality principle. Indeed, explaining an action by the actor's self-interest is explaining it by invoking this actor's reasons, but in the realm of physics and in a world from which the rationality principle is absent, nothing is done *in order to* obtain more or for any other *reason*. Post-Aristotelian physicists never invoke anything akin to falling bodies' self-interest when they explain their attraction to the Earth.

As we have seen in the two preceding chapters of this book, some economists have tried to explain such economic phenomena with the help of natural selection and some others are expecting neuroscience to develop explanations of these phenomena, which would be more akin to scientific ones. However, while the results of these attempts may be judged promising, they remain much too limited and ambiguous for clearly justifying the dismissal of explanations based on the rationality principle. I will come back to these questions in the concluding considerations of this book, but for now it is time to evaluate rational explanations in light of theories of explanation that were developed in philosophy of science.

Hempel's unified theory of explanation

This situation raises a particularly troublesome epistemological problem. If social sciences can develop a different kind of 'scientific explanation' based on principles totally different from those on which the scientific character of explanations provided by natural sciences is grounded, one may question either the scientific character of these alleged scientific explanations or the very notion of a 'scientific' explanation. If there are various ways to explain scientifically, how might one neutralize the pretensions of astrologers and other charlatans who claim that they provide 'scientific' explanations as well? In this context, it is hardly surprising that the question of the nature of a scientific explanation has occupied an important place in the philosophy of science, but since it is full of ambiguities, it has constantly divided philosophers of science for more than a century. The most sophisticated debates took place between philosophers of physics, but since a parallel debate was taking place regarding explanation in history, a discipline in which the role of the rationality principle is as important as it is in economics, I will start by considering this latter debate. After discussing the problem in this context and applying the results to economics (where few similar debates took place), I will try to clarify various problems by considering and discussing later developments in the debate among philosophers of physics. This transition from explanation in history (or in economics) to explanation in physics (and vice versa) will be greatly facilitated by the fact that debates in both domains were provoked by papers published by Carl Hempel regarding scientific explanation.

Hempel's deductive-nomological (DN) model of explanation was actually set forth for the first time in a paper addressing the problem of explanation in history (Hempel 1942) though it was fully explicated only six years later in a paper written with Paul Oppenheim (Hempel and Oppenheim 1948). As was recalled in the introduction of the present book, according to Hempel, a scientific explanation must be derived from a set of well established facts together with at least one empirical law. But as early as the 1950s, the philosopher William Dray, joined by a few other philosophers influenced by R. G. Collingwood's ideas regarding history (Collingwood 1946), contested Hempel's view and claimed that an explanation can be perfectly valid without the help of any law (Dray 1957). According to Dray, historians in particular invoke typically 'rational explanations' based on agents' rationality rather than on any law. One might also recall that a significant part of the considerations raised in this debate were anticipated by German philosophers involved at the end of nineteenth century and at the beginning of the twentieth in the debate concerning the alleged opposition between the natural sciences which allow us to explain (*erklären*), and the human sciences which allow us to understand (*verstehen*). In the nineteenth century, however, human sciences were mostly focused on the interpretation of biblical and classical texts, whereas, in the mid-twentieth century, the context was quite different, due to the important development of social sciences, whose pretension was also to explain. Therefore, the debate between Hempel and Dray did not directly refer to understanding, but concerned only two different views of explanation, one being typical of natural sciences and the other of history. Before trying to see whether these two views can be made compatible or not, let us recall the essentials of each of them.

Hempel's models are very well known, but since most theories of scientific explanation can be considered as reactions to these models, I think it is worthwhile to recall – with a few more details – the ideas on which they are founded and to illustrate why, in spite of their shortcomings, they are much more than purely formal schemes. According to Hempel's Deductive-Nomological (DN) model, two elements are required to have a scientific explanation: at least one law covering the phenomenon to be explained (designated as the explanandum), which justifies its being called nomological, and deducibility of this explanandum, which justifies its being called deductive. In such a view, a scientific explanation is nothing but an argument in virtue of which the explanandum can be logically deduced from a set of well confirmed facts together with some empirically established laws. While apparently purely formal, this theory allows us to put our finger on a central element of a scientific explanation. Let me briefly re-illustrate the logic of Hempel's argumentation, using this time an adaptation of one of Hempel's own examples borrowed from automobile mechanics.

Suppose that you are totally ignorant of mechanics and that, while taking out your car on a chilly morning, you notice a peculiar liquid flowing underneath it. You conclude that this liquid is coming from your car and that this is bad news. Looking for an explanation, a set of alternatives comes to mind: your car is a poorly maintained 'lemon'; a gang of local vagrants have amused themselves by perforating some part of your car; it was caused by malignant and powerful extraterrestrial creatures arriving in a UFO; the perforation might have been the result of an evil curse cast on you by a sorcerer who was insulted by your sceptical attitude regarding voodoo practices during your recent visit to Haiti. You consider all of these alternative explanations when a friend well versed in mechanics, passes you on the street and immediately looks below the hood. Your friend observes that the liquid (pure water without antifreeze) is leaking from your antiquated radiator, which clearly has burst the previous night. After reminding you that the temperature dropped below zero last night, this friend provides you with a scientific explanation for this unfortunate event. According to one law of physics, any quantity of water submitted to a temperature below zero centigrade will change into a larger volume of ice, which will necessarily break any container too small for it and too weak to withstand the mounting pressure. Since all the facts involved are effectively present and the law empirically established, the conclusion is irresistible: the breaking of the radiator should have been predictable to anybody with an awareness of the relevant facts on the previous night, since it is simply a matter of what happens regularly in such circumstances. The point here is that the explanation is clearly a scientific one, which means that you may put aside thoughts about lemons, vagrants, UFOs and sorcerers, since, now, you hold a scientific explanation.[2]

It is difficult indeed to resist such an explanation, but what makes it an explanation at all? Why does this deductive argument satisfy our need for explanation? It would be a mistake to attribute its virtue to the deductive power as such. Hempel himself, realizing that most scientific explanations in modern physics, and especially in quantum physics, are based on statistical laws, introduced his Inductive-Statistical (IS) model in order to cope with this situation (see in particular, Hempel 1965: Part 3). The remarkable fact about this move is that the deductive dimension of the DN model was sacrificed in order to preserve its nomological dimension. With the IS model, a strict deduction is no longer possible, though a relatively safe inductive conclusion can be reached, given the high probability implied in the statistical law involved. This law is now a statistical one, but it remains a law that emphasizes the regularity of the phenomenon to be explained. Hempel and his successors provide a great number of examples of both DN and IS explanations drawn from modern physics, but it is interesting to note that these kinds of scientific explanation can also be met, though clearly less frequently, in social sciences, including economics. Suppose that you want to buy an artwork by your favourite painter and that, influenced by the dramatic, continuous drop in the price of computers, you expect and wait for a similar drop in the price of the painting you have in mind. And suppose that the painter dies and that his death generates more interest in his painting. You go to the gallery and discover with great disappointment that the price of the painting has gone up considerably. You look for an explanation and consider various alternatives. Perhaps the gallery holder knew of your fondness for this painter and increased its price in order either to make an excessive profit or to punish you for something you had done which profoundly hurt him in the past; or perhaps a kind of fatal doom or genetic misfortune is there to block any favour that life offers you. An economist friend of yours rejects these foolish explanations and replaces them with a scientific one. This well informed economist observes that the greater notoriety of this painter has increased the demand for paintings whose production was interrupted by death and adds that there is a statistical law of demand according to which if the demand for a good whose supply is fixed increases, then the price of this good will increase. From this, it is easy to induce that the increase in price for these paintings should have been expected since it is simply a matter of what happens regularly in these circumstances. Why, in such a situation, look for far-fetched explanations? Thus, we can say that explanations conforming to either one of the Hempelian models are explanations because they convincingly let us see that the explanandum is nothing more than a case of a standard phenomenon which happens every time (or almost every time) a similar situation prevails. Given such a situation, it would be silly to keep looking for an explanation since what happened is precisely what was expected according to this law.

The role of rational explanations in social sciences

It is interesting to consider now the views of William Dray, not so much in order to emphasize his objections to Hempel's thesis, but to illustrate that a quite different type of explanation, exemplified by what Dray calls a 'rational explanation', which is clearly based on the rationality principle, might be scientifically significant, even though it looks very similar to a common-sense type of explanation. Here again, the classical example used by the author will help in understanding in what sense such a claim can be sustained. Dray took as an example the explanation, proposed by the historian G. M. Trevelyan, of the fact that in 1688 Louis XIV, a particularly opportunist and ambitious French King, refrained from invading Holland, a country he coveted, and this in spite of the fact that King William of Holland was fully occupied by the conquest of England. Trevelyan, who estimated, apparently on the basis of quite satisfying evidence, that the king's ambition extended to all of Europe and not only to tiny Holland, offered the following explanation: '[Louis XIV] calculated that, even if William landed in England, there would be civil war and long troubles, as always in that factious island. Meanwhile, he could conquer Europe at leisure.'[3] For Dray, the important point is that, in such an example, no covering law was available to Trevelyan and none whatsoever was necessary, because what such an explanation 'aims to show' is that the thing done by Louis XIV 'made perfectly good sense from his own point of view', not that a similar thing would necessarily have been done by other conquering kings (or even by Louis XIV himself) in similar circumstances. Therefore, since it is not based on a law, an explanation of this kind does not imply that it would have been possible to predict that Louis XIV would have done what he did.

Before discussing the titles of such an explanation to be treated as scientifically significant, let us consider a relatively similar one found in economics. The standard explanation of the phenomenon associated with the so-called Giffen goods illustrates this fairly well. For sure, the problem at hand is more theoretical than Trevelyan's, but this is normal when passing from history to a science based on generalized phenomena such as economics. Whereas the quantity demanded of any good normally decreases when the price of this good goes up, it was noted on rare occasions that the quantity of potatoes bought by poor people paradoxically increased when their price went up. The standard textbook explanation is as follows: potatoes are a widely consumed 'inferior good' and the consumption of such inferior goods may increase in spite of rising prices if the income effect of such price increases outweighs its substitution effect. One might argue that in this case, in contrast with Louis XIV's case, we have a lawlike statement concerning the relative impact of income and substitution effect, but it would be excessive to claim that this statement corresponds to an *empirical* law. Like the explanation of the shortage of apartments at low rental price discussed in the Introduction to this book, the explanation of the Giffen goods phenomenon draws its force not from this 'law' but from the fact that consumers are supposed to be rational. Indeed, if it is rational to consume less potatoes when their price increases, it is also rational, when discovering the negative effect on one's available income of this price increase, to abandon the consumption of more expensive superior goods and replace the latter by still more potatoes, which, in spite of their increased price, remain cheaper than those superior goods. This explanation parallels Trevelyan's because, in both cases, there is puzzling behaviour to explain (not invading Holland when it is left unprotected and buying more potatoes when their price is higher) since, in the described situation, the opposite behaviour (invading Holland and buying less potatoes respectively), at first glance, seems more appropriate. In both cases, it is the rationality principle that plays the decisive role in the explanation (since Louis XIV is rational, he refrains from invading Holland in order to benefit from the absence of William; since consumers are rational, they abandon expensive superior goods and buy more potatoes). In both cases, this becomes sensible only once a flawed assessment of the situation is corrected by instead adopting a more encompassing description of the situation: the king is in a better position to invade all of Europe if William remains out of the picture; consumers take into account the effect of increased prices on their incomes and not only the fact that it is sensible to consume less of any good whose price increases. Moreover, one must note that, in both cases, it is the same rationality principle that was the *source* of the puzzling situation requiring an explanation: *given their alleged rationality* and the previous assessment of the situation, it looked reasonable to think that the king should have invaded Holland and that consumers should buy less potatoes.

On what basis can one claim that the behaviours of Louis XIV and of our consumers have been explained? Clearly it is because, in both cases, a puzzling situation, one caused by an apparent contradiction between what happened and what was logically expected, turned out – due to the cognitive content and the logical considerations conveyed by the explanation – to appear perfectly normal since what had happened corresponded fairly well to what should have been expected in the now differently understood circumstances. Incidentally, in some sense, it is for the same reason that DN or IS explanations work. The leaking car and the increased price of paintings were seen as puzzling events since they contradicted what was expected, but, due to the information and to the logical considerations provided by relevant explanations, these events turned out to be perfectly normal given their exact correspondence to what should have been expected under the correctly understood circumstances. In spite of their opposition to such rational explanations, Hempelians would not have great difficulty agreeing on the functional similarity between the two alleged kinds of explanation since they believe that explanations based on the rationality principle, and even on common sense, frequently qualify as explanation 'sketches', which provide what could be characterized as an explanation's substantial components (see Hempel 1942: section 5.4). Thus, their disagreement does not concern the explanatory but the scientific character of such rational explanations.

Why rational explanations might qualify as 'scientific' explanations

What makes Hempelian explanations more scientific than those associated with common sense? Essentially two things: in a scientific explanation (1) all the facts invoked are, in principle, empirically well established, and (2) the explanandum is correctly derived with the help of at least one empirical law. The first point can make a radical difference between Hempelian and common-sense explanations, but not between the former and the rational explanations used by historians and economists. At least in principle, historians establish their facts with the best critical techniques available, while economists, if they were explaining a phenomenon with the help of an argument of the type illustrated in the Giffen goods case, would normally manage to establish their facts with the best econometrical techniques. Given the particular difficulties associated with the assessment of human behaviour, one may argue that, actually, natural scientists establish their facts in a more compelling way than historians and economists, but this is not a reason to invoke a difference of principle on this matter. In any case, it is the second point which is most crucial. The function of empirical laws is to reduce the explanandum to simple law-covered cases by assuring that at any time the situation is present, the explanandum is to be expected (and even predicted). Without these laws, the reasons why one expects that the fact described by the explanandum will occur seem to vanish. This is why Hempel claimed that, in order to qualify as scientific, Trevelyan's explanation should be supported by a general law according to which, in a situation similar to Louis XIV's, any rational agent would invariably (or with high probability) refrain from invading a country like Holland (Hempel 1963: 155). Only the addition of such a premise would have permitted a *prediction* of Louis XIV's action. This law-based predictability seems important indeed, because if it is admitted that Louis XIV could have, in the same circumstances, chosen to invade Holland, how can we say that the fact that he did not is explained? Such a hypothetical law could have one of the two following bases. It might be a statistical law based on the observation of leaders' decisions in a situation similar to Louis XIV's, but this possibility can be forgotten because, if one follows Dray's argumentation (Dray 1957: chapter 2), whereas such a law would normally have to be based on a number of situations similar on *all* relevant grounds, specific historical situations, such as the one involving Louis XIV's decision, would hardly be exemplified by cases *other* than the case that is considered. Moreover, even in the most similar cases, the possibility that the opposite decision might have been made cannot be excluded. In the case of the Giffen goods example, some economists would probably be prepared to contemplate a statistical law according to which consumers, after experiencing a decrease in available income caused by the rise in the price of a widely consumed inferior good, abandon the consumption of superior goods and increase their consumption of *this* inferior good. However, this lawlike proposition, which appears reasonable but virtually non-testable given its acknowledged atypical and almost anecdotal character, can hardly be considered an empirical law. Alternatively, a law could be based on neurophysiological considerations which would allow us to conclude that, in that situation, Louis XIV necessarily chose not to invade. However, even if some scientists may hope that, at some stage in the future, it will be possible to explain all human decisions this way, this possibility appears, at this moment in time, like a Laplacean dream and, in the absence of the still tremendous amount of knowledge necessary to establish it, the required law would simply consist in a sheer denial of the (at least apparent) fact that, in many situations, human beings can decide either way.

What happens if no empirical law of the proper type is available to historians or even to economists? Should we conclude that they fail to provide the scientific explanations they pretend to offer? Or does the Hempelian challenge force us to reassess the very meaning of an explanation? Could Trevelyan's explanation be characterized as scientific without the help of any law? What principle, if it were not a law, would allow us to infer that the decision *not to invade* must now be considered as the one expected of Louis XIV? Clearly, the 'principle of action',[4] referred to by Dray in this context, implicitly derives from the rationality principle, which implies that (rational) people make rational decisions and normally perform actions compatible with such decisions. Such a principle suggests that Louis XIV, who, after all, is considered to be a rational person, makes rational decisions. Hempel's strategy (1963: 155) was to tentatively consider that an empirically grounded reformulation of a principle of this kind might play the role of the covering law in an explanation such as Trevelyan's, but there is unfortunately no ground that would allow us to treat the rationality principle as an empirical law. It seems reasonable to claim that human beings are rational at least in the minimal sense of being not stupid and of being guided by intentional motivations, as economists readily admit, but should we give scientific credibility to the idea that a particular individual such as Louis XIV is rational to the point of making the decision which seems the most appropriate in a given circumstance? Surely not, but let us put the question a little more realistically. Without being in position to invoke a law, can we claim that Louis XIV is the kind of person who is rational enough to make decisions that qualify as rational?

In order to answer this question, we should take into consideration a remarkable fact, one that does not seem to have been underscored in the discussion about this type of explanation. It is the fact that the rationality principle, on the basis of which the decision not to invade is now seen as the decision to be expected, is precisely the same principle on the basis of which the decision *to invade* was previously seen as the decision to be expected. It is precisely *because Louis XIV was considered a rational person* that his decision not to invade conflicted with what appeared to be the logically expected decision, namely to invade, and it was this conflict that required an explanation. But, if, once our knowledge of the facts is rectified, it is exactly the same view about his rationality that allows us to conclude that what he did actually corresponds to what was expected and is therefore explained, there is no point in inquiring about the empirical status of this view about his rationality. Had we no reason to trust it, it would be less the explanation than the question itself which would lose its very meaning: why would someone who is not at all convinced that Louis XIV is one of those rational persons who normally avoids 'silly' decisions be particularly puzzled by an alleged inappropriate decision of this king? It is only if we accept, at least hypothetically, that Louis XIV was a rational person who normally avoids silly decisions that a problem is raised by his (apparently irrational) decision not to invade. Thus, joined with the empirically documented facts revealed by Trevelyan's analysis, a principle, which is *necessarily accepted* if there is a problem to solve and anything to explain, allows us to conclude that we hold an explanation which removes the problem and the puzzlement. Since, in this explanation, only empirically established facts and a necessarily accepted principle are involved, there is no compelling reason to deny that it should no longer be considered to be a simple common-sense explanation and that it is sensible to treat it as a scientific explanation, at least in the sense of being based on the best techniques available in the circumstance for deriving the safer conclusion about this explanandum.

As for the case of Giffen goods, it is similar to that of Louis XIV. There is no such thing as an empirical law according to which people experiencing a decrease in available income due to an increase in the price of a largely consumed good will increase their consumption of this good as a substitute for the forced diminution of their consumption of a superior good. This proposition, which appears reasonable even though it so rarely concerns observable situations, cannot seriously be considered an empirical law. It is probable that too many people will continue consuming more or less in accordance with their habitual consumption patterns to leave room for even a statistical law of this type. However, if an explanation was required, it is because the supposedly well observed phenomenon (increased potato consumption) was contrary to what is expected on the basis of the relevant application of the rationality principle, according to which people are rational enough to reduce their consumption of a good whose price increases significantly. However, once the economist has established that the income effect of this price reduction is important enough to induce a rational consumer to replace superior goods by still cheaper potatoes, it is precisely the *same* rationality principle that allows us to explain that the increase in potato consumption is exactly what should be expected. Were the principle that people are rational to be rejected, the increased consumption of more expensive potatoes would not be perceived as a puzzling situation demanding explanation, since it would be admitted from the start that variations in consumption are more or less randomly determined and have nothing to do with people's rational endeavour to be intentionally motivated in their consumption choices. However, since we have assumed that the economist's explanation of a situation involving Giffen goods is based on facts established with the best empirical methods available, together with this rationality principle (accepted with the very acceptation of the existence of problem to solve), there is no compelling reason to deny the scientific quality of this explanation either. Note, however, that accepting the scientific quality of such explanations does not mean that they are definitely true, since no scientific explanation is definitely true and all can be and are challenged.

The situation is quite different regarding the radiator and the price of artworks since there the laws invoked to conclude that the observed event was to be expected were absolutely not involved in what raised the problem: on the contrary, in these cases, it is the ignorance of those laws (the deterministic law of dilatation of water turning into ice and the statistical law of demand applied to goods of fixed supply), and not their acceptance as was the case with the rationality principle, which raises a problem requiring an explanation. Thus, it seems that the principle of inference which allows an explainer to conclude that an explanandum is satisfactorily explained can be either an empirical law expressing some observed regularities (as in the cases of the radiator and the price of artwork) or a principle that is pre-admitted, because it is itself a condition for the very existence of the problem to be solved (as in the cases of Louis XIV's decision and of the Giffen goods).

Hempel's theory challenged by Salmon: relevance versus expectation

Clearly, the attribution of such a scientific quality to explanations that are not based on any law is not compatible with the Hempelian ideal of a specific and unique definition of a scientific explanation. However, the authority of Hempelian views has been slowly but considerably eroded by an increasing number of objections which have weakened the integrity of most of its tenets. Thus, before returning to the discussion of the status of rational explanations, it is appropriate to look at the important developments in the theory of explanation which have taken place in the philosophy of natural sciences, especially during the 1970s and 1980s. It would be beyond the scope of the present study to systematically discuss the variety of arguments which have been proposed in order to point out insufficiencies in the Hempelian standard theory and which have forced philosophers to develop, during this period, new theories of scientific explanation. I will recall only three of the most famous counterexamples which have eloquently brought to light these insufficiencies. The Hempelian thesis according to which explanation and prediction are two faces of the same argument was probably the most frequently challenged, using counterexamples such as the fact that, long before Newton, mariners could predict the tides with the help of a law derived from the observation of the moon's positions and phases, while being totally unable to provide an explanation for such a phenomenon (Salmon 1989: 47). Other examples illustrate still more clearly that a perfectly well formed DN argument cannot be an explanation. The most often cited among these examples is probably the one involving a flagpole, whose height can be correctly deduced, but hardly explained, from the length of its shadow together with elementary trigonometric laws. It is clear that many examples of this kind can be found in economics as well. Whenever we observe a continuous increase in the price of a fix-supplied good, we can correctly *deduce* from the (correctly inverted) 'law' of demand that there is an increase in demand for it, but it would be absurd to conclude from this deduction that the increase in price *explains* the increase in demand: it is evidently the latter together with the inelastic supply that explain the increase in prices. Correct inference from a law (together with relevant facts) is far from being a sufficient condition of an explanation. Thus, not all correct inferences are explanations, but should all explanations be inferences? It does not seem to be the case, which means that a correct inference is not a necessary condition of an explanation either. This was clearly illustrated in a paper published in *Science* by Michael Scriven (1959: 480) who observed that, paresis being a sickness developed in about 25 per cent of those whose syphilis was left untreated with penicillin, one can reasonably claim that the absence of penicillin treatment of one's syphilis *explains* one's later paresis. However, Scriven added, this implies that an alleged law, according to which untreated syphilitics will develop paresis, is falsified in 75 per cent of cases. This example also illustrates in a different way that explanation and prediction must be dissociated since, in spite of the fact that paresis is correctly explained by untreated syphilis, one would be safer in predicting that an untreated syphilitic will *not* develop paresis. More generally, one can say that rare events, which happen only, but far from always, in rare circumstances, can frequently be explained by the presence of these circumstances, even if they cannot be predicted, or inferred from them.

Given these difficulties in Hempel's theory of explanation, the idea that an explanation is either a deductive or inductive *argument* from which the explanandum can be inferred has been seriously questioned. Wesley Salmon is among those who radically rejected this view (Salmon 1971a: 9; 1989: 101–107). According to him, the crucial element for an explanation is not the high probability which allows us to infer the explanandum, but the relevance of the factors involved with respect to the event to be explained. To illustrate his point, he used the following example (which was his favourite). It is perfectly true that any man who takes contraceptive pills will never become pregnant, a truth from which the observed fact that contraceptives-taking John Jones never became pregnant can be safely deduced. Nonetheless, this application of Hempel's criteria cannot be accepted as an explanation of Jones' non-pregnancy![5] To take an economics-related example, let us say that an astrologer claims that consumption will increase each time interest rates drop drastically during a particular conjunction of the stars. It is clear that a correct deduction from this probably unfalsified law cannot be invoked as an explanation of the eagerness to consume following a drastic interest rates reduction announced by the National Bank precisely when such a star conjunction prevails! Clearly, in both examples, one must disentangle the factors relevant to the explanation (manhood, interest rate reduction) from those which are not explanatory (contraceptive, star conjunction). What seems very easy when these far-fetched examples are considered raises a serious problem when it comes to defining unambiguous criteria in a theory of explanation.

According to Salmon, if a spurious argument like the one concerning Jones' pregnancy can apparently satisfy Hempel's requirements for a scientific explanation, it is because Hempel's IS explanation theory puts the emphasis on high probability, whereas what really matters in explanation is not high probability but relevance. Therefore, Salmon devoted a book including papers by Jeffrey and by Greeno (Salmon *et al.* 1971) to developing a new theory of explanation, the statistical relevance (S-R) theory, from which irrelevant factors such as Jones' ingestion of contraceptives are eliminated. When defending this theory, Salmon was so firmly convinced that high probability has nothing to do with explanation that he repeatedly claimed that (1) a relevant explanatory factor is one which changes the prior probability of an event either by increasing it *or even by reducing it* and therefore that (2) being explained has nothing to do with being expected. Let us consider these two points in turn, but in reverse order.

Before coming back to the core of Salmon's S-R theory, I would like to discuss more specifically his rejection of the idea that expectation has something to do with explanation. In a sense, it seems natural to consider that the fact that the occurrence of an event is expected is a good criterion of the fact that it is explained. This is true both for Hempelians, who claim that an expected explanandum is precisely what, according to a law, happens in given circumstances, and for those who invoke rational explanations, who claim that the expected action corresponds to the rational thing to do in those circumstances. But if it is *relevance* rather than inference, whether based on deduction, induction or on rationality principle, which is determinant for an explanation, it seems that we are forced to conclude with Salmon that expecting an event (due to an inference which, for Hempelians, should even make it predictable) and explaining it are two quite different things. Influenced by Richard Jeffrey's thesis according to which when we toss dice, for example, the explanation of an improbable result is of exactly the same type as the explanation of a probable result since in both cases pure chance is invoked (Jeffrey 1969), Salmon did not hesitate to claim that 'showing that the outcome is highly probable, and that it was to be expected, has nothing to do with the explanation' (1989: 62). I think, however, that this conclusion overshoots the mark, since it rests on an unwarranted assimilation of 'being expected' into 'being predicted'. Were someone playing Russian roulette (only once), my best prediction would be that the person will not be killed since the chance of survival in this case is five over six. If the person were to survive, I would naturally say that this fact is not puzzling at all given its relatively high probability. However, if the person were actually killed, I would say that such an event could not be predicted, though it would be odd to be puzzled by it and to say that such an event was totally unexpected. One may be reluctant to accept this distinction between prediction and expectation, but if I recommend to someone to play Russian roulette and this person is killed, I have little doubt that pleading that I did not *expect* such a tragic result will be scornfully rejected as foolish, whereas the claim that my best *prediction* was that the person was to survive will be judged perfectly sane while totally irrelevant in the circumstance. Were I invited to engage in this kind of experience myself, I would surely decline the invitation, since I would expect a deadly result to a degree quite sufficient not to try, though I would still admit that my best prediction concerning the consequences of going through with it is that I would survive. I would say that, in this situation, death is a disjunctively expected result. *Disjunctive expectation* is not so strange a notion: when a coin is tossed, it seems odd to say that, since no result is highly probable, it is impossible to expect any result at all; it seems more sensible to say that we expect either heads or tails, even though we cannot predict any one of these possible results. Salmon and those who reject any association between expectation and explanation took the verbs to expect and to predict as strictly synonymous. There remains, however, the above described semantic difference between them, which is illustrated by the fact that one event can be expected to the same degree as others, but cannot be predicted to the same degree as others: expecting either a heads or a tails is a meaningful description of the particular situation implied by tossing a coin, but predicting either a heads or a tails is meaningless since it is not predicting anything. The point is that there is a crucial difference between an expectation, which is the relatively *passive state* of someone who necessarily expects either this or that, and a prediction, which is the *performance* of someone who pretends to know that an occurrence will happen.

One could object that if expectation is dissociated from high probability in such a fashion, I should refrain from air travel as much as from Russian roulette, since I should expect a crash, being aware that such an event happens in, let us say, one case in a million. But this situation is totally different and this difference has nothing to do with the degree of probability. In the Russian roulette example, the possible results (in terms of the chamber that is drawn) are exactly at par. One is not more mysterious than the other. If death occurs, it would be silly to demand an explanation for the occurrence of such a result, a result that was sufficiently expected, at least in the sense of being absolutely not puzzling. Naturally, the fact that someone agrees to play Russian roulette needs to be explained, but this is a quite different matter, having nothing to do with the fact that death rather than survival be the actual result. Playing Russian roulette is statistically relevant in the explanation of death since it increases dramatically the probability of the involved person's death in the next hour (in contrast, for example, to playing chess, which does not significantly modify this probability), but if it is explanatory, it is because it transforms this dreadful potential event, which was, until then, unexpected, into an (already overly) expected (though not predictable) event. The case of a plane crash is very different. If a crash occurs, it is not at all silly to demand an explanation even when we objectively know that the chances of such an event occurring are one in a million. The event is considered possible, but not really expected. It is therefore puzzling and the committee in charge of its explanation will not rest until new information on relevant factors transforms this unexpected event into an event which, given this information, should have been expected and consequently explained. The explanation provided will possibly show that, under the circumstances, the plane had a nine out of ten chance of crashing, which will be considered a fair explanation, but this does not mean that high probability as such is an essential element of the explanation; what is explanatory and what transformed the event into an expectable event is rather the particular conditions under which the plane found itself, the knowledge of which being what allows experts to determine this high probability. If one invents a sophisticated version of Russian roulette (one which, for example, emits at random a lethal radioactive element) in which the probability of death is exactly one in a million, the very improbable event of death would count among the expected results and its eventual occurrence would be fully explained (it would be unjustified to demand more of an explanation). Similarly, one who buys a lottery ticket can safely enough predict not winning, but nonetheless expect to win, at least in such a way that if it turned out that the ticket were the winning one, no particular explanation would be required for the understanding of this improbable eventuality.

In fact, what I call disjunctive expectation to characterize situations in which one expects either something or something else is closely related to Jeffrey's and Salmon's somewhat unintuitive thesis that 'we understand the low-probability outcomes of any given stochastic process just as well as we understand the high-probability outcomes' (Salmon 1989: 67). Therefore, without endorsing Salmon's S-R theory of explanation as such, I maintain that when it concerns stochastic processes, such as those associated with the tossing of dice or the disintegration of radioactive atoms, Salmon's claim is perfectly true since the occurrence of an improbable event is not, as such, more mysterious or more puzzling than the occurrence of a probable event. However, this is precisely the reason why, in contrast with Salmon, I say that, when their occurrence is purely a stochastic matter (as in the case of Russian roulette), improbable events, *while unpredictable*, are (disjunctively) *expected* and do not require a supplementary explanation, just as probable events are. But when their occurrence is commanded by other factors (as is the case of the plane crash), improbable events remain puzzling and unexpected until an explanation transforms them into expectable ones. The difference between my wording and Salmon's might not be so important, since in both formulations, the *necessary* connection between high probability and explanation is rejected and the idea that probable and improbable stochastic events are explained in the same way is warranted, but the wording I propose seems to me more intuitive and, together with the insistence on the difference to be made between stochastic (where all possible results are expected, once its stochastic character is understood, as in the Russian roulette case) and non-stochastic processes (where those results are not necessarily expected, as in the plane crash case), it allows us to avoid objections such as those that can be opposed to the central thesis of Salmon' S-R theory, towards which it is now time to turn.

The key idea of Salmon S-R theory rests on a comparison between the prior probability of the event to be explained with its (posterior) probability obtained once relevant factors are taken into account. Even though the probability that John Jones did not become pregnant once he had ingested contraceptive pills is 100 per cent, this undisputable fact does not explain his non-pregnancy, because it changes nothing of the prior probability (which was equally 100 per cent) of a man avoiding pregnancy. However, as willingly admitted by Salmon, the notion of relevance is not so easy to define. For example, one could claim that, according to this view, a sudden drop in a barometer reading is a relevant factor in the explanation of an oncoming storm since this barometer drop changes considerably the probability of a storm occurring. To deal with such a case, in which both the storm and the barometer drop are actually explained by atmospheric conditions, Salmon introduced the notion of screening off (1971b: 55 and 1989: 65–66). Roughly speaking, it can be said that the drop in the barometer reading is screened off by atmospheric conditions if the probability of the storm given both of these events is equal to the probability of the storm given the atmospheric conditions alone, an equality which is clearly obtained in this case (assuming that the barometer works properly). In relation to Salmon's attempt to solve the problem of irrelevancies in the theory of explanation, it would be interesting to consider the techniques of econometricians, who, by way of sophisticated mathematical tools, have developed means of discriminating between true and false correlations and of excluding irrelevant factors from economic models. However, while it is in no way my intention here to discuss econometric models, I will nonetheless recall that developing efficient methods of excluding irrelevancies from scientific explanations is not the same as explicating the very structure of a scientific explanation apt to cope with such irrelevancies.

In any case, if high probability no longer plays a decisive role in an explanation, the idea that an explanation is an argument concluding in the explanandum could hardly be maintained. What is a determinant is no longer what allows us to conclude that the explanandum will surely happen, but rather what allows us to conclude that something is changed in the possibility of its occurrence. It was in order to emphasize the fundamental character of this change in perspective that Salmon was brought to radically, and mistakenly according to me, dissociate the fact of being explained from the fact of being expected, because, for him, expectation was linked to high probability. Therefore, Salmon characterized an explanation as an 'assemblage of facts *statistically relevant* to the fact-to-be-explained *regardless of the degree of probability* that results' (1989: 67, Salmon's emphasis). However, the probability of a single event has to be measured in relation to reference classes resulting from more or less arbitrary partitions. Taking this into account, Salmon defines the notion of statistical relevance in the following way: 'such partitions can be effected by a property C which divides the class A into two subclasses, $A.C$ and $A.\bar{C}$. A property C is said to be *statistically relevant* to B within A if and only if $P(A.C,B) \neq P(A,B)$' (Salmon 1971b: 42, Salmon's emphasis).

With the help of this definition, it is possible to illustrate more precisely what Salmon means when he says that an explanation has nothing to do with the degree of probability. Let us consider his example (ibid.: 64) of an equal mixture of uranium 238, which has one chance out of ten of producing a click on a Geiger counter in a given period of time, and of Polonium 214, which has nine chances out of ten of producing the same result. This mixture is such that its chance of producing a click in a given period is somewhere between the two probabilities mentioned above. Let us say that it is 0.5. If a click is produced during this period, it might be interesting to know whether it was produced by the disintegration of a polonium or uranium atom. The best way to understand what is involved here is to make an appropriate partition of the mixture. Whereas a partition between the right side and the left side of the mixture would be irrelevant since it would not change the probability of a click, the situation would be quite different with a partition between polonium and uranium because the degree of radioactivity of either of these components is statistically relevant given that their respective probabilities of obtaining a click are considerably changed. Nonetheless, if this probability is increased from 0.5 to 0.9 in the case of polonium, it is reduced from 0.5 to 0.1 in the case of uranium. Of course, the click might be explained by the disintegration of a polonium atom, but it might also have been produced by the disintegration of a uranium atom. And even though the latter event is much less probable than the former, it must be explained in exactly the same fashion, namely through the probability, however small, that it can be produced by chance. This systematic indifference to the degree of probability remains a cumbersome feature of Salmon's theory and it was the source of many objections to it. For example, in a paper entitled 'Causal Laws and Effective Strategies', Nancy Cartwright observed (1979: 425) that 'what makes uranium count as a good explanation for the click in the geiger counter' is evidently not the low probability but rather the causal law according to which 'uranium causes radioactivity' (ibid.). She illustrates her point by observing that the survival of some among a group of plants sprayed with a defoliant effective at 90 per cent cannot be explained by the fact that they have been sprayed in this way, even though, according to Salmon's rule, this spraying was statistically relevant since it reduces the probability of survival to 0.1, in the same way as the partition between polonium and uranium does when it comes to the probability of a click. Using a more or less similar example, Peter Achinstein, for his part, has proposed a more intuitive way of partially conciliating these views. According to him, one should say that the disintegration of uranium causally explains the radioactive click indeed, but that the statistical law according to which uranium 238 has one chance out of ten to produce a click in a given period of time (non causally) explains the *possibility* that this event occurs (Achinstein 1983: 253).[6] In any case, Salmon's S-R model faced other difficulties, both in relation to the definition of a proper partitioning of the reference class and to the explanation of theoretical laws, in such a way that, even at the early stages of the development of this model, its author became progressively convinced of 'the necessity of appealing to causal mechanisms' (Salmon 1989: 106) in order to develop a new theory of explanation.

The role of causality

Salmon, as well as Cartwright, who criticized his views on statistical relevance, solved the paradoxes raised by probabilistic explanations by 'appealing to causal mechanisms'. There is no doubt that the view that explanation is the eliciting of causal mechanisms that bring about the phenomenon to be explained can neutralize most counterexamples plaguing either DN, IS or S-R theories. Since the defoliant clearly does not cause the plants' survival, there can be no question of invoking it in order to explain that survival. Similarly, since mariners did not know the cause of tides, they were unable to explain it. Since the length of a shadow does not cause the height of a flagpole, it cannot explain this height. Since the drop in a barometer reading does not cause a storm, nor does it explain it. Since Jones' contraceptives did not bring about his non-pregnancy, it does not explain it either. In contrast, since, in some sense, the absence of penicillin treatment for syphilis actually causes paresis, the former explains the latter, irrespective of the fact that, in most similar cases, this causal link does not hold since no paresis is observed. Thus, at least at first glance, it seems difficult to dissociate explanation from causality. One can even say, though not without raising some specific problems, that Louis XIV's decision not to invade Holland was explained by Trevelyan through his eliciting of events taking place in Europe that caused the king's rational decision. Similarly, various explanations provided by economists can be presented as an eliciting of features of economic situations causing economic agents' decisions, as was illustrated and discussed in a paper by Daniel Hausman (2001: 314–315 and 321–323).

Salmon realized that the explicitly causalist character of his new theory of explanation places it in a quite different class from many of those developed since Hempel's theory, the latter included. He therefore proposed a threefold classification of epistemic, modal and ontic conceptions of scientific explanation (Salmon 1984: 15–20 and chapter 4; see also 1989: 86 and 118–121). The modal conception, according to which an explanation must establish a relation of 'nomological necessity' between the event-to-be-explained and its antecedent conditions, is illustrated in D. H. Mellor's theory of explanation (Mellor 1976), and will not be considered here. According to Salmon, 'the epistemic conception is oriented toward the notion of scientific expectability' (1989: 120). In other words, it is a conception for which an 'explanation could be described as an argument to the effect that the event-to-be-explained was to be expected by virtue of the explanatory facts' (Salmon 1984: 16). Salmon admitted, however, that this conception cannot be described univocally. He therefore distinguished three versions of this conception: information-theoretic, inferential and erotetic. The information-theoretic version, for which it is the transmission of information involved in an explanation that is the key element, is illustrated in James G. Greeno's theses (Greeno 1970). Here again, since the present chapter is largely a discussion of the two other versions and of the third conception, this first version of the second conception will not be discussed either. Hempel himself, for whom it was so important to present explanations as arguments from which the explanandum can be derived, is the most illustrious representative of the inferential version. The third version, which Salmon calls 'erotetic', and according to which an explanation is essentially an answer to a question, usually a why-question, is illustrated by R.B. Braithwaite, by Sylvain Bromberger and, more systematically, by Bas van Fraassen whose theses will be examined later in this chapter. Not all those associated with the three versions of the epistemic conception are as eager as Hempel to claim that an explanation is an argument, but they tend to consider that an explanation is primarily related to knowledge and is even, in some respects, knowledge-dependent. In contrast, the third conception, adopted by Salmon, is characterized as 'ontic' because it claims that 'explanations exist in the world' (Salmon 1989: 86) or, put less radically, that it reports facts existing in the world. In such a conception, an explanation has nothing to do with an argument; it simply, by any means, exhibits that events-to-be-explained 'fit into the causal structure of the world' (Salmon 1977, quoted in Salmon 1984: 19; see also 1984: 121) or, put more generally, it brings to light the causal mechanisms which bring about a given event.

Salmon is perfectly aware that the idea of defining explanation by reference to causes is not original, recalling that it goes back at least to Aristotle (Salmon 1984: 135). And he is equally aware that the notion of cause is not particularly easy to manipulate in a philosophically satisfying way. Everyone is familiar with the fact that David Hume found the notion of causality highly questionable. One might also mention Auguste Comte, one of the fathers of the philosophy of science, who considered one of his main contributions to be the freeing of philosophy from the notion of cause which, according to him, should definitively be replaced by the notion of law. However, this somewhat cumbersome metaphysical notion cannot so easily be dispensed with. It reappeared with John Stuart Mill (Mill 1961 [1865]) and made its way into modern philosophy of science in spite of objections raised by some analytical philosophers.

In this context, it is clear that Salmon's contribution does not reside in the idea of introducing the notion of causal explanation as such, but in his sophisticated attempts to reinterpret the notion of cause in a more satisfying way. He proceeds by turning attention away from causal relations between events to causal processes and to causal conjunctions and interactions between phenomena. Concerning causal processes, the problem is to distinguish genuine processes from pseudo-processes. An example of a pseudo-process would be the continuous movement of the shadow of a moving car, whose movement is, in contrast, a genuine causal process (Salmon 1984: 143). Drawing on Einstein's special theory of relativity, Salmon underscores the fact that only genuine processes can transmit signals, whereas pseudo-processes are unable to do so. Being unable to transmit messages, pseudo-processes may move at any velocity, even faster than light, since their movement does not correspond to the movement of some particle whose velocity would be strictly limited by Einstein's famous principle (Salmon 1984: 140–143 and 1989: 107–108). In order to better characterize the notion of transmission of a causal process (Salmon 1989: 107–109), Salmon invokes what he calls his '*at-at theory of mark transmission*' (inspired by Bertrand Russell's solution of Zeno's paradoxes) according to which a mark 'that is imposed at point A in a process is *transmitted* to point B in that same process if, *without additional interventions*, the mark is present at each intervening stages in the process' (Salmon 1989: 110, Salmon's emphasis). And in order to deal specifically with the problem of common cause, the theory was completed by a probabilistic discussion (inspired by Reichenbach's work on the topic) concerning forks of conjunctions and interactions between phenomena. Thus, with the help of a conceptual analysis, only sketchily described here, Salmon proposes an 'ontic' theory according to which scientific explanation is an elicitation of spatiotemporally continuous genuine causal processes which, through a correctly identified net of forks, produce the phenomenon to be explained.

This theory, however, like its predecessors, has been subjected to various criticisms. For example, Philip Kitcher (1985: 638) is bothered by the circular character of Salmon's discussion of marks, which, while being the key element in Salmon's criterion of genuine causal process, can hardly be characterized without invoking a causal interaction. This brings him to conclude that 'although Salmon has made progress in meeting the [Humean] challenge, a familiar type of difficulty seems to remain'.[7] More radically, Bas van Fraassen, equally unconvinced of Salmon's analysis of genuine processes and of marks propagation,[8] raises questions about the viability of the causal conception when it comes to applying this view to explanations provided by quantum mechanics[9] – in contrast to relativity theory which, as van Fraassen admits, reinforces Salmon's causal theory (van Fraassen 1985: 650). In his book, Salmon himself had acknowledged this frustrating difficulty (Salmon 1984: 279 and 1985: 653) without considering it fatal, even though it appears to limit dramatically the scope of a causal theory of explanation. Van Fraassen also observes that many scientific explanations, especially those based on 'laws of coexistence' such as Boyle's law of gases, do not seem to be causal explanations in Salmon's sense, since the latter apparently involves the 'temporal development of some process or interaction'.[10] Salmon readily admits this fact in his 1984 book in which he quotes Boyle's as well as Kepler's laws in this regard, but he consistently, though not very convincingly, claims that these laws 'do not, by themselves, do much in the way of explaining other phenomena' (ibid.: 136). In any case, it is not clear that Salmon would reject the idea that some explanations disclose underlying non-causal mechanisms, a possibility of which he seems to be aware, at least in his later writings (see Salmon 1989: 134). At a more general level, van Fraassen raises a problem, which could be addressed to any ontic theory, concerning the determination of what information is to be included in the explanation. If explanation consists in bringing to light the causal process and its network of forks, how might one limit the amount of information considered relevant to this explanation? For van Fraaassen, who defends a pragmatic (erotetic) conception according to which an explanation is nothing but an answer to a why-question, this amount of information depends on the background of the questioner. However, in regard to Salmon's ontic conception, van Fraassen observes that 'what the relevant information is depends on the event to be explained, and not on facts about the questioner' (van Fraassen 1985: 640). But it is difficult to see how the event to be explained can determine by itself which among the multitude of elements related to its occurrence might be included in the explanation. Salmon argues that this problem should be largely resolved with the help of some concepts introduced by Peter Railton (Salmon 1985: 653), but analysing this still ambiguous solution is beyond the scope of the present discussion. Let us conclude, in any case, that a causal theory of explanation may solve most traditional difficulties associated with the Hempelian theory of explanation, but will not do so without raising serious problems of its own, not to mention particular problems which might appear in attempts to apply it to rational explanations provided by social sciences, in which genuine processes propagating causality from reasons to actions are even more difficult to manipulate.[11]

Van Fraassen's pragmatic theory of explanation

Let us see now whether van Fraassen's theory may fare better in this regard. Van Fraassen readily admits that his conception of explanation is 'much more liberal' than Salmon's 'when it comes to the form of the explanation in general' (1985: 650) though, according to him, this fact does not diminish the severity of the standards applied when it concerns the evaluation of the explanation. According to van Fraassen, an explanation is nothing but an answer to a why-question; such an answer may therefore take extremely varied forms, depending on the nature of the question and of the interests and background of the questioner, both of which determine what is the relevant information to be included in the explanation. For example, the fact that the analysis of causal processes was perceived as the canonical form of explanation in classic physics does not preclude that quantum mechanics can provide perfectly satisfying answers to those who have the background required to understand this kind of explanation, in spite of the fact that causal processes cannot be analysed in quantum mechanics in the same way as they are in classic physics. Similarly, as van Fraassen had argued in his critique of Salmon's causal theory, the laws of coexistence, which are not causal, can nonetheless be used to answer certain types of why-questions; I presume this might be the case with the why-question of someone who would be puzzled by the increased pressure exerted by a particular gas when being unaware of the fact that the temperature of this gas is rising. As for explanations in human and social sciences, they may take any form that the question raised by the questioner requires. Van Fraassen is even ready to admit that an explanation may take the form of a story that tells 'how things did happen and how the events hang together' (1980: 113). Incidentally, this was the thesis of some analytical philosophers of history, such as Arthur Danto (1965: chapter 11), and it is an idea on which the adepts of the rhetorical approach in economics have capitalized. More generally, van Fraassen does not hesitate in claiming that there is no difference between a scientific and a common-sense explanation insofar as their form or even 'the sort of information adduced' by them is concerned. However, one can identify a certain type of explanation as 'scientific' by requiring that such an explanation draw 'on science to get this information (at least to some extent) and, more importantly, that the criteria of evaluation of how good an explanation it is, are being applied using a scientific theory' according to rules which van Fraassen carefully exposes (1980: 155–156).

Van Fraassen's conception is thus admittedly epistemic and context-dependent. Before analysing more technical aspects of van Fraassen's theory, let us consider a moment this question of context-dependence which is central in other pragmatist theories of explanation as well (see in particular Achinstein 1983). It is difficult not to admit a certain degree of context-dependence when characterizing explanations. For example, in the event of a plane crash, the explanation that should be offered to an uneducated member of a victim's family could hardly be the same as the explanation required by the engineers who designed the plane, even though in both cases genuinely satisfying explanations should be provided. It is true that context-dependence might be seen as a weakness for a number of philosophical theories, but in a theory of explanation, there is a prima facie argument in favour of such an epistemic approach by the very fact that an explanation essentially concerns knowledge. Causality is, by definition, an ontic reality, but explanation designates a process through which information is conveyed from one person to another. The question at stake here is whether the selection of appropriate information should be determined by facts of the external world or, as claimed both by Bas van Fraassen and Peter Achinstein, by the interest and background of the questioner. For sure, the theory of explanation must not be a psychological one, which means that it should not consist in a description of what is going on in the mind of the questioner once the explanation is provided. The problem that an explanation solves can hardly be defined otherwise than by reference to the interests and background knowledge of the questioner, which does not mean that explicating what is an explanation must be a matter of describing the psychological process involved. Put in a very general way, I would say that a theory of explanation should determine what type of informational and logical considerations are required to allow one who finds a question puzzling (given one's interests and background knowledge) to realize that such puzzlement no longer has any (logically admissible) reason to persist. A psychologist might consider that the relevant analysis of the explanation should consist in determining what is going on, both at an emotional and intellectual level, in the mind or in the brain of the questioner when a state of puzzlement is succeeded by a state of intellectual satisfaction. In contrast, a philosopher will analyse the kind of considerations that are logically required – either in the form of an argument, of an assembly of facts, of an elicitation of causes or in any other form – to allow a hypothetically rational questioner (whose interests and background knowledge have been taken into account) to realize that what was judged puzzling in a state of things, at least in its initial description, no longer has any logically acceptable foundation. Economists are familiar with distinctions of this type between psychological and non-psychological approaches: the theory of decision, for example, deals with situations which cannot be characterized otherwise than by reference to the interests and background knowledge of deciders. But once the problem is posed in such a way, both, psychologists and economists find themselves in constant disagreement since psychologists are eager to describe with the greatest possible precision what takes place in the minds of moderately rational individuals, whereas economists are only interested in the logical implications of a rational decision. In spite of the interdisciplinary sensibility of both participants, the debate about models of rationality between the psychologist Daniel Kahneman and the economist Charles Plott (Kahneman 1996a,b; Plott 1996a,b) provides another remarkable illustration of such an opposition. Be that as it may, as for van Fraassen's theory of explanation, it is admittedly epistemic and pragmatic, but it cannot be charged with psychologism.

Let us look more closely at van Fraassen's theory consisting in the logical analysis of what constitutes an appropriate answer to a why-question, an analysis which necessarily implies a discussion of the characteristics of the why-question itself. In order to illustrate this, let us consider the following why-question which might be addressed to an economist: 'Why did the price of fuel increase in Canada last June?' Since, as emphasized by van Fraassen, not all why-questions can be answered, it is important to examine the presuppositions of the question. A presupposition of a question is defined by van Fraassen as 'any proposition which is implied by all direct answers' to that question (1980: 140), a direct answer being an answer which 'gives enough information to answer the question completely, but no more' (ibid.: 138). A first presupposition of a why-question capable of being answered is simply the truth of what van Fraassen calls the topic of the question, which is, in our example, the proposition saying that 'the price of fuel increased in Canada last June'. A second presupposition concerns what van Fraassen calls a contrast class. For example, the propositions 'the price of fuel decreased in Canada last June' and 'the price of fuel remained stable in

Canada last June' along with the topic ('the price of fuel increased in Canada last June') are members of a contrast class pertaining to that question. The second presupposition of an acceptable why-question is that, with the exception of the topic, all other members of the contrast class are false. However, an interesting feature of a why-question, which, according to van Fraassen, was first underscored by Bengt Hanson (van Fraassen 1980: 127), is that such questions may have more than one contrast class, each of which requires quite a different explanation. For example, the propositions 'the price of milk increased in Canada last June', 'the price of fuel increased in Canada last May', 'the price of fuel increased in France last June' are members of three different sets of contrast classes, each of which includes the topic proposition itself and, eventually, some other propositions contrasted to other members of its class through the same part of the proposition. I think that a supplementary specification is required if we want to claim that all of the members of a contrast class except the topic are false. Naturally, 'the price of fuel increased in Canada last June' and 'the price of fuel increased in Canada last May' could both be true, but were this the case, one should conclude that both could not be members of the same contrast class. This restriction makes sense since the puzzlement associated with the fact that the price of fuel increased last June in Canada cannot have been generated by the fact that the price of fuel increased last May as well. The contrast class is the class of those propositions which, through the kind of contrast they entertain with the topic, determine the very meaning of the question. The question and the explanation clearly differ depending on whether the questioner is puzzled because conditions allowed one to expect a decrease in the price of fuel, which nonetheless increases, or because it is precisely last June that an expected increase occurs whereas it did not occur during the previous months, or because the increase occurs in Canada whereas other countries were not affected. It seems to me that this notion of contrast class is particularly clarifying when it comes to analysing the various explanations typically provided by social sciences. Suppose that the topic of a question is 'there was famine in Chad in 1986' (date and country chosen arbitrarily for the sake of the example). It is easy to identify three different contrast classes concerning respectively: the famine, Chad and 1986. Let us consider the last two of them. The first includes 'there was famine in Mali in 1986', 'there was famine in Niger in 1986', etc.; the second includes 'there was famine in Chad in 1985', 'there was famine in Chad in 1987', etc. All of these four last sentences are supposed to be false. If the question emphasizes the contrast class including the propositions concerning Mali and Niger, the explanation might refer to something like the carelessness of the Chad Government, but if it is the contrast class including propositions concerning 1985 and 1987 that is emphasized, it is rather explanations such as an exceptional drought affecting the Saharan countries in 1986 that should be considered.[12]

According to van Fraassen, the last fundamental presupposition of an acceptable why-question concerns explanatory relevance. A why-question presupposes that, in a given context, at least one proposition (the core of an eventual answer) is relevant to the topic with respect to the contrast class involved. Even when a single contrast class is considered and when, consequently, the question bears on the same element of the topic, quite different considerations, depending on the interests and the background knowledge of the questioner, are likely to make an answer relevant, and this can totally change the meaning of the question and the content of the requested explanation. This fact is clearly illustrated by the example of the engineer and the members of victims' families who required different explanations of a plane crash, the former in order to improve the design of planes, the latter in order to find peace of mind and to identify who was responsible for the accident. For his part, van Fraassen refers to the case of a mechanical versus a functional explanation given in response to the question 'Why does the blood circulate through the body?' (1980: 142). He also illustrates his point with the example of the various kinds of factors which, depending on the interest of the questioner, can explain the warping of a conductor in a power station: human error, closure of a switch, moisture condensing on the switches, or standing conditions such as the presence of a sufficiently strong magnetic field to have made the event possible, or even the function fulfilled by this conductor in the station. As clearly seen from this last example, the determination of what is relevant in this sense implies a choice of the relevant factors among those which play a role in a usually very complex causal network. The magnetic field, the closure of the switch and human error are some factors which might constitute the necessary conditions of the event, but an explanation must invoke only those among which, in van Fraassen's words, make the answer 'relevant (in this context) to the topic with respect to [the involved] contrast class' (ibid.: 142).

The idea of considering the particular interests of the person requesting the explanation as the key element in the solution to the problem of choosing relevant (or salient) factors in an explanation is not new. Van Fraassen mentions N. R. Hansen as invoking such interests in a similar context in a book published in 1958 in which he takes the example of an automobile accident in order to distinguish the causes set out respectively by a physician (multiple haemorrhages), by a barrister (driver negligence), by a carriage-builder (brake system defect) or by a civic planner (presence of tall shrubbery at the turning of the road). It is interesting to note that, at the same period, philosophers of history, in their discussion of causality, treated this problem in roughly the same fashion. Edward Hallett Carr, for example, considers the same kind of automobile accident and discusses it in very similar terms (Carr 1961: 137–140). In a more systematic study devoted to causation in the law and in history, H. L. A. Hart and Tony Honoré propose, in order to illustrate the same point, the example of the man who, after eating parsnips, suffered indigestion explained by his wife as the result of eating a vegetable she described as indigestible and by his physician as the result of the ulcerated condition of his stomach.[13] In a book of methodology written before he died during the Second World War, the historian Marc Bloch, one of the founders of the *Annales* school of history, considers the case of a man who falls into a precipice when walking on an Alpine path and discusses the various elements necessary to explain this fall. Though he did not explicitly associate any one of the excluded elements with specific interests, he observes that, for the historian of the event, the unfortunate step was the appropriate cause to be invoked, even though it is not more necessary than other antecedent conditions such as the existence of gravity and the seasonal migration of sheep flocks, which was responsible for the laying out of the path (Bloch 1954: 190–191). For all these authors, who refer to a remarkably varied set of criteria, the most important aspect of the question is to determine the criterion that allows one to select the factor that qualifies as 'the cause' of an event. Van Fraassen, for his part, illustrates this variety of criteria by citing those invoked in writings published between 1953 and 1957 by L. W. Beck, Ernest Nagel, R. B. Braithwaite and David Bohm (van Fraassen 1980: 125, including appropriate references). Though van Fraassen's analysis of explanatory relevance – only the main lines of which are exposed here – does not pretend to determine what is the most appropriate criterion for choosing such a cause, this analysis integrates into a sophisticated pragmatic theory of explanation the kind of context-dependence that is responsible for this variety of criteria.

Solutions and objections

Van Fraassen is particularly confident that his theory of explanation has solved two persistent problems, namely the problem of asymmetry and the problem of rejection of demands for explanation, the former being solved by him in a quite original relativistic fashion and the latter being rarely considered by those who adopt less pragmatic approaches.[14] Let us first consider this last problem. A demand for explanation can be rightfully rejected, but this same demand can become legitimate at some other period. As an example of a question whose rejection was well grounded, van Fraassen gives that of the question posed by the Aristotelians to the followers of Galileo regarding the reason 'why does a body free of impressed forces retain its velocity?' (van Fraassen 1980: 111). As mentioned at the beginning of this chapter, he also mentions the question why there is such a thing as a gravitational force, a question which was considered legitimate even in Newton's time but which, at a later stage, was classed as 'intrinsically illegitimate', just like the question about the retention of velocity (ibid.: 112). With Hempel's DN or IS theories or with Salmon's causalist theories, it is difficult to take into account such a phenomenon since these theories, be they epistemic or ontic, tend to be context-independent. But for van Fraassen's theory, which is overtly context-dependent, the rejection can be explained by the absence of at least one of the required presuppositions of the why-question. Let us recall that, according to these presuppositions, the background knowledge accepted in a given context must imply both the truth of the topic and the falsity of the other members of the contrast class, and must not imply the denial of the relevance to the topic (with respect to the contrast class involved) of any proposition (likely to become the core of an eventual answer) (van Fraassen 1980: 145–146). It is clearly because the denial of the relevance of any proposition concerning the appropriateness of a gravitational force was not yet implied by the background knowledge accepted in Newton's time, but was implied by the background knowledge accepted at a later stage that the demand for an explanation regarding this question was accepted in Newton's time and rejected later. At first glance, this way of speaking may sound a bit tautological, but it allows us to integrate rejections of demands for explanation into a theory of explanation that makes room for context-dependence and to formulate in the very language of this theory the criteria justifying such rejections.

It is a quite different type of solution that van Fraassen proposes for the problem of asymmetry. This problem, illustrated by the flagpole example evoked above, is satisfactorily solved by a causalist theory of explanation such as Salmon's theory, insofar as we forget problems associated with the notion of causality as such. Given his warnings against an ontic theory, one presenting explanation as describing causal processes going on in the real world, van Fraassen could not invoke the direction of such causal processes to solve the problem the way Salmon did. Consistent with his context-dependence pragmatist approach, he instead refuses to reject flatly the idea that the length of the shadow could explain the height of the flagpole. To illustrate this bold position, he tells a charming story involving a tower designed by a gentleman in such a way that its height projected a shadow covering the spot where he had ignominiously killed one of his servants a long time ago (van Fraassen 1980: 132–134). Though this story is not particularly typical of stories concerning the relation between a tower and its shadow, it illustrates fairly well the fact that, even when the direction of the causal link seems to be self-evident, an explanation does not necessarily have to follow the same direction to be an appropriate answer to a why-question. Naturally, that does not mean that the height of the tower was caused by a posterior event, namely the projection of a shadow, whose length involved in the argument was necessarily obtained only once the tower had attained its full height. If something 'caused' its height, it is clearly the designer's previous desire to bring about his secret goal by means of a shadow's length. However, according to van Fraassen's theory, what is at stake does not concern the direction of the causal process, which, whatever its exact nature, goes necessarily from the tower to the shadow rather than in the reverse direction; it concerns the explanation, which is not to be inseparably linked to causality, as is the case in a causalist (and ontic) theory. Thus, the height of the tower causes the length of the shadow, but, in this fictional example, the length of the shadow nonetheless explains the height of the tower, since it is the key element of a correct answer to a legitimate why-question about the height of the tower.

Less far-fetched illustrations of such a situation are frequently found in economics. For example, when it comes to analysing a government's tax cut, it would seem normal to claim that such a tax cut caused the increased economic activity which was observed during the following months, but it would be odd to say that this stimulated economic activity is the cause of the tax cut, which preceded it. Nonetheless, if the Minister of Finance is asked by a member of parliament why he decided to incautiously reduce the State's resources, the minister might answer that it is the desired increase in economic activity (presently observed) which explains the implementation of the tax cut. Incidentally, such an answer will look particularly appropriate to anyone convinced that revitalized economic activity generates still more taxes for the State and that this fact has guided the Minister of Finance's decision to cut taxes in the first place. In any case, the point is that if the tax cut *causes* the bullish mood of the economy, it is the latter which is nonetheless cited in order to *explain* the tax cut. Finally, if Salmon's theory can make room for Dray's rational kind of explanation, insofar as one is prepared to consider as a genuine causal process the impact of Louis XIV's state of mind on his decision not to invade, with van Fraassen's pragmatic approach, this kind of explanation is unconditionally legitimized. Whether or not it is the case that Louis XIV's decision caused (through its impact on the continuation of King William's activities) a state of affairs favourable to the conquest of Europe, it would be odd to say that this posterior state of affairs caused his decision. However, whether subsequently followed by an actual conquest or not, this (expected) posterior state of affairs was nonetheless the key element in Trevelyan's explanation of Louis XIV's decision.

In fact, in each of these three examples, a state of affairs or an event (the tower height, the tax cut and the king's decision) is *explained* by the posterior realization of another state of affairs (the spot-hiding length of the shadow, the increased economic activity and the favourable military situation). It seems clear that, in each case, the *cause* of what is explained has to be looked for in the state of mind of the main actor (desire to hide the site of a crime, desire to revitalize the economy and desire to exclude a dangerous enemy from countries to be subdued). This view regarding causality corresponds exactly to what Salmon – following Larry Wright on this point – means when he maintains that causes are never posterior to their effects and that an explanation can be described as an elicitation of a cause, *even when* teleological and functional explanations are involved (Salmon 1989: 111–114). Van Fraassen would obviously agree with this, even though he would tend to interpret this elicitation of an efficient cause in a purely empirical rather than an ontological way. Indeed, in his curious tower and shadow story, he readily acknowledges that the 'efficient cause' is far from being posterior to its effect, since it is its designer's 'desire' to hide an unpleasant spot (1980: 132). However, he might add that, being answers to why-questions, explanations may refer to *any* sort of cause, regardless of the kind of mechanism involved, insofar as the cause referred to is relevant with respect to the correctly interpreted question to be answered. More precisely, van Fraassen, for whom 'Aristotle's fourfold typology of causes'[15] is a source of inspiration, would say that, in the above examples, it is the 'functional role' (the Aristotelian final cause) which corresponds to the relation of relevance implied by such why-questions. Relevant answers to such questions do indeed bear on the goal, or the reasons, that motivated someone to undertake a given action (the construction of a tower at an excessive height, the implementation of a tax cut, the unexpected refusal to invade a country). If such a goal is usually revealed or induced through various clues, it is immediately characterized and illustrated by the state of affairs that normally results from the action. Therefore, this state of affairs, presented as the content of an intention, can be retained as the core of an appropriate answer to the question.

Van Fraassen's radically epistemic theory was subjected to various objections. I will consider here only three of them, namely two on which Salmon places particular emphasis, and another one raised by Achinstein. The first objection raised by Salmon concerns the role of why-questions. Various authors, long before the publication of van Fraassen's thesis, had suggested that explanations might be answers not strictly to why-questions but to some other types of questions as well. William Dray devoted the last chapter of his 1957 book to showing that, though he assumed throughout most of this work that an explanation is an answer to a why-question, other kinds of questions, among which how-possibly questions, are also requests for explanation (Dray 1957: chapter 6). In this connection, Salmon mentions other authors and other types of questions (Salmon 1989: 137–138). One could attempt to neutralize this objection by reformulating questions of other types in such a way that they are transformed into why-questions,[16] but this might be difficult, especially when one considers that, as illustrated by Salmon (ibid.: 137), a how-possibly question may be quite satisfactorily answered by alternative potential explanations. Such potential explanations might show how an event that is puzzling because it was reputed impossible can look perfectly possible once the questioner is brought to envisage a sequence of possible events or, alternatively, other sequences of equally possible events. One cannot refer to both alternatives as *the* answer to a why-question, but one can perfectly propose these two alternatives as two possible answers to a how-possibly question. With such questions, the event to be explained can even be purely hypothetical: someone may explain to me how an event which never happened and that I consider impossible is perfectly possible in principle. This kind of explanation is frequent in a theoretically oriented science like economics. The upward sloping demand curve associated with Giffen goods might be such an example, but one can also mention the debate about reswitching, which concerns the sheer possibility of this quasi hypothetical phenomenon. It would be difficult to transform into why-questions the questions raised in this debate without forcing the meaning of the word as would be the case if one were to ask 'why is reswitching possible?' instead of 'how is reswitching possible?' (or how could reswitching be possible?) when there is no observed case of reswitching to be explained. I think a better way of defending van Fraassen's theory of explanation would be to generalize it by claiming that an explanation is an answer to a puzzlement-induced question. How-possibly questions as well as why-questions, and as well as a few other types of questions, are puzzlement-induced, as suggested by Dray who, on occasions, uses the term 'puzzlement' in connection with such questions.[17] This is evidently not true of all questions. For example, the question 'What is the capital of Jordan?' or 'Which is the highest mountain in North America?' are not puzzlement-induced and consequently they are not requests for explanations. It is true that such generalizing of van Fraassen's theory would require slightly adapting notions of contrast class and of relevance, but this adaptation would not be so difficult to bring about. For example, van Fraassen's three presuppositions could be straightforwardly transposed to a how-possibly question, except that the topic might be only hypothetically true and the other members of the contrast class might as well be only hypothetically false. Thus, I will consider that, scientifically grounded or not, explanations are answers to puzzlement-induced questions.

Before discussing Salmon's second objection, let us consider the objection raised by Peter Achinstein (1983: 183–185). It concerns the possibility that an explanation that satisfies all van Fraassen's criteria for a good explanation might be an incorrect one. These criteria are the following: the answer provided to the why-question (or to the puzzlement-induced question) must (1) be true, (2) favour the event *A* to be explained more than any other event that could have occurred instead of *A*, and (3a) be more probable and (3b) have more chance to produce *A* than any other reason and (3c) be not screened off as irrelevant or superfluous by a more probable reason.[18] Achinstein's point is that the explanandum may have been brought about by an event different from the one invoked by the explanation satisfying those criteria, in such a way that the latter would be insufficient for deciding that the explanation is the appropriate one. According to him, another event, another cause, while being a much less probable candidate for explanation, may accidentally and surreptitiously have caused the event to be explained, in such a way that van Fraassen's criteria are not sufficient. And if a correct explanation can be based on this other less probabilistically attractive cause, the criteria are not necessary either. Achinstein illustrates his point with the example of a man, christened Jones, who dies a few hours after having ingested a pound of arsenic but whose death was caused by a car accident whose probability of causing his death was clearly less than that associated with arsenic, in such a way that the explanation of the death by the arsenic may satisfy all van Fraassen requirements without being the correct explanation, whereas the explanation based on the accident, which does not satisfy them is the correct one.

More generally, when multiple causes can produce an event, even if all the reasons based on probability incite us to privilege one of them as the explanation of this event, it is always possible that another set of circumstances, while in a less probable fashion, has independently produced it. Such a situation may easily arise in economics. Suppose we observe a important drop in the demand for motorcycles in days following an announcement by government of a significant increase in the fee for a motorcycle licence; it is reasonable to explain this phenomenon by the increased fee, whose probability of producing such a result is higher than the probability associated with other possible causes. But suppose that the same day a very popular movie star dies in a motorcycle accident in such a way that many people are emotively turned away from their desire to buy a motorcycle before learning anything about the tax increase. And suppose that these potential buyers are precisely those who would have been discouraged from buying were they informed of the fee increase and that those who were not influenced by the accident are too fanatically devoted to the motorcycle to be influenced by the fee increase. Then, economists who are required to explain the phenomenon would normally explain it as an effect of the fee increase announcement which, according to the best estimate, is much more likely – at least, let us assume that – to influence potential buyers than the quite exceptional impact of the accident is. Their explanation would satisfy all van Fraassen criteria for a correct explanation, but it will not be the *correct* one.

But to what extent is this possibility damaging for a theory of explanation like van Fraassen's? Explanation given in these examples are answers to why-questions related to a singular fact (why did Jones, who was in very good health up to now, suddenly die? Why did the demand for motorcycles suddenly decrease?). Explainers are informed of a few things (Jones has ingested a pound of arsenic; an important fee increase on motorcycle licences has been announced), but they are not aware of other things (Jones' involvement in a car accident; the announcement of a tragic motorcycle accident involving a movie star); or, at least, they have no opportunity of knowing, respectively, whether the car accident was mortal or whether the movie star's death had an impact on motorcycle fans. In this situation, according to van Fraassen's criteria, the explanations based on arsenic or on a fee increase may be evaluated positively. These explanations may even be declared acceptable as scientific explanations. They remove any puzzlement about the event to be explained, and once they are understood, it no longer makes sense to be puzzled by the fact that Jones is dead or by the fact that the demand for motorcycles has decreased; it would be foolish to persist in demanding explanations of these facts. However, by hypothesis, we know that these explanations are not correct.

But science is a progressive process and, as convincingly emphasized by Karl Popper, scientificity cannot be defined by truth, nor scientific arguments by their correctness understood as truthfulness. If we consider that the explanations based on arsenic or on a fee increase are not correct, it is because they do not refer to the *true* causes of the events, causes that we know by hypothesis. If such is the case, these arguments might be accepted as 'scientific' in the sense of being, in the present state of knowledge, a valuable piece of scientific analysis, a bit like a contemporary historian of science may say that certain Newtonian explanations were not 'correct' without denying their undisputable scientific character. In any case, it remains from this discussion that the fact that the content of an explanation that satisfies all van Fraassen's criteria for a good explanation is true is *not sufficient* to warrant the correctness of this explanation, whereas the fact that the content of an explanation based on causality is true is fully sufficient to warrant its correctness. But this conclusion is far from surprising, because causality is precisely the criterion of correctness adopted by Achinstein, at least in this counterexample (the explanation based on car accident is the correct one, because it is the accident that has *caused* the death). But if such is the case, the evaluation of a causalist theory of explanation becomes purely a tautological affair. An explanation that consists in identifying the true cause of an event is necessarily a correct explanation since the explanation of an event is judged correct if and only if it identifies its true cause. It is probably for this reason that Achinstein says that it is dubious that such an account be 'welcome to most of those seeking models of explanation' (1983: 185). Thus, van Fraassen's theory avoids being involved in such a hardly illuminating tautology, even though it cannot provide criteria allowing us to evaluate whether an explanation is 'correct'. But does it allow us to discriminate between scientific and pseudo-scientific explanations? This is what is contested by Salmon's second objection, which was presented in a paper written with Kitcher.

This objection to van Fraassen's theory concerns the criteria which allow one to characterize an explanation as a scientific one. This problem is particularly acute since this theory is applicable to common sense, as well as to scientific explanation. The fact that an answer to a why-question can take so many forms renders the need for a characterization of a scientific explanation particularly pressing. For van Fraassen, calling an explanation scientific 'is to say nothing about its form or the sort of information adduced', but rather to claim that it 'draws on science' to get the information on which it is based, and 'more importantly' that it is evaluated as a good explanation with criteria 'applied using a scientific theory' (1980: 155–156). I recall that, for him, an explanation must be 'evaluated as telling, good or better' with the help of the criteria discussed above, which left their author not fully confident. These criteria, as we have seen, concern respectively, its truth, the degree to which it favours the topic of the question more than other members of the contrast class and the degree to which it should be preferred over other possible answers in regard to its probability, its relation to the topic and its relative relevance (van Fraassen 1980: 146–151). Kitcher and Salmon have challenged the trustworthiness of these conditions for being a 'scientific' explanation by objecting that a carefully devised astrological explanation of the fact that John F. Kennedy died exactly on November 22, 1963 could perfectly fulfil all of them (Kitcher and Salmon 1987: 322ff. and Salmon 1989: 141ff.).

Since any answer to this objection will bear on the question of whether the astrological 'explanation' really draws on science, there is little doubt that van Fraassen's difficulty in defining criteria of a scientific explanation is closely related to the well known difficulties of solving the long-standing problem of demarcation.[19] But if a conclusion is emerging from the unending debates about the latter problem, it seems to be that one must renounce perfectly defined criteria and be content with using a pragmatic and conventional mode of demarcation between science and pseudo-science (see Laudan 1983) – and, consequently, between scientific and pseudo-scientific explanations. Therefore, objections such as Kitcher and Salmon's that consist in discrediting van Fraassen's criteria of demarcation between science and pseudo-science by claiming that they can be satisfied by a pseudo-science such as astrology are a bit ambiguous since the latter is presented indisputably as *a pseudo-science, and in no way a genuine science*, apparently on the basis of a not fully compelling convention. Indeed, were one admitting that astrology can be considered to be a science, the criteria would not be discredited; but if one claims that astrology is just a pseudo-science, in the name of which other criteria can this be established by one who is so prompt to admit that astrology can easily satisfy so carefully designed criteria?

Naturally this ambiguity does not solve the problem raised by the objection to van Fraassen's criteria, because the very fact of being unable to determine criteria that can allow us to clearly distinguish science from non-science is a predicament for a theory that aims to characterize scientific explanations; however, it strongly presses one who uses this objection to present a theory that can formulate fully satisfactory criteria of demarcation. Thus, since Kitcher and Salmon object to van Fraassen that a pseudo-science such as astrology is a counterexample that can successfully pass his criteria, it is crucial for their objection to be completed by more compelling criteria allowing them to maintain that astrology is indisputably a sheer pseudo-science and not a science. In fact, Salmon avoids the intricacies associated with the problem of demarcation thanks to his own theory of explanation defined by an elicitation of genuine causal processes. Since the latter are defined themselves with the help of his causal *at-at* theory, which constitutes a kind of criterion that the alleged causality invoked by astrologers could hardly satisfy, no other criteria seem to be required to disentangle scientific explanations from astrological ones. According to the realist approach adopted by Salmon, the elicitation of such causal processes is necessarily a scientific explanation since science itself is understood as an analysis of true causes of phenomena, a situation similar to the one that we met when discussing Achinstein's objection. In this view, causal processes exist in the world in which, at least in principle, they can be discovered and elicited in order to provide, by this very fact, objective and genuinely scientific explanations. However, since this theory has its own shortcomings as we have seen above, and, in particular, since explanations provided by quantum mechanics cannot satisfy the requirements of this causal theory, this situation renders it cumbersome to reject pseudo-sciences in the name of the fact that their alleged causal processes cannot satisfy criteria that quantum mechanics cannot satisfy either.

Causality versus context-dependence

An ontic theory such as Salmon's raises another more general problem. Salmon is probably right when suggesting that science is nothing other than an analysis of true causes of phenomena; therefore deducing from this that a scientific explanation should be an elicitation of these causes is an attractive thesis. However, determining which causes should be elicited is, nevertheless, an important problem for such a theory, which is, in fact the problem that van Fraassen raised in his objection to Salmon, referred to above, about the determination of what information is to be included in the explanation. Even if we accept the *at-at* theory of causes, we must acknowledge that the chains of linked events that terminate in the event to be explained are multiple and that each of these chains are made up of a multitude of events. The famous fable used to vulgarize chaos theory, according to which the flapping of a butterfly's wings can cause a storm in the antipodes is possibly a fanciful exaggeration, but it nonetheless illustrates the intricacies of causal connections which link together all of the events happening in the world. What is elicited in a Salmonian explanation is nothing other than a segment of an extremely complex causal net. And what should be considered as the relevant causal process bringing out the event to be explained and whose elicitation constitutes the relevant explanation is necessarily a particular segment, chosen among a multitude of others, of such a causal net. How could the identity of this particular segment be revealed if it is not by being declared *relevant to the answer* of a puzzlement-induced question or, if one prefers, by being declared explanatory with respect to this particular question? Otherwise, on what basis could one effectuate this necessary segmentation of a causal net, which is made up of interconnected causal links which cannot even be denumbered? The Salmonian *at-at* theory of causation could not help since the multiple *at-at* intermediary positions cannot be denumbered either. Thus, it is not sufficient to claim that a satisfactory explanation supposes that causes are elicited. A choice must be made among the multiple causes or causal factors. Of course, this does not mean that the explainer can freely construct any causal process. It simply means that the question of relevance, so important in van Fraassen's approach, is still with us and cannot be eliminated.

This situation might be clarified to some extent by revisiting the over-discussed metaphysical question concerning the traits of a world free of human consciousness. In such a world, the multitude of events would continue to be linked together (through chains of contiguities) in a network of multifarious connections. Indeed, these connections, which, in our world, are observed or inferred empirically by scientists, are not freely invented by them; consequently, they should still be working in a world without consciousness. The moon would continue to produce tides in exactly the same way as it did for conscious beings. In this sense, the entities and events that we used to consider as the *cause* of the tides would still be there. In the wording of Salmon's *at-at* theory, at each intervening stage in the causal process that produces tides, the characters of the marks involved would have no reason to be changed by the absence of any conscious beings. However, this does not mean that the *relevant* causal links would be right there, waiting for a conscious mind to pick them out and, in this way, integrate them into explanations. Indeed, the *required structuring* of those infinite amounts of contiguous marks (whatever their exact nature may be) which goes from the moon (artificially taken in isolation in such a world) to the oceans and the tides would no longer be there in the absence of a conscious mind. The physical impact of the sequence of events in the causal net would not be affected, but the structure of the hardly identifiable segment of this causal net, whose elicitation constitutes an explanation, would no longer be there. Thus, if one can say, in a somewhat metonymical fashion, that the attraction of the moon *explains* the tides, one cannot say that this explanation of the tides can be *discovered* in a world in which such an explanation would already be present in the form of a set of causes. Indeed, since it depends on the interest and background knowledge of the particular question of a questioner, the relevant segment of the causal net can be tailored and structured only by the person providing a relevant answer to a question, and therefore an appropriate explanation.

According to van Fraassen's context-dependent theory of explanation, this is because 'the correct answer [to a why-question] consists in the exhibition of a single factor in the causal net, which is made salient in that context [...]' (1980: 132). Clearly, for van Fraassen – who incidentally opens his review of Salmon's book on causal explanation by claiming that his 'agreement with Salmon is much more extensive than [his] disagreement' (1985: 639) – the elicitation of the (relevant) cause of the phenomenon to be explained cannot be dispensed with, any more in his theory than in Salmon's. In fact, if we admit that, while pointing essentially towards causes, an explanation cannot be reduced to an elicitation of these causes, because it necessarily depends on the content of the question that has provoked it, we may either emphasize the difference that remains between these two theories or acknowledge that conciliation is possible.[20]

Whether conciliated or not, the very existence of these two theories of scientific explanation might have consequences for the significance of the ideal of a unified science. The point is not to deny that if explanations based on neuroscience were successfully substituted for all rational explanations, science would constitute a more unified entity. The point is rather that the significance of the unification resulting from such a hypothetical substitution is not so clear if we consider the difficulty of establishing a unified theory *of scientific explanation* and the fact that such explanations must remain context-dependent whatsoever. As for rational explanations, they are typically context-dependent explanations that can also be treated as elicitations of causes if we admit that reasons can be considered to be causes. As we have seen, when developed by competent economists, sociologists or historians they can also rest on well established premises. These facts may be not sufficient to satisfy those who aspire to provide social sciences with more typically scientific foundations, but they may help us to understand why it is sensible to say that social sciences' rational explanations allow us to understand a number of phenomena in the most satisfying way that is currently, and possibly ever, available.

Epilogue

No one would deny that, in the first decade of the twenty-first century, economics looks considerably different as a discipline from what it was during the 1960s and even the 1980s. It is true that Samuelson's and Friedman's methodological views which, in spite of their important differences, have dominated these decades, still exert a non-negligible influence on most contemporary economists, but so many new currents, new tools and new approaches made their way into the economic literature that the discipline seems to have been totally transformed. For many analysts of economic thought, this development corresponds to a return to pluralism. I do not contest this interpretation since it is true that many currents of thought such as Keynesianism, or even Marxism, which had lost their appeal in the preceding period seem to have found a new life after being more or less adjusted to correspond to the new economic wisdom; moreover, new approaches, inspired by feminism, ecology or other trends usually associated with heterodoxy, occupy an increasingly respected place in economic research. However, it is not this pluralist context that I want to emphasize here, but rather the fact that new objects are now discussed and new tools are now commonly used by mainstream as well as by heterodox economists. In any case, it is not my intention, far from it, to present a survey of these various new developments. I, rather, intend to briefly consider three of the most representative among them in order to see whether the ideas developed in this book, mostly in the context of analyses of a more traditional kind, can fit with the new context of economic research.

Theses summarily recapitulated

To start with, let us recall what the main theses of this book are. The first of these claims that the whole economic theory is based on the idea that people are rational, but adds that there is no need for this rationality to be conceived as a capacity to maximize. In fact, the required rationality can even be said to be minimal, not only because actual human actions are guided by a relatively modest degree of rationality, but because typical theoretical models, which correspond to an idealized picture of economic relations, can be perfectly well construed as requiring nothing more than a minimal degree of rationality. They can be construed as describing all the relevant parameters of a situation in such a way that idealized agents have only to give their consent to decisions that the model itself presents as preferable; agents have, for example, to decide to avoid increasing production when the model implies that the cost of producing supplementary units is clearly greater than the revenue expected, etc. Put otherwise, instead of interpreting models as deriving from optimal decisions of agents endowed with powerful computing capacities, one can interpret them as idealised descriptions of situations in which optimal decisions are literally pointed out to the agents.

To be rational does not mean to maximize, which would require that agents have knowledge of the multitude of relevant data involved in really maximizing a decision; as we have seen, pushed to the limit, such a requirement would imply that the agent be endowed with an impossible and self-contradictory omniscience. Nor does it mean to be consistent in making choices, which also implies that agents are omniscient; indeed, without omniscience, they would have various things to learn, and learning can be a source of inconsistency. Being rational simply means having the capacity to decide in a way that makes sense, which means having the capacity, when making decisions, to choose means after evaluating them as appropriate for reaching goals, which, for whatever reasons, have been previously judged worthwhile.

Now, if rationality is so important for economics, it is because it is the basis for most explanations of economic phenomena that economists have developed. Basing economic explanations on rationality supposes that agents are rational *individuals* and that social phenomena result to a significant extent from individual (rational) actions. Naturally, since, in a society, a great number of agents make rational decisions oriented towards various goals, the consequences of their actions are intermingled between themselves in such a way that final consequences are largely unwanted by the agents. This is the gist of methodological individualism, which has nothing to do with reductionism and which does not preclude that, conversely, social intercourse plays a crucial role in the shaping of individuals. Indeed, there is little doubt that social relations strongly influence the development of individuals, but this is not a reason for denying that social structures are explained in the last resort by the interfering of individual actions which are themselves explained by the reasons that guide rational individuals. It is also clear that individual agents are far from being immutable sources of decisions: they are subject to continuous learning in such a way that their preferences, and consequently their decisions, can and do change with their increasing but always limited knowledge. Such are the individual agents whose rational behaviour allows us to explain various but not all dimensions of economic phenomena.

One might prefer that economists use other kinds of explanations, more akin to those that have made the natural sciences successful, but up to now, explanations of economic phenomena *as such* (movements of prices or of various rates, equilibria, organization of labour and of firms, etc.) rest on the rationality principle. Of course, intensive research is done to develop other kinds of explanations, based, for example, on neuroscience, but when it comes to *explaining* economic phenomena as such (in contrast, for example, with the neurobiological basis of decision making), it is the relatively rational behaviour of individuals involved that is usually invoked. Similarly, for many decades, other attempts have been made to ground economic explanations on natural selection. It cannot be denied that a kind of selection may provide a complementary background to rational explanations by explaining the survival, or at least the success, of individuals and firms whose majority of choices turned out to be well adapted to their economic environment. It is also true that, if a few relatively unrealistic assumptions are accepted, this type of selection could explain that an equilibrium might obtain within certain widely defined limits. However, when it comes to explaining actual economic phenomena as they develop in a realistically short term, it is rational explanations that are invoked to explain the relatively efficient development of actual economies, in such a way that, in these cases, the arguments based on natural selection are revealed to be insufficient and superfluous.

Nonetheless, one may understand why many economists and methodologists do not judge rational explanations to be satisfactory. While such explanations can allow relatively reliable predictions in certain circumstances, they tend to generate rather vague and unstable predictions in many domains that interest economists. Moreover, as frequently underscored by Alexander Rosenberg, whatever the degree of reliability that can be granted to these predictions, they can hardly be improved upon with the development of knowledge as the predictions of natural sciences can. Moreover, rational explanations suppose interpretations that are not required, at least to the same degree, in explanations typical of natural sciences; indeed, reasons must be interpreted and cannot be directly observed as many – but far from all – physical causes can.[1] A consequence of these considerations is that rational explanations work relatively well when it comes to explain economic situations after the fact, but perform rather poorly in predictions. And another consequence is that the ideal of a unified science, which has heuristically inspired generations of philosophers, cannot be satisfied if this type of explanation is maintained. However, given the difficulty of establishing a satisfactory theory of explanation even in natural sciences and given that, according to various respectable theories, rational (or equivalent) explanations are the most appropriate ones when human actions are concerned, it seems excessive to postulate that explanations in economics must be modelled on explanations in natural sciences.

Three kinds of contributions typical of contemporary economics

In a nutshell, these are the theses of the present book. Let us now consider the three fields of research evoked above, whose recent development has so considerably transformed contemporary economics. I have in mind behavioural economics, game theory and neuroeconomics. In fact, none of them should be perceived of as a brand new kind of analysis. Behavioural economics has generalized the programme of experimental economics developed in the recent decades and its insistence on the psychological bases of economics was even anticipated to some extent by research done in the 1950s such as that of George Katona (1951). Game theory was also introduced to economics in the 1950s with Von Neumann and Morgenstern's celebrated book and it was used more and more in economics since the 1980s. Neuroeconomics is newer and was systematically developed as such mostly in the twenty-first century, but it is essentially a new name given to the application of research, initiated during the last decades of the twentieth century, to economics. Be that as it may, these relatively new approaches are quite typical components of what constitutes the new visage of contemporary economics. Indeed, whereas they were more or less considered marginal additions to mainstream economics before, let us say, the mid-1990s, they occupy an important place in the research programmes developed in most sectors of economic analysis since then. Moreover, in recent years these three approaches became more and more closely interrelated[2] in such a way that their importance for contemporary economics is correspondingly increased.

Behavioural economics

For many decades of the twentieth century, neoclassical economics developed successive models one of whose most emphasized merits was associated with the fact that they progressively eliminated any trace of psychology. Therefore the analysis of the interface between psychology and economics was not only neglected but overtly avoided by most economists of the first three quarters of the twentieth century until the development of experimental economics, in which analyses of economic behaviour and applications of the latter were systematically developed with the help of 'laboratory' experimentations and other psychological tools. Before this period, this field, which concerns the very genesis of economic behaviour, had attracted so few researchers, at least among economists, that when it became an acceptable domain of research for economists to whom psychology started to inspire less suspicious sentiments, a multitude and a great variety of questions were investigated during a relatively short period as testified by the recent collective book entitled *Advances in Behavioral Economics* (Camerer, Loewenstein and Rabin 2004). However, as observed by two of its editors, Colin Camerer and George Loewenstein (ibid.: 5), most of the ideas associated with behavioural economics 'return to the roots of neoclassical economics after a century-long detour'. They would surely add, however, that this 'return' corresponds to a much more general approach that includes field observations as well as experiments in laboratory conditions and that draws from a number of psychological insights that bear on very varied questions related to economic behaviour.

In the typical results of this kind of research, it would be difficult to see a source of objections that might be systematically raised against the ideas proposed here. Most work associated with behavioural economics has clearly illustrated that, when making choices, people rarely maximize and are far from being consistent. However, as we have seen, these results, which are highly damaging for the mainstream economic conceptions of rationality, usually do not induce experimentalists to deny that people are rational. Since these analysts of human behaviour aim to explain this behaviour, they have no choice but to develop models according to which people are rational in the sense that they find ways that they judged more straightforward and satisfactory for reaching their goals (rule of thumb, lexicographic order, untypical reactions to risk, utility function adapted to specific tastes, unusual sense of fairness, etc.). To be called explanatory, such models must imply that the behaviour to be explained is guided by principles that can be understood by analysts. For sure, understanding that individuals choose to let themselves be guided by untypical rules or principles may suppose that it is admitted that people have an imperfect power of decision making and a limited knowledge of the parameters involved in the decision to be made, but it nonetheless means that people manage in some way to make satisfactory decisions, and consequently that they are far from being stupid.

It would be unfair to claim that all these attitudes correspond to what I have described as minimal rationality, but it is clear that, in this context, economic decisions are not a matter of maximization or consistency, and that explaining is a matter of understanding whatever principle or rationale guides such decisions. This rationale can vary widely with situations and with people, but it must be close enough to what is usually meant by rationality to allow the analyst to claim that an explanation of the behaviour is provided; otherwise the only conclusion would be that no rational explanation of the phenomenon involved is possible. Indeed, suppose, for example, that it was discovered experimentally that some people choose to lose money *without any kind of perceptible compensation* such as altruism, facility, avoidance of anxiety or whatever; arriving at such a conclusion would be equivalent to concluding that the behaviour of those people remains unexplained because it is clearly irrational. But this is precisely the type of failure that many experimentalists try to avoid by explaining the situation with the help of models that invoke weak degrees of rationality. Therefore, unless we accept Ross' well informed but not very compelling argument according to which behavioural economics may easily lead to eliminativism (Ross 2005: 190–211), it seems reasonable, without claiming that behavioural economics provides a direct support to the ideas defended in this book, to say not only that it does not systematically hurt them, but that it promotes a vision of economics that, at least from certain points of view, is not so far from the one on which they are founded.

Game theory

At first glance, those ideas might face more embarrassing questions raised by game theory in spite of the fact that, as is well known, the latter is not a branch of science covering a particular domain, but rather an extremely rich toolbox, which, in principle, can be used in any sector of analysis. It is true that explanations provided by classical game theory are based on the rationality attributed to players who aim to obtain a payoff, which is not necessarily the maximal one but the most satisfactory, given various strategic considerations. However, the notion of minimal or moderate rationality seems to be hardly compatible with the kind of rationality attributed to players, which typically implies a powerful deductive capacity and an iterative common knowledge of a kind that is rarely realised even by the most brilliant minds.

This demanding type of rationality is indeed associated with theoretical models of games, just as rationality-maximization or rationality-consistency is associated with neoclassical economic models. But why should it not be possible to interpret these theoretical pieces the way I have interpreted typical economic models? We have seen that with such a construal, it is only required of agents that they make a minimally rational move by choosing the most favourable options (according to their usually unambiguous preferences), which are proposed by the model itself. A fairly obvious answer is that whereas in typical economic models, decisions (or actions) correspond to punctual moments in a theoretical structure that describes all the complexity of the situation, models proposed by game theory – especially when they are presented in an extensive form – are nothing but a step by step analysis of the rational and strategic decisions (or actions) themselves. Therefore such models could hardly be construed as if players have simply to give their adherence to a solution that would be suggested by the rest of the model. In a centipede game, for example, sophisticated players, guided by backward induction and by the common knowledge that each player is a strict maximizer, should in a first round paradoxically choose to keep a very small sum for themselves, which, in a succession of rounds, might be multiplied many times through a (risky) succession of exchanges between players. No doubt such counterintuitive but perfectly logical decisions could hardly be associated with minimal rationality. However, one should acknowledge that actual games are played by players who normally do not let themselves be guided by this uncompromising rationality. Experiments done by behavioural economists have shown that players engaged in somewhat sophisticated games rarely behave as the strategic rationality of the theory suggests. David Kreps, who does not hesitate to invoke common sense in his discussions of games (Kreps 1990: 82, 88–89, 102–103, 117), recalls that even sophisticated players in centipede games rarely follow the unintuitive prescription of the theory (ibid.: 78). He also shows that the very notion of maximization becomes highly ambiguous in such games (ibid.: 81, 117–118).

Of course, if actual economic situations were really *explained* through sophisticated strategic decisions, it is clear that it would not be sufficient to attribute minimal rationality to the agents, but such cases seem to be relatively rare. In fact, many game theory models – for example, those corresponding to simple cases of Nash equilibrium, including prisoner's dilemmas – could easily be interpreted as requiring a degree of rationality not very far from minimal, if we admit that wondering in a pessimistic mood what an opponent would risk doing and then opting for the safer option is not a particularly sophisticated behaviour.

Game theory has considerably expanded the understanding of the complex and sometimes paradoxical choices associated with rational behaviour in economic as in other contexts, but when it comes to explaining actual economic phenomena, it is frequently a less sophisticated application of rationality that is invoked. In any case, in game theory, at least in the classical game theory, rationality remains the key element of explanation. Moreover, a brand of methodological individualism, in a sense more radical than the one I have defended, seems to be tacitly implied by many models developed in game theory, still more unequivocally than by traditional microeconomics.[3] Even when organizations are involved, as when it is a question of the relations between a monopolist and possible entrants, the explanation of the consequences of the confrontation of their strategic decisions is provided as if decisions were made by individual players who conceive the adapted strategies and manage in such a way that the latter are adopted by their firms. On these various fronts, it is difficult to see in what sense classical game theory might endanger the substance of ideas developed in the present book.

However, it is no longer possible to discuss contemporary game theory without considering how players, and sometimes the games themselves, evolve when games are repeated. The origin of evolutionary game theory is usually attributed to John Maynard Smith who, in his groundbreaking book, *Evolution and the Theory of Games*, applied game theory to the development of evolutionary stable strategies in animal populations. Maynard Smith did not hesitate to claim that 'game theory is more readily applied to biology than to the field of economic behaviour for which it was originally designed' (Maynard Smith 1982: vi). Soon after that, however, economists and other social scientists found many applications for evolutionary game theory, especially for the analysis of the evolution of strategies through repeated games.

At first glance at least, these applications can be seen as a serious challenge to the role of rationality in social sciences. Herbert Gintis even claims that '[E]volutionary game theory deploys the Darwinian notion that good strategies diffuse across populations of players rather than being learned by rational agents' (Gintis 2009: xvi). However, it should be made clear first that rational explanations are normally inappropriate when it comes to explaining the origin of dispositions in people (whether by diffusion or otherwise), which may have been developed over centuries by virtue of natural selection. What is more to the point is the way people are likely to change their (rational) strategies through playing games repeatedly. Even though, in the games involved, players may more or less passively follow strategies that turned out to be successful in a given population in the past, without having to make the sophisticated calculations that are required in certain classical games, they have to make decisions at some point. Players in repeated prisoner's dilemma games can hardly avoid choosing either cooperation or defection even though the strategy that is diffusing strongly suggests what the appropriate choice is to them. Gintis and other evolutionary game theorists would probably acknowledge this fact, but not without observing that animals and computers can do the same. It is true that at a strictly formal level, it is difficult to disentangle these different types of 'choices'. But unless you admit that computers and all animals involved are conscious in the sense that they can judge, evaluate, regret, be disappointed and change their minds accordingly, their 'rational choices' can be more efficient than those of human beings, but they cannot be said to be rational in the sense that human choices are rational. And it is only when such a genuine rationality is invoked that rational explanations are meaningful and can be treated as autonomous explanations. We may consider that we have 'rationally' explained that agents have decided to choose *A* rather than *B* because, after an appropriate evaluation that has to be made explicit, they found it rational to choose *A* rather than *B*, and not because an unconscious mechanism drove them to adopt this choice. In the context of a diffusion process, we may say that, through this process, agents have learned a more appropriate strategy. Nothing excludes that they were in a position to learn in such a way because they are rational but far from omniscient; and the rationality required is rather minimal in the sense that they must simply be rational enough to choose a strategy that clearly turns out to be more rewarding.

From the point of view related to learning, evolutionary game theory, because it must make room for changes in preferences (usually due to learning) is compatible with the notion of minimal rationality, and possibly, while not so easily, with rationality-maximization, but what about rationality-consistency? In fact, changes in preferences *might* be made compatible with consistency, but only if all possible contents of knowledge were previously identified and made part of the situation. If such were the case, one might claim 'I am not inconsistent since I choose *A* over *B* with knowledge *X* after having chosen *B* over *A* with knowledge *Y*'. However, if consistency was understood this way, one should conclude that no real learning may occur in this context since all possible knowledge would already be contemplated.[4] In fact, in the real world, which is neither close nor completed, such an inventory of possible knowledge is in principle not realizable and even inconceivable; therefore, we can safely conclude that the notion of rationality-consistency is clearly incompatible with *true* learning, and that, consequently, it cannot easily be made compatible with evolutionary game theory. In any case, it is not my intention to enter in the subtleties of the debates concerning learning in game theory; I only want to underscore the fact that referring to rationality without being a slave to the limitations associated with rationality-consistency removes what is one of the main difficulties that economists can hardly avoid meeting when they quite legitimately try to introduce learning into their models. Of course, these considerations do not eliminate other challenges raised by evolutionary game theory, but the latter are closely associated with fundamental philosophical conceptions concerning the very nature of consciousness, which cannot be discussed further in the present book.

Neuroeconomics

Among the new developments in contemporary economics, neuroeconomics, which explores the interface between economics and neuroscience, seems to constitute a more important and direct challenge to rational explanations. In a particularly well articulated book, Paul Glimcher (2003) presents a critically commented history of the origins of this interface up to his own works, which analyse the regular way specific neurons in a primate's brain's cortex are fired depending on decisions that have to be made for solving different tasks. Here is not the place to analyse Glimcher's remarkable findings, but it is worthwhile underscoring the fact that various concepts developed mathematically in economics (expected utility) and in game theory (mixed strategy) are fruitfully applied to the behaviour of monkeys. Glimcher is possibly overenthusiastic about these astonishing results when he describes how monkeys solved the problems to which he submits them: 'the monkey should solve this problem by performing an expected utility calculation' (Glimcher 2003: 326). Since Bayes' theorem was involved in the efficient solution, he does not hesitate to say:

> So if he is to perform the task efficiently [what was effectively done] the monkey's guess must reflect more than just what he saw. It must represent the outcome of a calculation that describes a posterior probability as a combination of prior knowledge and current observation.
>
> (Glimcher 2003: 325)

Glimcher concludes that 'the monkey should solve this problem by performing an expected utility calculation' (ibid.: 326). And another task requires 'twice as many calculations' from the monkey (ibid.: 326). Naturally neither monkeys nor their neurons, which were associated with these tasks in Glimcher's experiments, do perform the types of operations that only some trained economists can perform. They do not perform them any more than billiards players perform the mathematical operations evoked by Friedman. It seems more sensible to say that they arrive at a correct solution because natural selection, over a multitude of centuries, has allowed animals who turned out to be capable of learning and developing similar skills to survive. Glimcher would very probably agree that such calculations do not have to be consciously and explicitly executed, but the language can be deceiving. Similarly, in experimental games in which monkeys have to deceive a computer playing the role of the opponent, they adopt the appropriate solution, which is the mixed strategy: they play randomly in order to become unpredictable. Human beings in similar games frequently adopt the same solution, because when engaged in a conflict, they are not stupid enough to reveal their strategy, and the only way to avoid revealing it is to use a mixed (randomized) strategy. Even though, in contrast with monkeys, human beings perform actual calculations in some circumstances, in all situations described above, they also adopt solutions that can be said to be (minimally) 'rational' without doing any actual computations, and it is on this basis that their behaviour can be explained. Whether the same thing can be said of the monkeys depends on whether a certain degree of consciousness can be attributed to them. I do not have to reach a conclusion regarding this question here, but my point is that, when explaining their behaviour, it is also a rational explanation requiring minimal rationality that we tend to invoke literally or metaphorically (depending on our answer to the previous question). The identification of the neurons that are fired when monkeys adopt such solutions is a spectacular and promising development in our understanding of the brain, which, however, does not clearly help those who want to understand *why* monkeys move their eyes in the direction associated with the highest expected reward and why monkeys and people adopt mixed strategies in certain circumstances. Put otherwise, even if neuroeconomists were to succeed in identifying all the connections between brain and behaviour, this would not imply that we would have an explanation of the meaning of conscious actions that could advantageously replace rational explanations. It is doubtful that the outsider who would know all the relations between our nervous systems (including the brain and all the sensorimotor elements), would be in a position to deduce the meanings that economic events have for us.

Glimcher's main achievement was probably his fruitful applications of the formalism of economics and game theory to neurological analyses, but one may also expect results from neuroeconomics that go the other way around: neurobiology should contribute to the development of economics. On this ground, the results seem less convincing. It is true that various methods of investigation have been more or less recently developed and that they mutually correct and reinforce themselves, as is clearly exposed in an authoritative paper by Camerer, Loewenstein and Prelec (2004: 557–558). The list of results obtained may impress by the number and variety of applications, because neuroeconomics is presented in this paper as a quite general analysis of the whole interface between body signals of any type and behaviour more or less directly related to economics. The multiple experimental studies pertaining to this vast domain have produced a number of interesting and useful results (ibid.: 562–572), which bring supplementary precision to more traditional concepts, new empirical bases for distinctions perceived only intuitively up to then, new ways of measuring certain data, supplementary information on the origin of emotions, suggestions for new research in under-analysed areas, finer knowledge of the mechanisms involved in phenomena such as addictions, which have interested economists, etc. These results are important and it would be irresponsible to denigrate them, but, at least up to now, they do not propose a new kind of explanation of economic phenomena that could be substituted for rational explanations. In a paper written in 2008, Camerer more ambitiously claims that '[t]he goal of neuroeconomics is to build up a mechanistic, behavioural and mathematical theory of choice and exchange' (Camerer 2008: 369). However, as is easily understood, when it is a question of a new science pointing towards such a formidable goal, the author can only present a few 'possibilities' along the lines of which this development might take place. He then acknowledges that these views are based on speculation but observes that '[it] is speculative, but at this point speculating is all we can do and is necessary to make progress' (ibid.: 373). Camerer is surely right on this point, but the prospect opened by these speculations on a possible theory should not justify the dismissal of the existing economic theory based on rationality.

Economics, rationality and rational explanations

It is true that these new trends in contemporary economics do not aim to reject the existing economic theory; they rather want to reinforce and complement it. It is only its foundation, namely rationality and rational explanations that, in this perspective, might be dismissed. We have already seen where the urge to proceed to this dismissal comes from. The ideal of a unified science remains highly attractive for many philosophers and economists. Moreover, by substituting explanations akin to those of natural sciences to rational ones, it might be possible not only to unify sciences but to neutralize what Rosenberg and other methodologists rightly perceived as the predicament of social sciences: its reliance on concepts which are not 'cut to joints' and on theories whose predictions can hardly be improved. However, if one does not consider that the urgency of forcing social sciences in a procrustean bed after downgrading the explanatory significance of human decisions overwhelms the need to understand the meaning of economic phenomena as well as the rational mechanisms that explain their development, one may continue, at least for a while, to explain these phenomena with the help of the rationality principle.

These new trends in contemporary economics, whether behavioural economics, classic or evolutionary game theory or neuroeconomics – that I have evoked much too sketchily to give a fair idea of their respective contributions – have provided us with highly interesting and *promising* new knowledge. However, the obsession with unified science, which they almost necessarily accentuate, tends to damage unduly the respectability of the explanations of economic phenomena obtained with the help of the rationality principle. It is true that these explanations are provided by economic analysis whose various branches and orientations are not necessarily contested by these new trends; nonetheless, it is what I just called the respectability of the very foundations of this kind of analysis, which is downgraded by the constant (but relatively unsuccessful up to now) attempt to replace them by more objective ones. I do not want to systematically defend economic theory to which so many justified critiques can be addressed and I still maintain that the way it has progressively identified rationality with maximization, and then with consistency, was the source of a lot of confusion. However, I also maintain that, in spite of its limitations as a science, economic theory has provided us with a number of idealized explanations of idealized economic phenomena. It is true that these explanations were based on concepts of rationality that economists have constructed to satisfy their need for an elegant formalism and that they have quickly pushed the principle of rationality in its full meaning under the rug. Nonetheless, these explanations of idealized phenomena have the merit of allowing us to understand the mechanisms involved in economic phenomena. However, when it comes to accounting for the fact that such explanations are a source of genuine new understanding, in spite of being quite different from natural science explanations, what must be invoked is not maximization or consistency but the principle of rationality in its minimal form, the principle that allows us to explain *why* people decide to do what they do, and why economic phenomena can be understood as unintended consequences of the interference of their multiple (minimally) rational actions.

Notes

Introduction

1 The rationality principle to which Karl Popper devoted a famous but controversial paper (Popper 1985: 361) was referred to by various economists under various names, for example by Fritz Machlup who, 30 years before, mentioned it under the name of 'assumption of rationality' or 'economic principle' (Machlup 1955: 16).
2 It is indeed a principle of this type that, rightly or wrongly, we usually invoke in order to explain, for example, why a dog (not stupid enough to lose such an opportunity) engages in more or less difficult performances required by its master, who associates the request with a reward.
3 For a systematic discussion of some of these laws see Kindleberger (1989). An earlier version of my views on economic laws appeared in French in Lagueux (2007).
4 Note that this has nothing to do with the fact that the gravitational constant varies according to the position considered on Earth. Since this fact depends on the distance between the centre of the Earth and the points on its not perfectly spherical surface, these differences can be dealt with by a correct application of the distance variable included in the law.
5 This view, which was first developed by David Lewis, was revisited by various philosophers of science including Carl Hempel and Nelson Goodman; Daniel Hausman refers to this point in Hausman (1992: 293).
6 In the *Principles of Economics* (V,V,2), Marshall calls *ceteris paribus* a 'pound' in which disturbing causes whose action would disrupt or overshadow the 'trend' that is considered, and therefore isolated, are temporarily gathered and neglected.
7 I borrow this example of a 'shortage created by the price ceiling' from Rappaport (1995: 432ff.), but I use it in a different theoretical context.
8 For the importance of emphasizing the role of mechanisms in explanation, see Cartwright (1995).
9 For a summary discussion of the succession and opposition of these two views on rationality, see Lagueux (2004), which develops an idea exposed in two working papers (Lagueux 1997 and Lagueux 2001b) derived from conferences presented respectively at Fribourg in 1997 and at the ESHET meeting held at Valencia in 1999. Since then, an authoritative and highly documented analysis of this displacement of the maximization view by the consistency view has been developed by Giocoli (2003) who aptly associates this move with a more fundamental displacement of an image of science construed as a system of force by an image of science construed as a system of relations.

1 Rationality in economics before the Second World War

1 The two first chapters of this book readapt and expand an earlier version of ideas published in Lagueux (2004).
2 This is not to deny that insane or neurotic moves can sometimes be predicted much more accurately than rational decisions, eventually on neurological bases, but these kinds of moves are typically not what goes on in a normal economy.
3 Smith (1937 [1776]: 279); I thank William Coleman (University of Tasmania) for having kindly drawn my attention to this passage that he had quoted in Coleman (1995: 126), which, incidentally, is a thoughtful assessment of the classical economists' perception of rationality.
4 Ricardo to Malthus, 22 October 1811, in Ricardo (1952 [1811]: 64), quoted by Coleman in the review of another work.
5 Marx, *Capital*, Book III, sections I and II (for the equality of profit rates, chapters IX and X).
6 It should be clear that, in this book, by 'modelling' I simply mean the process through which economic theories have been expressed with the help of mathematical models. I do net refer to the operation in which, according to most logicians and philosophers of science, scientific theories are interpreted through models in the sense that their axiomatic theorems are made true under this interpretation.
7 It is clear, however, that this so-called law can hardly be considered as a genuine law. It is better understood as a condition of intelligibility, for which the crucial point is not its empirical truth but its unavoidability. The difference between these two perspectives is not immaterial: *we are no longer referring to a conquest of the intellect, but rather to an acknowledgement of its limits.* To maintain that marginal utility is decreasing is not to pretend to have established a law comparable to the law of falling bodies; it is to claim that if human beings were systematically to behave according to a principle of *increasing* marginal utility, it would be impossible to explain such a situation with the type of explanation the social sciences has been provided up to now. I have discussed such a hypothetical case in Lagueux (1988 and 2006a).
8 Menger (1976 [1871]: 149), emphasis added; on this point, see Kirzner (1990: 99).
9 These 'goods of higher order' are characterized as those which 'do not have the capacity to satisfy human needs directly, but which are nevertheless used for the production of goods of first order, and can thus be put in an indirect causal connection with the satisfaction of human needs' (Menger 1976 [1871]: 57; see also 63).
10 Menger (1976 [1871]: 148). The index of this book mentions pp. 53, 67–71, 86, 105, 108, 120, 147–148, 216, 224, 273, 283 for the entry 'Error' and other page references are added for the entries 'Irrationality', 'Uncertainty' and 'Risk'.
11 In *Value and Capital*, however, Hicks proposes to look at the exchange the other way around and to refer consequently to the *diminishing* marginal rate of substitution in order to keep his terminology closer to the usual one (Hicks 1946 [1939]: note 1 on page 20). I thank Clément Lemelin for drawing my attention to this point.
12 I discuss Friedman's thesis in Lagueux (1994) (and in Chapter 6 of this book).
13 Machlup (1955: 17). Machlup quotes Max Weber and Alfred Schuetz in order to vindicate this last claim.
14 For a technical discussion of this type of infinite regress, see Mongin (2000, part 4).

2 The hardly consistent story of rationality-consistency

1 See Pollak (1968), Blackorby *et al.* (1973), Peleg and Yaari (1973) and Hammond (1976).
2 For an early challenge to the rational character of consistency, see May (1954: especially 5–8).
3 See Schick (1986: 117), Anand (1987: 200–201) and Mongin (2000: 85) for various versions of this objection.

4 *Capital*, Book one, third section, chapter VII, part I.
5 It is in order to show that, in this case, intransitivity generates irrationality that Davidson *et al.* (1955: 145) introduced what will be called the money pump argument whose shortcomings have been discussed above.
6 For a discussion of Tversky's approach, see Mongin (2000: 80ff.).
7 Other contributions defend the rationality of behaviour conflicting with both independence and transitivity axioms, for example Anand (1987), or of other kinds of apparently irrational behaviour, for example Bar-Hillel and Margalit (1988).
8 Tversky and Kahneman (1986: 138). It is interesting to note that, in his famous methodological work, Robbins was already conscious of the significance of the 'marginal utility of not bothering about the marginal utility' (Robbins 1952 [1932]: 92).
9 Not only were many psychologists and economists engaged in a debate about this case, as illustrated below, but some methodologists of economics discussed the example of preference reversals as a particularly significant result in experimental economics; see, for example, Hausman (1992: chapter 13), Hausman and Mongin (1997: 259ff.) and Ross (2005: 177ff.).
10 See Lichtenstein and Slovic (1971 and 1973), which are based on the findings of Slovic and Lichtenstein (1968).
11 This axiom must not be confused with the 'context independence axiom' referred to above; on this point, see Hausman (1992: 23 and 16).
12 Note that this idea was more or less explicitly present in the original Lichtenstein and Slovic paper (1971: 54).
13 For a few considerations on the role of scope in this context, see Hausman and Mongin (1997).

3 Can methodological individualism survive?

1 For recent contributions, see Heath (2005) and Hodgson (2007); for a less recent one in French, see Petroni (1991).
2 This estimate is wrong since, as is well known, at the very least by those who are familiar with the highly influential methodological work of Lionel Robbins, even though *homines oeconomici* are supposed to make decisions according to their perception of their best interest, this interest can perfectly be understood as altruistic (Robbins 1952 [1932]: 95).
3 For Marx, see Elster (1985); I developed a first version in French of this argument regarding both of them in Lagueux (2001a: 696–701), which proposes also early versions of the arguments of the next two subsections.
4 See Marx, *Capital*, Book I, chap. 14 (in section 4) on the production of relative surplus value.
5 For a criticism of this view that is based on similar considerations but applied in a quite different theoretical context, see Ross (2005: 216ff.).
6 Among others, Watkins (1953: 26 and 1957: 113), who was among the first authors to devote important papers to methodological individualism strongly insisted on this link between this methodology and unwanted consequences. See also Dray (1967: 54).
7 Geoffrey Hodgson (2007: 220, 222) claims that methodological individualism understood in this fashion is misnamed since an individualism that makes room for explanations requiring interaction between people is not a pure individualism and therefore cannot easily be distinguished from approaches that are not considered individualistic. He is right, but my point is not to defend the appropriateness of the label, but the appropriateness of the methodology itself for economics, whatever name is the most appropriate for it. In any case, as we will see, it is the methodology and not its label that is challenged by the authors mentioned at the beginning of this chapter.
8 See especially the chapter entitled 'The Results of Human Action but not of Human Design' in Hayek (1967: 96–105).

9 See references in Hayek (1967: 99 and 1978: chapter 15).
10 See, for example, Elster (1986: 61), Satz and Ferejohn (1994: 82), Hodgson (1998: 161), Davis (2003: 36), Kincaid (1997: 32).
11 Quoted by Davis (2003: 36) from Kincaid (1996: 145ff.); see also Kincaid (1997: 5 and 14). Kincaid however claims that methodological individualism *is* reductionist since he refers to a more radical form of this methodological approach. But when he refers to a conception somewhat closer to the one I defend, he seems to admit that it is not reductionist (cf. 1997: 16).
12 Walter Block, a supporter of Austrian economics, has taken care, in a somewhat too harsh and crude fashion, to answer to Nozick's remarks by claiming that the methodological individualism of Austrians is in no way a Crusoe type of approach nor, consequently, an absurd attempt to reduce social behaviour to a Crusoe and Friday kind of relation, and the latter to Crusoe behaviour in isolation, and so forth (Block 1980: 399).
13 Mirowski (2002: 439–440 and 443–448); in fact, in these pages, Mirowski is not directly charging methodological individualism; he is rather severely criticizing various views about the Self; but, in some passages, for example on p. 440, he seems to associate both questions with one another.
14 Elster (1987 [1985]); see also Davidson (1982: 300–305) and Hargreaves Heap (1989: 103–112).
15 See Elster (1987 [1985]: 10, 13, 14, 23, 24, 26–27 and especially 30). Hargreaves Heap, whose main argument grants a significant place to multiple selves, acknowledges also that the two selves he refers to are actually parts 'of the same person' (1989: 106).
16 On this point, Ross quotes G. Berns: 'it is possible that the rational agents are the neurons, not the person' (Berns 2003: 156, quoted by Ross 2005: 330).
17 If we consider that only computers – but not interests, neurons and bugs – are put on the same footing as human beings, then we are back to the case of Mirowski's fourth Self discussed above.
18 One should understand 'centrally controlled' in its very collective nature and not by individual dictators or members of another type of government.
19 As I have argued, methodological individualism is only a strategy of explanation; insofar as consciousness and rationality are attributed to eventual post-human individuals involved, this strategy should still be valid, but the rationality principle as presently used by social sciences concerns essentially human beings. If ever it becomes clear that other kinds of individuals present a similar type of consciousness and rationality, it will be appropriate then to evaluate whether this principle should still play an equivalent role in the analysis of social relations concerning them.

4 Is still some room left for irrationality?

1 An earlier version of some of the examples used in this chapter appeared in Lagueux (1995).
2 See, for example, Klant (1984), Rotwein (1986) and Kaufmann (1937).
3 Robbins (1952 [1932]: 94–99); Robbins does not couch his argument in terms of rationality, but this notion is implied by the way he uses the notion of 'economic men'.
4 Aristotle develop the notion of akrasia in *Nichomachean Ethics* 1152 a 25–27; in this passage, he claims that, by weakness of the will, some people act in a way that contradicts a firm resolution. This kind of irrational behaviour, frequently named 'incontinence' has been referred to by most of those who have discussed irrationality.
5 Elster (1984 [1979]). In a somewhat different context, Ulysses' decision regarded as the paradigmatic example of self-binding was previously referred to by Strotz who quotes the relevant passage of the Odyssey at the beginning of his paper (1955–56: 165). In another context, Elster refers to this passage of Strotz.

6 In a personal communication, in which he reacted to an earlier version of this part of the present discussion, Jon Elster observed quite correctly (and illustrated this very clearly with many examples drawn from another book from him, namely Elster, 1989) that 'there are always costs involved in binding oneself' and he concludes from this 'therefore, it would be better if one could just realize the aim directly'. Of course, it would be *better*, but would it be more rational for all that? If someone is impeded by some constraints from realizing 'the aim directly' and, after taking account of all the costs involved, manages to realize it in a very clever but indirect way, in what sense is it sensible to say that such a response is less rational than the direct response of a person who does not have to face these constraints? This is the question I try to reformulate in the following paragraphs.
7 For a recent discussion of irrational time preferences associated with a consistency conception of rationality, see Ross (2005: 182–185).
8 Popper (1985: 361); this text, which can be read in David Miller's anthology entitled *Popper selections*, is the English version of a paper that was previously published in French (Popper 1967) under the title 'La rationalité et le statut du principe de rationalité'. The English version appeared first in the anthology *A Pocket Popper*, published by Fontana in 1983. However, since this edition was withdrawn some years later, now it is only in *Popper selections* that this text presently exists, and all references in the present text concern this 1985 version edited by David Miller. I thank the latter for providing me with the information about the role of Fontana.
9 The text of this lecture delivered at Harvard in 1963 was published by Notturno only in Popper (1994) under the title 'Models, instruments and truth: the status of the rationality principle in the social sciences'.

5 Minimal *and* maximal rationality: loosely defined concepts?

1 An earlier French version of some ideas exposed in this chapter was published in Lagueux (2005).
2 On this paradox, see Cherniak (1986: 51–52 and 71).

6 Why unrealism of assumptions remains a predicament

1 An early version of the argument developed in the first parts of this chapter was published in Lagueux (1994).
2 For examples of papers underscoring these innovating aspects of Friedman's essay, see Hirsch and de Marchi (1990), Nadeau (1992), Mäki (2009c) and some other chapters of Mäki (2009a).
3 According to Mäki (2009b: 62), it is Bear and Orr (1967) who characterized Friedman's methodological tenet as a form of 'instrumentalism' for the first time. This might have been proposed independently by Wong and Boland, see Wong (1973); Wong was, on this ground, probably indebted to Boland who, however, wrote his own paper (Boland 1979) at a later date.
4 I do not want denounce realism as such, but only a doctrine according to which any theoretical construction must be derived from descriptively realist postulates.
5 Since it became so usual to use the term 'instrumentalism' to refer to Friedman's thesis, even though I maintain that this thesis differs substantially from what philosophers of science usually call instrumentalism, I tend to write 'instrumentalism' with quotation marks to refer to what I describes sometimes more explicitly as Friedman's brand of instrumentalism or as Friedmanian 'instrumentalism'. It is probably to avoid such a potentially equivocal designation that Mongin chose to characterize Friedman's thesis as a 'methodological unrealism' (Mongin 1986) or as an 'unrealism of assumptions thesis' (Mongin 1988) rather than as an 'instrumentalism'.
6 On this substantial difference between instrumentalism in physics and in economics,

see Hausman (1998). In more general terms, Rosenberg underscored a similar ambiguity for all 'positivist' interpretations of economics (Rosenberg 1976: 148–152); but see a critical discussion of this general statement in Mongin (1988: 308–310) and, by Rosenberg, a short comment on this point in Rosenberg (1988b: 380).

7 Friedman seems to consider that both words can be used indifferently (Friedman 1953: 7).

8 This idea was immensely influential up to our time; for example, Robert Aumann, one of the most respected economists and game theorists of our time claimed that 'In science one never looks at assumptions; one looks at conclusions' (Aumann 2005: 736).

9 See also Friedman (1953: 34) where, in a similar context, it is a question of 'misunderstanding of economic theory and misdirection of efforts to repair supposed defects'.

10 Fritz Machlup makes a similar distinction (Machlup 1955: 10–18) and concludes that 'the fundamental assumptions of economic theory are not subject to a requirement of independent empirical verification, but instead to a requirement of understandability' (ibid.: 17). This formulation is surely acceptable, but one should not conclude from this that one does not have to be worried if the fundamental assumption adopted is blatantly contradicted by economic behaviour.

11 In somewhat different terms, Tjalling Koopmans briefly made a similar objection to Friedman's position when urging him 'to exploit all the evidence we can secure, direct and indirect' (Koopmans 1957: 140; see also 138).

12 'A hypothesis is important if it "explains" much by little, that is, if it abstracts the common and crucial elements from the mass of complex and detailed circumstances surrounding the phenomena to be explained and permits valid predictions on the basis of them alone. To be important, therefore, a hypothesis must be descriptively false in its assumptions' (Friedman 1953: 14).

13 For an interesting analysis of Friedman's falling body example, see Mäki (2009c: 99–101).

14 On this point see Rosenberg (1988a: 77–79).

15 Of course, Friedman's example could be used to show that a theory assuming perfect competition can be applied successfully in cases sufficiently close to perfect competition, which, like the vacuum, is an antecedent condition and not the *fundamental* assumption of the theory. However, this point is not contested, at least by the main participants in the debate about realism of assumptions.

16 It was the results of such inquiries that Lester (1946: 63–82) opposed to marginal analysis in the seminal article which was, for Friedman, a paradigmatic example of misplaced concern about the unrealism of assumptions. When discussing this question, Friedman (1953: 15 and 31) contests that so much valuable evidence exists regarding alleged discrepancies between 'businessmen's actual market behavior' and 'the implications of the hypothesis being criticised' (ibid.: 31); ironically, this passage is apparently the only one where Friedman seems to admit that behaviours are implications (and not assumptions) of the theory, given that the actual market behaviour can hardly be in discrepancy with something other than another behaviour, but Friedman presents this entity as the *implications* of the hypothesis being criticized. But if this hypothesis assumes that people are maximizers and if Friedman really considers that explanative assumptions are 'wildly inaccurate descriptive representations of reality' (ibid.: 14), it seems difficult to see why he does not also admit that the 'businessmen's actual behavior' does not fit very well with the kind of behaviour that should be the normal implication of maximization.

17 For a more systematic discussion of such a 'positivist' version of Friedman's argument, see Mongin (1988).

18 Hausman (1998: 188) also uses the example of Ptolemaic astronomy to substantiate a similar claim.

19 In contrast with Alchian (1950: 214) who used the same example in a related context, Friedman does not explicitly refer to natural selection in the discussion of this example, but he does refer to this theory in discussing his next example (the billiards player) with a similar argument (Friedman 1953: 22). I will come back to this question in Chapter 8 of this book.
20 See especially Winter (1964: 239–242).
21 I call 'behavioural' those implications (of an economic theory) which concern the behaviour of entrepreneurs (on the average), but which Friedman does not seem to regard as implications at all.
22 In fact, Friedman admits that some inquiries about businessmen's behaviour (and even about their motives) can be 'extremely valuable in suggesting leads to follow in accounting for divergences between predicted and observed results; that is, in constructing new hypotheses or revising old ones' (Friedman 1953: 31, n. 22), but this does not fit very well with his condemnation of the 'misdirection of intellectual effort' that he associates with this kind of inquiry.
23 For the role of the absence of a more satisfactory hypothesis in Friedman's argumentation see Friedman (1953: 9, 17, 31).
24 For examples (not necessarily equivalent in their reference to instrumentalism) taken in literature, see: Boland (1979), Coddington (1979), Mingat, Salmon and Wolfelsperger (1985) and, to some extent, Caldwell (1982).
25 For a classical discussion of instrumentalism in the philosophy of science, see Popper (1963).
26 See, in particular, Churchland and Hooker (1985).
27 Daniel Hausman is one of the very rare authors who put van Fraassen's constructive empiricism in relation with the debates concerning instrumentalism in economics (Hausman 1998). A paper by Thomas Boylan and Paschal O'Gorman (1997) also refers to van Fraassen's constructive empiricism, but this reference concerns a different debate in economics.

7 Explaining in the absence of rationality

1 Except for two substantial pages by Richard Langlois (1986: 237–240) and some discussions in a paper by Sydney Winter (Winter 1964: especially 240, n. 1), it seems that little has been published on this debate. An early version of my views on this debate developed in the first subsections of this chapter was published in Lagueux (1993a).
2 The question of the validity of equilibrium theory is not at issue in this chapter; the only point being discussed concerns the possibility, when postulating irrationality, of obtaining an equilibrium similar to the one allegedly obtained when postulating rationality.
3 For the detailed analysis, see Becker (1962: 2–7).
4 Fisher (1925), Phillips (1950) and Boulding (1966). Fisher's and Phillips' models were even materially constructed, Fisher's machine being conserved at Yale University and Phillips' apparatus at the London School of Economics; on some implications of these models, see Lagueux (1992).
5 John Dupré makes a somewhat similar argument in order to emphasize the fact that adaptation should not be (even metaphorically) presented as a kind of design as, according to him, evolutionist psychologists wrongly tend to do (Dupré 2001: 78).
6 For a clear and well illustrated analysis of theoretical problems associated with intentionality, see Rosenberg (1988a: 41–49).
7 A first draft of the ideas exposed in the last part of this chapter appeared in a section of Lagueux (2008) published online.
8 See, for example, Dennett (1989 [1987]: 15); see also Ross (2005: 38).

9 For a presentation of these three types of stances, see Dennett (1989 [1987]: 16–18 and 38–40).

10 Ross had previously characterized functionalism as an approach that claims that the 'propositional content of a given belief [...] must be a *function* of that belief's *role* in a general network of intentional states' (Ross 2005: 40, emphasis added).

11 According to Ross (Ross 2005: 43), an objection of this type was put forward by John Searle. Ross apparently refers to a passage (Searle 1980: 418, among other passages relatively akin) where Searle claims 'our attribution of intentional meaning to states of artifacts is parasitic on the fact that we are already intentional interpreters.' This claim, however, was part of Searle's defence of his famous Chinese room argument, and not immediately, in contrast with the objection I mentioned above, an objection addressed to Dennett's thesis on intentional stance. In any case, according to Ross, the strategy of Dennett's answer to Searle was to explain how people, designed by natural selection with a brain that is an exceptionally versatile computer, can have intentional states, just like computers (Ross 2005: 44; see Dennett 1989 [1987]: chapter 8 and Lagueux 2008: 33–34). Whatever the merits of such an answer to Searle's argument, it could hardly be considered a direct answer to the objection I evoked, which does not directly concern the possibility of people or computers *having* intentional *states* or not, but the fact that human beings can *take* intentional *stances* to start with.

12 'Public language' designates here a social mode of communication transmitted from generation to generation (Ross 2005: 288), which must be distinguished from an internal 'language of thought' (ibid.: 53) and also from 'emotional signalling systems' (ibid.: 300).

8 Rationality and natural selection in economics

1 For a recent analysis of both Winter's intervention and Nelson and Winter's book, see Vromen (2009: 275–281).

2 The kind of rationality which Alchian was ready to make room for was also very close to what I have called minimal rationality; see Alchian (1950: 218 and 219).

3 In his 'Comments and Criticism' about Satz and Ferejohn's paper, Daniel Hausman denounces among other things this superficial compatibilism (Hausman 1995: 99–100).

4 An early French version of the argument developed in the last part of this chapter was published in Lagueux (1998b) and a still earlier one appeared in Lagueux (1993c).

5 This is true of the selection mechanism as such, even though the idea of the transmission of acquired traits makes more sense in economic theory (through imitation) than in Lamarck's biological theory.

9 Theories of explanation applied to economics

1 For examples of this type, see van Fraassen (1980: 111–112) who also quotes Kuhn (1970: 107ff.). I thanks Yves Gingras who draw my attention to some implications of the criterion for accepting such examples.

2 For an analysis and discussion of Hempel's DN model with applications to economics, see Mongin (2002).

3 Trevelyan (1938: 105) quoted by Dray (1957: 122); see also Dray (1963: 109).

4 This is the expression used by Dray (1957: 132) who refers to 'rational explanations' but, as far as I am aware, not to the rationality principle as such.

5 Salmon (1971b: 34 and 1989: 50). Robert Nadeau drew my attention to the fact that Hempel's view on partitions should be scrutinized in order to grant full justice to this author on this question; it does not seem, however, that this would preclude the fact that some explanations cannot be reducible to a logical inference.

6 Peter Railton also discusses a Cartwright-inspired example by claiming that the spraying 'is part of the explanation of survival', while denying that it is 'a probabilistic

cause of survival', the latter expression being reserved 'for factors that do raise the probability of an event in the circumstances' (Railton 1981: 238). A probabilistic explanation, in contrast, 'is a form of explanation in its own right, charged with the distinctive task of dealing with phenomena that came about by chance' (ibid.: 237). No doubt my example of playing Russian roulette counts among such phenomena, but not a plane crash, which requires a causal explanation. Incidentally, Railton's distinction between 'phenomena that came about by chance' and 'deterministic' phenomena corresponds exactly to the distinction between stochastic and non-stochastic phenomena, which I refer to, in my discussion of expectation.

7 In his rejoinder, Salmon acknowledges this hardly avoidable difficulty, and hopes that a satisfactory solution may be found (Salmon 1985: 652).

8 Van Fraassen (1980: 120–121) criticizing Salmon (1978), a paper which already expressed the essential of the discussion of this point developed in Salmon (1984).

9 Van Fraassen (1985: 643–651); on this point, see also Achinstein (1983: 253).

10 Van Fraassen (1980: 122; see 122–123). Peter Achinstein (1983) devotes a large part of his chapter on causal explanation to maintain, with detailed illustrations, that many kinds of explanations are not causal (228–243), after explicitly rejecting the idea that causal explanations work 'because "to explain" means "to utter a sentence expressing a causal proposition"' (227).

11 For an (almost classical) attempt to show that reasons *can* be causes and a discussion of arguments favouring the contrary thesis, see Davidson (1980: 3–19).

12 For a brief discussion of the application of van Fraassen's thesis to economics, see also Hausman (2001: 320–321).

13 Hart and Honoré (1985 [1959]: 35–37); in the same discussion, these authors present (p. 35) a case quite similar to the example of famine in Chad that I have used to illustrate the question of contrast classes, but, since they did not distinguish the question concerning contrast classes from that concerning relevance, their examples are lumped together as cases of context-dependence.

14 Peter Railton and Peter Achinstein are among the few other theoreticians of explanation who have explicitly addressed this problem (Railton 1981: 248 and Achinstein 1983: especially chapter 9). However, Achinstein's analysis is concluded by the acknowledgement that explaining, as such, does not require having limits, whose existence remains 'an empirical issue' (ibid.: 321). Relevant writings of both of these authors appeared relatively little time after the publication of van Fraassen's book.

15 Van Fraassen (1980: 131); see also Kitcher and Salmon (1987: 326), where allusion is made to a personal communication of van Fraassen on this point, and van Fraassen (1989: 186) for an implicit reference to Aristotle's four causes theory ('preceding events, standing conditions, material composition, or functional role'). Van Fraassen's reference to Aristotle's four types of causes might introduce some confusion since what modern philosophers usually call a 'cause' corresponds uniquely to Aristotle's 'efficient cause'. It seems clear, however, that van Fraassen has found in this theory a tentative typology of relevance relations rather than the basis of a redefinition of the notion of cause.

16 Even though Hempel showed that how-possibly questions can be reinterpreted in order to be dealt with by covering laws explanations (Hempel 1965: 428–430), it might be more difficult to transform them into why-questions in such a way that they could, in the spirit of van Fraassen's thesis, require an answer which would straightforwardly illustrate what is an explanation.

17 Dray (1957: 165); see also Dray (1963: 108). It would be worthwhile (but out of the scope of the present analysis) to relate the possible generalization of van Fraassen's theory proposed here to Dray's most general views on explanation (in contrast with his views on 'rational' explanation) and also to Bromberger's analysis of answers to various kinds of questions (Bromberger 1966) as well as to Achinstein's generalized approach of explanation (Achinstein 1983).

18 Van Fraassen (1980: 146–147) proposes these criteria which should be met by an explanation that is not necessarily correct, but 'evaluated as telling, good or better'; moreover, he admits that he has 'rather less confidence' in them than in the rest of his theory (1980: 146); see also van Fraassen (1989: 186).

19 On the ambiguities of the demarcation problem, see Lagueux (1998a).

20 A conciliation might also be attempted with the help of Achinstein's model of explanation that makes room for both causal processes and context-dependence (Achinstein 1983) or of Peter Railton's notion of an 'ideal explanatory text' (Railton 1981), which Salmon presents as helpful for 'reconciling the views of the pragmatists and the realists' (Salmon 1989: 161) and which seems congenial to most of van Fraassen's theses on explanation, but the discussion of these possibilities would be beyond the scope of this chapter.

Epilogue

1 For an interesting discussion of this point, see Hollis (1994: 225–229).

2 For example, a few chapters of Camerer, Loewenstein and Rabin (2004) are devoted to behavioural game theory; Fudenberg (2006) which is an assessment of the latter paper, discusses its relations with neuroeconomics (705–707). This interrelation is particularly evident from the point of view of behavioural economics that makes room for methods of game theory and for results of neuroeconomics.

3 Gregory Berns even question the utility of game theory – whose applications are governed by the 'assumption of rationality' – given 'its very failure in social domains' (Berns 2003: 155).

4 In a totally different theoretical context, Ken Binmore made a distinction of this kind; see especially (Binmore 1993: 324–325).

References

Achinstein, P. (1983) *The Nature of Explanation*, Oxford: Oxford University Press.

Ainslie, G. (1992) *Picoeconomics: the Strategic Interaction of Successive Motivational States within the Person*, Cambridge: Cambridge University Press.

Alchian, A. (1950) 'Uncertainty, Evolution and Economic Theory', *Journal of Political Economy*, 58: 211–222.

Alchian, A. (1953) 'Biological Analogies in the Theory of the Firm: Comment' *American Economic Review*, 43: 600–603.

Anand, P. (1987) 'Are the preference axioms really rational?', *Theory and Decision*, 23: 189–214.

Archibald, G. C. (1959) 'The State of Economic Science', *British Journal for the Philosophy of Science*, 10: 58–69.

Aumann, R. (2005) 'An interview with Robert Aumann' by Sergiu Hart, *Macroeconomic Dynamics*, 9: 683–740. Online available at: www.ma.huji.ac.il/~hart/abs/aumann.html (accessed 18 August 2009).

Backhouse, R. (2009) 'Friedman's 1953 essay and the marginalist controversy' in U. Mäki (ed.), *The Methodology of Positive Economics, Reflections on the Milton Friedman Legacy*, Cambridge: Cambridge University Press, pp. 217–240.

Bar-Hillel, M. and Margalit, A. (1988) 'How Vicious are Cycles of Intransitive Choice?', *Theory and Decision* 24: 119–145.

Bear, D. V. T. and Orr, D. (1967) 'Logic and Expediency in Economic Theorizing', *The Journal of Political Economy*, 75: 188–196.

Becker, G. (1962) 'Irrational Behavior and Economic Theory', *Journal of Political Economy*, 70: 1–13.

Becker, G. (1963) 'A Reply to I. Kirzner', *Journal of Political Economy*, 71: 82–83.

Becker, G. (1976) *The Economic Approach to Human Behavior*, Chicago: The University of Chicago Press.

Berns, G. (2003) 'Neural Game Theory and the Search for Rational Agents in the Brain', *Behavioral and Brain Sciences*, 26: 155–156.

Binmore, K. (1993) 'De-Bayesing Game Theory' in K. Binmore, A. Kirman and P. Tani (eds) *Frontiers of Game Theory*, Cambridge, MA: The MIT Press, pp. 321–339.

Blackorby, C., Nissen, D., Primont, D. and Russell, R. (1973) 'Consistent Intertemporal Decision Making', *Review of Economic Studies*, 40: 239–248.

Bloch, M. (1954) *The Historian's Craft* (translation from the French *Le métier d'historien* by Peter Putnam), Manchester: Manchester University Press.

Block, W. (1980) 'On Robert Nozick's "On Austrian Methodology"', *Inquiry*, 23: 397–444.

Boland, L. A. (1979) 'A Critique of Friedman's Critiques', *Journal of Economic Literature*, 17: 503–522.

Boudon, R. (1986) 'Individualisme et holisme dans les sciences sociales' in P. Birnbaum and J. Leca (eds), *Sur l'individualisme: Théories et méthodes*, Paris: Presses de la fondation nationale des sciences politiques, pp. 45–59.

Boulding, K. (1966) *Economic Analysis*, Vol I: *Microeconomics*, fourth edition, New York: Harper & Row.

Boylan, T. and O'Gorman, P. (1997) 'Kaldor on Method: a Challenge to Contemporary Methodology', *Cambridge Journal of Economics*, 21: 503–517.

Bromberger, S. (1966) 'Why-Questions' in R. Colodny (ed.), *Mind and Cosmos*, Pittsburgh: University of Pittsburgh Press, pp. 86–111.

Caldwell, B. (1982) *Beyond Positivism, Economic Methodology in the Twentieth Century*, London: Allen & Unwin.

Camerer, C. (2008) 'The Potential of Neuroeconomics', *Economic and Philosophy*, 24: 369–379.

Camerer, C., Loewenstein, G. and Rabin, M. (eds) (2004) *Advances in behavioural Economics*, Princeton, NJ: Princeton University Press.

Camerer, C., Loewenstein, G. and Prelec, D. (2004) 'Neuroeconomics: Why Economics Needs Brains', *Scandinavian Journal of Economics*, 106: 555–579.

Carr, E. H. (1961) *What is History?*, New York: A. A. Knopf and Random House.

Cartwright, N. (1979) 'Causal Laws and Effective Strategies', *Noûs*, 13: 419–437.

Cartwright, N. (1983) *How the Laws of Physics Lie*, Oxford: Clarendon Press.

Cartwright, N. (1995) 'Ceteris paribus Laws and Socio-Economic Machines', *The Monist*, 78: 276–294.

Cherniak, C. (1986) *Minimal Rationality*, Cambridge, MA: The MIT Press.

Churchland, P. (1984) *Matter and Consciousness: A Contemporary Introduction to the Philosophy of Mind*, Cambridge, MA: The MIT Press.

Churchland, P. M. and Hooker, C. A. (eds) (1985) *Images of Science, Essays on Realism and Empiricism, with a Reply from Bas C. van Fraassen*, Chicago: The University of Chicago Press.

Coase, R. (1976) 'Adam Smith's View of Man', *The Journal of Law and Economics*, 19: 529–546.

Coddington, A. (1979) 'Friedman's Contribution to Methodological Controversy', *British Review of Economic Issues*, 2: 1–13.

Coleman, W. (1995) *Rationalism and Anti-Rationalism in the Origins of Economics*, Aldershot, Hants: Edward Elgar.

Collingwood, R. G. (1946) *The Idea of History*, London: Oxford University Press.

Conlisk, J. (1996), 'Why Bounded Rationality?', *Journal of Economic Literature*, 34: 669–700.

Danto, A. (1965) *Analytical Philosophy of History*, Cambridge: Cambridge University Press.

Davidson, D. (1963) 'Actions, Reasons, and Causes' in D. Davidson (1980) *Essays on Actions and Events*, Oxford: Oxford University Press, pp. 3–19.

Davidson, D. (1982) 'Paradoxes of Irrationality' in R. Wollheim and J. Hopkins, *Philosophical Essays on Freud*, Cambridge: Cambridge University Press, pp. 289–314.

Davidson, D., McKinsey, J. C. C. and Suppes, P. (1955) 'Outline of a Formal Theory of Value, I', *Philosophy of Science*, 22: 140–60.

Davis, J. (2003) *The Theory of the Individual in Economics: Identity and Value*, London: Routledge.

Dennett, D. (1989 [1987]) *The Intentional Stance*, Cambridge, MA: The MIT Press.

Dennett, D. (1991a) *Consciousness Explained*, Boston: Little, Brown & Co.

Dennett, D. (1991b) 'Real Patterns', *The Journal of Philosophy*, 88: 27–51.

Dray, W. (1957) *Laws and Explanation in History*, Oxford: Oxford University Press.

Dray, W. (1963) 'The Historical Explanation of Actions Reconsidered' in S. Hook (ed.), *Philosophy and History, A Symposium*, New York: New York University Press, 105–135.

Dray, W. (1967) 'Holism and Individualism in History and Social Science' in P. Edwards (ed.), *The Encyclopedia of Philosophy*, London: Macmillan, Vol. 4, pp. 53–58.

Dupré, J. (2001) *Human Nature and the Limits of Science*, Oxford: Clarendon Press.

Elster, J. (1983) *Sour Grapes, Studies in Subversion of Rationality*, Cambridge: Cambridge University Press, and Paris: la Maison des sciences de l'homme.

Elster, J. (1984 [1979]) *Ulysses and the Sirens, Studies in rationality and irrationality*, Cambridge: Cambridge University Press, and Paris: la Maison des sciences de l'homme.

Elster, J. (1985) *Making Sense of Marx*, Cambridge: Cambridge University Press.

Elster, J. (1986) 'Marxisme et individualisme méthodologique' in P. Birnbaum and J. Leca, (eds), *Sur l'individualisme: Théories et méthodes*, Paris: Presses de la fondation nationale des sciences politiques, pp. 60–76.

Elster, J. (ed.) (1987 [1985]) *The Multiple Self*, Cambridge: Cambridge University Press.

Elster, J. (1989) *Nuts and Bolts for the Social Sciences*, Cambridge: Cambridge University Press.

Enke, S. (1951) 'On Maximizing Profits: A Distinction between Chamberlin and Robinson', *American Economic Review*, 41: 566–78.

Enke, S. (1953) 'Comment', *American Economic Review*, 43: 603.

Fisher, I. (1925) *Mathematical Investigations in the Theory of Value and Prices*, New Haven, CT: Yale University Press.

Friedman, M. (1953) 'The Methodology of Positive Economics' in M. Friedman, *Essays in Positive Economics*, Chicago: University of Chicago Press, pp. 3–43.

Friedman, M. (1962) *Price Theory*, Chicago: Aldine.

Fudenberg, D. (2006) 'Advancing Beyond *Advances in Behavioural Economics*', *Journal of Economic Literature*, 44: 694–711.

Gintis, H. (2009) *Game Theory Evolving*, second edition, Princeton, NJ: Princeton University Press.

Giocoli, N. (2003) *Modelling Rational Agents*, Cheltenham: Edward Elgar.

Glimcher, P. (2003) *Decisions, Uncertainty, and the Brain*, Cambridge, MA: The MIT Press.

Greeno, J. (1970) 'Evaluation of Statistical Hypotheses Using Information Transmitted', *Philosophy of Science*, 37: 279–293 (reprinted under the title 'Explanation and Information' in Salmon, Jeffrey and Greeno, 1971, *Statistical Explanation and Statistical Relevance*, Pittsburgh: University of Pittsburgh Press, pp. 89–104).

Grether, D. and Plott, C. (1979) 'Economic Theory of Choice and the Preference Reversal Phenomenon', *American Economic Review*, 69: 623–638.

Hammond, P. (1976) 'Changing Tastes and Coherent Dynamic Choices', *Review of Economic Studies*, 43: 159–73.

Hands, W. (1985) 'Karl Popper and Economic Methodology, A New Look', *Economics and Philosophy*, 1: 83–99.

Hargreaves Heap, S. (1989) *Rationality in Economics*, Oxford: Blackwell.

Hart, H. L. A. and Honoré, T. (1985 [1959]) *Causation in the Law*, Oxford: Clarendon Press.

Hausman, D. (1988) '*Ceteris Paribus* Clauses and Causality in Economics' in *PSA 1988: Proceedings of the Biennal Meeting of the Philosophy of Science Association*, Vol. 2: Symposia and Invited Papers, pp. 308–316.

Hausman, D. (1992) *The Inexact and Separate Science of Economics*, Cambridge: Cambridge University Press.

Hausman, D. (1995) 'Comments and Criticism', *The Journal of Philosophy*, 92: 96–102.

Hausman, D. (1998) 'Problems with Realism in Economics', *Economics and Philosophy*, 14: 185–213.

Hausman, D. (2001) 'Explanation and Diagnosis in Economics', *Revue Internationale de philosophie*, 217: 311–326.

Hausman, D. and Mongin, P. (1997) 'Economists' Responses to Anomalies: Full-Cost Pricing versus Preference Reversals' in J. Davis (ed.), *New Economics and its History*, annual supplement to vol. 29 of *History of Political Economy*, Durham, NC: Duke University Press, 255–272.

Hayek, F. (1952 [1942–44]) 'Scientism and the Study of Society', Part one of *The Counter-Revolution of Science: Studies on the Abuse of Reason*, Glencoe, IL: The Free Press, (slightly modified version of three papers published under this title in *Economica*, 1942, 1943 and 1944).

Hayek, F. (1967) *Studies in Philosophy, Politics, and Economics*, Chicago: The University of Chicago Press.

Hayek, F. (1978) *New Studies in Philosophy, Politics, Economics and the History of Ideas*, Chicago: The University of Chicago Press.

Heath, J. (2005) 'Methodological Individualism', in *Stanford Encyclopedia of Philosophy*, ed. Edward N. Zalta. Online available at: http://plato.stanford.edu/entries/methodological-individualism/ (accessed 12 August 2009).

Hempel, C. (1942) 'The Function of General Laws in History', *Journal of Philosophy*, 39: 35–48 (republished in C. Hempel, *Aspects of Scientific Explanation, And Other Essays in the Philosophy of Science*, New York: Free Press and London: Collier-Macmillan, pp. 231–243).

Hempel, C. (1963) 'Reasons and Covering Laws in Historical Explanation' in S. Hook (ed.), *Philosophy and History, A Symposium*, New York: New York University Press, pp. 143–163.

Hempel, C. (1965) *Aspects of Scientific Explanation, And Other Essays in the Philosophy of Science*, New York: Free Press and London: Collier-Macmillan.

Hempel, C. and Oppenheim, P. (1948) 'Studies in the Logic of Explanation', *Philosophy of Science*, 15: 135–175 (reprinted with modifications and with a 1964 Postscript in C. Hempel (1965): *Aspects of Scientific Explanation, And Other Essays in the Philosophy of Science*, New York: Free Press and London: Collier-Macmillan, pp. 245–295.

Hicks, J. R. (1946 [1939]) *Value and Capital*, Oxford: Clarendon Press.

Hicks, J. R. and Allen, R. G. D. (1934) 'A Reconsideration of the Theory of Value', Part I, *Economica*, 1 (New Series): 52–76.

Hirsch, A. and de Marchi, N. (1990) *Milton Friedman Economics in Theory and Practice*, Ann Arbor: The University of Michigan Press.

Hodgson, G. M. (1991) 'Economic Evolution: Intervention contra Pangloss', *Journal of Economic Issues*, 25: 519–533.

Hodgson, G. M. (1993) *Economics and Evolution: Bringing Life Back into Economics*, Ann Arbor: The University of Michigan Press.

Hodgson, G. M. (1998) 'Evolutionary Economics' in J. Davis, W. Hands and U. Mäki (eds), *The Handbook of Economic Methodology*, Cheltenham: Edward Elgar, pp. 160–167.

Hodgson, G. M. (2007) 'Meanings of Methodological Individualism', *Journal of Economic Methodology*, 14: 211–226.

Hollis, M. (1994) *The Philosophy of Social Science, An Introduction*, Cambridge: Cambridge University Press.

Hollis, M. and Sugden, R. (1993) 'Rationality in Action', *Mind*, 102: 1–35.

Holt, C. (1986) 'Preference Reversals and the Independence Axiom', *American Economic Review*, 76: 508–515.

Houthakker, H. S. (1950) 'Revealed Preference and the Utility Function', *Economica*, 17: 159–174.

Hume, D. (1970 [1752]) 'On the Balance of Trade' in E. Rotwein (ed.), *David Hume Writings on Economics*, Madison: University of Wisconsin Press, pp. 60–77.

Hume, D. (2000 [1739]) *A Treatise of Human Nature*, Oxford: Oxford University Press.

Jeffrey, R. (1969) 'Statistical Explanation vs. Statistical Inference' in N. Rescher, *Essays in Honor of Carl G. Hempel*, Dordrecht: D. Reidel, pp. 104–113. (reprinted in Salmon, Jeffrey and Greeno, 1971, *Statistical Explanation and Statistical Relevance*, Pittsburgh: University of Pittsburgh Press, pp. 19–28).

Jevons, S. (1957 [1871]) *The Theory of Political Economy*, fifth edition, New York: Sentry Press (Augustus M. Kelly reprints, 1965).

Kahneman, D. (1996a) 'New Challenges to the Rationality Assumption', in K. J. Arrow, E. Colombatto, M. Perlman and C. Schmidt (eds), *The Rational Foundations of Economic Behaviour*, London: Macmillan, pp. 203–219 with a Comment by Charles Plott, pp. 220–224.

Kahneman, D. (1996b) 'Comment', in K. J. Arrow (eds), *The Rational Foundations of Economic Behaviour*, London: Macmillan, 251–254.

Katona, G. (1951) *Psychological Analysis of Economic Behavior*, New York: McGraw Hill.

Kaufmann, F. (1937) 'Do Synthetic Propositions a Priori Exist in Economics, A reply to Dr. Bernardelli', *Economica*, 4: 337–342.

Keynes, J. M. (1936) *The General Theory of Employment, Interest and Money*, London: Macmillan.

Kincaid, H. (1996) *Philosophical Foundation of the Social Sciences: Analysing Controversies in Social Research*, Cambridge: Cambridge University Press.

Kincaid, H. (1997) *Individualism and the Unity of Science, Essays on Reduction, Explanation, and the Special Sciences*, Lanham, MD: Rowman & Littlefield.

Kindleberger, C. (1989) *Economic Laws and Economic History*, Cambridge: Cambridge University Press.

Kirzner, I. (1962) 'Rational Action and Economic Theory', *Journal of Political Economy*, 70: 380–385.

Kirzner, I. (1963) 'Rejoinder', *Journal of Political Economy*, 71: 84–85.

Kirzner, I. (1990) 'Menger, Classical Liberalism, and the Austrian School of Economics', in B. Caldwell, *Carl Menger and his Legacy in Economics* (annual supplement of H.O.P.E., no. 22), Durham, NC: Duke University Press, pp. 93–106.

Kitcher, P. (1985) 'Two Approaches to Explanation', *The Journal of Philosophy*, 82: 632–639.

Kitcher, P. and Salmon, W. (1987) 'Van Fraassen on Explanation', *The Journal of Philosophy*, 84: 315–330.

Klant, J. J. (1984) *The Rules of the Game, The Logical Structure of Economic Theories*,

Cambridge: Cambridge University Press (first edition in Dutch in 1973 as a doctorate thesis, and then in 1979).

Koopmans, T. C. (1957) *Three Essays on the State of Economic Science*, New York: Mcgraw-Hill.

Kreps, D. M. (1990) *Game Theory and Economic Modelling*, Oxford: Clarendon Press.

Kuhn, T. (1957) *The Copernican Revolution: Planetary Astronomy in the Development of Western Thought*, Cambridge MA: Harvard University Press.

Kuhn, T. (1970) *The Structure of Scientific Revolutions*, second edition, Chicago: The University of Chicago Press.

Lagueux, M. (1988) 'Apriorisme et empirisme en science économique', *Fundamenta Scientiae*, 9: 217–230.

Lagueux, M. (1992) 'What's Wrong with Metaphors in Economics?: the Case of Hydraulic Metaphors' in T. Lowry (ed.), *Perspectives on the History of Economic Thought*, vol. VIII, Aldershot, Hants.: Edward Elgar, pp. 35–50.

Lagueux, M. (1993a) 'Kirzner versus Becker: Rationality and Mechanisms in Economics' in R. Hebert (ed.), *Perspectives on the History of Economic Thought*, vol. IX, Aldershot, Hants: Edward Elgar, 37–50.

Lagueux, M. (1993b) 'Popper and the Rationality Principle', *Philosophy of the Social Sciences*, 23: 468–480.

Lagueux, M. (1993c) 'Natural Selection and Economics', *Methodus*, 5: 93–100.

Lagueux, M. (1994) 'Friedman's "Instrumentalism" and Constructive Empiricism in Economics', *Theory and Decision*, 37: 147–174.

Lagueux, M. (1995) 'How Could One Be Irrational?' in M. Marion and Robert Cohen (eds), *Quebec Studies in the Philosophy of Science*, book II: *Biology, Psychology, Cognitive Science and Economics*, Dordrecht: Kluwer; pp. 177–192.

Lagueux, M. (1997) *Omniscience and Rationality in Microeconomics*, Cahiers du département de philosophie, Montréal: Université de Montréal. Online available at: www.philo.umontreal.ca/textes/Lagueux_Omniscience.pdf (accessed 12 August 2009).

Lagueux, M. (1998a) 'Demarcation' in J. Davis, W. Hands and U. Mäki (eds), *The Handbook of Economic Methodology*, Cheltenham: Edward Elgar, pp. 95–100.

Lagueux, M. (1998b) 'Rationalité et sélection naturelle en économie', *Philosophiques*, 25: 163–180.

Lagueux, M. (2001a) 'Individualisme, subjectivisme et mécanismes économiques', *Dialogue*, 40: 691–722.

Lagueux, M. (2001b) *What Does Rationality Mean for Economists?*, Cahiers d'épistémologie no 2001–09, Montreal: Université du Québec à Montréal. Online available at: www.er.uqam.ca/nobel/philuqam/dept/page_perso.php?id=13 (accessed 8 January 2010).

Lagueux, M. (2002) 'Information Costs, Deliberation Costs and Transaction Costs: a Parallel Treatment' in S. Boehm, C. Gehrke, H. Kurz and R. Sturn (eds), *Is There Progress in Economics?* Cheltenham: Edward Elgar, pp. 356–367.

Lagueux, M. (2004) 'The Forgotten Role of the Rationality Principle in Economics', *Journal of Economic Methodology*, 11: 31–51.

Lagueux, M. (2005) 'L'agent économique: rationalité maximale ou minimale, *Cahiers d'économie politique*, 49: 143–157.

Lagueux, M. (2006a) 'L'apriorisme des Autrichiens', *Cahiers d'économie politique*, no. 51: Les économistes autrichiens (1870–1940): 69–90.

Lagueux, M. (2006b) 'Popper and the Rationality Principle' in I. Jarvie, K. Milford and D. Miller (eds), *Karl Popper: A Centenary Assessment*, Volume III, Aldershot: Ashgate Publishing, pp. 197–208.

Lagueux, M. (2007) 'Y a-t-il des lois en économie?' in A. Berthoud, B. Delmas and T. Demals (eds), *Y a-t-il des lois en économie?*, Villeneuve d'Ascq: Presses Universitaires du Septentrion, pp. 63–67.

Lagueux, M. (2008) 'Are we Witnessing a Revolution in Methodology of Economics? About Don Ross's recent book on Microexplanation', *Erasmus Journal for Philosophy and Economics*, 1: 24–55. Online available at: http://ejpe.org, (accessed 12 August 2009).

Langlois R. (1986) 'Rationality, Institutions, and Explanation' in R. Langlois (ed.), *Economics as a Process*, Cambridge: Cambridge University Press, pp. 225–255.

Laudan, L. (1983) 'The Demise of the Demarcation Problem' in R. Cohen and L. Laudan (eds), *Physics, Philosophy and Psychoanalysis, Essays in honor of Adolf Grünbaum*, Dordrecht: D. Reidel, pp. 11–127.

Lester, R. A. (1946) 'Shortcomings of Marginal Analysis for Wage-Employment Problems', *American Economic Review*, 36: 63–82.

Lichtenstein, S. and Slovic, P. (1971) 'Reversals of Preferences between Bids and Choices in Gambling Decisions', *Journal of Experimental Psychology*, 89: 46–55.

Lichtenstein, S. and Slovic, P. (1973) 'Response-Induced Reversals of Preference in Gambling – an Extended Replication in Las Vegas', *Journal of Experimental Psychology*, 101: 16–20.

Loomes, G. and Sugden, R. (1983) 'A Rationale for Preference Reversal', *American Economic Review*, 73: 428–432.

Machlup, F. (1946) 'Marginal Analysis and Empirical Research', *American Economic Review*, 36: 519–554.

Machlup, F. (1947) 'Rejoinder to an Antimarginalist', *American Economic Review*, 37: 148–154.

Machlup, F. (1955) 'The Problem of Verification in Economics', *Southern Economic Journal*, 22: 1–21.

Mäki, U. (ed.) (2009a) *The Methodology of Positive Economics, Reflections on the Milton Friedman Legacy*, Cambridge: Cambridge University Press.

Mäki, U. (2009b) 'Reading *the* Methodological Essay in Twentieth Century Economics: Map of Multiple Perspectives' in U. Mäki, *The Methodology of Positive Economics, Reflections on the Milton Friedman Legacy*, Cambridge: Cambridge University Press, pp. 47–67.

Mäki, U. (2009c) 'Unrealistic Assumptions and Unnecessary Confusions: Rereading and Rewriting F53 as a Realist Statement' in U. Mäki, *The Methodology of Positive Economics, Reflections on the Milton Friedman Legacy*, Cambridge: Cambridge University Press, 90–116.

Marschak, T. A. (1978) 'On the Study of Taste Changing Policies', *American Economic Review*, 68: 386–391.

Marshall, A. (1949 [1890]) *Principles of Economics*, London: Macmillan.

Marx, K. and Engels, F. (1947 [1846]) *The German Ideology*, Parts I & III, New York: International Publishers.

May, K. (1954) 'Intransitivity, Utility, and the Aggregation of Preference Patterns', *Econometrica*, 22: 1–13.

Maynard Smith, J. (1982), *Evolution and the Theory of Games*, Cambridge: Cambridge University Press.

McPherson, M. (1987) 'Changes in Tastes' in *The New Palgrave, A Dictionary of Economics*, vol. 1, London: Macmillan, pp. 401–403.

Mele, A. (1987) *Irrationality, An Essay on Akrasia, Self-deception, and Self-control*, Oxford: Oxford University Press.

Melitz, J. (1965) 'Friedman and Machlup on the Significance of Testing Economic Assumptions', *Journal of Political Economy*, 73: 37–60.
Mellor, D. H. (1976) 'Probable Explanation', *Australasian Journal of Philosophy*, 54: 231–241.
Menger, C. (1976 [1871]) *Principles of Economics* (translated from German by J. Dingwall and F. Hoselitz), New York: New York University Press.
Menger, C. (1985 [1883]) *Investigations into the Method of the Social Sciences with Special Reference to Economics* (translation from German by F. J. Nock), Urbana: University of Illinois Press.
Mill, J. S. (1948 [1836]) *Essays on some Unsettled Questions of Political Economy*, London: London School of Economics.
Mill, J. S. (1961 [1865]) *Auguste Comte and Positivism*, Ann Arbor: University of Michigan Press.
Mingat, A., Salmon, P. and Wolfelsperger, A. (1985) *Méthodologie économique*, Paris: Presses Universitaires de France.
Mirowski, P. (2002) *Machine Dreams, Economics Becomes a Cyborg Science*, Cambridge: Cambridge University Press.
Mises, L. von (1944) 'The Treatment of "Irrationality" in the Social Sciences', *Philosophy and Phenomenological Research*, 4: 527–545.
Mises, L. von (1976) *Epistemological Problems of Economics*, New York: New York University Press.
Mongin, P. (1986a) 'La controverse sur l'entreprise (1940–1950) et la formation de "l'irréalisme méthodologique"', *Économies et sociétés* (Cahiers de l'I.S.M.E.A., PE, no. 5), 20: 95–151.
Mongin, P. (1986b) 'Simon, Stigler et les théories de la rationalité limitée', *Rationality and Society, Rationalité et Société*, 25: 555–606.
Mongin, P. (1988) 'Le réalisme des hypothèses et la Partial Interpretation View', *Philosophy of the Social Sciences – Philosophie des sciences sociales*, 18: 281–325.
Mongin, P. (1992) 'The "Full-Cost" Controversy of the 1940s and 1950s: A Methodological Assessment', *History of Political Economy*, 24: 311–356.
Mongin, P. (2000) 'Does Optimization Imply Rationality?', *Synthese*, 124: 73–111.
Mongin, P. (2002) 'La conception déductive de l'explication scientifique et l'économie', *Theory and Methods/Théorie et Méthode*, 41: 139–165.
Morgan, M. (1997) 'The character of "rational economic man"', *Dialektik, Enzyklopädische Zeitschrift für Philosophie und Wissenschaften*, 1: 77–94.
Musgrave, A. (1981) '"Unreal Assumptions" in Economic Theory: The F-Twist Untwisted', *Kyklos*, 34: 377–387.
Nadeau, R. (1992) 'Friedman et son discours de la méthode' in M. Lavoie and M. Seccareccia (eds), *Milton Friedman et son oeuvre*, Montréal: Presses de l'Université de Montréal, pp. 131–150.
Nadeau, R. (1993) 'Confuting Popper on the Rationality Principle', *Philosophy of the Social Sciences*, 23: 446–467.
Nagel, E. (1963) 'Assumptions in Economic Theory', *American Economic Review, Papers and Proceedings*, 53: 211–219.
Nelson, R. R. and Winter, S. G. (1982) *An Evolutionary Theory of Economic Change*, Cambridge, MA and London: Belknap Press of Harvard University Press.
Nozick, R. (1974) *Anarchy, State, and Utopia*, New York: Basic Books Inc.
Nozick, R. (1977) 'On Austrian Methodology', *Synthese*, 36: 353–392.

Peleg, B. and Yaari, M. E. (1973) 'On the Existence of a Consistent Course of Action when Tastes are Changing', *Review of Economic Studies*, 40: 391–401.
Penrose, E. (1952) 'Biological Analogies in the Theory of the Firm', *American Economic Review*, 42: 804–819.
Penrose, E. (1953) 'Rejoinder', *American Economic Review*, 43: 603–609.
Peters, T. and Waterman, R. (1982) *In Search of Excellence*, London: Routledge & Kegan Paul.
Petroni, A. (1991) 'L'individualisme économique', *Journal des économistes et des études humaines*, 2: 25–61.
Phillips, A. W. (1950) 'Mechanical Models in Economic Dynamics', *Economica*, 17: 283–305.
Plott, C. (1996a) 'Rational Individual Behaviour in Markets and Social Choice Process', in K. J. Arrow, E. Colombatto, M. Perlman and C. Schmidt (eds), *The Rational Foundations of Economic Behaviour*, London: Macmillan, pp. 225–250, with a Comment by Daniel Kahneman, pp. 251–254.
Plott, C. (1996b) 'Comment', in K. J. Arrow and alia (eds), *The Rational Foundations of Economic Behaviour*, London: Macmillan, pp. 220–224.
Pollak, R. A. (1968) 'Consistent Planning', *Review of Economic Studies*, 35: 201–208.
Popper, K. (1963) 'Three Views Concerning Human Understanding', in K. Popper, *Conjectures and Refutations: The Growth of Scientific Knowledge*, New York: Harper Torchbooks, 97–119.
Popper, K. (1967) 'La rationalité et le statut du principe de rationalité' in E. M. Classen (ed.), *Les fondements philosophiques des systèmes économiques, textes de Jacques Rueff et essais rédigés en son honneur, 23 août 1966*, Paris: Payot, pp. 142–150.
Popper, K. (1968 [1934–35]) *The Logic of Scientific Discovery* (second edition, first English edition, 1959; translated from German by K. Popper with the assistance of J. and L. Freed), New York: Harper & Row.
Popper, K. (1985) 'The Rationality Principle' in D. Miller (ed.), *Popper Selections*, Princeton, NJ: Princeton University Press, pp. 357–365.
Popper, K. (1994) 'Models, Instruments, and Truth' in K. Popper, *The Myth of the Framework*, ed. M. A. Notturno, London: Routledge, pp. 154–184.
Railton, P. (1981) 'Probability, Explanation, and Information', *Synthese*, 48: 233–256.
Rappaport, S. (1995) 'Economic Models and Historical Explanation', *Philosophy of the Social Sciences*, 25: 421–441.
Ricardo, D. (1951 [1815]) *An Essay on the Influence of a low Price of Corn on the Profits of Stock*, in The *Works and Correspondance of David Ricardo*, vol IV, Cambridge: Cambridge University Press, pp. 2–41.
Ricardo, D. (1951 [1817]) 'On the Principles of Political Economy and Taxation' in The *Works and Correspondance of David Ricardo*, vol. I, Cambridge: Cambridge University Press.
Ricardo, D. (1952 [1811]) 'Ricardo to Malthus, 22 October 1811' in The *Works and Correspondance of David Ricardo*, vol. VI, Cambridge: Cambridge University Press, pp. 63–65.
Robbins, L. (1952 [1932]) *An Essay on the Nature and Significance of Economic Science*, second edition (1935), London: Macmillan.
Rosenberg, A. (1976) *Microeconomic Laws, A Philosophical Analysis*, Pittsburgh: University of Pittsburgh Press.
Rosenberg, A. (1988a) *Philosophy of Social Science*, Boulder, CO: Westview Press.
Rosenberg, A. (1988b) 'The Past Recaptured: Mongin on the Problem of Realism in

Economics', *Philosophy of the Social Sciences – Philosophie des sciences sociales*, 18: 379–381.
Rosenberg, A. (1992a) *Economics – Mathematical Politics or Science of Diminishing Returns?*, Chicago: The University of Chicago Press.
Rosenberg, A. (1992b) 'Neo-classical Economics and Evolutionary Theory: Strange Bedfellows', in *PSA 1992*, vol. 1 (Philosophy of Science Association), pp. 174–183.
Rosenberg, A. (1994) 'What is the Cognitive Status of Economic Theory?' in Roger Backhouse (ed.), *New Directions in Economic Methodology*, London: Routledge, pp. 216–235.
Ross, D. (2005) *Economic Theory and Cognitive Science – Microexplanation*, Cambridge, MA: The MIT Press.
Ross, D. (2008) 'Reply to Lagueux: on a Revolution in Methodology of Economics', *Erasmus Journal for Philosophy and Economics*, 1: 56–60. Online available at: http://ejpe.org (accessed 12 August 2009).
Rotwein, E. (1986) 'Flirting with Apriorism: Caldwell on Mises', *History of Political Economy*, 18: 669–673.
Salmon, W. (1971a) 'Introduction' in Salmon, Jeffrey and Greeno, *Statistical Explanation and Statistical Relevance*, Pittsburgh: University of Pittsburgh Press, pp. 3–17.
Salmon, W. (1971b) 'Statistical Explanation' in Salmon, Jeffrey and Greeno, *Statistical Explanation and Statistical Relevance*, Pittsburgh: University of Pittsburgh Press, pp. 29–87.
Salmon, W. (1977) 'A third Dogma of Empiricism', in R. Butts and J. Hintikka (eds) *Basic Problems in Methodology and Linguistics*, Dordrecht: D. Reidel, pp. 149–166.
Salmon, W. (1978) 'Why ask, "Why?" – An Inquiry concerning scientific Explanation', *Proceedings and Addresses of the American Philosophical Association*, 51: 683–705.
Salmon, W. (1984) *Scientific Explanation and the Causal Structure of the World*, Princeton, NJ: Princeton University Press.
Salmon, W. (1985) 'Conflicting Conceptions of Scientific Explanation', *The Journal of Philosophy*, 82: 651–654.
Salmon, W. (1989) *Four Decades of Scientific Explanation* in P. Kitcher and W. Salmon, *Scientific Explanation*, vol. XIII of Minnesota Studies in Philosophy of Science, Minneapolis: University of Minnesota Press, pp. 3–219. (This text was also published independently by University of Minnesota Press.)
Salmon, W., Jeffrey, R. and Greeno, J. (1971) *Statistical Explanation and Statistical Relevance*, Pittsburgh: University of Pittsburgh Press.
Satz, D. and Ferejohn, J. (1994) 'Rational Choice and Social Theory', *The Journal of Philosophy*, 91: 71–87.
Schick, F. (1986) 'Dutch Bookies and Money Pumps', *The Journal of Philosophy*, 83: 112–119.
Scriven, M. (1959) 'Explanation and Prediction in Evolutionary Theory', *Science*, 30: 477–482.
Searle, J. (1980) 'Mind, Brains and Programs' (including Searle's introductory paper, Open Peer Commentary and Searle's Response), *The Behavioral and Brain Sciences*, 3: 417–457.
Sen, A. (1987) 'Rational Behaviour' in *The New Palgrave, A Dictionary of Economics*, vol. 4, London: Macmillan, pp. 68–76.
Simon, H. (1957) *Models of Man*, New York: John Wiley & Sons.
Simon, H. (1976) 'From Substantive to Procedural Rationality' in S. Latsis (ed.), *Method and Appraisal in Economics*, Cambridge: Cambridge University Press, pp. 129–148.

Simon, H. (1978) 'Rationality as process and as product of thought', Richard T. Ely lecture, *American Economic Association, Paper and Proceedings*, 68: 1–16.

Slovic, P. and Lichtenstein, S. (1968) 'Relative importance of probabilities and payoffs in risk taking', *Journal of Experimental Psychology*, 78: 1–18.

Smith, A. (1937 [1776]) *An Inquiry into the Nature and Causes of the Wealth of Nations*, New York: Modern Library.

Stigler, G. (1961) 'The Economics of Information', *Journal of Political Economy*, 69: 213–225.

Stigler, G. and Becker, G. (1977) 'De Gustibus Non Est Disputandum', *American Economic Review*, 67: 76–90.

Stigum, B. (1990) *Toward a Formal Science of Economics*, Cambridge, MA: The MIT Press.

Strotz, R. H. (1955–56) 'Myopia and Inconsistency in Dynamic Utillity Maximization', *Review of Economic Studies*, 23: 165–180.

Sugden, R. (1985) 'Why be Consistent? A Critical Analysis of Consistency Requirements in Choice Theory', *Economica*, 52: 167–183.

Trevelyan, G. M. (1938) *The English revolution, 1688–1689*, London: Oxford University Press.

Turgot, A. R. J. (1898 [1766]) *Reflections on the Formation and the Distribution of Riches*, (translated from French by W. J. Ashley), New York: Macmillan and Co.

Tversky, A. (1969) 'Intransitivity of preferences', *Psychological Review*, 76: 31–48.

Tversky, A. and Kahneman, D. (1986) 'The Framing of Decisions and the Psychology of Choice' in J. Elster (ed.), *Rational Choice*, New York: New York University Press, pp. 123–141.

Tversky, A., Slovic, P. and Kahneman, D. (1990) 'The causes of preference reversal', *American Economic Review*, 80: 204–217.

Ullmann-Margalit, E. (1978) 'Invisible Hand Explanations', *Synthese*, 39: 263–291.

van Fraassen, B. (1980) *The Scientific Image*, Oxford: Clarendon Press.

van Fraassen, B. (1985) 'Salmon on Explanation', *The Journal of Philosophy*, 82: 639–651.

van Fraassen, B. (1989) *Laws and Symmetry*, Oxford: Clarendon Press.

Vromen, J. (2009) 'Friedman's Selection Argument Revisited' in U. Mäki, *The Methodology of Positive Economics, Reflections on the Milton Friedman Legacy*, Cambridge: Cambridge University Press, pp. 257–284.

Walras, L. (1954 [1874]) *Elements of Pure Economics; or, the Theory of Social Wealth* (translated from French by William Jaffé), Homewood, IL: Richard D. Irwin.

Watkins, J. W. N. (1953) 'Ideal Types and Historical Explanation', *British Journal for the Philosophy of Science*, 3: 22–43.

Watkins, J. W. N. (1957) 'Historical Explanation in the Social Sciences', *British Journal for the Philosophy of Science*, 8: 104–117.

Weisbrod, B. (1977) 'Comparing Utility Functions in Efficiency Terms or, What Kind of Utility Functions Do We Want?', *American Economic Review*, 67: 991–995.

Weizsäcker, C. C. von (1971) 'Notes on Endogenous Change of Tastes', *Journal of Economic Theory*, 3: 345–372.

Winter S. G. (1964) 'Economic "Natural Selection" and the Theory of the Firm', *Yale Economic Essays*, 4: 224–272.

Wong, S. (1973) 'The "F-Twist" and the Methodology of Paul Samuelson', *American Economic Review*, 63: 312–325.

Woodward, J. (2002) 'There is no Such Thing as a Ceteris Paribus Law', *Erkenntnis*, 57: 303–328.

Index